MRC

SOCIAL & PUBLIC HEALTH SCIENCES UNIT

4 LILYBANK GARDENS

GLASGOW G12 8RZ

British Social Attitudes

Attitudes The 20th REPORT

The *National Centre for Social Research* (NatCen) is an independent, non-profit social research institute. It has a large professional staff together with its own interviewing and coding resources. Some of NatCen's work – such as the survey reported in this book – is initiated by the institute itself and grant-funded by research councils or foundations. Other work is initiated by government departments, local authorities or quasi-government organisations to provide information on aspects of social or economic policy. NatCen also works frequently with other institutes and academics. Founded in 1969 and now Britain's largest social research institute, NatCen has a high reputation for the standard of its work in both qualitative and quantitative research. NatCen has a Survey Methods Centre and, with the Department of Sociology, University of Oxford, houses the Centre for Research into Elections and Social Trends (CREST).

The contributors

Arturo Alvarez Rosete
Research Officer at the King's Fund

John Appleby
Chief Economist at the King's Fund

Michaela Brockmann
Research Officer at City University

Catherine Bromley
Senior Researcher at NatCen, Scotland and Co-Director of the *British Social Attitudes* survey series

Ian Christie
Associate of the New Economics Foundation and visiting professor at the Centre for Environmental Strategy, University of Surrey

Rosemary Crompton
Professor of Sociology at City University

John Curtice
Research Consultant at NatCen, Scotland, Deputy Director of CREST, and Professor of Politics at Strathclyde University

Geoffrey Evans
Professor and Official Fellow in Politics, Nuffield College Oxford

Sonia Exley
Researcher at NatCen and Co-Director of the *British Social Attitudes* survey series

Steve Fisher
Lecturer in Political Sociology and Fellow of Trinity College Oxford

Anthony Heath
Professor of Sociology at the University of Oxford and Co-Director of CREST

Lindsey Jarvis
Research Director at NatCen and Co-Director of the *British Social Attitudes* survey series

Alison Park
Research Director at NatCen and Co-Director of the *British Social Attitudes* survey series

Catherine Rothon
Research Officer for CREST at the University of Oxford

Tom Sefton
Research Fellow at the ESRC Research Centre for Analysis of Social Exclusion (CASE) at the London School of Economics

Ben Seyd
Senior Research Fellow at the Constitution Unit, University College London

Paula Surridge
Lecturer in Sociology at the University of Bristol

Katarina Thomson
Research Director at NatCen and Co-Director of the *British Social Attitudes* survey series

Richard D Wiggins
Professor of Social Statistics at City University

Ted Wragg
Professor of Education at Exeter University

British Social Attitudes

Attitudes

The 20th
REPORT

Continuity and change over two decades

EDITORS

Alison Park

John Curtice

Katarina Thomson

Lindsey Jarvis

Catherine Bromley

SAGE Publications
London · Thousand Oaks · New Delhi

NatCen
National Centre for Social Research

SAGE Publications Ltd
6 Bonhill Street
London EC2A 4PU

SAGE Publications Inc.
2455 Teller Road
Thousand Oaks, California 91320

SAGE Publications India Pvt Ltd
B-42, Panchsheel Enclave
Post Box 4109
New Delhi 100 017

British Library Cataloguing in Publication data

A catalogue record for this book is available from the British Library

ISSN 0267 6869
ISBN 0-7619-4277-7

Library of Congress Control Number available

Printed in Great Britain by The Cromwell Press Ltd, Trowbridge, Wiltshire

Contents

6   Pass or fail? Perceptions of education

7   Charting change in British values

List of tables and figures

Chapter 1

Chapter 2

Chapter 3

Chapter 4

Chapter 5

Chapter 6

Chapter 7

Chapter 8

Chapter 9

Chapter 10

Chapter 11

Conclusion

Appendix I

Introduction

This report analyses and describes the findings of the latest *British Social Attitudes* survey. The series began in 1983 and, some 50,000 interviews later, we mark its twentieth year by paying particular attention to the myriad ways in which Britain's attitudes and values have changed over the last two decades – and to the many areas in which they have remained remarkably constant over time.

Changing Britain?

How has Britain changed over the last two decades? In this introduction, we briefly consider some of the most important demographic, political and social changes that have occurred over this period – many of which, as we shall see later, have had important implications for our attitudes and values.

The labour market is one area which has radically changed over the last twenty years. In the early 1980s, unemployment was at its peak, with twelve per cent of the labour force unemployed in 1984, well over double the rate now (five per cent). The nature of the work available has also changed markedly, with structural changes in the economy (particularly the shift from manufacturing to service sector industries) resulting in a sharp increase in more middle-class 'white collar' occupations, and a concomitant decline in working-class 'blue collar' ones. The steepest increase has been in professional and managerial occupations – in 1986, 22 per cent of people were classified as belonging to this group, compared with nearly a third now (32 per cent), making it the single largest social class in Britain. Meanwhile, the 'working class' has shrunk considerably. As described in our *19th Report*, so too has union membership (Bryson and Gomez, 2002). In Chapter 7, we consider whether these sorts of changes mean that the notion of different 'classes' no longer applies in modern Britain.

Such labour market changes have been accompanied by shifts in the attributes of those entering the labour force. Perhaps the most dramatic has been the marked increase in the proportion of graduates; in 1986, seven per cent of

British Social Attitudes respondents had a degree – now 16 per cent do so. This reflects the fact that, by 2003, more than one pupil in three was entering the higher education sector, compared with one in seven two decades earlier. Just what this means for attitudes to education is discussed in Chapter 6. Meanwhile, the proportion of women, particularly mothers, in the labour market has continued to increase. Chapter 8 considers how attitudes towards gender roles have shifted over the same period.

The rewards of work have also changed. Since the mid-1980s, average incomes have increased by 50 per cent. But this has been accompanied by a marked increase in income inequality, leading some to argue that we are now more tolerant of inequality than in the past. In Chapter 4, we consider whether or not this is the case, focusing particularly on whether British society has become more accepting of inequality in the wake of Margaret Thatcher's period in office.

Of course, it is not just the labour market that has changed. So too have other aspects of British society. Over the last decade, Britain's ethnic minority population grew by just over 50 per cent, and now represents eight per cent of the population of the United Kingdom. Whether such increased ethnic diversity has lead to a change in levels of racial prejudice in Britain is explored in Chapter 9.

Car ownership has expanded. At the end of 2000, there were over 24 million cars registered in the UK, twice the total for 1975. Over 70 per cent of households had regular use of a car. Car use dominates our travel patterns, accounting for 85 per cent of all passenger kilometres in 2000 (ONS, 2001). At the same time, evidence of the deleterious consequences of car use (such as its contribution to global warming and poor air quality) has grown. In Chapter 3, we examine how attitudes to public and private transport have changed over time, and how far we have come to accept that car use might need to be curbed.

Other important changes form the backdrop to more than one chapter in this report. Demographically, British society is ageing, the result of lower fertility rates and increased life expectancy, combined with fluctuations in the birth rate over time. The number of people aged 65 and over in the UK has increased by 51 per cent since 1961, to 9.4 million in 2001 (Summerfield and Babb, 2003). We are less religious too; in 1983, only 31 per cent of *British Social Attitudes* respondents said they did not regard themselves as belonging to any particular religion, but by 2002 this had increased to 41 per cent. Family life has changed, with notable increases in the proportions of people who cohabit, are divorced, or remain single. As outlined in our *18th Report*, cohabitation rates have increased particularly dramatically, from five to 15 per cent of all couples between 1986 and 1999 (Barlow *et al.*, 2001). The proportion of children born outside marriage has increased, with a quarter of children now born to cohabiting families. In 1983, 65 per cent of *British Social Attitudes* respondents were owner-occupiers; by 2002, this group included nearly three-quarters of the sample (74 per cent). Conversely, the proportion in 'social housing' (that is, those renting from local authorities or housing associations) fell from 27 to 16 per cent. Technologies have changed, and increased affluence has meant that increasing numbers have earlier access to them. The new technologies of 1983 were the compact disc and camcorder; since then, we have witnessed the exponential rise of the mobile phone and the Internet, both of which have had profound implications for the way in which we live our lives.

It is not just Britain that has changed. So too has the world in which it operates. In 1983, the Berlin Wall still divided Europe, symbolising the continued conflict between 'East' and 'West'. That year, Yuri Andropov was President of the USSR and Ronald Reagan was the President of the USA. There was widespread global concern about security and, not surprisingly, a major theme in the first *British Social Attitudes* questionnaire was nuclear weapons and nuclear disarmament. Now, of course, the Cold War has been replaced by a quite different international conflict, and much of Eastern and Central Europe is on the verge of joining a European Union, most of whose members have adopted a common currency. Britain now lives in a 'globalised' world in which more of its citizens take foreign holidays, restrictions on the movement of capital are few and far between, and worldwide communication is facilitated by the Internet. Just how our attitudes towards Europe have evolved against this backdrop is discussed in Chapter 10.

Politically too, 1983 seems very long ago. Margaret Thatcher's Conservative Party enjoyed their second election victory, winning 44 per cent of the vote and all but wiping out Michael Foot's Labour Party as an electoral force in the south of England. Labour's share of the vote that year, at 28 per cent, was not far off the 26 per cent achieved by the alliance between the newly formed Social Democratic Party and the Liberals. The aftermath of the election saw Michael Foot resign, to be replaced by Neil Kinnock (who, in turn, would be replaced by John Smith after another election defeat in 1992). These defeats were to persuade the Labour Party of the need to reform itself before it could end the Conservatives' apparently endless success and, in 1997, New Labour secured a record-breaking victory under the leadership of Tony Blair. But how far was the Conservatives' success underpinned by an ideological drift to the right to which Labour had to accommodate itself before winning power? Chapter Eleven considers this by comparing public opinion during Margaret Thatcher's premiership and Tony Blair's period as Labour leader.

In the aftermath of the 1983 election, the focus was largely upon how those who had voted (73 per cent of the electorate) had chosen to cast their ballots. But by 2001, fewer than six in ten (59 per cent) voted at all, the lowest level since 1918. Not surprisingly then, the attention paid to those who did *not* vote has almost equalled that paid to those who did. The extent to which these developments mark a crisis of political participation is explored in Chapter 5.

Throughout the last twenty years, one subject has been pre-eminent in the country's political debate – the appropriate balance between taxation and spending. Policy, of course, has been far from constant. Under Margaret Thatcher's regime, income tax rates fell. But, more recently, the Labour government has increased national insurance to help fund large increases in public spending. Chapter 1 examines how attitudes to taxation and spending have changed, looking in particular at attitudes towards welfare benefits and their recipients. Meanwhile, Chapter 2 focuses upon one of the most popular nominees for any extra public spending, the National Health Service, and assesses the extent to which attitudes to the NHS are affected by spending levels.

Our thanks

Over the years, the *British Social Attitudes* series has developed a widely acknowledged reputation as *the* authoritative map of contemporary British values. In achieving this, it owes a great deal to its many generous funders. We are particularly grateful to our core funder – the Gatsby Charitable Foundation (one of the Sainsbury Family Charitable Trusts) – whose continuous support of the series from the start has given it security and independence. Many other funders have also made long-term commitments to the study and we are ever grateful to them as well. In 2002 these included the Department of Health, the Department for Transport, the Departments for Education and Skills, Trade and Industry, and Work and Pensions, and the Office of the Deputy Prime Minister. Thanks are also due to the Institute of Community Studies. We are also very grateful to the Economic and Social Research Council (ESRC) who provided funding for two modules of questions that year, one examining political legitimacy and participation (funded through its Democracy and Participation Programme) and a second which examined employment, the family and work–life balance.

The ESRC also supported the *National Centre*'s participation in the *International Social Survey Programme*, which now comprises 42 nations, each of whom help to design and then field a set of equivalent questions every year on a rotating set of issues. The topic in 2002 was the family and changing gender roles, the British results of which are explored in Chapter 8.

One recent spin-off from the *British Social Attitudes* series has been the development of an annual *Scottish Social Attitudes* survey. This began in 1999 and is funded from a range of sources along similar lines to *British Social Attitudes*. It is closely associated with its British counterpart and incorporates many of the same questions to enable comparison north and south of the border, while also providing a detailed examination of attitudes to particular issues within Scotland. Three books have now been published about the survey (Paterson *et al.*, 2000; Curtice *et al.*, 2001; Bromley *et al.*, 2003).

The *British Social Attitudes* series is a team effort. A research group designs, directs and reports on the study. This year, the group bid farewell to a valuable colleague, Sonia Exley, now at Nuffield College, Oxford. The researchers are supported by complementary teams who implement the sampling strategy and carry out data processing. They in turn depend on fieldwork controllers, area managers and field interviewers who are responsible for getting all the interviewing done, and on administrative staff to compile, organise and distribute the survey's extensive documentation. In this respect, particular thanks are due to Kerrie Gemmill and her colleagues in the *National Centre*'s Operations Department in Brentwood. Other thanks are due to Susan Corbett and her colleagues in our computing department who expertly translate our questions into a computer-assisted questionnaire. Meanwhile, the raw data have to be transformed into a workable SPSS system file – a task that has for many years been performed with great care and efficiency by Ann Mair at the Social Statistics Laboratory in the University of Strathclyde. Many thanks are also due to Lucy Robinson and Fabienne Pedroletti at Sage, our publishers.

Last, but by no means least, we must praise the anonymous respondents across Britain who gave their time to take part in our 2002 survey. Like the 50,000 or so respondents who have participated before them, they are the cornerstone of this enterprise. We hope that some of them will one day come across this volume and read about themselves with interest.

The Editors

References

Barlow, A., Duncan, S., James, G. and Park, A. (2001), 'Just a piece of paper? Marriage and cohabition', in Park, A., Curtice, J., Thomson, K., Jarvis, L. and Bromley, C. (eds.), *British Social Attitudes: the 18th Report*, London: Sage.

Bromley, C., Curtice, J., Hinds, K. and Park, A. (eds.) (2003), *Devolution – Scottish Answers to Scottish Questions?*, Edinburgh: Edinburgh University Press.

Bryson, A. and Gomez, R. (2002), 'Marching on together? Recent trends in union membership', in Park, A., Curtice, J., Thomson, K., Jarvis, L. and Bromley, C. (eds.), *British Social Attitudes: the 19th Report*, London: Sage.

Curtice, J., McCrone, D., Park, A. and Paterson, L. (eds.) (2001), *New Scotland, New Society? Are social and political ties fragmenting?*, Edinburgh: Edinburgh University Press.

Office for National Statistics (ONS) (2001), *Social Trends 2001*, London: The Stationery Office.

Paterson, L., Brown, A., Curtice, J., Hinds, K., McCrone, D., Park, A., Sproston, K. and Surridge, P. (2000), *New Scotland, New Politics?*, Edinburgh: Edinburgh University Press.

Summerfield, C. and Babb, P. (eds) (2003), *Social Trends No 33*, London: The Stationery Office.

1 What we want from the welfare state

Tom Sefton *

When the Conservative Party came to power in 1979, they argued that excessive public expenditure was at the heart of Britain's economic difficulties and that the levels of taxation needed to finance past rates of growth in public spending had become unsustainable (Burchardt and Hills, 1999). Since then, the welfare state has come under considerable pressure as successive governments have questioned the way different aspects of it are funded and provided. Social security has attracted particular attention as it became widely recognised that the system established by Beveridge was no longer appropriate for the late 20th century, given the changes in the social and economic climate that have taken place since 1945 (DSS, 1998). At the same time, the social demands that led to a steady growth in public spending have not gone away: as incomes rise, people want better education and health care services, whilst higher unemployment and an ageing population have further added to the pressure on resources. As Glennerster puts it, "it is not merely that the lid [on welfare spending] has been put on, but that the steam pressure in the pot has been rising too" (Glennerster, 1998: 311).

The broad aim of the Conservative Party's social policy in the 1980s and early 1990s was to roll back the state, ostensibly by targeting spending more effectively on the poor. This was in part an attempt to reduce public expenditure for the reasons discussed above, but the aim was also ideological: the Conservatives were keen to promote choice and consumerism, including greater use of privately funded and/or provided welfare services, and they sought to emphasise personal responsibility and reduce welfare dependency by cutting back on fraud and making life on benefits less attractive.

In many respects, the New Labour government has sought to adapt rather than reverse this broad thrust of policies. It committed itself to the Conservative's fiscally conservative spending plans for its first two years in office and declared

* Tom Sefton is Research Fellow at the Economic and Social Research Council Research Centre for Analysis of Social Exclusion (CASE) at the London School of Economics.

that Labour was no longer a 'tax and spend' party (although in the 2001 Budget, it announced a rise in national insurance contributions to fund higher spending on the NHS). Reducing welfare dependence is still high on the political agenda, but is couched in terms of promoting opportunity: 'a hand up, rather than a handout'. Paid work, rather than income redistribution is seen as the best route out of poverty. The emphasis on personal responsibility (e.g. to look for work) has, if anything, been strengthened under Labour with more conditions being attached to the receipt of certain benefits.

Commentators disagree about how fundamental the restructuring of the welfare state has been in practice. Those who emphasise the changes have talked about a 'new' welfare state, while those who stress the continuities refer to a 'resilient' welfare state (Powell, 1999). However, all would agree that there have been some significant changes over the last twenty years, even if these have not always matched the political rhetoric. These include tighter controls on public spending, the decline of social housing, the growth in private pensions, the increased involvement of the private sector in the provision, and in some cases the funding, of welfare services, and greater means-testing and conditionality of benefits.

The 1986 *British Social Attitudes Report* argued that there was "a collectivism of attitude" towards the role of the welfare state which was shared by about two-thirds of the population and by people of quite different ideological viewpoints (Bosanquet, 1986). We are now in a position to examine whether this consensus around the core elements of the welfare state has weakened or strengthened over the intervening period, against the backdrop of rising incomes and expectations, changing economic orthodoxy, and a change in government. The first two sections of this chapter focus on attitudes towards public spending and spending priorities. The following section looks at whether previously divided opinions on the social security system – the most contentious aspect of the welfare state – have swung decisively in one direction or the other. The final section considers the increasing use of private welfare services and whether this has affected people's attitudes towards the welfare state.

We might expect trends in public opinion to have followed one of three different trajectories, depending on public reactions to changing government policies. The first possibility is that the public are resistant to any attempt to reduce or redefine the role of the welfare state. Under this scenario, people would become increasingly frustrated by the perceived under-funding of public services, translating over time into a growing dissatisfaction with public services and increased support for higher public spending. The second possibility is that government policies have led or reflected public attitudes towards the welfare state. In this case we would expect to see broad agreement with current levels of public spending, a hardening of attitudes towards benefit claimants and support for a 'modernised' and/or more stream-lined welfare state. The third possibility is that both these trends are present among different people – public opinion would then have become more divided over time, perhaps along ideological grounds. A distinct and growing group of private welfare users may have emerged with very different attitudes towards public spending and the welfare state. In this case, we would now see no broad consensus either way over the role and operation of the welfare state. We shall use this chapter to examine whether there is any evidence of these three changes happening.

Attitudes towards public spending

The *British Social Attitudes* survey contains a general question on taxation and spending on the welfare state which has been asked consistently over the history of the survey series:

> *Suppose the government had to choose between the three options on this card. Which do you think it should choose?*
> * *Reduce taxes and spend less on health, education and social benefits*
> * *Keep taxes and spending on these services at the same level as now*
> * *Increase taxes and spend more on health, education and social benefits*

When the first *British Social Attitudes* survey was carried out in 1983, the majority of respondents (54 per cent) felt that taxes and spending on the welfare state should be kept at the same level. Around a third (32 per cent) felt they should be higher and about a tenth (9 per cent) said they should be lower. During the 1980s, the balance shifted clearly in favour of higher taxes and welfare spending. By 1991, nearly two-thirds (65 per cent) of respondents said that government should increase taxes and spending and only three per cent said they should reduce them. Except for a downward blip in 2000, support for higher taxes and spending has remained strong ever since (this is shown by the black line in Figure 1.1).

The 2001 Budget incorporated an explicit policy of raising direct taxes to finance higher spending on selected public services, marking a decisive shift away from the prudence and fiscal constraint that has characterised government spending plans over the previous twenty years (Taylor-Gooby and Hastie, 2002). We might therefore have expected public support for higher taxes and spending to have fallen in the most recent survey. Some people who had previously supported higher taxes and spending might have felt that the increases announced by the government were sufficient and that further increases were no longer justified. However, this did not happen; support for higher taxes and spending actually increased in 2002 and now stands at 63 per cent – about the same level as in 1997. This could be interpreted as a vote of confidence for the government's more expansive fiscal policy. Alternatively, and less favourably, it could be seen as a measure of people's continued dissatisfaction with public services and continued demand for even more public spending. It is also possible that public opinion simply has not yet responded to these changes and that there is a lag in changes in attitudes: the actual tax increases and much of the increased spending only came into effect from April

2003, after the 2002 *British Social Attitudes* survey fieldwork had been carried out.

Be that as it may, trends in attitudes towards public spending appear to be quite closely related to general levels of (dis)satisfaction with public services, with a slight lag, as shown in Figure 1.1. Periods when support for higher spending has increased (in the 1980s, second half of the 1990s, and post-2000) follow periods of growing dissatisfaction with the National Health Service. Similarly, support for higher public spending fell off in the early 1990s and again in the late 1990s when satisfaction with the NHS had been rising. Dissatisfaction with the performance of secondary schools has followed a similar trend over the last decade – falling in the early 1990s, rising in the mid–1990s, falling in the late 1990s and then rising again since 2000. This supports the view that demands for higher spending are driven at least in part by dissatisfaction with public services.

Figure 1.1　Dissatisfaction with health and education and attitudes towards public spending, 1983–2002

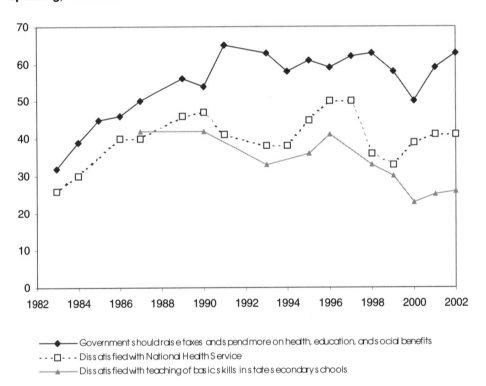

————◆———— Government should raise taxes and spend more on health, education, and social benefits

- - -□- - - Dissatisfied with National Health Service

————▲———— Dissatisfied with teaching of basic skills in state secondary schools

Not only do the trends over time match, but those individuals who are least satisfied with the NHS are generally more likely to favour higher taxes and public spending, presumably because they believe that under-funding is part of the problem. However, support for higher spending has risen most among those who say they are *satisfied* with health services. In 2002, 62 per cent of those who were satisfied with the NHS felt that government should increase taxes and spend more on health, education and social benefits – an increase of 33 percentage points since 1983, compared to an increase of 21 percentage points amongst those who are dissatisfied with the NHS. Thus, people's attitudes towards public spending appear to be strongly influenced by general perceptions about the quality of public services, as well as their own personal level of satisfaction.

In addition to the general question about taxation and spending on the welfare state, the *British Social Attitudes* survey also regularly asks a number of more specific questions about welfare benefits and redistribution. For example, respondents are asked to agree or disagree with the following two statements:

> *The government should spend more money on welfare benefits for the poor, even if it leads to higher taxes*

> *Government should redistribute income from the better-off to those who are less well off*

Figure 1.2 Attitudes towards spending on welfare benefits and redistribution, 1986–2002

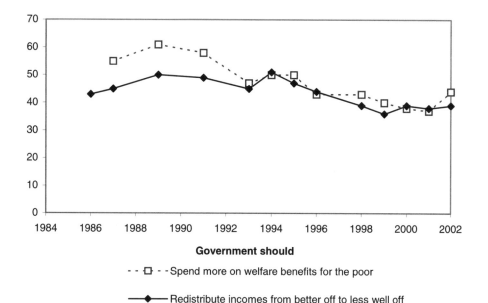

Government should

- - ☐ - - Spend more on welfare benefits for the poor

——◆—— Redistribute incomes from better off to less well off

Strong and sustained support for higher spending on "health, education, and social benefits" contrasts with a decline in support for more spending on welfare benefits for the poor. As seen in Figure 1.2 above, this has been falling since the late 1980s (though even after the decline, more people favour higher spending than favour lower spending). There is also a decline over the same period in the proportion of people agreeing that the government should seek to redistribute income. One way of interpreting these trends is that when people say they want more spending on health, education, and social benefits, they mean higher spending on services in kind, not social benefits or, at least, not those social benefits that are targeted at poor households.

The decline in support for spending on welfare benefits for the poor was much greater among certain groups within the population, in particular younger people and Labour supporters. The next table shows that, in 1987, almost three-quarters of those who identified with the Labour Party said they would support an increase in welfare spending on the poor; by 2002, this had fallen to half – a fall of 23 percentage points. For those who identified with the Conservative Party, the corresponding fall was just one percentage point (albeit from the much lower level of 38 per cent). Similarly, the rise in support for public spending on health, education, and social benefits was much more muted among Labour supporters. In the case of attitudes towards redistribution, views were unchanged among Conservative supporters, while support fell by 20 percentage points among Labour supporters.

Table 1.1 Changing attitudes towards welfare spending and redistribution by party identification, 1987-2002

% who agree that the government should ...	1987	Base	1996	Base	2002	Base	Change 1987–2002
... increase taxes and spend more on health, education and social benefits							
Conservative	35	506	49	859	55	728	+20
Labour	64	337	68	1324	69	1187	+5
... spend more money on welfare benefits even if this means higher taxes							
Conservative	38	1095	26	1012	37	856	-1
Labour	73	824	56	1528	50	1400	-23
... redistribute income from better off to those who are worse off							
Conservative	21	986	22	859	21	728	0
Labour	69	699	58	1324	49	1187	-20

This comparison is slightly misleading since the composition of Labour Party supporters also changed over this period: the Labour Party was attracting new supporters whose views on welfare spending and redistribution were probably more conservative than those of 'traditional' supporters. Nevertheless, attitudes towards public spending and redistribution appear to be less divided along ideological grounds than was the case in the 1980s. During this same period, the Labour Party has gradually distanced itself from an explicit policy of income redistribution, culminating in a firm commitment not to raise the higher rate of income tax. In his book on the 'third way', Powell argues that New Labour has sought to redefine redistribution in terms of opportunities, as opposed to incomes, quoting from a statement made by Gordon Brown in 1996:

> For too long, we have used the tax and benefit system to compensate people for their poverty rather than doing something more fundamental – tackling the root causes of poverty and inequality ... the road to equality of opportunity starts not with tax rates, but with jobs, education ... (Powell, 1999:17–18)

It is possible that Labour supporters have been persuaded that this new approach to tackling poverty is better than one of income redistribution and have modified their views accordingly. Alternatively, New Labour may have adapted their policies to be more in tune with changing public attitudes. Either way, reduced support for spending on welfare benefits for the poor may reflect a lack of enthusiasm for this particular instrument of redistribution, rather than the objective of redistribution itself.

As seen in Table 1.2, there is widespread support for higher spending on benefits for certain 'deserving' groups, such as parents who work on low incomes, disabled people and pensioners – who constitute the majority of poor households. Even among those who said they did not support higher spending on welfare benefits for the poor in general, two-thirds said they would like more government spending on benefits for pensioners, and over half favoured higher spending on benefits for disabled people and parents working on very low incomes. Thus, people seem happy for redistribution to take place as a 'side-effect' of supporting particular vulnerable groups. This corroborates the findings of recent qualitative research on attitudes towards public spending and redistribution, which found that, whilst few of those who participated in the focus group discussions supported redistribution for its own sake, most believed that people's basic needs should be met whether or not they had enough money to pay and recognised that this would mean that some people put less in and take more out of the welfare state than others (Hedges, forthcoming).

There is far less support for spending on benefits for single parents and unemployed people, perhaps because these groups are seen as less 'deserving' or because people now believe that other policies, such as the New Deal, are the most appropriate way to assist these groups. As the next table shows, even among those who supported more spending on welfare benefits in general, only a third wanted more spent on the unemployed. Respondents hugely overestimate the amount spent on benefits for the unemployed. The 2001 *British Social Attitudes* survey showed that almost half (44 per cent) of respondents believed that benefits for unemployed people comprised the largest share of the social security budget, whereas in reality they account for only around six per cent of the total – less than a tenth of the amount spent on retirement pensions and less than half that spent on children or disabled people (Taylor-Gooby and Hastie, 2002). This may explain why there is less support for spending on welfare benefits, as opposed to public spending more generally, given that spending on unemployed people is much less popular than spending on other groups of benefit recipients and is becoming less popular over time.

Table 1.2 Public attitudes towards welfare spending on poor or vulnerable groups

	% who say they would like to see more government spending on benefits for:					
	Retired people	Disabled people who cannot work	Parents who work on very low incomes	Single parents	Unemployed people	*Base*
Of those who **agree** that government should spend more on welfare benefits for the poor	79	78	78	47	33	*1314*
Of those who **disagree** that government should spend more on welfare benefits for the poor	67	56	58	27	7	*739*

At the same time, there is evidence that the attitudes of younger age groups towards the welfare state are diverging in important respects from those of older age groups. As seen in the next table, the proportion of 18–34 year olds who felt that more should be spent on welfare benefits for the poor fell by 17 percentage points between 1987 and 2002, compared with a fall of six percentage points among those aged 55 or over. The same trend is evident in a number of related questions, including attitudes towards public spending on health, education and social benefits and redistribution from better off to less well off households. The table also shows that most of these changes occurred during the first part of this period (between 1987 and 1996). Thus, a significant age differential seems to have emerged in attitudes towards public spending, which was not evident in the 1980s. Further analysis confirms that these differences between younger and older age groups are now statistically significant even after taking account of a range of other factors that may also influence people's attitudes towards public spending. (For further details of this multivariate analysis, see the appendix to this chapter.) The effect on attitudes towards public spending of being in the 18–34 age group (relative to the reference group of 35–54 year olds) is roughly equivalent to the effect of being a Conservative, as opposed to a Labour, supporter.

Table 1.3 Changing attitudes towards welfare spending and redistribution by age group, 1987–2002

% who agree that the government should ...	1987	Base	1996	Base	2002	Base	Change 1987–2002
... increase taxes and spend more on health, education, and social benefits							
Age:　18–34	51	885	53	1035	55	900	+4
35–54	53	1024	65	1261	67	1249	+14
55+	46	933	60	1309	64	1282	+18
... spend more money on welfare benefits even if this means higher taxes							
Age:　18–34	48	399	32	875	31	745	-17
35–54	57	478	46	1111	45	1086	-12
55+	59	402	51	1091	53	1065	-6
... redistribute income from better off to those who are worse off							
Age:　18–34	50	781	44	875	34	745	-16
35–54	42	917	46	1111	38	1086	-4
55+	42	792	43	1091	43	1065	+1

The survey questions are very general, so it is not possible to tell whether younger people are becoming less enthusiastic about the welfare state in general (relative to older age groups) or whether their responses are driven by a reaction against particular forms of public spending. Previous *British Social Attitudes* surveys have asked a separate set of questions about whether people would favour higher spending on specific items, including health, education, old age pensions, and unemployment benefits. The next table shows the proportion of respondents who would like to see more spending on each of these areas, broken down by age group. This shows that the age differential in attitudes towards public spending changed across all areas of spending in the period up to 1996. In the case of health care and old age pensions, support for higher spending fell among 18–34 year olds, but rose among other age groups. In the case of education and unemployment benefits, support for higher spending among the youngest age group either rose by less or fell by more than among older age groups.

Table 1.4 Changing attitudes towards spending on public services by age group, 1985–1996

	1987	Base	1996	Base	2002	Base	Change 1987–2002
% who say that much more should be spent on health							
Age: 18–34	37	535	38	380	36	275	-1
35–54	32	536	34	429	44	364	+12
55+	36	459	35	410	45	348	+9
% who say that much more should be spent on education							
Age: 18–34	25	535	28	380	29	275	+4
35–54	23	536	27	429	34	364	+11
55+	16	459	24	410	29	348	+13
% who say that much more should be spent on old age pensions							
Age: 18–34	20	535	18	380	15	275	-5
35–54	19	536	24	429	22	364	+3
55+	37	459	38	410	42	348	+5
% who say that more or much more should be spent on unemployment benefits							
Age: 18–34	44	535	40	380	32	275	-12
35–54	35	536	38	429	32	364	-3
55+	39	459	40	410	37	348	-2

Unfortunately, this set of questions has not been asked since 1996. However, the 2001 survey asked respondents whether they would support either a 1p or 3p increase in income tax to finance higher spending on various items, including those listed in Table 1.4. The age differentials are as great, if not greater, than in 1996 (although it is not possible to make direct comparisons, because the questions are worded differently). For example, only a quarter (27 per cent) of 18–34 year olds said they would strongly favour a 1p increase to pay for higher spending on health, compared with over two-fifths (43 per cent) of 35–54 year olds, and half (50 per cent) of those aged 55 or over. In the case of pensions, the corresponding figures were 10 per cent, 15 per cent and 31 per cent.

Thus, the evidence does indeed point to a general decline in support for the welfare state amongst younger people compared with older generations. This finding is consistent with the response to another question about whether the creation of the welfare state is one of Britain's proudest achievements. In 2002, only a third (35 per cent) of 18–34 year olds agreed with this statement, compared with half (52 per cent) of 35–54 year olds and two-thirds (69 per cent) of those aged 55 or over. This is also consistent with changing attitudes towards the social security system, which show a divergence over time between younger and older age groups. We shall return to this point later in the chapter.

This difference in attitudes may be confined to this particular cohort of young people. Several commentators have previously remarked that the children who grew up knowing only Conservative governments – 'Thatcher's children' may as adults have rather more 'conservative' views than their parents who grew up in the 1960s and 1970s (Gordon *et al.*, 2000). Alternatively, this trend may signal the beginning of a long-term decline in support for the welfare state – with successive generations being less favourable towards public spending and the welfare state. This assumes that current and future generations of young people will continue to be less enthusiastic about the welfare state as they grow older compared with previous generations.

Spending priorities

The previous section focused on public attitudes towards overall levels of spending on public services and welfare benefits. This section examines the priorities attached to different areas of public spending and how these have changed over time.

Table 1.5 First or second priorities for extra government spending, 1983–2002

	1983	1987	1991	1996	2002	Change 1983– 2002
	%	%	%	%	%	
Health	63	79	74	80	79	+16
Education	50	56	62	66	63	+13
Help for industry	29	12	10	9	4	-25
Housing	21	24	21	12	10	-11
Social security	12	12	11	8	5	-7
Defence	8	4	4	2	3	-5
Police and prisons	8	8	6	11	14	+6
Roads	5	3	5	3	6	+1
Public transport	3	1	5	6	13	+10
Overseas aid	1	1	1	1	2	+1
Base	*1761*	*2847*	*2918*	*3620*	*3435*	

As seen in Table 1.5, the priority given to different spending areas has changed markedly over the last two decades. In the 1980s, the importance attached to health and education increased at the expense of help for industry. The latter in part reflected the improvement in the economy from the early 1980s, but also a change in economic orthodoxy that no longer favoured state support for ailing industries. (Support for state help for industry only increased slightly during the recession at the beginning of the 1990s before falling off again as the economy recovered.) As we have already seen, the increasing support for spending on health and education coincided with growing dissatisfaction with the National Health Service and low levels of satisfaction with schools. During the 1990s, the biggest increases were for police and prisons and, more recently, public transport, while housing fell down people's list of priorities.

Table 1.6 Changes in overall spending priorities by sub-group, 1983–2002

	Change in percentage who say their first or second priority for extra government spending would be ...					
	Health	Education	Housing	Social security	Public transp.	Base
All	+16	+13	-11	-7	+10	1761,3434
Age group						
18–34	+16	+13	-8	-6	+11	525,900
55+	+16	+11	-13	-6	+10	607,1282
Household type						
Without children	+17	+12	-13	-7	+11	1289,2522
With children	+13	+16	-7	-5	+8	472,913
Income [+]						
Low	+23	+16	-12	-13	+8	269,830
High	+13	+7	-10	-2	+15	294,511
Tenure						
Owner-occupier	+18	+11	-10	-5	+10	1148,2433
Social sector tenant	+9	+14	-7	-6	+8	491,658
Party identification						
Conservative	+17	+10	-10	-3	+12	676,856
Labour	+14	+17	-15	-11	+10	584,1400

+ Household income levels were defined as follows: 1983 high: £12,000+, low: £3,000 or below; 2002 high: £44,000+, low: £10,000 or below.

First base shown in each row is for 1983; second base is for 2002.

How these changes are mirrored across different subgroups of the population is shown in the table above. All subgroups are giving a higher priority to spending on health, education, and public transport and a lower priority to housing and social security. This is true even among those groups with a vested interest in those areas that are becoming less popular. For example, the priority attached to social security has fallen most dramatically among those on low incomes who would be most likely to benefit most from higher spending in this area. Similarly, the priority attached to housing fell significantly among tenants in social rented housing as well as owner-occupiers. Thus, there appears to be a strong consensus about *changes* in overall spending priorities over time.

The same is broadly true for the priorities attached to different groups of benefit recipients over time. The next table shows that, for nearly all sub-groups, benefits for pensioners and children have become a higher priority over the last twenty years, whilst benefits for lone parents and unemployed people have become a lower priority. The latter is consistent with a hardening of attitudes towards recipients of unemployment benefits, especially among younger people, As we shall see in the next section, this is apparent in people's responses to a range of other questions about the social security system.

Table 1.7 Changes in priorities for social benefits spending by subgroup, 1983–2001

	Change in percentage who say their first or second priority for extra government spending on social benefits would be ...					
	Pensions	Disabled	Children	Single parents	Unem-ployed	*Base*
All	+12	-1	+15	-7	-20	*1761,3287*
Age group						
18–34	+6	+3	+22	0	-30	*525,793*
55+	+10	-1	+8	-8	-12	*607,1222*
Household type						
Without children	+12	+1	+13	-8	-19	*1289,2410*
With children	+9	-6	+21	-1	-24	*472,877*
Income +						
Low	+1	-3	+7	+3	-10	*269,662*
High	+13	-5	+20	-13	-19	*294,545*
Economic status						
In work	+13	-5	+22	-9	-21	*935,1766*
Unemployed	-7	+7	+12	+18	-29	*124,127*
Retired	+7	0	+7	-7	-11	*272,814*
Party identification						
Conservative	+14	-2	+16	-16	-16	*676,743*
Labour	+11	+3	+15	-4	-28	*584,1481*

+ Household income levels were defined as follows: 1983 high: £12,000+, low: £3,000 or below; 2001 high: £38,000+, low: £8,000 or below.
First base shown in each row is for 1983; second base is for 2001.

The level of unemployment was much lower at the end of the period, which might also explain the reduced priority attached to unemployment benefits.

Interestingly, the greatest fall in support is among unemployed people themselves – the proportion of unemployed people who said that benefits for the unemployed were their first or second priority for higher spending on social benefits fell by 29 percentage points between 1983 and 2001.

However, there are some notable differences between subgroups. For example, at the beginning of this period higher income groups and Conservative supporters were *more* supportive of benefits for single parents than lower income groups or Labour supporters. This position had reversed by the end of the period, perhaps because of the changing composition of single parents, in particular the growing proportion of never-married single parents.

Attitudes towards social security

In his chapter on the 1983 *British Social Attitudes* survey, Bosanquet noted that the claiming and take-up of benefits generated strongly held opinions with substantial differences along party lines – for example, on questions about the adequacy of benefits and the amount of fraud (Bosanquet, 1984). Is this still the case twenty years later?

The position of the Conservative governments in the 1980s and early 1990s was clear: dependence on benefits was not only bad for the economy, but also gave adverse incentives to the unemployed, who were less likely to seek jobs if they could get by on benefits. As noted in the introduction to this chapter, New Labour took on board many of these arguments in developing its approach to reforming the benefits system. With a mixture of 'sticks' (e.g. stronger obligations to look for work) and 'carrots' (e.g. more assistance in looking for work and financial incentives to 'make work pay'), the Labour government has attempted to create a more active welfare state, based on the principle of 'work for those who can, security for those who can't', with a strong emphasis on the former.

The 1994 *British Social Attitudes* survey showed little evidence that the public had bought these arguments. According to Lipsey, "detailed questioning fails to suggest that a majority of the public believe that welfare spending is either wasteful or that it acts as a disincentive" (Lipsey, 1995: 4). However, the 1998 survey highlighted a dramatic shift in public opinion on the level of unemployment benefits, which appears to have occurred shortly after the 1997 election (Hills and Lelkes, 1999). Respondents are asked:

> *Opinions differ about the level of benefits for unemployed people.*
> *Which of these two statements comes closest to your own view ...*
> *... benefits for unemployed people are **too low** and cause hardship,*
> *or, benefits for unemployed people are **too high** and discourage them*
> *from finding jobs?*

As seen in Figure 1.3, the public went rather suddenly from believing that unemployment benefits were too low and caused hardship prior (up to 1997) to believing they were too high and discouraged work (in 1998). But, by 2000 the position had been reversed again. One theory has been that people's responses in the 1998 survey were strongly influenced by recent high profile ministerial statements about welfare reform, which stressed the problems with the benefits system, and that public attitudes appeared to be reverting to where they had been before, once the political prominence of this issue subsided (Hills, 2002).

Figure 1.3 Benefits for the unemployed are too high or too low, 1983–2002

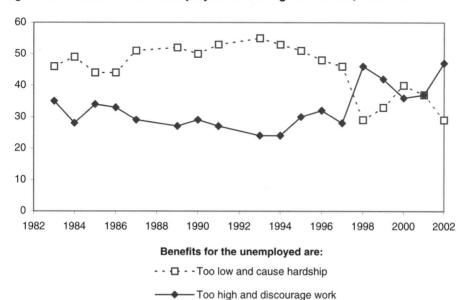

Benefits for the unemployed are:

- - ☐ - - Too low and cause hardship

——◆—— Too high and discourage work

Two years on, the figures are back to something similar to the 1998 level, so it now looks as if there has indeed been a decisive shift in this indicator since the mid-1990s, although the responses to this question are unusually volatile.

Figures 1.4 and 1.5 show two further indicators where more people are now choosing a much tougher line on the incentive effects of the benefits system. More people now agree that if welfare benefits were not so generous people would learn to stand on their own two feet (44 per cent) than disagree with this statement (30 per cent), whereas the corresponding figures in 1987 were 33 per cent and 45 per cent. A clear majority (65 per cent) now believe that most unemployed persons "around here" could find a job if they really wanted one, whereas the proportion who agreed with this statement fluctuated between 30 and 50 per cent during the late 1980s and early 1990s.

Figure 1.4 "If welfare benefits weren't so generous, people would learn to stand on their own two feet", 1987–2002

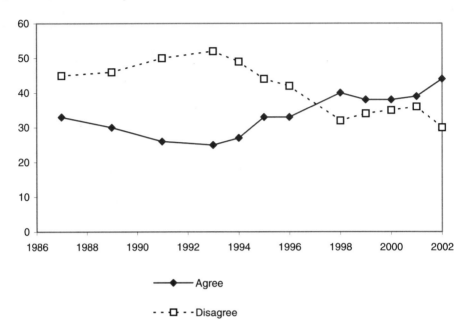

Figure 1.5 "Around here, most unemployed people could find a job if they really wanted one", 1987–2002

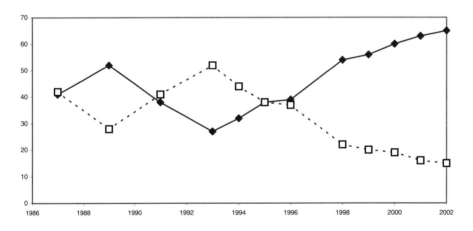

Concerns about fraud and abuse of the system have also been growing over the same period. The proportion of people who believe that large numbers of people are falsely claiming benefits is very high and has been growing over time – from two-thirds (67 per cent) in 1987 to four-fifths (81 per cent) in 2002. And more people now agree that most people on the dole are fiddling in one way or another (38 per cent) than disagree (28 per cent). In 1987, when this question was first asked, it was the other way round: 32 per cent agreed and 40 per cent disagreed.

Attitudes towards benefit claimants tend to harden during periods of economic growth and soften during a recession, so that some increase in these indicators would be expected to come with the recovery from the recession of the early 1990s. Some indicators are particularly sensitive to the economic cycle; for example, the question about whether most unemployed people around here could find a job if they really wanted. But, even in this case, the position in 2002 is very different to that in the boom at the end of the 1980s, which also followed a sustained period of economic growth. Moreover, the consistency of this trend across a range of different indicators supports the idea that there has been a marked change in public attitudes towards the benefits system, over and above the effect of the economic cycle.

Table 1.8 Attitudes towards the benefits system by party identification, 1987–2002

% who agree that	1987	Base	1996	Base	2002	Base	Change 1987–2002
Benefits for the unemployed are too low and cause hardship							
Conservative	32	1095	29	1012	17	856	-15
Labour	72	824	62	1528	36	1400	-36
If welfare benefits weren't so generous, people would learn to stand on their own two feet							
Conservative	47	506	52	859	58	728	+11
Labour	17	337	21	1324	37	1187	+20
The welfare state makes people nowadays less willing to look after themselves[*]							
Conservative	67	506	65	859	66	840	-1
Labour	35	337	31	1324	42	1220	+7

* Answers in the last columns are for 2000 (when this was last asked).

This change in attitudes has not been confined to particular subgroups, but is evident across all income groups, social classes, and supporters of the main political parties. However, as seen in the Table 1.8, these changes have been greater among those who identify with the Labour Party. This is partly because the composition of Labour supporters has changed over this period, as already discussed, but also, perhaps, because statements about the failure of the system have recently been coming from Labour ministers and may, therefore, be more credible or acceptable to people who had previously held contrary views (Hills, 2002).

At this point in time, it appears that people's attitudes towards the benefits system are less divided on ideological grounds than they have been over the last twenty years.

The hardening of attitudes towards benefit claimants is also more pronounced among younger age groups. As shown in the next table, the proportion who agree that benefits for the unemployed are too low and cause hardship fell by 29 percentage points between 1987 and 2002 amongst those aged 18–34, but only by 16 percentage points amongst those aged 55 or over. Similarly, the proportion who believe that if benefits were less generous people would learn to stand on their own two feet rose by 19 percentage points for those in the younger age group and by only four percentage points for those in the older age group.

Table 1.9 Attitudes towards the social security system by age group, 1987–2002

% who agree that:	1987	Base	1996	Base	2002	Base	Change 1987-2002
Benefits for the unemployed are too low and cause hardship							
Age: 18–34	61	885	50	1035	32	900	-29
35–54	51	1024	51	1261	32	1249	-19
55+	40	933	41	1309	24	1282	-16
If welfare benefits weren't so generous, people would learn to stand on their own two feet							
Age: 18–34	22	399	30	875	41	745	+19
35–54	33	478	28	1111	41	1086	+8
55+	45	402	42	1091	49	1065	+4
The welfare state makes people nowadays less willing to look after themselves[*]							
Age: 18–34	36	399	37	875	43	766	+7
35–54	55	478	41	1111	46	1102	-9
55+	67	402	54	1091	62	1108	-5

* Answers in the last columns are for 2000 (when this was last asked).

This might help to explain why support for increased spending on welfare benefits for the poor has fallen most among the younger age group, as discussed earlier in the chapter. As shown in the next table, those who are concerned about the disincentive effects of the system or believe it is subject to widespread fraud and abuse are much less likely to favour higher spending on benefits for the poor than those who do not express these concerns. For example, among those who think that "if welfare benefits weren't so generous, people would learn to stand on their own two feet", only just over a third think that the government should spend more on welfare benefits for the poor. Among those who disagree, the figure is almost two-thirds. This does not necessarily mean that changing attitudes towards the benefits system are the *cause* of the decline in support for welfare spending on the poor, but the two trends seem to be closely related.

Table 1.10 Attitudes towards spending on welfare benefits for the poor by related attitudes

		The government should spend more money on welfare benefits for the poor		
		Agree	**Disagree**	*Base*
Unemployment benefits are				
Too high and discourage work	%	35	36	*1313*
Too low and cause hardship	%	61	14	*850*
If welfare benefits weren't so generous, people would learn to stand on their own two feet				
Agree	%	37	38	*1259*
Disagree	%	62	18	*864*
Around here, most unemployed people could find a job if they really wanted one				
Agree	%	40	32	*1819*
Disagree	%	61	20	*446*
Most people on the dole are fiddling in one way or another				
Agree	%	40	34	*1093*
Disagree	%	57	22	*818*

Use of private welfare

The Conservative governments of the 1980s and 1990s were keen to promote private sector involvement in welfare. Council housing was the only part of the welfare state subject to wholesale privatisation, but financial incentives were used to encourage private provision in other areas – for example, tax relief and

rebates to employees who opted out of the State Earnings Related Pension
Scheme (SERPS) and tax reliefs on private medical insurance for those aged 60
or over. The New Labour government, whilst adopting a more cautious
approach to private welfare, has accepted a greater role for the private sector in
the delivery of welfare, particularly in respect of pensions. This favourable
policy environment, as well as rising incomes and expectations, has contributed
to a growth in the use of private welfare over the last twenty years. For
example, the proportion of respondents who have private medical insurance
doubled since 1983 – from 10 per cent to 21 per cent. The proportion whose
children have attended private school has doubled since 1987 – from four per
cent to eight per cent. And nearly three-quarters of (non-retired) respondents
now expect most of their income in retirement to come from private pensions or
savings.

**Figure 1.6 Attitudes of private welfare users towards spending on the welfare
state, 1986–2002**

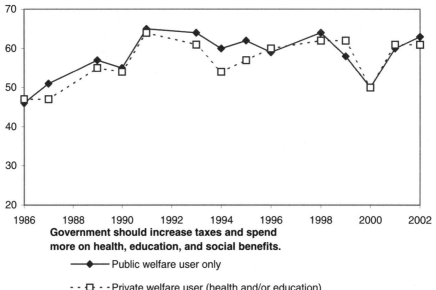

Government should increase taxes and spend
more on health, education, and social benefits.

——◆—— Public welfare user only

- - ☐ - - Private welfare user (health and/or education)

This trend might be expected to have implications for attitudes towards public
welfare. It would be natural to assume that users of private welfare services
would be less supportive of public services than others, either on ideological
grounds or because they may see little reason to support services they are less
likely to use themselves. But we find that this is, in fact, not the case, at least
not for health and education. Figure 1.6 compares the attitudes of public and
private welfare users towards public spending on health, education, and social
benefits taken as a whole. The two groups show similar levels of support for

increased taxes and spending throughout this period. (Only in two years – 1994 and 1995 – is the difference statistically significant.)

Moreover, as shown in the next table, analysis of the 2001 *British Social Attitudes* survey suggests that the attitudes of private welfare users towards public spending are not very different to those who rely on public provision. Those with private medical insurance are just as likely to favour (or strongly favour) a 1p increase in income tax to pay for higher spending on the National Health Service as those without private insurance. Similarly, those who attended a private school or whose child(ren) attended a private school are equally supportive of higher spending on schools. Therefore, concerns that the increasing use of private welfare services could over time erode support for core public services, like health and education, do not appear to be justified.

Table 1.11 Attitudes towards higher public spending by use of private welfare, 2001

% who would support a 1p increase in income tax to pay for higher spending on		Strongly in favour	In favour	Neither	Against	Strongly against	*Base*
National Health Service							
No private medical insurance	%	38	44	9	6	2	*886*
Private medical insurance	%	43	42	6	6	2	*228*
Schools							
State education only	%	18	55	14	10	2	*1381*
Child or self went to private school	%	23	49	11	4	3	*276*
Pensions							
Not retired, mainly state pension	%	18	50	16	12	2	*369*
Not retired, mainly private pension	%	12	48	21	17	2	*812*
Retired, state pension only	%	36	40	11	13	1	*338*
Retired, private pension	%	31	34	13	21	1	*72*

These findings are consistent with previous research by Burchardt and Propper, which found little evidence that there is strong support for reducing public spending on health or education, even among users of private services (Burchardt and Propper, 1999). One reason for this is that users of private health care and education also make considerable use of state services, for example NHS emergency services or state primary schools. Another possible explanation is that some private welfare users may be strong supporters of public welfare, who would prefer higher state spending to achieve better public services, but opt out because they are not satisfied with the quality of public services.

Only in the case of pensions is there some evidence that those with private pensions (or those who expect most of their income in retirement to come from private pensions) are less likely to support higher public spending on pensions than those who are (or expect to be) dependent on a state pension. But the differences are relatively small: 60 per cent of those who expect to rely on a private pension are in favour of a 1p increase in income tax to pay for higher spending on state pensions, compared with 68 per cent of those who expect to rely mainly on the state pension.[1]

Pensions is an area where successive governments have made particular efforts to increase the role of private provision and has been described by this government as the most successful example of a public–private partnership (DSS, 1998). Public attitudes on this issue appear to be in a state of transition. On the one hand, the next table shows that an overwhelming majority of people believe that the government has a continuing responsibility to ensure an adequate standard of living for old people and attach a high priority to higher spending on retired people. As already noted, those who have or expect to have a private pension are only marginally less likely to hold these views. The strongly adverse public reaction when the government increased the state pension by (just) 75 pence in the 2001 Budget indicates the continued sensitivity of this issue. There is evident disappointment with the existing state provisions – over half of respondents (54 per cent) express the view that governments have been unsuccessful at ensuring a decent standard of living for the old.

Table 1.12 Attitudes towards government's responsibility for and spending on the elderly

		Definitely	Probably	Probably not	Definitely not	Base
Whether it should be the government's responsibility to provide a decent standard of living for the old	%	79	17	1	0	1911
		Much more	More	Same as now	Less	Much less	
Whether would like to see more or less spending on benefits for retired people	%	19	54	23	2	0	3435
		Government		Person's employer		Person and family	
Who should be mainly responsible for ensuring that people have enough money to live on in retirement*	%	62		7		29	3287

* Answers to this question are for 2001 (when this was last asked).

On the other hand, a high proportion of (non-retired) respondents say they expect that their income in retirement will come mainly from private sources. As seen in the next table, among those aged 55 or over (and not yet retired), the proportion that expects to rely mainly on a private pension (45 per cent) is significantly higher than the proportion of retired households who are actually in receipt of a private pension (18 per cent). The proportion that expects most of their retirement income will come from private sources is even higher among younger age groups. (Almost two-thirds of the under 55s expect to rely on occupational or private pensions.) This suggests that successive generations are adapting their expectations to the new policy environment, although younger respondents may also be less than clear about their plans for retirement.

Table 1.13 Main expected source of income in retirement

When you have retired, where do you think most of your income will come from?		State pension	Occupational or personal pension	Other savings and investments	Base
All	%	24	58	12	2464
Age: 18–34	%	16	62	17	900
35–54	%	24	62	9	1240
55+	%	43	45	9	321

When asked (in 2001) whose responsibility it should be to ensure that people have enough money for retirement, a significant minority of respondents (36 per cent of all respondents and 42 per cent of 18–34 year olds) said it should be mainly up to the person and their family or their employer (and not the government) to do so. This is significantly higher than the proportion of people who felt that it should mainly be up to families or employers to pay for their own health care (11 per cent) or to ensure that unemployed people (11 per cent), sick people (15 per cent), or their carers (11 per cent) have enough money to live on, suggesting that people think differently about pensions than about other areas covered by the national insurance system. Unfortunately, the same question has not been asked in previous surveys, so it is not possible to tell whether opinions on this matter have always been different or whether they have changed over this period.

In summary, there is little evidence that the increasing use of private health care and education has reduced support for spending on 'core' public services, such as health and education. Most people also believe that government has a responsibility to provide an adequate standard of living for retired people, although the majority of people do not expect that they themselves will rely on the state pension as their main source of income when they retire, especially among younger age groups. This could be interpreted as an implicit acceptance that the state will play a diminishing role in providing for people in their retirement, something that is already explicitly acknowledged by the significant minority of people who believe that that families or their employers – not the state – should be mainly responsible for ensuring people have enough money to live on in their retirement. This suggests that governments have succeeded in gradually shifting the accepted boundaries between public and private provision in this area.

Conclusions

The introduction identified three possible trends in attitudes towards public spending and the welfare state over the last twenty years: resistance to any attempt to reduce or redefine the role of the welfare state; support for a 'modern', more stream-lined, welfare state; or else a growing divide between these two positions. What we have found is, in fact, evidence of elements of all three, depending on which aspect of the welfare state is the focus of attention.

Firstly, there has been public resistance to the attempts by successive governments to restrict spending on public services. Support for increased taxes and spending rose during the 1980s, when controls on public spending were tightest, and has remained at a high level ever since. Furthermore, there is evidence that support for higher spending is driven by general dissatisfaction with public services. Periods when support for higher spending increased have followed periods of growing dissatisfaction with the National Health Service and state schools. Recent announcements of direct tax increases to finance higher spending do not appear to have dampened the public's enthusiasm for higher spending on public services, although this may yet change once the tax increases really take effect. In the longer term, it remains to be seen whether recent increases in spending will satisfy the public's desire for better health and education services and, if not, whether there will be a reaction against further increases in public spending.

In other respects, changes in public attitudes appear to be in sympathy with governments' attempts to create a more 'modern' welfare state. The decline in support for spending on welfare benefits for the poor and for redistribution, more generally, especially among Labour supporters, occurred at around the same time as the Labour Party was shifting its policy stance away from direct income redistribution towards a more preventative approach to tackling poverty. People continue to favour higher spending on benefits for specific vulnerable groups, such as disabled and retired people, but, like this government, they have become more selective about who should benefit from increased spending.

There is also evidence of a decisive shift in attitudes towards the benefits system. Successive governments from both parties have emphasised the disincentive effects of the system and the need to reduce welfare dependency and this appears to be in tune with, and perhaps driving, public attitudes.

In addition, there is some evidence that government policies have gradually changed the accepted boundaries between public and private provision in some areas, such as housing and, more recently, pensions. The majority of people of working age do not expect to be dependent on the state pension as their main source of income when they retire, especially among younger age groups. This could be interpreted as an implicit acceptance that the state will play a diminishing role in providing for people in their retirement.

The third scenario postulated a growing divide in public attitudes towards the welfare state. Here the picture is rather more surprising. The increase in support for higher spending on public services has been concentrated among Conservative supporters, whilst the hardening of attitudes towards benefit claimants has been concentrated among Labour supporters, so that on both issues public attitudes towards the welfare state are now *less* divided on ideological grounds than was the case twenty years ago. Nor does the increased use of private health and education services appear to have undermined support for 'core' public services. There is little evidence that a significant and distinct class of private welfare users is emerging with very different attitudes towards public spending and the welfare state.

However, there does appear to be a growing divide in attitudes towards the welfare state along a different dimension within society: age. Over this period, younger people have become less favourable towards increases in public spending and harder in their attitudes towards the benefits system, relative to older generations. This difference in attitudes may be confined to this particular cohort who grew up in the 1980s – 'Thatcher's children'. Alternatively, this trend may signal the beginning of a long-term decline in support for the welfare state – with successive generations being less enthusiastic about a welfare state that increasingly falls short of their rising expectations. In the process of modernising the welfare state, governments may be losing the support of those on whom the future of the welfare state depends.

Notes

1. The above analysis was repeated using the other sub-sample of respondents who were asked if they would support a 3p increase in income tax to pay for higher spending in each of these areas and the conclusions are the same. (Although the sample of retired people with private pensions is small, the consistency of the results between the two sub-samples gives them additional credibility.)

References

Bosanquet, N. (1984), 'Social policy and the welfare state', in Jowell, R. and Airey, C. (eds.), *British Social Attitudes: the 1984 Report*, Aldershot: Gower.

Bosanquet, N. (1986), 'Interim report: public spending and the welfare state' in Jowell, R., Witherspoon, S. and Brook, L. (eds.), *British Social Attitudes: the 1986 Report*, Aldershot: Gower.

Burchardt, T. and Hills, J. (1999), 'Public expenditure and the public/private mix', in Powell, M. (ed.), *New Labour, New Welfare State?*, Bristol: The Policy Press.

Burchardt, T. and Propper C. (1999), 'Does the UK have a private welfare class?', *Journal of Social Policy*, **28(4)**: 643–665.

Department for Social Security (1998), *A New Contract for Welfare: New Ambitions for Our Country*, Cm 3805, London: The Stationery Office.

Glennerster, H. (1998), 'Welfare with the lid on?', in Glennerster, H. and Hills, J. (eds.), *The State of Welfare: The Economics of Social Spending*, Oxford: Oxford University Press.

Gordon, D., Adelman, L., Ashworth, K., Bradshaw, J., Levitas, R., Middleton, S., Pantazis, C., Patsios, D., Payne, S., Townsend, P. and Williams, J. (2000), *Poverty and Social Exclusion in Britain*, York: Joseph Rowntree Foundation.

Hedges, A. (forthcoming), *Exploring Public Attitudes towards Redistribution: a Qualitative Study*, London: Centre for Analysis of Social Exclusion/National Centre for Social Research.

Hills, J. (2002), 'Following or leading public opinion? Social security policy and public attitudes since 1987', *Fiscal Studies*, **23(4)**: 539–558.

Hills, J. and Lelkes, O. (1999), 'Social security, selective universalism and patchwork redistribution', in Jowell, R., Curtice, J., Park, A. and Thomson, K. (eds.), *British Social Attitudes: the 16th Report – Who Shares New Labour Values?*, Aldershot: Ashgate.

Lipsey, D. (1995), 'Do we really want more public spending?', in Jowell, R., Curtice, J., Brook, L. and Ahrendt, D. (eds.), *British Social Attitudes: the 11th Report*, Aldershot: Dartmouth.

Powell, M. (ed.), (1999), *New Labour, New Welfare State? The 'third way' in British social policy*, Bristol: The Policy Press.

Taylor-Gooby, P. and Hastie, C. (2002), 'Support for state spending: has New Labour got it right?', in Park, A., Curtice, J., Thomson, K., Jarvis, L. and Bromley, C. (eds.), *British Social Attitudes: the 19th Report*, London : Sage.

Acknowledgements

The *National Centre for Social Research* is grateful to the Department for Work and Pensions, and its predecessors, for their financial support which has enabled us to ask many of the questions reported in this chapter over the years, although the views expressed in the chapter are those of the author alone.

The author is grateful to John Hills for helpful comments on a previous draft of this chapter.

Appendix

Attitudes towards public spending on welfare

Logistic regression estimates (odds ratios): probability of agreeing that government should increase taxes and spend more on health, education, and social benefits.

	1983	1987	1991	1996	2002
Aged 18–34	0.917	0.863	0.718**	0.727**	0.628**
	-0.87	-1.48	-3.16	-3.33	-4.67
Aged 55+	0.843	0.735*	0.707**	0.863	1.03
	-1.26	-2.31	-2.65	-1.09	-0.21
Female	1.036	1.196*	1.056	1.042	1.335**
	-0.4	-2.04	-0.62	-0.52	-3.59
Child in household	1.312**	1.240*	1.259*	1.161	1.047
	-2.73	-2.17	-2.2	-1.5	-0.47
Conservative	0.373**	0.335**	0.477**	0.446**	0.588**
	-10.07	-10.94	-7.68	-8.73	-5.47
Liberal	0.758*	0.997	0.908	1.02	1.510**
	-2.27	-0.02	-0.7	-0.15	-2.91
No party identification	0.601**	0.430**	0.539**	0.429**	0.597**
	-3.08	-5.1	-3.86	-6.29	-4.27
Low income	1.411*	1.039	0.775	0.917	0.94
	-2.55	-0.29	-1.82	-0.8	-0.56
High income	1.256*	1.041	1.12	1.002	0.964
	-2.04	-0.34	-0.98	-0.02	-0.32
Social class I/II	0.907	1.323**	1.041	1.261*	1.061
	-0.94	-2.78	-0.4	-2.51	-0.62
Social class IV/V	0.84	0.929	0.981	0.982	0.806*
	-1.7	-0.72	-0.19	-0.19	-2.04
Unemployed	1.239	1.445*	1.191	1.399	1.537*
	-1.35	-2.06	-0.95	-1.75	-1.98
Retired	0.928	1.165	1.112	1.132	0.926
	-0.49	-0.97	-0.73	-0.84	-0.52
Other	0.998	1.117	1.025	1.169	1.209
	-0.01	-0.88	-0.21	-1.33	-1.47
Scotland	0.854	0.907	1.129	0.792	1.549**
	-1.05	-0.64	-0.78	-1.61	-2.92
North	1.009	0.872	0.942	0.793*	0.958
	-0.08	-1.27	-0.55	-2.3	-0.41
Midlands	0.943	0.962	0.987	1.053	1.16
	-0.48	-0.31	-0.1	-0.44	-1.26
Wales	0.849	1.33	0.985	0.937	1.129
	-0.8	-1.52	-0.08	-0.35	-0.68
London	0.823	1.296	1.456*	0.91	0.993
	-1.32	-1.76	-2.47	-0.7	-0.05
Base	*2793*	*2668*	*2754*	*3461*	*3326*
Log likelihoods	-1758.0	-1739.8	-1746.9	-1984.7	-1869.0

T-values in italics.
* = significant at 5% level; ** = significant at 1% level,

1. Reference categories are as follows: 35–54 year olds, male, Labour supporter, middle income group, social class III, in work, and living in the South of England.

2. Low and high-income groups correspond broadly to the bottom and top 20 per cent of household incomes in each year. In 2002, low income is defined as a gross annual income of £10,000 or below. High income is defined as an annual income of £44,000 or more.

2 The NHS: keeping up with public expectations?

John Appleby and Arturo Alvarez Rosete

In 1983, the NHS spent just over £15 billion. Now, two decades on, it spends £65 billion – over twice as much in real terms, and a significantly greater proportion of the country's wealth (Her Majesty's Treasury, 1989; Secretary of State for Health, 2003). Such increased spending has bought increased numbers of NHS staff, with medical and dental staff numbers rising by nearly 70 per cent since 1983. It has also allowed the NHS to treat more people – 80 per cent more inpatients and day cases, 20 per cent more outpatients and 30 per cent more new accident and emergency patients. Consultations with GPs have increased by 13 per cent, and the number of prescriptions by nearly 70 per cent. In addition, a key measure of performance – waiting times – have reduced substantially over the last twenty years. In the early 1980s, the average waiting time for inpatients was about ten months; by 2002, it had fallen to around four months. More resources for the NHS has – unsurprisingly – meant more health care. And while it is difficult to accurately quantify health care's contribution to the population's *health*, the NHS must take some of the credit for a halving of the infant mortality rate over the last twenty years, the increase in life expectancy at birth of around five years for men and four for women, and a drop in overall mortality rates of around eight per cent.

The facts, one might suppose, speak for themselves. Over the last twenty years health services across the UK have improved and so too has our health. And yet, people's opinions and perceptions of the NHS have not only *not* improved, they have worsened. At the time of the first *British Social Attitudes* survey in 1983, the proportion of people who were satisfied with the NHS (55 per cent) outweighed the proportion who were dissatisfied (25 per cent) by two to one. By contrast, in 2002, these two groups were (at 40 and 41 per cent respectively) more or less the same size. Any of the nine different Secretaries of State for Health since 1983 would surely sigh in exasperation at an apparently ungrateful public.

 John Appleby is Chief Economist at the King's Fund. Arturo Alvarez Rosete is a Research Officer at the King's Fund.

There are, of course, many possible explanations for this apparent contradiction between reality and perception. The public may be unaware of the improvements in the NHS. Alternatively, they may know the facts, but feel the performance measures most commonly cited do not properly capture what most concerns them about the NHS and health care. They may, indeed, simply not believe what official statistics have to say on the matter. Changing – that is, increasing – expectations must also surely play a part in any explanation.

Perhaps, more fundamentally, declining levels of satisfaction indicate that people are increasingly questioning the very notion of a tax-funded health care system? Certainly, over recent years, there has been no shortage of suggestions from various think tanks as to alternative ways to pay for health care – from voucher systems enabling individuals to purchase their own care, to encouraging greater take up of private medical insurance through tax breaks (cf. Green, 2000; Lea, 2000; NERA, 2001; Conservative Party, 2003;). And, of course, the promotion of such alternative systems can help promulgate a rather negative view of the performance of the current system – it's broke and needs fixing. But how disenchanted are we with the way the NHS is funded? And do we *really* want to change the universal nature of the services it provides?

We begin by examining and unpacking some of the detailed survey results for 2002, setting them in their historical context and examining possible explanations for the way in which satisfaction with the NHS has changed over time. We also consider the ways in which the headline trends in satisfaction with the NHS mask important variations; between individual NHS services, different age groups and those with different political affiliations, to give but a few examples. And, secondly, we examine whether changes in satisfaction with the NHS are associated with a more fundamental shift in attitudes concerning the nature of the NHS itself. We consider what kind of NHS we want. Should it remain funded largely from general taxation and if so, what priority should it be given over other public services for extra funding?

Satisfaction with the NHS: why does it change?

We begin by considering general satisfaction with the NHS. To assess this, we ask:

> All in all, how satisfied or dissatisfied would you say you are with the way in which the National Health Service runs nowadays?

As Table 2.1 shows, responses to this question have varied markedly over time. In the early 1980s, for example, 'net' satisfaction (that is, the proportion who are satisfied minus the proportion who are dissatisfied) was generally positive. In the 1990s, however, net satisfaction became negative, meaning that more were dissatisfied with the NHS's performance than were satisfied. This peaked in 1997, when the third who expressed satisfaction were dwarfed by the half who expressed dissatisfaction. Since then, attitudes appear to have settled down to a more or less even split between the proportions satisfied and dissatisfied.

It is worth noting that between 1997 and 1998 the survey recorded the largest *fall* in a single year in the proportion who were *dissatisfied* with the NHS – from a half in 1997 to 36 per cent the following year (Mulligan and Appleby, 2001). It is hard to overlook the fact that this same period also heralded the first change in political administration since the survey series started, with the fall of the Conservative government in 1997 and the first election of a Labour government in eighteen years. This prompts speculation as to whether there is a link between satisfaction rates and politics, speculation which is borne out when we look at how the attitudes of different party identifiers have changed since 1986. In fact, the surge in net satisfaction with the NHS between 1997 and 1999 was wholly due to increased satisfaction among *Labour* identifiers after Labour's election victory (Conservative identifiers became marginally less satisfied over this period). And, since 1999, the *erosion* of net satisfaction has been due to Conservative identifiers becoming more dissatisfied with the NHS (Labour identifiers' attitudes have barely changed between 2000 and 2002). As noted in previous *British Social Attitudes* Reports (Bosanquet, 1988; Mulligan and Appleby, 2001), this suggests that general attitudes towards the NHS may tell as much about government popularity as they do about the NHS *per se*.

Table 2.1 Satisfaction with the NHS, 1983–2002

	'83	'86	'89	'91	'94	'97	'98	'00	'02
Very/quite satisfied	55	40	36	40	44	34	42	42	40
Neither satisfied nor dissatisfied	20	19	18	19	17	15	22	19	18
Very/quite dissatisfied	25	39	46	41	38	50	36	39	41
Net satisfaction (satisfaction minus dissatisfaction)	+20	+1	-10	-1	+6	-16	+6	+3	-1
Base	*1719*	*3066*	*2930*	*2836*	*3469*	*1355*	*3146*	*3426*	*2287*

While the public's views about politics, politicians and government no doubt help shape their views about the state of the NHS, other factors also contribute. So we turn now to consider some other possible explanations for the twists and turns since 1983 in levels of public satisfaction with the NHS.

Satisfaction with different NHS services

The NHS is, of course, made up of a range of different services, making it potentially dangerous to rely only upon a single question about the system as a whole. For this reason, we also ask people how satisfied they are with each of a range of different services – including primary care services (general practitioners and dentists) and inpatient and outpatient hospital services:

> *From your own experience, or what you have heard, please say how satisfied or dissatisfied you are with the way in which each of these parts of the National Health Service runs nowadays ...*

Figure 2.1 plots the proportion expressing satisfaction with each of these services since 1983. For comparison, it also shows the results of the general NHS question considered earlier. Two points stand out. Firstly, satisfaction with individual services is, and has always been, higher than satisfaction with the NHS overall. But, secondly, all show generally downward drifts since 1983. General practice remains the service with which the highest proportion of people are satisfied (72 per cent in 2002), but even here satisfaction has fallen some ten points since the early 1990s. Dentistry – despite a rise in satisfaction in 2000 – shows the steepest decline in satisfaction since 1983, possibly a reflection of the increasing problems faced by many over the years in accessing dentists willing to carry out work on the NHS.

Figure 2.1 Satisfaction with individual NHS services, 1983–2002

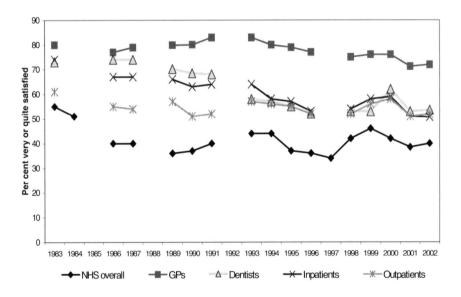

To varying degrees, trends in satisfaction with individual services mirror those in satisfaction with the NHS overall. This is less true of satisfaction with GPs and dentists, but is very much the case in relation to satisfaction with inpatient services and, to an even greater extent, outpatient services.[1] The reasons behind this may simply reflect a coincidence of opinion about these services, or may also indicate a rather narrow – but not surprising – tendency to think primarily of hospital-based services when asked about the NHS in general.

Satisfied customers?

To what extent does satisfaction with the NHS reflect the experiences of those who come into contact with it? One fairly consistent finding throughout the survey series has been that those with recent experience of NHS services, either themselves or through a close family member, tend to be more satisfied than those without such experience (Mulligan and Appleby, 2001). The next table illustrates this, using data from 2002. The most dramatic differences relate to *outpatient* experience; among those with this sort of recent experience (by recent, we mean within the last year), 44 per cent express satisfaction with the NHS as a whole, compared with only a third of those without such experience. As a result, the net level of satisfaction among the former is +4 (because the proportion who were satisfied outweighed the proportion who were dissatisfied), compared with a level of -9 among those who had no recent outpatient experience. Similar differences, though less pronounced, are also evident when considering those with recent GP and inpatient experience.

Table 2.2 Use of NHS services within last year and satisfaction with NHS

	GP visit?		Outpatient?		Inpatient?	
	Yes	*No*	*Yes*	*No*	*Yes*	*No*
	%	*%*	*%*	*%*	*%*	*%*
Very/quite satisfied	41	32	44	34	42	39
Neither satisfied nor dissatisfied	17	26	16	22	15	20
Very/quite dissatisfied	42	39	40	43	43	41
Net satisfaction (satisfaction minus dissatisfaction)	-1	-7	+4	-9	-1	-2
Base	*1755*	*124*	*1166*	*671*	*651*	*1145*

The differences between the overall satisfaction rates found among those with, and without, recent GP or outpatient experience are largely due to the fact that those *without* recent contact are more likely than those with such contact to sit on the fence and say that they are "neither satisfied nor dissatisfied" (rather than being because they are more likely to be dissatisfied). So recent contact with these services appears to firm up the opinions of the 'floating' patient. However, when it comes to recent inpatient experience, the picture is slightly less clear-cut.

In summary, therefore, trends in satisfaction with the NHS overall seem to relate most closely to people's opinions about hospital services (particularly outpatient services). Moreover, those with recent *experience* of different NHS services are more satisfied with the NHS than those without experience. However, while such connections are interesting, they cannot on their own 'explain' trends in overall satisfaction. So we turn now to consider a more direct and intuitively plausible relationship, that between NHS funding levels and public opinion.

NHS funding and satisfaction

It has been claimed that a connection exists between actual NHS funding levels and public satisfaction with the services it offers (Judge *et al.*, 1997; Mulligan and Appleby, 2001). It is certainly true that there have been periods in which satisfaction rates have risen in line with generous financial settlements and fallen in line with parsimonious ones (most notably in the 1990s). However, looking back over nearly two decades, there is little significant connection between the two other than in a handful of years, either graphically or statistically. This is shown in Figure 2.2 which plots changes from one year to the next in NHS volume spending (which takes account of NHS-specific inflation) and in actual cash spending, alongside overall satisfaction ratings for the NHS.[2] We have divided the graph into five sections, each corresponding to a particular government's time in office during the period. Interestingly, while there is evidence of cyclical peaks and troughs in funding over the course of different parliaments, in only two out of the five general elections did funding move in the 'expected' way – that is, increasing just prior to the election date. Moreover, in one of these elections – 1997 – the incumbent government lost power.

Perhaps this discontinuity between NHS spending and public awareness simply reflects a time lag? Though plausible, this does not prove to be the case; even when we lag our funding variables (whether cash or volume funding) one, two or three years behind, they are still not closely linked to levels of public satisfaction.

So, although there are particular years where funding and satisfaction levels rise and fall in a way that might be expected were there an association between them, there are also years where changes in satisfaction went the 'wrong' way or changed in the 'right' way, but only very weakly (given the change in spending). In particular, over the last few years, funding has risen substantially and yet, while satisfaction rates have generally moved in the expected direction, the magnitude of the changes has not matched that of the funding of the NHS.

In general, therefore, it seems that public satisfaction with the NHS is not directly driven to any great extent by changes in the level of funding of the NHS. This may seem counter-intuitive, but may simply reflect a relative ignorance of the facts, a general cynicism of politicians' claims about funding or a lack of conviction about the connection between the financial inputs to the NHS and its outputs.

Figure 2.2 UK NHS funding and overall rate of satisfaction with the NHS, 1983–2002

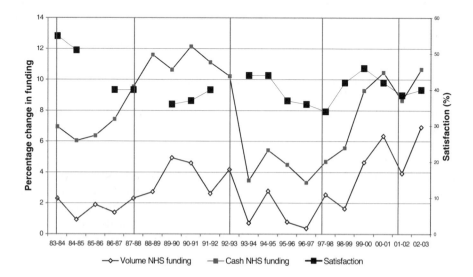

Generational and lifecycle changes

We turn now to explore the extent to which satisfaction with the NHS is associated with wider societal changes in attitudes. In particular, we focus upon a long-established link between *age* and satisfaction, with older groups tending to express more satisfaction with the NHS than younger ones. This is as true now as it was in 1983; in 2002, for instance, just over a third of 18–24 year olds were satisfied with the NHS overall, compared with just over a half of the 65 plus age group.

  Why might this be? Some suggest that it reflects younger people's higher expectations of the NHS, making them harder to please than their older counterparts. Perhaps people's greater satisfaction could result from their awareness of life without an NHS; indeed, their gratitude for its existence (Exley and Jarvis, 2003). Both these explanations hint at some degree of 'generational' difference, whereby different generations (or birth cohorts) are 'shaped' in some way by their experiences during their formative years and tend to maintain these distinctive views as they get older. Conversely, it might be the case that there are 'lifecycle' processes at work, whereby satisfaction increases as people get older. We have already come across one plausible reason for this; greater use is made of the NHS as people age, and satisfaction is generally higher amongst those with recent experience of the NHS.

Untangling lifecycle from generational differences is important, as both have very different implications for how social attitudes might change over time. If *generational* influences predominate, we should expect to find gradual change over time, as younger and less satisfied generations replace older and more satisfied ones. However, if *lifecycle* influences matter more, we should not expect to see such change, as the impact of one birth cohort getting older and becoming more satisfied would be counteracted by the entry of another, younger and less satisfied, birth cohort into the adult population.

Unfortunately, it can be very difficult to untangle generational and lifecycle 'effects' from one another (Park, 2000). It is made particularly complex by what are called 'period effects' – that is, general shifts in view that affect everybody (and not just particular age groups). However, we can attempt to shed some light on these processes by looking at satisfaction levels among the same birth cohorts in 1983 and 2002 and seeing whether these have changed over time. This is shown in Table 2.3.

The first row in the table shows that, overall, the proportion who express satisfaction with the NHS has fallen by 15 points between these two years. The subsequent rows show the views of the different birth cohorts described in the first column. If we look, for instance, at the cohort born between 1958 and 1967, the table shows that 56 per cent were satisfied with the NHS in 1983 (when they were aged between 18 and 24) but that, by 2002 (they were aged between 35 and 44), only 40 per cent were satisfied.

Table 2.3 Satisfaction with the overall running of the NHS by birth cohort, 1983 and 2002

			1983	**2002**	**Difference**
All			55	40	-15
Cohort	*Age 1983*	*Age 2002*			
1978–1984	Under 4	18–24	–	36	n.a.
1968–1977	6–15	25–34	–	36	n.a.
1958–1967	18–24	35–44	56	40	-16
1948–1957	25–34	45–54	47	35	-12
1938–1947	35–44	55–64	52	41	-11
1928–1937	45–54	65–74	52	49	-3
1918–1927	55–64	75–84	48	57	+9
Pre 1918	65+	–	70	–	n.a.

n.a. = not applicable

What does this tell us? The clearest message is that period effects have been at work between 1983 and 2002 – as evidenced by the fact that satisfaction levels among nearly all the age groups declined over time. So the changing levels of satisfaction with the NHS that we have found are not simply a reflection of older, more satisfied, generations 'dying out' – they are changes which have affected everybody. However, the table also shows that this fall in satisfaction shrinks as we move from younger to older cohorts, and is not evident at all in our oldest cohort. This is likely to reflect *lifecycle* changes, with the increased use of the NHS made by people as they age acting as a slight counterbalance to the overall period effect. It is also possible that the oldest generations in the table, growing up in the early days of the NHS, have an attachment to it that has also prevented them from becoming too dissatisfied over time.

What kind of NHS do we want?

So far we have attempted to explain changes in satisfaction with the overall running of the NHS by examining significant changes in the political landscape, satisfaction with particular NHS services, and changes in levels of NHS funding. We have also attempted to disentangle possible period and lifecycle effects with respect to changes in satisfaction. All these factors, to some extent, provide hints as to why satisfaction has changed over the last two decades, but no definitive answers. So we turn now to examine whether changes in satisfaction with the NHS – and the general downward drift in satisfaction over time – reflect more fundamental changes in beliefs about the twin defining aspects of the service – redistributive funding from general taxation and universal access.

A number of important and long running questions in the *British Social Attitudes* series relate to views about spending and taxation. Since the series began in 1983, these have shown there to be very strong public support for state provision of welfare services, funded through taxation. Moreover, *The 19th Report* showed that health has consistently been the public's top priority for extra spending (Taylor-Gooby and Hastie, 2002). As Figure 2.3 shows, in 2002 there was a small drop in the priority accorded to health, but support remains historically high and has always placed health first above other spending areas such as education, police and prisons, housing, and public transport. (See also Table 1.5 in the chapter by Sefton in this Report).

Interestingly, respondents' top five spending priorities for extra government resources are exactly matched by the government's 2002 spending review plans. Of the £23.7 billion increase in total departmental spending between 2002/3 and 2003/4 (which excludes social security payments, income support, tax credits and other annually managed expenditure), health takes the largest share (28.2 per cent) followed by education, transport, criminal justice and then housing (Her Majesty's Treasury, 2002).

Figure 2.3 Health as first or second priority for extra public spending, 1983–2002

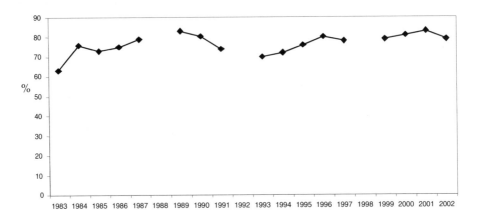

Perhaps, as Taylor-Gooby and Hastie suggest (2002), government spending priorities are in part *driven* by public opinion on these matters. Alternatively, the causation could be reversed, with the public's attitudes to spending priorities being driven (at least in part) by previous government spending decisions.[3] In reality, causation almost certainly flows both ways, with past public opinion influencing current government spending, and past government spending influencing current public opinion. This is demonstrated when we examine the relationship between the priority given by the public to greater spending on health, and actual government spending on health over the last two decades. In fact, up to 35 per cent of the change in spending on the NHS in any single year is *positively* associated with the extent to which health was prioritised by the public the *previous* year. In other words, if health is a top public priority one year, there tends to be higher government spending on it the following year. Conversely, up to 60 per cent of the proportion of the public ranking the NHS as a first or second spending priority in any one year is *negatively* associated with changes in cash spending on the NHS *three years previously*. So, if there is high spending on health in any one year, health tends to attract lower support for additional spending three years down the line. Further details of these analyses can be found in the appendix to this chapter.

This suggests that the government is quicker to react to public opinion than the public are to government spending plans. It also implies that we should expect to see a *decline* in the priority attached to increasing NHS spending over the next few years, as the impact of the current government's spending plans for the NHS filter through into the public's consciousness (in fact, the fieldwork for the 2002 survey was carried out just after the Budget in which the Chancellor announced large increases in NHS spending for the next five years – to be paid for by increases in national insurance contributions from 2003).

Of course, these sorts of relationships should generally be treated with caution. The determinants of both government spending and public attitudes to such spending are considerably more complex and numerous than we implicitly suggest here. There is, for example, quite a strong *negative* association between the level of public satisfaction with the NHS overall and changes in the proportion of the public stating that the NHS should be a top priority for funding.[4] In other words, the more satisfied people are with the NHS, the less likely they are to prioritise it for extra funding, switching their attention to other spending areas – and, conversely, the less satisfied they are with the NHS, the more likely they are to prioritise it for more funding.

However, it remains clear that, for the last twenty years, the public has expressed a strong desire for a well-funded NHS. Moreover, as discussed in Chapter 1, there remains a clear majority in favour of increasing taxation in order to spend *more* on health, education and social benefits, demonstrating a willingness to continue funding health care through general taxation.

We turn now to examine trends in support for another defining aspect of the NHS – universal access. We assess this by asking:

> *It has been suggested that the National Health Service should be* **available only to those with lower incomes.** *This would mean that contributions and taxes could be lower and most people would then take out medical insurance or pay for health care. Do you support or oppose this idea?*

As the next table shows, nearly three-quarters are *opposed* to the idea of restricting the NHS to those on lower incomes, a slightly higher proportion than was the case in 1983.

Table 2.4 Attitudes towards a 'two-tier' NHS, 1983–2002

	'83	'86	'89	'90	'94	'96	'98	'00	'02
Support (a little/a lot)	29	27	22	22	20	21	26	23	24
Oppose (a little/a lot)	64	67	74	73	78	77	72	74	73
Base	1719	3066	2930	2698	3469	3620	3146	3426	2287

So it seems that the sort of NHS we want is one that receives priority above all other government spending programmes for any extra resources, and which is funded through general taxation. And a key defining feature of this NHS remains one of universal access, with no 'opting out' of tax obligations.

Accounting for public opinion

In our attempts to explain trends in satisfaction with the NHS, we have established the existence of long-running trends in support for a well-funded

NHS, which is funded from taxation and which retains its universal access and concomitant tax obligation. We have also considered the possible relationship between changes in overall satisfaction and a number of factors. In particular, we have considered the possibility that trends in satisfaction reflect trends in support for the government of the day, that satisfaction with *particular* NHS services drives trends in overall satisfaction, that changes in funding levels influence satisfaction, and, finally, that generational or lifecycle changes in attitudes help explain the general downward drift in satisfaction with the NHS over the last twenty years.

All of these factors, to a lesser or greater extent, appear, if not directly causal, then at least associated with changes in satisfaction over time. However, quite apart from the problem of determining the *direction* of causation in some cases (NHS funding may influence satisfaction, but satisfaction may also influence NHS funding, for instance), there are other factors which we have not been able to take account of, and which might matter a great deal. Two stand out as particularly important. The first relates to what it is that the public *expect* from the NHS – as this might clearly have changed over time, it might well have affected people's attitudes towards the NHS. The second relates to the impact of media stories about the NHS, and the role that these can play in shaping public opinion and attitudes towards it (Philo, 1999). Capturing these dimensions will be important if we are to improve upon our current understanding of attitudes towards the NHS.

Conclusions

Since 1983, attitudes to the NHS have shown patterns of both great stability and considerable change. Most notably, levels of satisfaction have declined considerably, and dissatisfaction has grown. In the early 1980s, net satisfaction was generally positive, while in the 1990s, it became negative, reaching its nadir in 1997. Since then, attitudes appear to have settled down to a more or less even split between the proportions who are satisfied and dissatisfied. In attempting to explain these trends, we have shown that connections and associations can be made between changes in satisfaction and a number of intuitively plausible factors. There have been periods over the last twenty years (most notably in the 1990s) when satisfaction rates fell, mirroring (in the early to mid-1990s) rather parsimonious financial settlements for the NHS, and then rose (in the late 1990s) reflecting, perhaps, rather more generous allocations between 1997 and 2000. There are also interesting connections between satisfaction and age – not just in any particular year, but over the whole period. All age cohorts bar our oldest (members of whom were aged 65 and over in 2002) recorded falls in satisfaction between 1983 and 2002. However, this 'period effect' was ameliorated somewhat, with older age groups indicating slightly lower reductions in satisfaction than younger groups – presumably reflecting the greater use made of the NHS as people age alongside the fact that recent users of the NHS tend to have more favourable views of the service than non-users.

Of course, the nature of opinion formation is complex, making it impossible to explain changes in satisfaction by taking account of only one factor at a time. This is clearly illustrated by the apparent association between changes in NHS funding and satisfaction which, as we have noted, appears strong in certain periods but weak in others. The inadequacy of this explanation is clear when we consider the last few years – years in which NHS funding has increased substantially, and yet there has been little change in satisfaction. In this respect, current government plans, following recommendations from the Wanless Report (2002), to increase health funding by over a third in real terms, and to increase spending on public and private health care from around nine to ten per cent of GDP, may, in themselves, do little to improve satisfaction rates, at least in the short term.

Money is not the only issue on which the public base their views of the NHS. For example, the role of expectations and the media in reporting on the NHS are also likely to influence public attitudes towards the NHS. The generally negative media stories concerning the NHS may play a part in explaining the consistent finding in *British Social Attitudes* surveys that those people with recent experience of the NHS tend to report significantly higher satisfaction rates than those without recent experience. Similarly, increases in the public's expectations of the NHS may also explain the gap between attitudes towards the NHS and the actual performance of the service over the last twenty years. The NHS may be doing more than it used to, but perhaps we expect it to do even more than that.

A superficial interpretation of these observation could be that the NHS – while improving – is in a sense failing. From here it is a short step to concluding that such failure arises from the two things that define its existence – being funded from general taxation and offering universal provision of its services. However, what is striking about the *British Social Attitudes* surveys over the last twenty years is the consistent and significant opposition to any erosion of the principles of universal provision and the implied expectation that the NHS should remain funded from taxation.

Consequently, for the moment at least, it would appear that the public remain unconvinced that there are credible alternatives to the NHS which satisfy their longstanding support for equity in funding and delivery of health care. Nevertheless, given the general drift downwards in satisfaction with the NHS (although with notable improvements in satisfaction with some specific aspects of its services) it cannot rely on support for its founding principles: the care it delivers must not only continue to improve, but, crucially, be seen to do so. Here, the government and the NHS face problems. The setting of explicit, well-publicised targets in recent years was intended, in part, to clearly demonstrate improvements in NHS performance and also to clarify the connection between financial inputs and health care outputs. In public relations terms, however, it is arguable whether this has been successful. The recent creation of the arms-length Commission for Healthcare Audit and Inspection, with a role to report on the performance of the NHS, is likely to help restore some credibility in this area. However, a review of the experience of using targets to drive up performance is now probably overdue.

More broadly, a range of new policies point towards an intention to distance the NHS from traditional political control and accountability. These include the introduction of greater patient choice, the creation of Foundation Trusts, and the (re)introduction of market mechanisms into the NHS, together with its associated radical overhaul of the way hospitals are to be reimbursed using fixed national tariffs. In addition, the retention of existing methods of funding and access criteria represent a recognition of the public's continuing support for fairness in funding and access to care. Whether, and how, this new devolutionary policy stance will affect the public's perceptions of the NHS is hard to judge. But if the decoupling of politics and the NHS is seen to be real, it is likely to re-focus the public's views of the NHS on its actual achievements and away from the general performance of the government.

Notes

1. Correlation coefficients over time follow between satisfaction with the overall running of the NHS and: GPs (0.16); dentists (0.19); inpatients (0.48); outpatients (0.68).
2. Some previous analyses of this relationship have focused upon volume spending (Judge *et a.l,* 1997) but it is more likely that the public – if aware of funding changes at all – are more familiar with percentage cash changes. This is because volume spending figures are reported at least one year *after* the year in which the spending and inflation occurred.
3. For example, higher increases in NHS spending one year tend to lead to a slightly smaller proportion ranking extra NHS spending as a top priority the following year.
4. The correlation coefficient is -0.69.

References

Bosanquet, N. (1988), 'An Ailing State of National Health', in Jowell, R., Witherspoon, S. and Brook, L. (eds.), *British Social Attitudes: the 5th Report*, Aldershot: Gower.

Conservative Party (2003), *Setting Patients Free*, London: Conservative Party.

Exley, S. and Jarvis, L. (2003), *Trends in Attitudes to Health Care 1983 to 2001*, London: *National Centre for Social Research*.

Green, D. (2000), *Stakeholder Health Insurance*, London: Civitas.

Her Majesty's Treasury (1989), *The Government's Expenditure Plans, 1989–90 to 1991–92. Chapter 14 – Department of Health*, London: HMSO.

Her Majesty's Treasury (2002), *Spending Review 2002: New Public spending plans, 2003–2006*, London: The Stationery Office.

Judge K., Mulligan J.-A. New, B. (1997), 'The NHS: New prescription needed?', in Jowell, R., Curtice, J., Park, A., Brook, L., Thomson, K. and Bryson, C., (eds.), *British Social Attitudes: the 14th Report - The end of Conservative values?*, Aldershot: Ashgate.

Lea, R. (2000), *Healthcare in the UK: The need for reform*, London: Institute of Directors.

Mulligan, J.-A. and Appleby, J. (2001), 'The NHS and Labour's battle for public opinion', in Park, A., Curtice, J., Thomson, K., Jarvis, L. and Bromley, C. (eds.), *British Social Attitudes: the 18th Report – Public Policies, Social Ties*, London: Sage.

NERA (2001), *Towards stakeholder health care*, London: NERA.

Park, A. (2000), 'The generation game', in Jowell, R., Curtice, J., Park, A., Thomson, K., Jarvis, L., Bromley, C. and Stratford, N. (eds.), *British Social Attitudes: the 17th Report - Focusing on Diversity*, London: Sage.

Philo, G. (ed.) (1999), *Message Received*, London: Longman.

Secretary of State for Health (2003), *The Government's Expenditure Plans. Departmental Report 2003*. Cm 5904. London: The Stationery Office.

Taylor-Gooby, P. and Hastie, C. (2002), 'Support for state spending: has New Labour got it right?', in Park, A., Curtice, J., Thomson, K., Jarvis, L. and Bromley, C. (eds.), *British Social Attitudes: the 19th Report*, London: Sage.

Wanless, D. (2002), *Securing our Future Health: Taking a Long-Term View*, Final Report, London: HM Treasury.

Acknowledgements

The *National Centre for Social Research* is grateful to the Department of Health for the financial support which enabled us to ask the questions reported in this chapter.

Appendix

The following table shows the R^2 results for simple linear regressions for various lagged years between annual changes in cash funding for the UK NHS and the percentage of *British Social Attitudes* respondents stating the NHS should be a first or second priority for extra government spending. The table shows that, for example, 32 per cent of the variation in cash spending is 'explained' by variations in the priority accorded to the need for NHS spending five years previously. Conversely, 60 per cent of the variation in the priority accorded to the need for extra NHS spending is 'explained' by variations in cash funding three years previously. Relationships between the two variables can be negative or positive (the former is indicated in bold) suggesting, for example, that decreases in funding in one year could be associated with a rise in those stating NHS funding should be a priority in a subsequent year (i.e. a negative association).

		Annual changes in cash spending on the UK NHS					
		Year t	Year t-1	Year t-2	Year t-3	Year t-4	Year t-5
% placing NHS as 1st/2nd funding priority	Year t	0.17	0.01	**0.17**	**0.60**	**0.31**	**0.08**
	Year t-1	0.35					
	Year t-2	0.18					
	Year t-3	0.00					
	Year t-4	**0.07**					
	Year t-5	**0.32**					

3 Stuck in our cars? Mapping transport preferences

Sonia Exley and Ian Christie [*]

The demand for mobility has risen steadily in the past half-century, fuelled by the growing availability and affordability of cars and air travel, and by the extension of the road and aviation networks. Demand for rail travel has also grown in recent years, despite the troubles of the railway system. The pressure on infrastructure has created conditions in which transport has become a political hot potato, and an area of public service about which politicians, industry experts and travellers can all agree on at least one thing – that the system is going to take a long time to improve. There are some clear reasons for this.

All of the major modes of transport have experienced significant difficulties in operation, and public transport services have not been able to compete easily with the attractions of car use. Privatisation of the rail system has led to many problems in maintenance of the network, and the costs of operation have increased. Although, in some areas, bus use has risen of late, it is still suffering from a negative image with at least part of the travelling public (Exley and Christie, 2002). Despite a downturn in the aviation sector as a result of international security fears over the last two years, air travel is expected to continue to grow, encouraged by the intense competition for customers that has produced the boom in cut-price operators.

Government and observers on all sides agree that there has been a long-term neglect of essential investment in the rail and road networks. The costs of modernising major infrastructure have risen considerably and the timetable for regenerating the railway network has had to be extended accordingly. The UK has been reported as being among the worst off countries in Europe for quality of public transport and for trouble with road congestion (Commission for Integrated Transport, 2001).

[*] Sonia Exley is a Researcher at the *National Centre for Social Research* and Co-Director of the *British Social Attitudes* series. Ian Christie is an associate of the New Economics Foundation and a visiting professor at the Centre for Environmental Strategy, University of Surrey.

There are two dimensions to debates about transport policy. The first concerns the *supply* side – investment in the means to allow people to travel. The second concerns the *demand* side of transport and is politically highly sensitive. Many analysts and campaigners, especially in the environmentalist lobby, contend that we are reaching the limits to expansion of transport infrastructure in the UK. Their argument is that catering indefinitely for what is potentially unlimited demand for mobility is unsustainable in a small country, and that the trend towards what geographer John Adams calls 'hypermobility' generates serious environmental and social problems (Adams, 2000). It has been argued that expansion of the road network erodes countryside and simply fuels demand for more car use and road freight (DETR, 1998; Goodwin, 1998). If so, all that extra road-building and other expansion in infrastructure achieves is temporary relief before demand is stoked up to new levels, after which we are faced with familiar congestion problems but at an even higher level.

The argument for a 'demand management' approach to mobility also points to pollution caused by vehicles. Although marginal gains in the efficiency of engines and reductions in the environmental impact of particular vehicles have been achieved and will continue to be achieved, these benefits tend to be outweighed greatly by absolute increases in use of cars and planes. Transport is the fastest growing source of emissions linked to the risk of global warming and climate disruption, and this is now a major concern in transport policy (DETR, 2000).

So, the challenge in transport policy is to improve the infrastructure but also to manage demand, and overall to make the transport system environmentally sustainable. This complex issue is very difficult for politicians and policy makers. It highlights a need for measures not only to improve roads and the public transport system, but also to influence demand and promote alternatives to the most problematic forms of growth in travel – car use and aviation. This implies that change is needed in many citizens' long-established habits and travel patterns.

In recent years the sheer difficulty of making effective changes on either the supply or the demand side in pursuit of 'sustainable mobility' has become apparent. Many problems tackled by the government since 1997 have so far proved intractable. In its first term, the government launched a White Paper on Transport (DETR, 1998) that was widely hailed as an important move towards an 'integrated transport strategy'. This was intended to face up to the unsustainability of ever-expanding road use and increased road-building. It would promote public transport, cycling, walking and changes in land use, while working towards reducing the need for travel. By 2002–03 it was clear that efforts to reduce demand for car use had not been sufficiently successful and that a limited programme of road-building and widening would be needed in badly congested areas. Those opposed to such a programme have argued that the government has not lived up to its White Paper ambitions and that it has been overcautious in its approach to demand management options such as road pricing.

How have public attitudes been affected by the years of mounting controversy about the quality of transport and measures to cope with congestion and rising car use? In this chapter, we explore attitudes towards transport use in general. We look at views about a variety of policies intended to promote changes in use of transport modes – especially to reduce car use – and, in particular, attitudes towards rail services, which have aroused some of the most heated debates of the last few years. In an effort to examine the degree to which Labour has managed to influence views since its election in 1997, we focus particularly on identifying changes in views on transport matters over the last six years.

Patterns of car use

Not surprisingly, travel patterns reflect the dominance of private cars in our transport system. Since 1993 the proportion of respondents saying they drive a car has risen by ten percentage points, from 60 to 70 per cent in 2002. Just one in six adults (17 per cent) now say they have no access to regular use of a car – a drop of six percentage points since 1993. Over the last decade, the incidence of two-car households has risen from 29 per cent in 1993 to 36 per cent in 2002.

The next table shows how our survey respondents get about from day-to-day: almost half (48 per cent) drive a car every day or nearly every day, and the figure for car use rises to well over half when those travelling as passengers are taken into account. Of car drivers in our sample, two-thirds (68 per cent) said they drive a car every day or nearly every day. This dwarfs the proportions who say they use local buses or trains on a near daily basis. The table also shows a substantial rise in car use from the early to the late 1990s, probably reflecting the growing divergence between the real costs of travelling by car, train and bus (Commission for Integrated Transport, 2003). Despite this the rise in car use seems to have levelled off in recent years and the figures for 2002 are not significantly different to those in 1998 or 2000.

Table 3.1 Patterns of transport use, 1993–2002

% who usually travel by each form of transport every day or nearly every day	1993	1996	1998	2000	2002
By car as a driver	38	42	48	47	48
By car as a passenger	10	9	9	10	11
By local bus	7	7	8	6	7
By train	2	3	2	2	3
Base	*1452*	*1235*	*1079*	*1133*	*1148*

As discussed in *The 19th Report*, car users have a distinctive social profile (Exley and Christie, 2002). Men are considerably more likely than women to drive regularly, although the gap is narrowing slightly. The likelihood of being a habitual driver rises with the level of education, income and social class.

Those in work, unsurprisingly, are much more likely to be regular drivers compared with the economically inactive and pensioners. People with children are much more likely to be regular motorists than those without. Country residents are more likely to be regular drivers than those living in urban areas, reflecting rural–urban differences in the availability and convenience of public transport alternatives.

Driving, then, is clearly linked to economic activity and earning power. As the country climbed out of the recession of the early 1990s, so car use grew. This makes the levelling off since 1998 all the more interesting.

How dependent are we on the car habit?

If the government is to achieve any success in managing the demand side of the transport equation, it is vital that the public's attitudes fall into line. Since car use so dominates the transport system, this has to translate into a willingness to use our cars less. In this section, we ask how important people think it is to see a reduction in our use of cars overall, and how difficult they think this would be to achieve.

Firstly, do people even agree that it is important to cut car use? Over the years, we have asked respondents how important they "think it is to cut down the number of cars on Britain's roads". The good news is that most people do think this *is* important, as seen in the next table. Consistently since 1996, over one-quarter of respondents have thought it "very important" (27 per cent in 2002) and a further two-fifths or more have seen it as "fairly important" (48 per cent in 2002). Only just under a fifth see it as "not very important" or "not important at all".

Table 3.2 How important is it to cut the number of cars on the road?

% saying very important or fairly important to reduce the number of cars	1996	1997	1998	1999	2000	2001	2002
All	72	75	79	74	75	73	75
Base	*1075*	*1086*	*889*	*819*	*978*	*922*	*1001*
Drives car every day/ nearly every day	65	75	77	68	71	70	72
Base	*445*	*441*	*400*	*347*	*430*	*406*	*458*
Does not drive car every day/ nearly every day	76	74	80	79	79	76	77
Base	*613*	*639*	*477*	*466*	*542*	*506*	*531*

The high point in the last few years for concern about cutting down the number of cars on Britain's roads was 1998, when almost eight in ten rated this challenge as very or fairly important, with 30 per cent saying "very important". Since then, there has been a slight *decrease* overall in the perceived urgency of the situation. One interpretation of this is that, since 1998, alternatives to the car such as trains have been reported as being crisis-prone and expensive, and also experienced as such by many people, and that this has hardened pro-car attitudes somewhat. Further support for this line of argument comes from the results we get from questions about the importance of building more motorways: in 1997, just 30 per cent agreed that this should be done, while in 2001 the proportion had risen to 38 per cent. Conversely, between 1997 and 2001 there was a *fall* in numbers opposing motorway construction, with just over one-third taking this stance in 2001.

Is it the car users who are resisting change? To a certain extent this is true, as can be seen in Table 3.2: those who do *not* drive cars daily or nearly every day are more likely than those who do to see a cut in the number of cars as important or very important. Regular train users are significantly more likely to say it is important to cut down the number of cars on the road, as are cyclists and those who walk regularly as part of their travel patterns. Women overall are also more likely to take this view. However, even among regular car users, some two-thirds or more have shared this perception since 1996.

To what extent does environmental virtue matter to people enough to curb car use? We ask several questions where the environmental dangers of car use are explicitly mentioned. As seen from the next table, the number who do *not* agree that "people should be allowed to use their cars as much as they like, even if it causes damage to the environment" outnumber those who agree by more than two to one. Moreover, the last decade has seen a rise of five percentage points in the proportions of the population taking the anti-car line. There has been a similar increase over the past decade in the proportions rejecting the view that "driving is too convenient to give up for the sake of the environment". But here, over a third agree with the proposition, a figure that has barely changed from the 1993 survey.

Table 3.3 Environmental impact of car use, 1991–2002

	1991	1993	1994	1997	2000	2001	2002
People should be allowed to use their cars as much as they like, even if it causes damage to the environment	%	%	%	%	%	%	%
Agree	19	n/a	17	n/a	20	n/a	20
Disagree	43	n/a	48	n/a	42	n/a	48
Driving one's own car is too convenient to give up for the sake of the environment	%	%	%	%	%	%	%
Agree	n/a	39	41	32	n/a	46	38
Disagree	n/a	23	28	31	n/a	24	33
Base	*1224*	*1261*	*975*	*1080*	*972*	*912*	*989*

n/a = not asked

In summary, then, there is a mixed message on car dependency. Curbing the car is important to most people, but attitudes have become somewhat more 'pro-car' in recent years. Attitudes are also associated, unsurprisingly, with people's habitual travel mode. Regular car users are more likely to agree that driving is too convenient to give up, while regular train users and pedestrians are less likely to agree.

One aspect to reducing car dependency is the extent to which people perceive alternatives. We talk more about public transport later in the chapter, but many journeys made by car are short ones, and most journeys of all kinds are short trips. Could people imagine doing without their car in this respect, at least? The incidence of cycling and walking (for journeys of at least 15 minutes by foot) has not changed much in the past ten years. In 2002, the proportion saying that they cycle every day or nearly every day stood at just under three per cent of respondents. One-third said they walk all or most days for trips of at least 15 minutes, a proportion that has varied little since 1995.

More specifically, we asked:

> *How much do you agree or disagree with this statement:*
> *Many of the short journeys I now make by car I could just as easily ...*
> > *... walk*
> > *... cycle, if I had a bike*
> > *... go by bus*

Unfortunately, the results are not encouraging – people seem to have become less inclined to abandon their cars. In 1993, 45 per cent of respondents agreed that they could just as easily walk on many of the short journeys they made by car. By 1997, the proportion had fallen slightly to 41 per cent, and by 2002, just 36 per cent agreed. The question about bicycles was first asked in 2000, when 41 per cent agreed that they could just as easily use a bike. In 2002, a small decline was seen, with 37 per cent agreeing, while the proportion disagreeing with the proposition rose from 38 to 43 per cent. As for substituting local bus use for short trips made by car, in the 1997 survey 31 per cent agreed that they could do this, but only one-quarter agreed with the idea in 2002, and 55 per cent disagreed that short trips made by car could just as easily be done by bus.

This perhaps reflects the ratchet effect of rising car use: when people get cars, it appears to make economic sense to use them as much as possible, breeding the habit of using cars for short trips. Moreover, the more other people use cars, the less appealing it is to walk in a congested and possibly more hazardous local environment. This may also affect bus use since a bus journey is likely to involve walks to and from bus stops.

Given these attitudes, it is hardly surprising that respondents are very resistant to any attempt to make them use their cars less. From time to time, we ask car users how inconvenient they would find it if they had to cut their number of regular car trips by a quarter and by half. As reported in *The 19th Report*, we find a very stable pattern, with over four-fifths of car users seeing reductions of one-quarter or one-half of their car trips as "very" or "fairly" inconvenient.   In response to the question about reducing trips by half, resistance rises – with around nine in ten regarding this as "very" or "fairly" inconvenient (Exley and Christie, 2002).

These results are sobering for those seeking to break the British love affair with the car. It should be noted that attitudes reflect car dependency in the light of the current context of transport services, and perhaps the findings might be altered if we were to see substantial improvements in public transport. Changing such a pattern of behaviour and attitudes will require policies that offer both a 'stick' for continued car use and a 'carrot' in terms of incentives for the alternatives, as well as a groundswell of public opinion that something has to give. Whether such conditions apply, we will explore in the next sections.

How serious is congestion for travellers?

Congestion has become a major political issue, above all in London, prompting the introduction in 2003 of a £5 congestion charge in the city centre, which might be the first of many similar schemes around the UK. But how serious is congestion in the eyes of the public?

The next table confirms what we found last year, namely that traffic congestion in towns and cities has actually been perceived as less of a problem in the last few years than it was in the late 1990s (Exley and Christie, 2002). Nevertheless, over half of respondents see traffic congestion in towns and cities as a serious or very serious problem for them. Motorway congestion is seen as less of a problem (although almost a third still see it as a serious or very serious problem), and there has not been a notable change in this since 1997.

Table 3.4 How bad a problem is congestion on motorways and in urban areas to the respondent, 1997–2002

	1997	1998	1999	2000	2001	2002
Traffic congestion on motorways is ...	%	%	%	%	%	%
... a very serious/serious problem	32	32	36	35	31	31
... not very serious/not a problem	67	66	63	64	69	68
Traffic congestion in towns and cities is ...	%	%	%	%	%	%
... a very serious/serious problem	70	67	71	72	52	57
... not very serious/not a problem	29	32	28	27	47	43
Base	*1355*	*1075*	*1031*	*1133*	*1099*	*1148*

How can we explain the improved perception of congestion in towns and cities? For some areas this could reflect actual progress in reducing congestion, for example, through better public transport services and diversion of traffic elsewhere. As we noted in last year's report (Exley and Christie, 2002), an alternative interpretation is that many people have simply become accustomed to high levels of congestion in towns, and that their perceptions of what is tolerable for them personally have been adjusted accordingly. However, the change could be in part an artefact of an alteration in our questionnaire. The order in which these questions were asked was changed in 2001; previously, it was asked immediately after a comparable question about rural congestion. It is possible that, by thinking about the countryside first, respondents then overstated congestion in towns. However, similar results were recorded in July 2001 by the Office for National Statistics Omnibus survey (ONS, 2001), and it is therefore quite conceivable that a striking shift in some perceptions of urban congestion has occurred. The extent to which this reflects success in traffic management on the one hand, and people becoming accustomed to town centre jams on the other, remains unclear.

However, congestion is not the only problem caused by traffic. Over a third of respondents (38 per cent) said that noise from traffic in towns and cities was a serious or very serious problem for them, and three-fifths (60 per cent) said this about exhaust fumes from traffic in towns and cities.

Since these questions focused on problems for the respondents themselves, the answers unsurprisingly differ by where people live, with those living in big cities significantly more likely than those in smaller cities, towns and villages to find traffic congestion a problem. Those in the South East of England also stood out as being a great deal more concerned with congestion in towns and cities (66 per cent in London and the South East perceived this to be a problem, compared with 57 per cent in Britain overall). They were also more concerned about exhaust fumes.

Regular car use is a factor that clearly affects perceptions. Those who used a car at least two days a week were much more likely than others to perceive congestion in both towns and cities and motorways to be a problem. Those who walked regularly as part of their travel patterns and those with children under 16 were significantly more likely to express concern about the levels of exhaust fumes in towns and cities, while car users were less likely to give this view. Lastly, those living in London and the South East were more likely than others to perceive traffic noise as a problem.

Managing the demand side: getting us out of our cars

The picture we have seen so far is one of high – although possibly levelling off – car ownership and use, high levels of 'car dependency', fairly high levels of concern about traffic congestion, albeit lower than they were some years ago, and low levels of use of public transport. One goal of both policy makers and campaigners for sustainable transport is to reduce the degree to which we are dependent on our cars, and to devise incentives to encourage people to use other modes of transport. What is the likely impact that people think particular policies for demand management might have on their own car use?

We asked about people's views on two kinds of measures – 'stick' attempts to manage demand by making driving more expensive and difficult, and 'carrot' policies to improve the quality of alternatives to the car. Car drivers were asked the following question:

> *I am going to read out some of the things that might get people to **cut down** on the number of car journeys they take. For each one, please tell me what effect, if any, this might have on how much **you yourself** use the car to get about.*

The findings need to be treated with caution, since questions are being asked about policies that are hypothetical. However, since the 2002 survey, London has seen the introduction of its pioneering congestion charging system, and similar schemes might become commonplace in coming decades. So there is much interest in public attitudes towards a range of options for demand management policies aimed at getting us out of our cars more often.

The next table shows the proportion of respondents who said they might use their car "a little less", "quite a bit less" or "give up using" their car if a particular 'stick' measure was adopted. By far the most effective policy would appear to be policy of gradually doubling the cost of petrol over the next ten years. In 2002, three-fifths said that this would lead them to cut back on car use, but its effectiveness varies between different groups, depending on how desperately they depend on their cars and their ability to pay. Those who are regular car users are more likely than non-regular car drivers to say it would make no difference (40 per cent compared with 31 per cent). Those in work and those who are retired are more likely than those who are out of work to say it would make no difference. People with children are also more likely to say that it would make no difference, as are respondents in the highest income bracket and those living in rural areas, where alternatives to regular car use are often thin on the ground. Those in younger age groups and on lower incomes are more likely to say that doubling fuel prices would make a difference to them, reflecting the sensitivity of both categories to financial pressures. It should be said, moreover, that there is hardly any support among the public for increasing the cost of petrol, as we shall discuss in more detail in the next section.

Respondents think that urban road pricing and tougher parking conditions would be less effective in reducing their car use than increased petrol prices. The proportion saying that more restrictions on parking would curb their car use has hovered around the two-fifths mark. More parking restrictions and penalties were more likely to be seen as a deterrent by those in urban areas and by those who are not in work.

The proportion who said that a £2 city centre congestion charge would change their driving behaviour fell in the 2001 and 2002 surveys, perhaps as the level of £2 began to seem rather low. The actual charge introduced in London in 2003 was, of course, £5 and from the 2003 survey we shall be asking about this. Even at the £2 level, congestion charging would make much more difference to those living in urban areas, and also to the economically inactive than those in work and those who are retired, highlighting the impact of increased trip costs on those with lower incomes. There is a clear income gradient in responses to this question – those in the lowest income bracket were most likely to change behaviour (just 44 per cent said a congestion charge would make no difference to them, compared with 56 per cent in the highest income quartile who said it would make no difference). However, in contrast to increases in petrol costs, road pricing is as effective at getting the regular drivers out of their cars as it is for those who only drive occasionally. And thus, although respondents think congestion charging is less likely to be effective at cutting their own car use than hikes in the petrol price, it may be a better way of reaching the core group of regular car drivers, many of whom seem to think that they would pay the higher petrol prices come what may.

Table 3.5 'Stick' policies to curb car use: what impact on drivers' habits, 1996–2002

% who say the measure might mean they would use their car less	1996	1998	2000	2001	2002
Doubling the cost of petrol over the next 10 years	60	59	61	63	60
Introducing a £2 city centre peak-time congestion charge	54	52	60	48	49
More severe parking penalties and restrictions	37	42	44	39	41
Base	967	678	780	686	736

In addition, this policy is more attractive than petrol price hikes because opposition is lower and has fallen in recent years. The high point of opposition was in 1999, when nearly two-thirds (62 per cent) of regular car drivers said they were opposed to the introduction of a £2 charge to enter or drive through a city or town centre at peak times. This has fallen to under half (45 per cent) in 2002 and is now no longer significantly higher than the opposition from non-regular car drivers (42 per cent). So while resistance to congestion charging is more likely than support (39 per cent of regular car drivers, 38 per cent of non-regular car drivers are in support), attitudes have softened – perhaps as a reflection of intensified debate on the prospects of congestion charging stimulated by arguments in London, and possibly a sign of acceptance by more drivers of the likelihood of wider use of road pricing. That said, the overall results over the past few years point to a slight *hardening* of opinion against 'stick' policies that aim to reduce car use. This is found when we consider the pattern of response to questions about increasing taxation generally on car use in order to reduce the problems of congestion. We asked respondents:

> *How much do you agree or disagree that for the sake of the environment, car users should pay higher taxes?*

The proportion agreeing with this was a quarter (24 per cent) in 1990; by 1997, it had fallen to a fifth (20 per cent); by 2002 just over one in seven (15 per cent) agreed with the proposition, while almost three-quarters (70 per cent) disagreed.

What explains this? As we argued last year, experience of – and media reporting of – public transport alternatives between 2000 and 2001 will have played a part. In this period the rail network entered a time of trouble following the disarray caused by the Hatfield crash in October 2000 and the autumn floods that year. In the face of rail crises and announcements that a full recovery of the network would take many years, many people might conclude that they would prefer to accept higher costs for driving rather than drive less and take to alternatives they perceive as less attractive. Moreover, the blanket coverage in the media of the 'fuel crisis' of September 2000 might also have played a part, with feelings running high among protestors about the costs of motoring.

Improving the supply side: attitudes to public transport investment

Improving public transport has been supported consistently by over nine in ten respondents (95 per cent in 2002) since Labour came to power in 1997; seven in ten regard this goal as "very important". As seen in the chapter by Tom Sefton in this book, the proportion putting it as their first or second priority for extra government spending (out of a list that includes health and education) has risen by ten percentage points, from three per cent in 1983 to 13 per cent in 2002, whereas demand for more spending on roads is virtually unchanged at six per cent.

We also ask specifically about the choice between extra spending on public transport and roads:

> *Thinking now of towns and cities. If the government had to choose …*
> *… it should improve roads or*
> *… it should improve public transport.*

The question is then repeated for country areas. When phrased like this, large majorities again put improve public transport ahead of roads. That said, the proportion backing road improvements as an urban priority rose by ten percentage points between 1996 and 2002, with a corresponding drop in the public transport-first camp from 72 to 62 per cent. In the countryside, two-thirds back public transport as the priority for improvements, a proportion more or less unchanged from 1996 to 2002.

So, the controversial issue is not whether public transport should be improved but how to pay for it. As seen in the next table, there is much less consensus about the means than there is about the aim. There is strong opposition to general 'stick' measures that would affect all drivers in all places – such as doubling the cost of petrol and cutting funds for road maintenance. Resistance to more targeted and localised measures that affect road users at the point of use – such as urban congestion charging – was weaker to start with, is weakening further, and has substantial minorities in support. Backing for peak-time road charging in urban centres rose considerably in 2002 over the 2001 result – from 30 per cent to 38 per cent, perhaps reflecting national exposure to the debate on proposals for London's congestion charge scheme. As we have argued in previous years, one interpretation of this pattern is that less targeted policies will tend to be seen as 'anti-car', whereas local, targeted measures are regarded as more appropriate and less hostile to what many people clearly see as an unavoidable aspect of their daily life. However, there is still a majority *against* each proposed policy to raise revenue for public transport.

Table 3.6 How should we fund improvements in public transport?

% who support the following ways of funding improvements in public transport	1997	1998	1999	2000	2002
Introducing a £2 city centre peak-time congestion charge	30	31	25	29	38
Cutting in half spending on new roads	30	30	21	19	20
Doubling the cost of petrol in the next ten years	12	12	8	7	12
Cutting in half spending on road maintenance	10	8	7	5	8
Base	*1080*	*877*	*813*	*972*	*989*

What effect do respondents say that better public transport services, however they are to be funded, might have on travel habits? The next table shows the pattern of attitudes of car drivers over the last six years. If we compare this with Table 3.5, we can see that people tend to prefer 'carrot' policies of better public transport, to the 'stick' of higher charges of different kinds on road use. At around three-fifths, the proportion who think that better local and long-distance public transport would make them use their car less, is comparable to the most effective 'stick' measure – doubling the cost of petrol. These figures have also risen substantially over time, showing perhaps at least a theoretical willingness to begin to reduce car dependency given favourable circumstances.

This increased willingness to switch to improved forms of public transport could reflect, continuing frustration with congestion among many drivers; however, as we have seen, the proportion of respondents seeing congestion as a serious problem for them has *fallen*. So possibly some of the responses we see in the next table are attributable to people offering what they feel is the 'correct' socially responsible answer. That said, overall the results can be seen as fairly encouraging for policy makers aiming to reduce car dependency. If improvements in local public transport systems, in particular, can be achieved, it seems there are many people who might be willing to switch at least some of the time from using their cars.

Table 3.7 'Carrot' policies to curb car use: what impact on drivers' habits, 1997–2002

% who say the measures might mean they would use their car less	1997	1998	1999	2000	2001	2002
Greatly improving the reliability of local public transport	54	61	63	65	65	64
Greatly improving long-distance rail and coach services	45	51	53	57	56	57
Introducing special cycle lanes on roads	22	24	27	28	21	22
Base	*768*	*639*	*620*	*689*	*686*	*786*

Unsurprisingly, people seem much more responsive to suggestions for 'greatly improving' services when price tags are not attached. In practice, would a *combination* of coercive and positive measures, dealing with both improvements to supply and management of demand, have a greater impact on willingness to change patterns of car use? To assess this issue, in 2001 we asked the following questions:

> *Now suppose that the two things on this card were done **at the same time**. What effect, if any, might this have on how much you yourself use the car? First, charging motorists £2 for entering town centres at peak times **but at the same time** greatly improving the reliability of local public transport?*

> *And what about charging motorists £1 for every 50 miles on motorways **but at the same time** greatly improving long-distance rail and coach services?*

Surprisingly, the addition of a stick does not make a major difference. So, as we have seen in Table 3.7, around two-thirds of car users (65 per cent) in 2001 thought that they would use their car less if local public transport were improved. This rose only marginally to 67 per cent if the stick of a congestion charge was added. However, it should be compared with the much lower figure of 48 per cent in 2001 (49 per cent in 2002) who thought they would use the car less if the congestion charge was introduced without the carrot of the better local transport (see Table 3.5). Therefore a mixture of 'carrot' and 'stick' would be appear to be beneficial.

It is, however, difficult to interpret some of these responses. Looking again at the figures for 2001 in Table 3.7, while we can see that 56 per cent thought they would use their cars less if long-distance rail and coach services were improved, this fell slightly to 53 per cent rather than increased when the comparable question was asked about what would happen if improvements were coupled with motorway charges. We can only conclude that hypothetical questions of this sort are fraught with danger as people find it hard to predict their own behaviour.

In summary then, some 'stick' approaches – especially congestion charging which is seen as likely to be moderately effective and is not subject to the same implacable opposition as some other stick approaches – can have an important role to play in reducing car dependency. But an absolutely key aspect of achieving a sustainable transport system is to convince the travelling public that public transport really has improved. Even if improved public transport services were to be offered, the challenge persists of changing attitudes towards them after years of bad publicity and growing price disadvantage relative to car use. Last year we examined attitudes towards bus services (Exley and Christie, 2002); below we turn our attention to public views about the railways. How do we feel collectively about this particular alternative to the car?

Let the train take the strain

The past decade has been a turbulent one for the British railway system, with intense controversy over the form and manner of its privatisation, well-publicised problems for train operators and for Railtrack and its successor, Network Rail, and a legacy of under-investment that makes for a combination of high fares, rising costs for maintenance and safety, and regular problems due to various mishaps on the lines. It is not a promising backdrop for policy makers trying to persuade motorists to use public transport in general and rail services in particular.

We saw earlier that just three per cent of respondents in 2002 say they travel by train daily or nearly every day. However, the proportion saying they *never* use the train has fallen in recent years, from three-fifths (59 per cent) in 1993 to just under half (46 per cent) in 2002. Correspondingly, the proportion saying they take train trips either at least once a month or "less often than that" has risen since 1993 from one-third (33 per cent) to just under half (44 per cent) in 2002. So there has at least been a rise in the *irregular* use of the trains.

This decline in people who never use the train merits further attention. The next table shows how this group has changed since 1993. Train use, however sporadic, has in fact become more common in *every* category shown in the table over the past decade. However, there are some clear patterns relating to earning power. Those with higher education qualifications show a much bigger shift from non-use of trains to occasional or regular use than do those with lower levels of formal qualification. Similarly, there has been a large fall in 'never use' among professionals and those in the third income quartile. (The top income group shows a smaller percentage drop, but this is from an already low base.) In age terms, it is those in middle age who have seen the largest fall.

Table 3.8 Characteristics of people who 'never' take the train, 1993 and 2002

% who never take the train	1993	Base	2002	Base	Change 1993–2002
Total	59	1452	46	1148	-13
Men	57	616	47	527	-11
Women	60	845	45	621	-15
In paid work	55	678	39	654	-16
Economically inactive	61	440	50	228	-11
Retired	66	331	62	259	-4
Professional	38	48	18	59	-20
Intermediate	52	306	36	349	-16
Skilled	60	693	53	458	-7
Partly skilled	66	238	54	186	-12
Unskilled	72	98	57	65	-15
Aged 18–33	48	391	34	260	-15
Aged 34–49	59	441	44	370	-15
Aged 50–64	66	260	46	267	-20
Aged 65+	68	359	65	249	-2
Income of less than £9,999	67	497	61	275	-6
£10,000–£19,999	61	377	55	236	-6
£20,000–£37,999	58	275	43	290	-15
£38,000 and above	34	127	29	233	-6
Higher education incl. degree	46	291	27	343	-19
A level or equivalent	40	150	36	151	-4
GCSE or equivalent	53	289	51	210	-3
Below GCSE level	71	703	63	421	-8

Of course, these factors are not independent of each other as those in professional jobs are also likely to be the ones with higher education and higher income. In order to untangle some of these effects, we created a logistic regression model which can take all the factors into account at the same time (see model 1 in the appendix to this chapter). This analysis confirmed that age is a key factor, with those in the eldest age group (65 and over) significantly more likely and those in the youngest age group significantly less likely to say they never take the train. The importance of income and education are also confirmed. Those in London and the South East, and those living with a train station nearby were significantly less likely to say they never travel by train, while regular car users (unsurprisingly) show up as being more likely to fall into this category.

These findings suggest that increases in train use have come to a large extent from people who are in well-paid occupations. This is in sharp contrast to the analysis in *The 19th Report* of bus use, where we found that people travelling by bus are likely to be in lower paid work, to be retired or economically inactive, and manual workers (Exley and Christie, 2002).

When we look at those who say they *regularly* use train services (at least 2–5 days a week), the picture is slightly different. What we see again is a clear gradient according to income, with the highest income quartile recording the highest use at ten per cent. Urban residents are again much more likely to use the train regularly – a fifth (18 per cent) of people in big cities, compared to one in twenty (six per cent) overall, reflecting the greater density of public transport networks in cities and higher levels of congestion on the roads. But the age profile is a bit different: the greatest regular train use is among the 18–33 age group (12 per cent), twice as many as among the 34–49 group (which displays high car use) and four times higher than among the 50–64 group.

Despite these increases, the low proportion of respondents regularly using train services is striking when we consider people's proximity to stations. Over one in five say they live less than half a mile from the nearest station, and overall two-thirds say they live within three miles of their nearest station. Proximity counts for little, however, unless people think the train service can provide them with what they want.

Perceptions of train services

How do people feel about the train system? The next table shows responses to a number of statements about the railway service.[1] There is some good news here: three-fifths of respondents think trains are a fast way to travel and a similar proportion think that it is easy to find out when the trains run. Nor is frequency a major grouse – the proportion who think the trains run often enough is greater than the proportion who think they do not. However, the table also reveals some serious problems with the image of the train service. Over half of respondents think that it is difficult to find out the cheapest fares. And over half doubt that the trains run on time or that the fares are reasonable. On the fraught question of the safety record, just under a third agree that the trains have a good safety record, while just over a third disagree.

Table 3.9 Attitudes towards rail travel

		Agree strongly	Agree	Neither agree nor disagree	Disagree	Disagree strongly
It is easy to find out what time trains run	%	7	52	13	18	3
Trains generally run often enough	%	2	38	15	30	5
Trains generally run on time	%	*	19	16	45	12
Train fares are fairly reasonable	%	1	15	11	42	23
Trains are a fast way to travel	%	6	54	15	15	3
It is difficult to find out the cheapest train fares	%	11	44	16	16	3
Trains have a good safety record	%	2	29	23	29	9

Base: 989

To examine the various factors underlying these attitudes, we used multiple regression (see models 2–8 in the appendix to this chapter), which reveals some interesting patterns and not necessarily ones that are very promising for the railways. While regular use of the trains does not attain significance in any of the models, economic activity and income do. Those in paid work (and therefore travelling to work each day) are significantly less likely to think that trains run often enough or on time, or are reasonably priced. These perceptions – whether justified or not – go a long way towards explaining why people drive to work instead of taking the train.

These attitudes bear the imprint not only of personal experience of the railways – and it is important to keep in mind that relatively few people do experience them day in, day out – but also of perceptions, based on media coverage of rail services' problems, and probably also in many cases on the complaints of family, friends and colleagues. That perception is more at work in some respects than real experience is evident in the response to the question on rail safety – in reality, very few casualties occur on the railways, and the response here is probably influenced by memories of major accidents such as the Hatfield and Potters Bar crashes. Road accidents lead to many more victims than we see on the railways, but the rail network has suffered from the massive coverage accorded to its few fatal incidents. Moreover, perceptions clearly play a major role in views on punctuality. In reality, despite many local difficulties, the majority of trains in the course of a year are reasonably punctual; however, travellers remember the frustrating delayed service more than the one that runs on time, and will tend to talk about the former rather than the latter.

That said, perceptions will affect actual behaviour, and Table 3.9 suggests that most people will continue to avoid regular contact with the rail network until they feel that it is more reliable, safe and affordable to use. The survey results above suggest that many more people could use rail than actually do, given proximity to stations, but they are unlikely to do so unless a combination of influences is put in place – improvements in train services, and policies to make car use less attractive. The same can be said for bus services (see last year's analysis of bus use, in Exley and Christie, 2002).

Conclusions

The responses to *British Social Attitudes* questions on transport amply illustrate why this is a policy area in which progress is very difficult to make. On the one hand there is some good news: people are concerned about the number of cars on the roads, and the great majority wishes to see significant improvements in public transport. Moreover, there appears to be a levelling off in car use in the last few years. There is certainly a decrease in the proportion of people who have never used the train, and trains have a positive image as a fast way of travelling. People are largely in favour of 'carrot' policies to make public transport more attractive, and there is a widespread expectation that such approaches would actually have the effect of reducing car use.

On the other hand there is the bad news: people show much less consensus about how improvements should be financed, with opposition to just about every policy that would cost them money. Our collective dependency on the car is still overwhelming. Although train use is up, there are many image problems to address, including unreliability, poor value for money and a dubious safety record.

For policy makers, politicians and campaigners for more sustainable mobility, perhaps the most disquieting result in this chapter is that attitudes towards the key issues do not seem to have changed much in recent years. Despite the intensity of debate and the frequency of troubles across the transport system, no consensus on how to solve the problems has emerged. The transport situation remains 'stuck': the pattern of results from our surveys indicates that there has been no breakthrough in the national debate on transport, no decisive shift in public perceptions that would lead us away from dependence on the car and towards acceptance of policies to curb car use. Government has acknowledged that some of its ambitions in the 1998 White Paper and its early statements on transport, in particular that of reducing car use overall, have suffered considerable setbacks. Taking decisive policy measures to make us less dependent on our cars calls for considerable political courage.

Would there be public backing for bolder moves from public authorities? There are indications in the data of what *might* be possible. Opposition to targeted measures to curb car use – notably urban congestion charging – is weakening and a reasonable number of car users, including some regular car users, think this would make them use their cars less. This is in contrast with more general measures, such as a hike in petrol prices, which although likely to be effective, are also associated with implacable opposition from car users. Findings indicate that the most effective measures may involve a combination of coercive measures and improvements in public transport.

Our findings thus suggest that there is the basis of support for a package of measures that combines varieties of targeted demand management with improvements in public transport. This is being put to the test now in London with the congestion charge and new strategies for public transport. Can decision-makers nationwide learn from the London experiment, and will it influence public attitudes? Time will tell; but the pattern of attitudes that entrenches the 'car culture' is going to remain hard to transform.

Notes

1. These questions were asked for the first time in 2002, so we are not able to chart changes over time in these attitudes.

References

Adams, J. (2000), *The Social Implications of Hypermobility*, Paris: OECD.

Commission for Integrated Transport (2001), *European Best Practice in the Delivery of Integrated Transport*, London: Department for Transport, Local Government and the Regions.

Commission for Integrated Transport (2003), *Ten Year Transport Plan: Second Assessment Report*, London: Commission for Integrated Transport.

Department for the Environment, Transport and the Regions (DETR) (1998), *A New Deal for Transport: the Government's White Paper on the future of transport*, London: The Stationery Office.

Department for the Environment, Transport and the Regions (DETR) (2000), *Climate Change: The UK Programme*, London: The Stationery Office

Exley, S. and Christie, I. (2002), 'Off the buses?', in Park, A., Curtice, J., Thomson, K., Jarvis, L. and Bromley, C. (eds), *British Social Attitudes: the 19th Report*, London: Sage.

Goodwin, P. (1998), 'We are at a historic crossroads', in Taylor, J. (ed.), *Can Prescott steer us through a transport revolution? Special supplement, New Statesman*, 22nd May.

Office for National Statistics (ONS) (2001), *Social Trends 2001*, London: The Stationery Office.

Acknowledgements

The *National Centre for Social Research* is grateful to the Department for Transport for their financial support which enabled us to ask the questions reported in this chapter, although the views in this chapter are those of the authors.

Appendix

Multivariate analysis

Models referred to in the chapter follow. Two multivariate techniques were used: logistic regression (model 1) and multiple regression (models 2 to 8). These techniques are explained in more detail in Appendix I to this Report.

For the logistic regression model, the figures reported are the odds ratios. An odds ratio of less than one means that the group was less likely than average to be in the group of interest on the dependent variable (the variable we are investigating), and an odds ratio greater than one indicates a greater than average likelihood of being in this group.

For the multiple regression models, it is the coefficients (or parameter estimates) that are shown. These show whether a particular characteristic differs significantly from its 'comparison group' in its association with the dependent variable. Details of the comparison group are shown in brackets. A positive coefficient indicates that those with the characteristic score more highly on the dependent variable and a negative coefficient means that they are likely to have a lower score.

For both methods, two asterisks indicate that the coefficient or odds ratio is statistically significant at a 99 per cent level and one asterisk that it is significant at a 95 per cent level.

Those variables which were selected as significant in predicting this are shown in order of the importance of their contribution. Variables which proved to be non-significant in the models have been dropped from the tables. All the models included the following variables:

Age
1. 18–33
2. 34–49
3. 50–64
4. 65+

Sex
1. Men
2. Women

Highest educational qualification
1. Degree or other higher education
2. A level or equivalent
3. GCSE level or equivalent
4. Lower than GCSE level

Household income
1. Less than £9,999
2. £10,000–£19,999
3. £20,000–£37,999
4. £38,000 and above
5. Unknown

Economic activity
1. Paid work
2. Economically inactive
3. Retired

Socio-economic group
1. Managerial/Professional
2. Intermediate
3. Small employer/own account worker
4. Lower supervisory/technical
5. Semi-routine/routine

Social Class
1.   I
2.   II/III
3.   IV
4.   V

Children under 16 living in household
1. No children
2. Children

Type of area
1. A big city
2. The suburbs/outskirts of a big city
3. A small city or town
4. A country village/farm/country home

Region
1. North England
2. Eastern/Midlands
3. Wales and South West
4. London and South East
5. Scotland

Regular car use
1. Does not use car at least 2–5 times a week
2. Uses car at least 2–5 times a week

Regular bus use
1. Does not use bus at least 2–5 times a week
2. Uses bus at least 2–5 times a week

Regular train use
1. Does not use train at least 2–5 times a week
2. Uses train at least 2–5 times a week

Nearby train station
1. Less than ½ mile
2. ½ mile up to 1 mile (15–30 mins walk)
3. More than 1 mile, up to 3 miles
4. More than 3 miles, up to 10 miles
5. Over 10 miles

Model 1 Predictors of taking the train 'never nowadays'

Category	B	S.E.	Wald	Odds ratio (Exp(B))	Sig
Baseline odds	-0.084	0.103	0.664	0.920	
Highest educational qualification			48.749		**
Degree or other higher education	-0.682	0.123	30.759	0.506	**
A level or equivalent	-0.193	0.151	1.644	0.824	
GCSE level or equivalent	0.240	0.130	3.426	1.271	
Lower than GCSE level	0.635	0.124	26.315	1.887	**
					**
Nearby train station			29.827		
Less than ½ mile	-0.609	0.148	16.898	0.544	**
½ mile up to 1 mile (15–30 mins walk)	-0.253	0.145	3.042	0.777	
More than 1 mile, up to 3 miles	-0.051	0.124	0.166	0.951	
More than 3 miles, up to 10 miles	0.518	0.137	14.235	1.678	**
More than 10 miles	0.395	0.179	4.879	1.484	*
					**
Region			18.814		
North	0.122	0.128	0.909	1.129	
Eastern/Midlands	-0.116	0.132	0.767	0.891	
Wales and South West	0.380	0.153	6.140	1.462	*
London and South East	-0.550	0.144	14.562	0.577	**
Scotland	0.164	0.193	0.726	1.178	
					**
Income			17.505		
Less than £9,999	0.359	0.162	4.899	1.431	*
£10,000–£19,999	0.190	0.142	1.784	1.209	
£20,000–£37,999	-0.139	0.128	1.181	0.870	
£38,000 and above	-0.598	0.151	15.674	0.550	**
Unknown	0.189	0.178	1.127	1.208	
Regular car use					
Uses regularly	0.300	0.082	13.414	1.350	**
Does not use regularly	-0.300	0.082	13.414	0.741	**
					*
Age			9.709		
18–33	-0.265	0.133	3.989	0.767	*
34–49	-0.005	0.130	0.001	0.995	
50–64	-0.158	0.125	1.596	0.854	
65+	0.429	0.156	7.506	1.535	**
Children under 16					
Children under 16 in household	0.190	0.091	4.409	1.209	*
No children under 16 in household	-0.190	0.091	4.409	0.827	*

Number of cases in model: 1076

Model 2 Correlates of agreeing that 'it is easy to find out what time trains run'

Individual characteristics (comparison group in brackets)	Standardised Beta coefficient
Age (65 and over)	
18–33	-0.144**
34–49	-0.240**
50–64	-0.118**
Children under 16 (no children under 16 in household)	
Children under 16 in household	0.101**
Regular car use (does not use regularly)	
Uses regularly	-0.083*

Number of cases in model: 970

Model 3 Correlates of agreeing that 'trains generally run often enough'

Category	Standardised Beta coefficient
Economic activity (retired)	
In paid work	-0.196**
Economically inactive	-0.171**
Socio-economic group (Managerial/Professional)	
Intermediate	0.010
Small employer/own account worker	0.001
Lower supervisory/technical	0.024
Semi-routine/routine	0.086*
Region (North)	
Eastern/Midlands	-0.038
Wales and South West	-0.085**
London and South East	-0.031
Scotland	0.016
Income (less than £9,999)	
£10,000–£19,999	0.004
£20,000–£37,999	-0.010
£38,000 and above	-0.078*
Unknown	-0.027

Number of cases in model: 970

Model 4 Correlates of agreeing that 'trains generally run on time'

Category	Standardised Beta coefficient
Economic activity (retired)	
In paid work	-0.238**
Economically inactive	-0.221**
Socio-economic group (Managerial/Professional)	
Intermediate	0.032
Small employer/own account worker	-0.016
Lower supervisory/technical	0.048
Semi-routine/routine	0.150**
Sex (men)	
Women	0.085**

Number of cases in model: 970

Model 5 Correlates of agreeing that 'train fares are fairly reasonable'

Category	Standardised Beta coefficient
Economic activity (retired)	
In paid work	-0.179**
Economically inactive	-0.181**
Socio-economic group (Managerial/Professional)	
Intermediate	0.035
Small employer/own account worker	-0.011
Lower supervisory/technical	0.044
Semi-routine/routine	0.142**
Region (North)	
Eastern/Midlands	-0.131**
Wales and South West	-0.129**
London and South East	-0.138**
Scotland	-0.006
Highest educational qualification (lower than GCSE level)	
Degree or other higher education	-0.095**
A level or equivalent	-0.052
GCSE level or equivalent	-0.006
Sex (men)	
Women	0.091**

Number of cases in model: 970

Model 6 Correlates of agreeing that 'trains are a fast way to travel'

Category	Standardised Beta coefficient
Economic activity (retired)	
In paid work	-0.227**
Economically inactive	-0.193**
Socio-economic group (Managerial/Professional)	
Intermediate	0.035
Small employer/own account worker	-0.007
Lower supervisory/technical	0.018
Semi-routine/routine	0.150**
Sex (men)	
Women	0.126**
Nearby train station (less than ½ mile)	
½ mile up to 1 mile (15–30 mins walk)	-0.047
More than 1 mile, up to 3 miles	0.038
More than 3 miles, up to 10 miles	-0.094**
More than 10 miles	-0.023
Region (North)	
Eastern/Midlands	-0.076*
Wales and South West	0.006
London and South East	-0.094**
Scotland	-0.022
Regular bus use (does not use bus regularly)	
Uses bus regularly	0.069*

Number of cases in model: 970

Model 7 Correlates of agreeing that 'it is difficult to find out the cheapest train fares'

Category	Standardised Beta coefficient
Economic activity (retired)	
In paid work	-0.170**
Economically inactive	-0.145**
Socio-economic group (Managerial/Professional)	
Intermediate	-0.035
Small employer/own account worker	-0.031
Lower supervisory/technical	0.025
Semi-routine/routine	0.111**
Nearby train station (less than ½ mile)	
½ mile up to 1 mile (15–30 mins walk)	-0.081*
More than 1 mile, up to 3 miles	-0.002
More than 3 miles, up to 10 miles	-0.024
More than 10 miles	0.052
Income (less than £9,999)	
£10,000–£19,999	-0.025
£20,000–£37,999	-0.007
£38,000 and above	-0.005
Unknown	0.067*

Number of cases in model: 970

Model 8 Correlates of agreeing that 'trains have a good safety record'

Category	Standardised Beta coefficient
Age (65 and over)	
18–33	-0.217**
34–39	-0.225**
50–64	-0.085*
Type of area (big city)	
The suburbs/ outskirts of a big city	-0.088**
A small city or town	0.018
A country village/ farm/ country home	-0.011
Socio-economic group (Managerial/Professional)	
Intermediate	-0.011
Small employer/own account worker	-0.077*
Lower supervisory/technical	-0.014
Semi-routine/routine	0.026

Number of cases in model: 970

4 Has Britain become immune to inequality?

Catherine Bromley [*]

Perhaps one of the most notable changes to have occurred since the *British Social Attitudes* survey series began has been the trend towards increased affluence, coupled with ever-widening income inequality. Since the mid-1980s, average incomes have increased by 50 per cent (Goodman and Shephard, 2002).[1] This has not gone unnoticed, with fewer now reporting difficulties coping on their household income than was the case two decades ago. As part of the 1984 *British Social Attitudes* survey, we asked respondents to choose between various possible descriptions of their household's income these days. Then, just under a quarter (24 per cent) said they were "living comfortably"; a similar proportion (26 per cent) said they were finding it difficult or very difficult to cope. By 2002, the proportion living comfortably had risen to four in ten (39 per cent), while those reporting difficulties had shrunk to 16 per cent.

Despite this increase in overall affluence, income inequality has increased, largely because of the varying rates at which different groups' incomes have grown. According to the Institute for Fiscal Studies, during the Thatcher era (1979–1990) the income growth of the richest 20 per cent in society was over eight times that of the poorest 20 per cent (Goodman and Shephard, 2002). By contrast, the period between 1991 and 1997, during John Major's premiership, saw the incomes of the poorest increase more than those of the richest (mainly as a result of economic recession). After the election of a Labour government in 1997, and as Britain moved out of recession and experienced stronger economic growth, income growth was fairly evenly distributed across all groups in society. However, as we shall see later, if incomes grow at similar rates, any gap between the incomes of richer and poorer groups will inevitably grow.

The *Gini coefficient* offers a useful way of examining changes in income inequality (for a discussion of this, and other measures, see Goodman *et al.*, 1997). This figure, ranging from zero to one, summarises the extent to which

---

[*] Catherine Bromley is a Senior Researcher at the *National Centre for Social Research*, Scotland, and is Co-Director of the *British Social Attitudes* survey series.

incomes in a society are equally distributed. A figure of one would mean that all
the income is earned by just one person, while everyone else has nothing; a
figure of zero means that incomes are evenly shared. Figure 4.1 shows the
British Gini coefficient figures for the period between 1970 and 2001–2. This
clearly demonstrates that income inequality fell in the 1970s, grew significantly
in the period between 1979 and 1992, fell during the recession of the early
1990s, and then began to steadily climb from the mid-1990s. The election of a
Labour government in 1997 did nothing to curb the growth of income inequality
and it now stands at a higher level than at any time in the past. Currently, the
poorest tenth in society receive three per cent of the nation's total income,
whereas the richest tenth receive more than a quarter (Goodman and Shephard,
2002).

**Figure 4.1 Income inequality in Britain measured by the Gini coefficent, 1970–
2001/2**

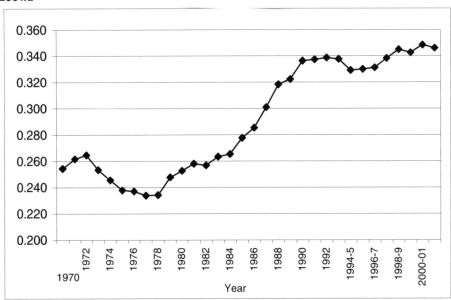

Incomes are measured before housing costs are taken into account, and are
standardised for family size.
Figures between 1970 and 1993 are taken from the Family Expenditure Survey, 1994
onwards Family Resources Survey. Data was supplied by the IFS (www.ifs.org.uk).
From 1994 onwards the years referred to are financial years, 1970–1993 are calendar
years.

Many have suggested that income inequality is an inevitable feature of modern
industrial societies; a consequence of the premium attracted by highly skilled
labour, coupled with the ease with which developing countries can compete for

low-skilled jobs by providing cheaper labour and materials (see Atkinson, 1999, for a fuller discussion of this). However, there is nothing inevitable about the increasing level of income inequality found in Britain over the last two decades (Hills, 1998; Atkinson, 1999). Between the mid-1980s and early 1990s, the rate of growth in Britain's income inequality was the fastest amongst those western countries for which data are available. Not only was the rate of growth in income inequality significantly lower in a number of other western societies, some – including Canada, Italy and the Netherlands – actually achieved reductions in inequality.

The politics of inequality

If increasing income inequality is not inevitable, there must clearly be some other explanation as to why some countries have experienced growing levels of inequality while others have not. One possibility, suggested in Polly Toynbee's book, *Hard Work – Life in Low-Pay Britain* (2003), is that the British public are increasingly accepting of inequality:

> Post-Thatcher, fewer people seem to question why incomes are distributed as they are. Conservative cultural domination of a generation has atrophied natural sensitivity to the unfairness of the accidents of birth or position.

Toynbee argues that, despite no longer being in power, the Conservative Party (and the Thatcher era in particular) has left a mark on British politics that has yet to be erased. This is the main question we address in this chapter. But, before we start, we briefly consider the different ways in which politics and policies have dealt with inequality over the last two decades.

We begin with the policies of the 1979–1990 Thatcher governments (and to a lesser extent the Major governments until 1997). These followed a distinct path, unrecognisable from what had gone before, especially in relation to economic policy. Up to the 1970s at least, the post-war era was characterised by a reasonably broad consensus, both about the general direction in which Britain was going, and about the means by which it should get there. This was brought to an end in the 1970s as Keynesian economic policy failed to find an answer to the new challenges posed by stagnant economic growth, high inflation and industrial unrest.

When Margaret Thatcher was elected in 1979 she was vocal in her support of new ways to manage the economy and to transform British politics. Her ideology and political style did not have a single source, being influenced both by her own personal experience as well as the work of economists such as Milton Friedman, Friedrich Hayek and Sir Keith Joseph. In so doing, she attempted to renegotiate the relationship between citizens and the state, reflecting her belief that people had been led to expect too much of government and, as a result, their own capabilities were being stifled. This belief helped unite four key tenets of Thatcherism (Kavanagh, 1990). The first was a determination to combat inflation and end the practice of having government-led incomes policies and formal agreements between industry, government and trade unions. The second was the limiting of the public sector and a move towards an overtly free market economy (involving tax and public spending cuts, privatisation of public utilities and the sale of council housing). The third was a sustained dismantling of trade union powers with the aim of freeing up the labour market. And the final part of the picture was an increased focus on law, order and national defence.

The impact of Thatcherism on Britain in the 1980s is unquestionable. It heralded a new ideological regime which challenged previously held orthodoxies and set about dismantling many of the hitherto traditional features of the British state (including the public utilities, council housing, strong trade unions and Keynesian economic policy). However, Thatcherism's impact on the period which followed is less clear-cut. The Labour Party's transformation into New Labour is undoubtedly a direct consequence of the party's continual electoral defeat in the Thatcher era. New Labour certainly has no appetite to re-introduce the kinds of tax rates, income or industrial policies which many hold responsible for the economic chaos that beset the 1970s. But some argue that Thatcherism's influence stretches further still and that politicians will inevitably have to embrace her political framework if they are to succeed (Cosgrave, cited in Kavanagh, 1990). This view seems particularly prescient when considering the distance that Labour has travelled since the 1970s on the matter of income inequality. Then, Denis Healey threatened to "tax the rich until the pips squeak". Contrast this with Tony Blair's refusal to answer directly a question posed repeatedly on *Newsnight* as to whether it is acceptable for the gap between the rich and the poor to widen:

> Paxman: Is it acceptable for the gap between rich and poor to get bigger?
> Blair: What I am saying is the issue isn't in fact whether the very richest person ends up becoming richer. The issue is whether the poorest person is given the chance that they don't otherwise have. [2]

And, in response to whether it was fair that the UK tax system taxed a person earning £34,000 at the same rate as someone earning £34 million (though clearly not the same amount), Blair's response was:

> ... the justice for me is concentrated on lifting incomes of those that don't have a decent income. It's not a burning ambition for me to make sure that David Beckham earns less money.

This is not to deny that Labour has expressly targeted the poorest in society, most notably through the introduction of Britain's first national minimum wage, the New Deal, and a host of tax credits designed to boost the incomes of working families. But the fault lines which run through both the parliamentary Labour Party and much of the party's membership, as well as the trade union movement, suggest that for many the transformation of the party over the last decade has been an uncomfortable process.

The extent to which the policies advanced in the name of Thatcherism ever fully achieved their intended aims, or even had that much popular support, has been questioned (Heath *et al.*, 2001). In particular, Thatcher's public spending policies, and her attempts to introduce free market principles to the health service and the education system were demonstrably out of tune with what many wanted at the time. This chapter explores whether (and how) attitudes towards inequality have changed over the last two decades and, particularly, whether 'Thatcher's children' (that is, those who entered the labour market at the height of the economic boom in the 1980s, and in the years following this) are more willing than others to accept income inequality than those who started their working life in the pre-Thatcher era. We then conclude by considering how people think income inequality should be addressed.

Is income inequality acceptable?

Then and now

Over the years, two key questions have been used to measure attitudes towards income inequality:

> *Thinking of income levels generally in Britain today, would you say that the gap between those with high incomes and those with low incomes is too large, about right, or, too small?*

> *How much do you agree or disagree that ordinary working people do not get their fair share of the nation's wealth?*

Figure 4.2 charts the trends in attitudes to these two questions. The most striking finding is the very high proportion who believe that the gap between those on high and low incomes is too large. Almost three-quarters (72 per cent) thought this in 1983, and it has been the view of no less than 80 per cent since 1989, peaking at 87 per cent in 1995. In 2002, 82 per cent took this view. When it comes to whether or not the "nation's wealth" is shared, just over six in ten agree that "ordinary working people" do not get their fair share. Views on this have varied little over time, never exceeding 70 per cent, and rarely dropping below 60 per cent.

Figure 4.2 Trends in attitudes to income inequality and wealth sharing, 1983–2002

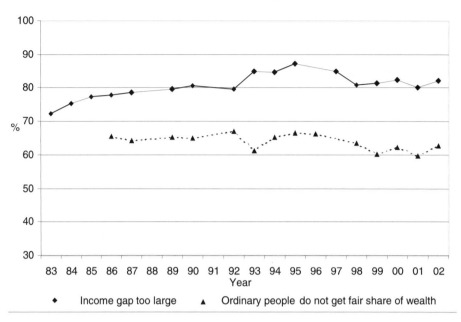

The scale in this chart starts at 30 per cent.

So far we have found little to support Toynbee's suggestion that fewer people nowadays question the way in which incomes are distributed, or that people are now less sensitive to the plight of those who are less well off. However, it might be thought curious that the proportion who express unhappiness with the gap between those with high and low incomes did not rise more over the period (given the marked rise in actual income inequality over the period, particularly during the 1980s). Might this be a *tacit* increase in public acceptance of inequality – assuming that people are aware of these kinds of trends? This seems improbable. True, the increase in inequality between 1984 and 2002 shown in Figure 4.2 is far more pronounced than the eight point increase over the same period in the proportion thinking that the gap between high and low incomes is too large. But, with a starting point as high as 72 per cent (1984), it would be very improbable that changes in attitudes could match actual changes in inequality.

Clearly there are difficulties when interpreting questions which require people to express views about current social and political 'reality', particularly when this reality is rapidly changing. So, to double-check our assertion that Thatcherism has not brought about a creeping acceptance of income inequality, we examine two additional questions, the responses to which are not as rooted in the context of the time. The first encapsulates a key strand of Thatcherite economic thinking, and was used by some to justify large income differentials:

How much do you agree or disagree with this statement? Large differences in income are necessary for Britain's prosperity

Another important principle of Thatcherism was that it is the responsibility of the *individual*, and not the state or society in general, to provide for people's needs in the long term. This is summed up perfectly in Norman Tebbitt's now infamous remark that the unemployed should "get on their bikes" and seek work. By shifting the focus away from the state and onto the individual, Thatcherism challenged the idea that phenomena such as poverty and inequality are the responsibility of – and perhaps even the *fault* of – governments and institutions. Indeed, perhaps one of the most successful features of Thatcherism, and the New Right agenda more broadly, was its ability to demolish the idea that social problems have a structural explanation. To assess this, we asked people whether they agreed or disagreed with the following statement about why inequality might exist:

Inequality continues to exist because it benefits the rich and powerful

The results are shown in Table 4.1. If Thatcherism *did* mould British public opinion about inequality, we should see an increase over time in acceptance of the need for large income differences. However, as the table shows, public support for this idea has actually fallen over time. In 1987, a quarter said they either "agreed strongly" or "agreed" with the assertion that income differentials are necessary; by 1999, this had fallen to just 17 per cent. Even in 1987, only a quarter agreed with the proposition, while nearly a half disagreed. And, at no time did any more than four per cent ever agree *strongly* with the proposition.

We can probably assume, with some degree of confidence, that anyone who agrees with the assertion that inequality persists because it benefits the powerful, accepts the notion that inequality has a structural and not individual explanation. And, as the next table shows, on the three occasions we have asked this question, around six in ten fall into this category. Although it is true that the proportion who say they agree *strongly* with the assertion has decreased over time, the fact that the overall level of agreement remained the same – and was the majority position – is a pretty definitive contradiction of the notion that people bought wholesale into the doctrines pursued by Thatcher in the 1980s.

Table 4.1 Attitudes to inequality, 1987, 1992 and 1999

% agree	1987	1992	1999
Large differences in income are necessary for Britain's prosperity	26	19	17
Inequality persists because it benefits the rich and powerful	59	61	58
Base	*1212*	*1066*	*804*

Income inequality and social cohesion

So far we have seen evidence of high levels of concern about the gap between rich and poor, and little support for the notion that income inequality is a necessary component of economic prosperity. But whether income inequality – that is, the size of the gap between the richest and poorest – actually matters is an issue of some debate. For some, what counts is that the incomes of those at the bottom end of the income distribution are sufficient to live on, and that they are not disproportionately excluded from the means by which they could progress through the social strata. Consequently (and as illustrated by the earlier quotation from Prime Minister Blair), it is the *absolute* incomes of these poorer groups which matters most, not how they fare relative to a millionaire football player or rich company director. However, others argue that it is income inequality *per se* (and not just absolute living standards) which is most important, not only because it affects people's outcomes and experiences in life, but also because it is an important barometer of social cohesion. By this account, an unequal society is a socially divided society, with clear distinctions between the 'haves' and the 'have nots'. Wilkinson (1999) cites many sources of cross-national evidence which point to there being a strong relationship between the extent of income inequality within a society and levels of poor health (notably heart disease), violent crime (especially homicide), domestic violence, racial discrimination, smoking and obesity. By this account, actual levels of poverty or the living standards of the poor matter less than levels of income inequality. As he states in relation to health (ibid.: 259):

> Health appears to be related less to people's absolute material living standards than to their position in society as expressed by their income.

Concern has also been expressed about high levels of inequality leading to the 'voluntary exclusion' of the very rich (Giddens, 1998). This could result from their withdrawal from various public services (such as the health service or education), or the development of fortress-like communities which impose a physical barrier between them and the rest of society. Trends such as these are clearly evident in countries like South Africa, but can also be seen in parts of some large British cities.

The fact that inequality might have implications for social cohesion poses some interesting questions in relation to attitudes towards inequality. The most obvious relates to finding out the amount of shared concern in Britain about income inequality. Is this an issue which brings together otherwise disparate groups, or are those who are less advantaged themselves more concerned about inequality than those who are more advantaged? Perhaps, for instance, concern about the gap between rich and poor is only evident among those on the poorer side of that gap, with more advantaged groups being far less concerned (or even supportive) of inequality? Alternatively, richer groups might also have concerns about inequality. Whether these are motivated by altruism, or by more pragmatic worries about the implications of inequality for society as a whole (or both), this would mean that even the most advantaged groups could be extremely concerned about inequality.

To address these issues we consider how attitudes to income inequality vary between different social class and income groups. In addition to looking at those living on different incomes, we also examine whether views vary according to a more subjective measure; how well a person feels they and their household cope on their current household income. This can be a more useful measure of economic hardship (as our measure of household income does not take into account the size of household, or housing and other living costs).

Even a very fleeting glance at the next table demonstrates that clear majorities in all groups think that the gap between those on high and low salaries is too large. In all cases, around three-quarters or more take this view, displaying a quite considerable degree of unanimity.

Table 4.2 Attitudes towards inequality by social class, self-rated economic hardship, and household income

The gap between high and low incomes is ...		... too large	... about right	Base
All	%	82	13	1148
Social class (NS-SEC)				
Managerial or professional	%	79	18	409
Intermediate occupations	%	87	8	146
Small employer or own account workers	%	77	15	93
Lower supervisory or technical staff	%	81	15	141
Semi-routine and routine manual occupations	%	86	8	331
Household income				
£38,000 or more	%	74	22	275
£20,000–37,999	%	86	11	236
£10,000–19,999	%	87	9	290
£9,999 or less	%	84	7	233
Self-rated hardship				
Living comfortably	%	77	18	419
Coping	%	84	12	530
Having difficulty	%	90	4	197

So there is little evidence here that this is an issue which markedly divides those in more and less advantaged positions. This said, some interesting variations remain. These largely follow the pattern we might expect, whereby those in less advantaged positions (in working-class occupations, on low incomes, or who are struggling financially) are the most likely to feel that income gaps are too large. The clearest relationship is with what we might call 'self-rated hardship', with those who are having difficulty in coping on their current household income being 13 percentage points more likely than those who are living comfortably to consider the gap between high and low incomes to be too large. This shows that those who find themselves in more precarious social or economic circumstances do seem to have the most acute concern about the gap between rich and poor. But this issue is not ignored by those who are more advantaged; they too are clearly concerned about the size of the gap between society's richest and poorest members.

Does this social unanimity still apply when we consider the views of different party supporters? After all, as we outlined earlier, the ways in which the main political parties in Britain have responded to inequality have varied considerably, both between parties and within the same party over time. Despite this, however, concern about inequality is not particularly politically divisive. As the next table shows, there is a broad consensus across the political spectrum that the gap between rich and poor is too large. That said, supporters of the Conservative Party do stand out as being the least likely to take this view, though seven in ten still do so.

Table 4.3 Attitudes towards inequality by party identification

The gap between high and low incomes is …		… too large	… about right	Base
All	%	82	13	1148
Party identification				
Conservative	%	71	25	284
Labour	%	88	7	444
Liberal Democrat	%	84	16	137
None	%	81	12	170

Although we have found only very limited evidence of social divisions in attitudes towards inequality, this might not have always been the case. So we turn now to examine whether or not different groups have varied in their views over time. Has, for instance, the rapid growth in income inequality over the past two decades changed the way different groups perceive this issue? Perhaps the relative unanimity we saw earlier is a recent phenomenon, a response to a changing, and less equal, social reality.

To assess this, we focus again upon respondents' perceptions of their own financial situation (as earlier this proved to be related to their views about inequality), and concentrate upon those who say they are "living comfortably" and those who say they are "finding it difficult to cope" on their present income.

As the next table shows, it is notable that concern about inequality has increased more among those who were living comfortably than it has amongst those who were having financial difficulties (although this at least partly reflects the fact that concern could not get much higher among this group). This trend towards increased concern among the better off is particularly evident in the mid- to late 1990s; by 1998, eight in ten of those who were living comfortably thought the gap between high and low incomes was too large, as did 85 per cent of those who were finding it hard to cope on their household's income. As a result, the 'gap' between the views of these two groups was, at six percentage points, at its smallest ever. Since then, concern among both groups has remained relatively stable – although some small shifts have taken place, these are not statistically significant.

Table 4.4   Trends in attitudes to income inequality by self-rated economic hardship, 1983–2002

% who think gap between high and low incomes is "too large"	1984	1986	1989	1992	1995	1998	2000	2002
All	75	77	80	80	87	81	82	82
Base	*1675*	*3100*	*3029*	*1445*	*1234*	*3146*	*2292*	*1148*
Self-rated hardship								
Living comfortably	68	70	72	71	80	79	78	77
Base	*388*	*756*	*832*	*376*	*299*	*1078*	*900*	*419*
Having difficulty	83	82	85	86	89	85	86	90
Base	*438*	*801*	*706*	*382*	*313*	*416*	*390*	*197*
Size of gap between two groups	15	12	13	15	9	6	8	13

We turn now to consider how the views of different party supporters have changed over time. Our particular interest here is two-fold. Firstly, we examine how the views of Conservative identifiers have changed over time, and whether these views are the same now as they were at the height of Thatcherism. And, secondly, we assess the extent to which the views of Labour supporters have changed as the party has modernised and modified its stance on inequality.

Among Conservative identifiers, there has been a sustained *increase* over time in the proportion who think the gap between rich and poor is too large, from 62 per cent in 1984 to 71 per cent nowadays (peaking at 78 per cent in 1995). Perhaps the most remarkable aspect of this is that, even at the height of Margaret Thatcher's premiership, over six in ten of her supporters considered the gap between high and low incomes to be too large. Meanwhile, the views of Labour supporters have remained fairly consistent throughout the period, albeit with a slight peak in the mid-1990s. So there is little sign here that changing

Labour Party policy is reflected in the views of its supporters. As a result of these changes, the gap between the views of Conservative and Labour identifiers has narrowed markedly. At its widest, 23 percentage points separated Labour and Conservative identifiers; at its lowest, in 1995, this gap stood at 13 points. Since then, the two camps have diverged slightly again, and the gap between them stands at 17 points.

Table 4.5 Trends in attitudes to income inequality by party identification, 1983–2002

% who think gap between high and low incomes is "too large"	1984	1986	1989	1992	1995	1998	2000	2002
All	75	77	80	80	87	81	82	82
Base	1675	3100	3029	1445	1234	3146	2292	1148
Party identification								
Conservative	62	65	68	68	78	72	74	71
Base	640	1054	1198	515	319	818	635	284
Labour	85	86	88	88	91	87	88	88
Base	595	1080	1017	510	561	1398	927	444
Liberal Democrat	85	85	89	85	94	87	90	84
Base	220	542	335	167	160	324	229	137
None	78	81	82	77	85	73	80	81
Base	105	226	215	110	108	367	293	170
Size of gap between Conservative and Labour	23	21	20	20	13	15	14	17

Income inequality in practice

Most of our discussion so far has focused upon attitudes towards reasonably abstract concepts. So we turn now to look at a range of specific occupations; at what people think earnings *are* within them, and at what they think earnings *should* be. We have already seen that a very high proportion think that the gap between those with the highest and lowest incomes is too large. But is this borne out when respondents pass judgement on the actual earnings of various occupations?

To assess this, we presented respondents with a number of different occupations and asked what they thought someone in that job was currently paid, and what they should be paid. Over the three occasions on which we have included these questions, a total of sixteen different occupations have been covered. But, because we are most interested in change (or lack of it) over time, we focus here on the five occupations which were included in all three years.

They are listed here in ascending order of how much people thought they should be, and what they thought they actually are, paid:[3]

- An unskilled worker in a factory
- A skilled worker in a factory
- A doctor in general practice
- A cabinet minister in the UK government
- The chairman of a large national corporation

The responses people gave enable us to identify the extent to which people think that certain occupations are overpaid and underpaid. They also allow us to compare what people see as an 'appropriate' gap between the incomes of different jobs with the gap that currently exists. Finally, and perhaps most importantly for our purposes, they also allow us to examine whether views about inequality have changed over time, or whether they have remained relatively stable. Whether people's assessments of incomes are actually correct is not what matters here; the key factor is their perceptions. As Sen (2000: 60) puts it:

> People's attitudes towards, or reactions to, actual income distributions can be significantly influenced by the correspondence – or the lack thereof – between (1) their ideas of what is normatively tolerable, and (2) what they actually see in the society around them.

The results in the next table are based upon comparing people's views about what particular jobs *are* paid with what they *should* be paid. For example, if a person's estimate as to what a skilled factory worker is paid was *less* than what they thought a skilled factory worker should be paid, this can be taken to indicate that they see skilled factory workers as underpaid. This exercise shows that company chairmen are consistently judged to be the most overpaid, with eight in ten thinking this in 1999 (when these questions were last asked). Following fairly closely are cabinet ministers, with around two-thirds seeing them as overpaid. Meanwhile, factory workers are underpaid (with skilled factory workers attracting near universal sympathy for their pay levels), and opinion is divided regarding doctors. While four in ten consider doctors to be underpaid, six in ten think their earnings are either appropriate or too high.

There are also some interesting (but small) changes of opinion over time. Between 1987 and 1992 there was a small but significant rise in the proportion of people who thought that company chairmen were overpaid, no doubt reflecting concerns about boardroom pay at the time of the recession in the early 1990s. However, since 1992 this has fallen back. Conversely, the view that GPs are overpaid fell from 28 to 20 per cent in 1999, with a corresponding rise in the proportions thinking they are paid about the right amount. Interestingly, perceptions of Ministerial pay were almost identical over the period, despite a distinct hardening in attitudes towards politicians and a considerable downturn in levels of trust in government (Bromley and Curtice, 2002).

Table 4.6 Perceptions of over- and underpaid occupations, 1987, 1992 and 1999

| | % who say each occupation is ... | | | | | | | | |
| | ... overpaid | | | ... underpaid | | | ... paid right amount | | |
	'87	'92	'99	'87	'92	'99	'87	'92	'99
Unskilled factory worker	6	5	3	72	73	76	23	22	21
Skilled factory worker	1	1	1	97	99	99	2	*	*
Doctor (GP)	28	25	20	39	39	42	33	36	38
Cabinet minister	68	67	67	12	12	12	20	22	22
Chairman of corporation	78	85	80	6	5	5	16	11	14

Base (ranges): 1987: 1000–1015; 1992: 903–915; 1999: 605–630

Having seen what people think of the individual earnings of these five occupations, we now turn to look at perceptions of the size of the gap between the highest and lowest earners, both in practice and in principle. This will help us reach a more definitive conclusion as to whether or not attitudes have changed over time. If the size of the gap that people judge to be acceptable *increased* between 1987 and 1999 that would indicate that income inequality has become more acceptable over time. Conversely, if the gap has not changed, or has decreased, this would confirm our earlier impression that views about income inequality are either stable or have become more critical. However, it should be noted that there is widespread acceptance of the fact that some occupations are paid more than others, and very little to suggest that there is any appetite for anything approaching a completely egalitarian distribution of earnings.

These results are shown in the next table. As company chairmen were consistently judged to have the highest pay, and unskilled factory workers the lowest, we focus upon the earnings gap between these two groups. We show the *median* incomes that people thought these occupations would and should earn in 1987, 1992 and 1999. In each year, the first column represents *perceived* actual earnings, while the following shows what people thought the case *should* be. The amount in pounds does not take into account average earnings inflation, and so conclusions cannot be drawn about income growth over the period.

Even the most cursory glance at the table shows that, in any given year, the gap perceived to exist between the pay earned by company chairmen and unskilled factory workers vastly exceeds what is seen to be appropriate. Moreover, the preferred way of closing this gap involves a significant reduction in the higher earner's income, accompanied by a relatively small increase in the lower earner's income. So, when it comes to the gap between those on low and high incomes, the 'problem' is very much seen to lie at the upper end of the income scale. It is not so much that those on low incomes are seen to be dramatically underpaid; rather, those on higher incomes are seen as being very overpaid. For example, in 1987 people perceived the actual income of a chairman before taxes (£60,000) to be ten times higher than that of an unskilled worker (£6,000). However, when asked what was appropriate, respondents thought the chairman should earn around £35,000 (a pay drop of £25,000) and the unskilled worker £7,000 (a pay increase of £1,000). These 'ideal' salaries would mean that the company director only earned five times what an unskilled worker would, rather than the ten-fold gap that was perceived to exist in reality. By 1992, company chairmen's earnings were perceived to be 12.5 times larger than those of unskilled workers (again, the *preferred* size of the difference was half the estimated size – six times). The corresponding figures for 1999 are 12.5 and 6.25.

Table 4.7 Perceived average earnings of unskilled factory workers and company chairmen, and what they should earn, 1987, 1992 and 1999

	1987		1992		1999	
	Does earn £	Should earn £	Does earn £	Should earn £	Does earn £	Should earn £
Unskilled factory worker	6,000	7,000	8,000	10,000	10,000	12,000
Chairman of corporation	60,000	35,000	100,000	60,000	125,000	75,000
Base	*1212*	*1066*	*804*	*1212*	*1066*	*804*

So, in each year, people saw the size of the gap between the highest and lowest paid occupations as *twice* the size they thought would be appropriate. The fact that this figure did not alter over time lends yet more ammunition to the case that people have *not* become more accepting of income inequality since, or because of, the Thatcher era.

Is there a Thatcher's generation?

So far we have found very little evidence to suggest that Thatcherism caused a sea change in public attitudes towards income inequality. However, it is possible that, even if the population as a whole is concerned about inequality, certain age groups might have become inured to the plight of the poorest in society. If this is the case, this might have implications for how attitudes might change in the future. We can explore this by focusing on particular generations – that is, people born (and, most importantly, reaching adulthood) [4] during specific periods of history. On some issues, these generations can have very distinct views compared to those held by previous or later ones. In this case, we might speculate that those who came of age during Thatcher's terms of office in the 1980s were imbued with a particularly unique set of values. This was, after all, an era which for the first time saw mass conspicuous consumption (for some at least), new economic opportunities and the rise of the super rich. Not surprisingly, then, much has been written about a so-called 'Thatcher's generation' (often nicknamed 'Thatcher's children'). We turn now to assess the extent to which this stereotype is backed up by our findings. We do this by comparing the views of six distinct generational groups:

- A 'post-Thatcher' generation born between 1973 and 1984, and who came of age between 1991 and 2002.

- A 'Thatcher' generation, born between 1961 and 1972, and who came of age between 1979 and 1990.

- A 'seventies' generation, born between 1952 and 1961, and who came of age between 1970 and 1979.

- A 'sixties' generation, born between 1942 and 1951, and who came of age between 1960 and 1969.

- A 'fifties' generation, born between 1932 and 1941, and who came of age between 1950 and 1959.

- A 'pre-1950s' generation, born before 1931, and who came of age sometime before 1950.

The next table looks at the responses of these six generational groups towards a range of the questions we have already considered. It finds no evidence of a Thatcher's generation who are more accepting of inequality. In fact, on the subject of income inequality, this generation tend to be *more* concerned than other groups. This confirms earlier studies which have found no evidence at all that those who grew up during the 1980s were any more accepting than average of economic inequality and disparities in income (Heath and Park, 1997). True, the Thatcher generation are slightly less likely than generations who came of age in the 1960s or earlier to think that "ordinary people do not get their fair share of the nation's wealth". But so too are the 'seventies' generation, making it hard to see Thatcherism as the root cause of any difference. It is, however, true that the Thatcher generation and its successor have different views about root causes of inequality than the generations before them. Half of those who came of age after 1979 agree that inequality persists because it "benefits the rich and powerful", compared with around six in ten for all previous generations.

  These results do not support the assertion that the Conservative domination of a generation has led people to accept income inequality more readily. The so-called Thatcher generation does not stand out in its views on this subject, although it is interesting that it is less likely to feel that inequality's persistence is for structural reasons.

Table 4.8 Attitudes towards income inequality across the generations

% agree	Year of turning 18					
	1991 and after	1979–1990	1970s	1960s	1950s	1940s and earlier
The gap between those with high and low incomes is too large*	78	85	80	85	84	80
Ordinary working people do not get their fair share of the nation's wealth*	59	61	59	66	69	67
Base	172	295	180	184	144	171
Inequality persists because it benefits the rich and powerful**	50	52	62	60	63	60
Base	434	763	443	474	367	415

*These questions were asked in 2002.
** This question was asked in 1999.

What should be done to reduce income inequality?

Having established that people are concerned about levels of income inequality, we turn now to explore what people think should be done to reduce it. We begin by considering whether people think government should play any role in this at all. After all, one of the key tenets of Thatcherism was the attempt to disassociate government from these kinds of responsibilities. Has this gradually become more acceptable over time? To assess this we ask respondents to respond to the following statement:

> *It is the responsibility of the government to reduce the difference in income between people with high incomes and those with low incomes*

As the next table shows, there is no sign of a turning away from government involvement. Between 1985 and 1999 there was always a majority (ranging from 51 to 65 per cent) in favour of the principle that the government should be responsible for *reducing* income differences.

Table 4.9 Whether government is responsible for reducing income inequality, 1985–2000

% agree	1985	1986	1987	1990	1992	1996	1999	2000
Government responsibility to reduce income differences between high and low incomes	51	59	63	56	64	51	65	58
Base	*1530*	*1321*	*1212*	*1197*	*1066*	*2027*	*804*	*972*

So, having established support for it being part of government's responsibility to reduce income inequality, we can now consider how they might go about this. One obvious strategy would be to redistribute income, as outlined in the following statement:

> *Government should redistribute income from the better off to those who are less well off*

When this question was first asked in 1986, just over four in ten agreed that income redistribution should take place. Support then increased, peaking at 50 per cent in 1989 and at 51 per cent in 1994. Since then, support has declined, and now fewer than four in ten support income redistribution by government.

Table 4.10 Attitudes towards redistribution, 1986–2002

% agree	1986	1987	1989	1991	1993	1994	1995	1996	1998	2000	2002
Government should redistribute from rich to poor	43	45	50	49	45	51	47	44	39	39	39
Base	*1321*	*2493*	*2604*	*2702*	*1306*	*2929*	*3135*	*3085*	*2531*	*2980*	*2900*

These findings leave us with a conundrum. We have found that (very) large proportions think the gap between rich and poor is too large, and that national wealth is not fairly distributed. We have also found support for government playing a role in reducing income differences. But how should we square this with the fact that less than half think income *should* be redistributed from higher to lower income groups? How then do people think that inequality might be alleviated?

One possibility is that people now believe there are means of reducing inequality which do not necessarily require income redistribution. This could, at least in part, be due to the kind of economic policies advanced by Blair and Brown since 1997, policies which have made a virtue of allowing the incomes of the very rich to grow without the threat of higher taxes. This, in combination with the introduction of a national minimum wage, a 10p starting rate of tax and numerous tax credits for those with low incomes, has perhaps led people to agree with Blair that the answer to combating poverty does not lie in making the very rich slightly less wealthy.

Alternatively, the issue at stake might be the very *word* redistribution, rather than the *concept*. In *The 16th Report*, Hills and Lelkes found that support for a reduced income gap between rich and poor diminished somewhat once redistribution was explicitly mentioned. So we turn now to consider public attitudes towards one of the most obvious ways of achieving redistribution in practice; taxation. To assess this, we asked:

> *Do you think people with high incomes should pay a <u>larger share</u> of their income in taxes than those with low incomes, the <u>same share</u>, or a <u>smaller share</u>?*
> *Much larger share*
> *Larger*
> *The same share*
> *Smaller*
> *Much smaller share*

The results suggest that people *do* support a highly progressive tax system – one in which the incomes of those at the top of the scale are taxed at a higher rate than those lower down, meaning that they not only pay more tax proportionately (because they have higher incomes) but also pay more of their income in taxes relative to those less well off. As the next table shows, in each year no less than three-quarters thought that those on high incomes should pay either a "much larger" or a "larger" share of their income in taxes – with around a fifth each year opting for a much larger share.

Table 4.11 Whether people on high incomes should pay a larger share of their income in taxes compared with people on low incomes, 1987, 1992 and 1999

	1987	1992	1999
	%	%	%
Much larger share	19	20	21
Larger share	55	58	55
Same share	21	18	20
Smaller share	1	1	*
Much smaller share	-	*	-
Base	*1212*	*1066*	*804*

The lack of change in responses to this question is notable, particularly as 1987 marked the height of the Thatcher–Lawson economic boom and was the very year in which the top rate of tax was reduced from 60 to the 40 per cent level still in place today. However, as the question does not require respondents to take account of rates of taxation at the time, we cannot be sure quite what they have in mind when they advocate those on higher incomes paying a "much larger share" of their income in taxes (and whether that share is greater than what is currently being paid). It is possible, for instance, that the meaning of "larger share" has changed somewhat over the period. What is undeniable, however, is widespread support for progressive taxation rates.

There is similarly widespread support for increased taxation in order to spend more on health, education, and social benefits (described in Chapter 1). This also implies strong public support for redistribution in practice, if not in word. Set against this, however, is the fact that support for more spending in the *most* redistributive areas, for instance welfare benefits, is considerably weaker than support for greater spending on health and education, spending which would benefit the better off as well as the poor (Taylor-Gooby and Hastie, 2002). Moreover, when advocating extra spending, people rarely imagine that they themselves will fall into the high income groups which might be required to pay a much larger share of their salary. However, as explored in *The 13th Report*, although support for large increases in public spending falls once the personal tax implications are spelt out, there still remains widespread support for additional public spending (Brook *et al.* 1996).

Conclusions

The evidence in this chapter suggests that income inequality is no more acceptable now than it was in the early 1980s. There was widespread concern then about the gap between high and low incomes – and, if anything, concern has grown since. True, it has not grown at quite the same rate as actual income inequality, but this largely reflects the fact that concern was already very high to begin with (meaning that it had only limited room to grow). And while there does now seem to be widespread aversion to the term 'redistribution', there is little evidence here to suggest that the *principle* is any less popular.

When given the chance to suggest appropriate wages for people working in particular occupations, people's solution to the 'wages gap' tends to be a dramatic lowering of salaries for higher income earners (rather than a very large increase in salaries for lower income earners). As these questions were last asked in 1999, views on these issues are now likely to be more damning still, given recent publicity surrounding multi-million pound boardroom pay deals and the unprecedented overturning in May 2003 of GlaxoSmithKline's Chief Executive's salary package following a shareholder revolt. Consequently, although the notion of a national *maximum* wage might sound far-fetched, UK companies might like to reflect on the attractiveness to their customers (and even their shareholders) of some form of wage restraint along these lines (Simms, 2003).

We found little to support claims (including those made by Polly Toynbee described earlier in this chapter) that Thatcherism has encouraged people to be less questioning, and more tolerant, of large gaps between rich and poor in society. The generation who came of age during the 1980s, at the height of Thatcher's time in office, are no less concerned about inequality than some of the previous generations (and are sometimes more so). The fact that Thatcherism cannot account for attitudes to inequality is not surprising; for a political era to cause such a fundamental shift in attitudes and values would require its messages (and, perhaps more importantly, its policies) to have affected everyone in a similar way. So, any attempt to draw inferences about the impact of Thatcherism on people's attitudes *en masse* will tend to fail because it takes account only of the narrow perspective of the opportunity and wealth it created for some people (and not the implications it had for less advantaged groups). However, had Toynbee's theory been that fewer *politicians*, rather than fewer people, now question why incomes are distributed as they are she might have been a little closer to the truth. As many past volumes in the *British Social Attitudes* series have told us, the notion that politicians' ideas and policies always equate with public concerns can often be ill-founded.

Notes

1. These figures relate to median equivalent incomes (before housing costs).
2. The interview was broadcast on 5 June 2001, two days before the general election. A transcript of this interview can be found at: http://news.bbc.co.uk/1/hi/events/newsnight/1372220.stm
   An accompanying note to the transcript contains a warning that the transcript was typed at speed and therefor might contain mistakes for which *Newsnight* accepts no responsibility.
3. In 1999 respondents were asked about 9 different occupations as well as their own, in 1992 and 1987 they were asked about 11 (but not their own). The analysis in this chapter is restricted to the five occupations which were asked about in all three years.
4. In order to standardise the analysis, we have treated 18 as the age of 'coming of age' for all cohorts.

References

Atkinson, A. (1999), *Is Rising Inequality Inevitable? A Critique of the Transatlantic Consensus*, WIDER Annual Lectures 3, Helsinki: UNU World Institute for Development Economics Research.

Bromley, C. and Curtice, J. (2002), 'Where have all the voters gone?', in Park, A., Curtice, J., Thomson, K., Jarvis, L. and Bromley, C. (eds.), *British Social Attitudes: the 19th Report*, London: Sage.

Brook, L., Hall, J. and Preston, I. (1996), 'Public spending and taxation', in Jowell, R., Curtice, J., Park, A., Brook, L. and Thomson, K. (eds.), *British Social Attitudes: the 13th Report*, Aldershot: Dartmouth.

Giddens, A. (1998), *The Third Way*, Cambridge: Polity Press.

Goodman, A., Johnson, P. and Webb, S. (1997), *Inequality in the UK*, Oxford: Oxford University Press.

Goodman, A. and Shephard, A. (2002), *Inequality and Living Standards in Great Britain: Some Facts*, London: Institute for Fiscal Studies.

Heath, A.F., Jowell, R.M. and Curtice, J.K. (2001), *The Rise of New Labour – Party Polices and Voter Choices*, Oxford: Oxford University Press.

Heath, A. and Park, A. (1997), 'Thatcher's children?', in Jowel, R., Curtice, J., Park, A, Brook, L., Thomson, K. and Bryson, C. (es.), *British Social Attitudes: the 14th Report – the end of Conservative values?*, Aldershot, Ashgate.

Hills, J. (1998), *Income and Wealth – the latest evidence*, Joseph Rowntree Foundation.

Hills, J. and Lelkes, O. (1999), 'Social security, selective universalism and patchwork redistribution', in Jowell, R., Curtice, J., Park, A. and Thomson, K. (eds.), *British Social Attitudes: the 16th Report – who shares New Labour values?*, Aldershot: Ashgate.

Kavanagh, D. (1990), *Thatcherism and British Politics – the End of Consensus?*, Oxford: Oxford University Press.

Sen, A. (2000), 'Social Justice and the Distribution of Income', in Atkinson, A. and Bourguignon, F. (eds.), *Handbook of Income Distribution Volume 1*, Elsevier.

Simms, A. (2003), 'Now for a maximum wage', *Guardian, 6 August*.

Taylor-Gooby, P. and Hastie, C. (2002), 'Support for state spending: has New Labour got it right?', in Park, A., Curtice, J., Thomson, K., Jarvis, L. and Bromley, C. (eds.), *British Social Attitudes: the 19th Report*, London: Sage.

Toynbee, P. (2003), *Hard Work – Life in Low-Pay Britain*, London: Bloomsbury.

Wilkinson, R.G. (1999), 'Putting the pieces together: prosperity, redistribution, health, and welfare', in Marmot, M. and Wilkinson, R.G. (eds.), *Social Determinants of Health*, Oxford: Oxford University Press.

Acknowledgements

Many of the questions discussed in this chapter formed part of modules designed for the *International Social Survey Programme (ISSP)*. The *National Centre for Social Research* would like to thank the Economic and Social Research Council (ESRC) for funding its participation in the *ISSP*, through its funding of the *Centre for Research into Elections and Social Trends (CREST)*. The author would like to thank the Institute for Fiscal Studies, and in particular Andrew Shephard, for supplying the data on income inequality; responsibility for its interpretation lies solely with the author.

5 Is there a crisis of political participation?

John Curtice and Ben Seyd [*]

There appears to be a crisis of political participation in Britain. Turnout at the last UK general election was, at 58 per cent, lower than at any other general election since 1918. Moreover, voters have been reluctant to go to the polls in every other kind of election held over the last six years. Unsurprisingly, then, politicians of all political persuasions have been asking themselves how they can 're-engage' the public with the political process.

This decline in electoral participation might seem particularly surprising given one of the key social changes to have occurred in Britain over the last two decades – the expansion of educational attainment. Education is supposedly a 'democratic good', meant to encourage adherence to democratic values, a sense of political competence and thus a greater propensity to vote (Almond and Verba, 1963; Wolfinger and Rosenstone, 1980). As Almond and Verba's study of *The Civic Culture* put it:

> The educated classes possess the keys to political participation and involvement while those with less education are less well equipped.

As Table 5.1 shows, in the mid-1980s nearly half the adult British population had no educational qualifications. Now, less than a quarter are in this position. Over the same period, the proportion with a degree has more than doubled (to 16 per cent), while those with at least an A level or its equivalent now comprise well over two-fifths of the adult population (rather than just over a quarter as they did two decades ago). So Britain has experienced a substantial increase in overall levels of educational attainment, something we might expect to produce an increase in electoral participation. That the very opposite seems to have happened is nothing less than a 'puzzle of participation' (Brody, 1978).

[*] John Curtice is Research Consultant at the *National Centre for Social Research*, Scotland, Deputy Director of the Centre for Research into Elections and Social Trends, and Professor of Politics and Director of the Social Statistics Laboratory at Strathclyde University. Ben Seyd is a Senior Research Fellow at the Constitution Unit, School of Public Policy, University College London.

Table 5.1 Highest educational qualification reached, 1986–2002

	1986	1989	1991	1994	1998	2000	2002	Change '86-'02
	%	%	%	%	%	%	%	
Degree	7	7	9	10	9	14	16	+9
A-level / other HE	21	24	25	26	30	26	29	+8
None	45	42	38	35	30	29	23	-22
Base	3100	3029	2918	3469	3146	3426	3425	

Of course, voting is not the only form of political participation open to individuals in a liberal democracy. They can also, for example, sign a petition, contact the media or go on a demonstration. Recent events, such as the fuel protests in September 2000, marches against the banning of fox hunting, and anti-war demonstrations prior to the onset of the Iraqi war in March 2003, have suggested that perhaps there *is* no puzzle of participation after all. Perhaps a better-educated and more politically competent society is more willing and able to participate in a range of political activities, activities that are seen as a more effective way of expressing one's view than simply putting a cross on a ballot paper (Inglehart, 1997).

However, if this is the case, then it raises different concerns about recent trends in participation in Britain. There is plenty of evidence that those who take part in non-electoral forms of political participation tend to be drawn disproportionately from the ranks of the better educated (Marsh, 1977; Marsh and Kaase, 1979; Heath and Topf, 1987; Parry *et al.*, 1992; Norris, 2002).[1] Consequently, if such non-electoral participation is becoming relatively more important, we might find growing social divisions in Britain between those who do and do not participate. Moreover, some argue that rising educational standards will mean that those without any qualifications will find it increasingly difficult to compete in the political market place (Dalton, 2002). If this is true, we should expect to find our divide widening still further. So perhaps we need to be concerned about a growing participation divide in Britain between, on the one hand, a group of well-educated 'super-activists' who are able and willing to engage in range of political activities, and, on the other, a substantial if diminishing group of the less well educated who are effectively excluded from the avenues of political participation.

These are the questions examined in this chapter. We begin by considering how it might have been possible for electoral turnout to have fallen despite rising levels of educational attainment. We then examine whether levels of non-electoral participation have indeed increased over the last twenty years. And, finally, we consider whether there is any evidence that education has come to matter more in determining who participates. In so doing, we are not aiming to provide a full account of the recent decline in electoral turnout (see Bromley and Curtice, 2002), or to explain why people protest (Marsh, 1977; Barnes and Kaase, 1979; Parry *et al.*, 1992). Rather, we seek to examine what impact, if any, one of the major changes of the last twenty years has had on patterns of political participation.

Personal efficacy

One key assumption underpins the proposition that rising educational levels should result in higher levels of participation. This is that higher levels of educational attainment bring with them a stronger sense of 'subjective' political competence. By this, we mean the sense that one has the ability and confidence to take political actions that could be effective in changing a government decision. So we begin by considering whether education does bring with it a sense of personal political efficacy. We then examine what impact rising educational levels have had on overall levels of efficacy.

As the next table shows, those with no educational attainment certainly are less likely than the better educated to feel personally efficacious. Those with no qualifications are currently twice as likely as those with a degree to agree strongly with the view "people like me have no say in what the government does", and are no less than eight times more likely to agree strongly that "sometimes government and politics seem so complicated that a person like me cannot really understand what is going on". Moreover, while these differences have fluctuated somewhat from year to year, there is no evidence that the gap between the most and least well educated has consistently become any narrower in more recent years. So the reasoning behind Almond and Verba's claim that the educated possess the 'keys to political participation' appears to remain as valid as it has ever been.[2]

However, the next table also tells us something else equally important. This is that the rise in educational attainment over the last twenty years has not been accompanied by any systematic long-term increase in personal efficacy. The proportion who strongly agree that politics and government seem complicated is just as high now as it was in the 1980s, while the proportion who believe they have no say in what the government does is if anything higher now.

So, while at any one point in time higher levels of educational attainment are associated with a stronger sense of political efficacy, it is not the case that the increase in educational attainment has resulted in more people feeling efficacious. The impact of the increase in educational attainment has in fact been wholly negated by changes in the level of personal efficacy within our educational groups, changes that are perhaps a response to the drop that has occurred in the extent to which people believe the political system is able and willing to respond to demands for change that may be made of it (Curtice and Jowell, 1997: 153; Bromley *et al.*, 2001; Bromley and Curtice, 2002).[3] And while none of this on its own points to any kind of crisis of participation, we can at least begin to see why a rise in educational attainment may not be sufficient to bring about a more participatory culture.

Table 5.2 Trends in personal efficacy and education level, 1986–2002

% strongly agree	1986	1987	1991	1994	1996	1998	2000	2002
People like me have no say in what government does								
All*	23	14	16	28	24	17	25	26
Education level								
Degree**	14	3	7	18	9	10	17	16
No qualifications***	26	20	21	30	32	24	28	32
% strongly agree								
Politics and government so complicated that a person like me cannot really understand								
All	17	13	16	22	22	15	18	17
Education level								
Degree	4	2	4	3	6	4	3	4
No qualifications	23	18	26	31	35	32	25	32
*Base	1548	3414	1445	1137	1180	2071	2293	2287
**Base	113	284	112	110	124	179	300	342
***Base	689	1342	576	458	406	654	740	609

Source: 1987: *British Election Study*

Electoral participation

But does how efficacious someone feels make any difference to whether or not they vote in the first place? Table 5.3 suggests that those who feel personally efficacious are somewhat more likely to vote (Parry *et al.*, 1992; Pattie and Johnston, 1998). Thus, among those who *disagree* with the statement "people like me have no say in what the government does" (and who therefore can be seen as having high levels of political efficacy), nearly three-quarters reported voting in the 2001 election, compared with fewer than six in ten among those who agreed strongly with the statement. But the strength of this link seems to vary from election to election, and indeed is never particularly strong. This may help explain why sometimes researchers have doubted whether any link exists at all (Heath and Taylor, 1999; Pattie and Johnston, 2001). Our findings suggest that, although a link exists, it is only amongst the minority with the lowest possible levels of personal efficacy that turnout is noticeably different from the norm. We should remember too that in 1997, and again in 2001, turnout fell across the board, quite irrespective of how efficacious someone felt. So the level of turnout can certainly change irrespective of trends in levels of personal efficacy.

Table 5.3 Voting and personal efficacy, 1987–2001

People like me have no say in what the government does	% voted					
	1987	Base	1997	Base	2001	Base
Agree strongly	85	491	75	374	57	242
Agree	86	1149	80	1033	69	480
Neither agree nor disagree	88	537	78	488	66	118
Disagree/disagree strongly	88	1191	84	518	72	254

Sources: 1987 and 1997: *British Election Study*

Given this, it is not surprising to find that in Britain, as in much of the rest of Europe (but not in the United States), there is little relationship between educational attainment and turnout (Heath and Topf, 1986; Parry *et al.*, 1992; Pattie and Johnston, 1998, 2001; Topf, 1999a). As the next table shows, among those with no educational qualifications the level of reported turnout in the 2001 election was just five points lower than it was among those with a degree. A similar pattern has applied to each election over the last two decades. In short, there is no reason to expect that an increase in educational attainment should have much impact on the level of turnout one way or another.

Table 5.4 Turnout and education level, 1987–2001

	% voted			
Education level	1987	1992	1997	2001
Degree	87	93	82	77
Base	305	255	301	497
No qualifications	85	85	79	72
Base	1560	1263	908	899

Source: 1987 and 1997: British Election Study

Still, we might ask why this should be the case, given the lower level of personal efficacy that exists amongst those with no educational qualifications? One of the key explanations that has been offered is that trade unions in Britain (as in much of the rest of Europe) have been able to mobilise the less well educated and persuade them of the merits of going to the polling station. This, it is argued, distinguishes Britain from the United States, which has both a weaker trade union movement and a more pronounced gap in turnout between more and less well-educated groups (Dalton, 2002: 54).[4] However, if this were the case, we might have anticipated an educational divide in levels of turnout to have opened up over the last twenty years as trade unions have declined.

In fact, there is little to substantiate this theory. As the next table shows, over the last twenty years, trade union membership has consistently been *higher* among the better educated than among the less well educated. And, at the same time, the decline in membership has occurred at more or less the same rate among all educational groups. So there is no reason here to anticipate that the decline in trade in union membership should have opened up an educational divide in electoral participation.

Table 5.5 Trade union membership by education level, 1986–2002

	% belong to a trade union				
	1986	**1991**	**1994**	**1998**	**2002**
All	24	21	22	19	18
Base	*3100*	*2918*	*3469*	*3146*	*3435*
Highest education level					
Degree/other HE	32	28	32	27	24
Base	*576*	*666*	*759*	*870*	*1015*
A level	26	22	22	22	18
Base	*266*	*280*	*419*	*311*	*440*
O level/CSE/GCSE	23	20	20	16	14
Base	*829*	*783*	*925*	*888*	*979*
None	21	17	18	13	12
Base	*1392*	*1134*	*1300*	*1009*	*895*

So perhaps we should stop looking for explanations as to why education makes no difference to turnout and instead accept that, in Britain at least, voting is not after all that demanding an act, and is certainly one that the less well educated can undertake perfectly well. However, if we accept this line of argument, it not only means that rising levels of educational attainment are no guarantee of *higher* turnout, but that they are also little defence either against other forces that might discourage electoral participation (Heath and Taylor, 1999; Bromley and Curtice, 2002; Franklin, 2002). And, if this is so, one may question how far innovations such as the inclusion of classes in civic education on the English national curriculum can be expected to increase turnout either.

Non-electoral participation

The picture is, however, very different once we move beyond the ballot box and look at trends in non-electoral participation. The next table shows, using our 2002 survey, the proportion of those with a degree and those with no qualifications who report ever having done each of eleven possible actions that might be undertaken by someone in response to a government action they believe is unjust and harmful (or in the case of stopping buying goods as a way of protesting against something a country or company has done). Graduates are far more likely than those without qualifications to have undertaken each of the activities. In fact, among those with no qualifications, few report ever having done anything other than sign a petition or boycott something in the shops.

5.6 Non-electoral participation by educational attainment

% saying they had	Education level	
	Degree	No qualifications
Stopped buying goods as a protest	70	34
Signed a petition	60	26
Given money to a campaigning organisation	34	7
Gone on a protest or demonstration	31	6
Contacted MP	29	9
Got involved in a campaigning organisation	29	8
Raised the issue in an organisation they already belong to	17	2
Contacted government department	12	2
Contacted the media	11	4
Spoken to an influential person	11	3
Formed a group of like-minded people	4	1
Base	342	609

So, once we move beyond the ballot box, educational attainment does make a considerable difference to the likelihood that someone will ever be involved in political activity. But why is this so? Is it, as Almond and Verba would suggest, simply because these groups are more efficacious? After all, whatever may be true about voting, virtually all other forms of political action are sufficiently demanding to require a degree of confidence in one's ability. Or is the process more complex than this? Inglehart's theory of cognitive mobilisation suggests that rising educational standards tend not only to increase people's sense of their own political abilities, but also to lower their regard for the political system itself, and in particular for 'hierarchical political institutions' (Inglehart, 1997). As a result, they have a greater *motivation* to engage in protest activities, as well as the confidence to do so. Similarly, Marsh has argued that the most politically active people are those who are both personally efficacious and disinclined to trust governments to do what is right. These 'efficacious cynics', he claims, believe in their own ability to effect change, but also "feel that politics is far too important to be left solely to the politicians, most of whom they actually mistrust" (Marsh, 1977: 123).

In practice, the simpler explanation proves to be the more convincing (see also (Parry *et al.*, 1992; Curtice and Jowell, 1997). The next table uses the same information as Table 5.6 but shows the average number of actions reported (excluding boycotting products as this is not an action directed at a domestic government) broken down by respondents' political efficacy and levels of trust in government. Efficacy clearly matters. Someone who strongly *disagrees* with the view that politics is too complicated to understand (and who is thus very efficacious) has, on average, undertaken nearly three activities, a sharp contrast to the figure of 0.8 actions undertaken by someone with the lowest level of efficacy. But these figures are not higher if people have low levels of trust in government – indeed for the most part they are slightly lower. In so far as it matters at all, it seems that, far from giving people the motivation to become involved politically, lack of trust promotes the feeling that getting involved is unlikely to be worth the effort.

Table 5.7 Non-electoral participation by personal efficacy and trust in government

Mean no. of actions taken	Trust governments to place the needs of the nation above party interest			
Politics and government so complicated that a person like me cannot understand	Just about always/most of the time	*Base*	Some of the time/ almost never	*Base*
Strongly agree	0.8	*73*	0.8	*339*
Agree	1.3	*230*	1.0	*768*
Neither agree nor disagree	1.3	*59*	1.2	*158*
Disagree	1.9	*163*	1.9	*322*
Strongly disagree	3.0	*38*	2.8	*78*

But what has happened to levels of non-electoral participation over the last twenty years? Has it increased in line with the rise in educational attainment? Or has it been held back by the failure of personal efficacy to increase during that period? Is non-electoral participation perhaps becoming a substitute for the ballot box? Or is the decline in electoral turnout part of a wider decline in political participation and engagement?

We have two sets of measures we can use to examine these questions. For most of the activities listed in Table 5.6 we have data going back twenty years. This shows both the extent to which people *would* take a particular action if "a law was being considered by parliament which you thought was really unjust and harmful", and the extent to which people had ever done so. So the first of these measures is an indication of apparent inclination or potential to engage in non-electoral protest activity; the second, an indication of the degree to which that potential has been realised in practice.

We begin with our measure of inclination or potential. The next table shows the proportion who said they would do each thing were an unjust or harmful law being considered by parliament. We also show a summary of the total number of things people said they would do.

Table 5.8 Trends in potential non-electoral participation, 1983–2002

% saying they would	1983	1986	1989	1991	1994	1998	2000	2002	Change '83–'02
Sign a petition	55	65	71	78	68	67	68	63	+8
Contact MP	46	52	55	49	58	59	49	51	+5
Contact media	14	15	14	14	22	21	22	27	+13
Go on protest or demonstration	8	11	14	14	17	21	16	18	+10
Speak to an influential person	10	15	15	17	15	18	17	19	+9
Form a group of like-minded people	6	8	19	7	10	9	7	8	+2
Raise the issue in an organisation they already belong to	9	10	11	9	7	9	10	11	+2
No. of actions									
None	12	10	8	6	7	7	7	7	- 5
One or two	72	65	61	64	58	54	59	58	- 14
Three or more	14	25	30	29	33	37	32	33	+ 19
Base	*1761*	*1548*	*1516*	*1445*	*1137*	*2030*	*2293*	*2287*	

As the last column of table 5.8 shows, in every case, more people say they would take a particular action now than said they would twenty years ago. Particularly noteworthy is a near doubling in the proportion who say they would contact the media (a reflection perhaps of the recent growth in opportunities for 'ordinary people' to get their views across to the media). True, the growth in reported willingness to take action has not followed a simple linear trend. Much of the increase happened in the 1980s (a period in which rising levels of educational attainment were *not* being counteracted by falling levels of personal efficacy). But at least some of the dividend that might have been expected from the rise in educational attainment appears to have been reaped.

Has this growth in protest potential been realised in action? Table 5.9 suggests it has. In six of the seven actions listed in the table, more people now report having done them than was the case in 1986. However, the increases are mostly small and, as we saw earlier, many of them largely occurred in the 1980s.

Table 5.9 Trends in actual non-electoral participation, 1986–2002

% saying they had	1986	1989	1991	1994	2000	2002	Change 1986-2002
Signed a petition	34	41	53	39	42	43	+9
Contacted MP	11	15	17	14	16	17	+6
Contacted media	3	4	4	5	6	7	+4
Gone on a protest or demonstration	6	8	9	9	10	12	+6
Spoken to an influential person	3	3	5	3	4	6	+3
Formed a group of like-minded people	2	3	2	3	2	2	0
Raised the issue in an organisation they already belong to	5	4	5	4	5	6	+1
No. of actions							
None	56	48	37	53	47	46	-10
One or two	38	43	53	38	43	42	+4
Three or more	5	7	8	8	9	11	+6
Base	1548	1516	1445	1137	2293	2287	

Moreover, apart from the relatively undemanding activity of signing a petition, most people have not engaged in these forms of protest activities most of the time.[5] Still, it is quite clear that the decline in turnout at recent British elections is not part of any wider refusal by the public to become involved in the political process. Rather, it seems that other forms of political participation are now somewhat more common than they once were.

This coincidence of a decline in electoral participation and an increase in non-electoral participation obviously raises questions as to whether the two are connected. Is the latter, perhaps, replacing the former? Are some turning away from the ballot box and demonstrating on the street instead? In truth, there is no evidence to support this. Rather, those who do take part in non-electoral political activities are actually *more* rather than less likely to vote in elections. In our 2002 survey, as many as 80 per cent of those who had undertaken three or more protest actions said they had voted in the previous general election, compared with just 65 per cent of those who had not engaged in any actions. The same finding applies among younger people, the group for whom the claim that non-electoral activity is a substitute for electoral activity is most common. So, among those aged under 35 who had *never* undertaken any form of non-electoral activity, reported turnout was 46 per cent; among those who had undertaken three or more, turnout was reported at 58 per cent. Consequently, non-electoral participation should be seen as an *add-on* to voting, and not as a substitute (Marsh, 1977; Bromley *et al.*, 2001).

What, however, we can also note from Tables 5.8 and 5.9 could be happening is that a new breed of 'super-activists' is emerging who engage in a much wider range of non-electoral activities than was commonly the case in the past. Certainly, the proportion of people who say they have undertaken three or more actions has more than doubled since 1986. Is this perhaps a sign that the education divide in non-electoral participation is widening, and that Britain now has an educated elite that is becoming even more active while perhaps those with no qualifications are being left behind?

It seems not. In Table 5.10, we show the number of actions reported by those with degrees and those with no qualifications on a number of occasions over the last two decades. We also show the 'education gap', which is simply the difference between the proportion of those with a degree reporting having undertaken three or more activities and the proportion of those with no qualifications doing so. This education gap proves to be largely the same in most years and certainly shows no evidence of a trend over time. So while non-electoral participation is far higher amongst the better educated, this is no more the case now than it was twenty years ago.

Table 5.10 Trends in number of actual non-electoral activities undertaken by education level, 1986–2002

No. of protest activities undertaken by...	1986	1989	1991	1994	2000	2002
... people with a degree						
None	28	28	22	23	26	27
One or two	47	34	56	54	49	48
Three or more	22	35	22	23	25	26
Base	*113*	*88*	*141*	*110*	*300*	*342*
... people with no qualifications						
None	62	58	49	69	58	63
One or two	34	37	46	27	38	34
Three or more	2	3	3	3	4	3
Base	*689*	*622*	*593*	*458*	*740*	*609*
Education gap	+20	+32	+19	+20	+21	+23

At the same time Table 5.10 also shows that the levels of participation within the two groups has not varied a great deal either. This suggests that the rise in non-electoral participation over the last two decades has been no less – but also no more – than we might have expected given the increase in educational attainment and the strength of the relationship between educational attainment and non-electoral participation. In fact, participation levels are somewhat higher now than they were in 1986 in some of the intermediate educational groups not shown in Table 5.10. So in truth, modest though it has been, the rise in non-electoral participation has been somewhat greater than accounted for by the rise in educational attainment alone. Evidently it is a mistake to believe that the rise in educational attainment has been sufficient to transform the pattern of non-electoral participation.

Conclusions

We began this chapter with a crisis and a puzzle. Britain appeared to be suffering a crisis of political participation and this appeared to be a puzzle given the expansion that has occurred in educational attainment over the last twenty years. Yet it seems that we have neither a crisis nor a puzzle. True, electoral participation may have fallen, but it has been accompanied by an increase in non-electoral participation, an increase that cannot itself be regarded as the cause of the decline in turnout. So the participation crisis in Britain is confined to the ballot box, and it is not part of a wider decline in the willingness of citizens to engage with the political system.

These divergent trends are perfectly compatible with the increase in levels of educational attainment that has occurred over the last twenty years. Educational attainment has never had, and continues not to have, much influence on electoral participation and so its expansion cannot be expected to insulate levels of turnout against whatever other forces that may be helping to depress them. On the other hand, education has always been associated with non-electoral participation, levels of which have duly risen by more or less the (modest) amount that we would expect given the extent of the rise in educational attainment.

What messages do our findings tell us about how levels of political participation in Britain might change over the next twenty years, particularly as the proportion of adults with educational qualifications continues to rise? One possible danger, that the less well educated will become increasingly politically marginalised, is not perhaps as great as we might have feared. Their relative chances of being involved in politics outside the ballot box do not seem to show any signs of becoming any lower than they are already. But, even so, voting remains the only form of political activity where levels of participation between groups from different educational backgrounds approach equity. So, if voting continues its recent decline, and non-electoral participation its increase, then there is an increased danger that the voices of the less well educated will become quieter still.

Certainly, a further rise in non-electoral participation seems quite likely, although in part this depends on there not being a decline in levels of personal efficacy. And a better-educated public would seem more likely to engage with the increasing attempts being made by government to consult with the public in the formulation of public policy. But, even so, and even amongst graduates, most forms of political activity are the preserve of a small minority, and are likely to remain so in the near future. Britain may become more like a participatory democracy in future, but most people, for most of the time, will still be relying on their elected representatives to make the right decision for them.

Notes

1. However, in contrast, Topf has argued that the relationship between education and protest may be weakening. Across west European countries, he reports a steady "de-skilling of political activism", as more and more people with low educational levels become involved in some form of protest activity (Topf, 1999b).
2. In addition to the trends shown in the table it should also be noted that there has been a decline in personal efficacy amongst all those whose level of educational attainment lies in-between that of the two groups shown in the table.
3. There is no evidence in our data to support the claim by Parry *et al.* (1992) that it is those with *middle level qualifications* that have the highest level of efficacy. For example, the proportion of those whose highest educational qualification is an 'A' level (or its equivalent) who strongly agree that "people like me have no say in what government does" is, at 23 per cent, in-between the equivalent figure for those with a degree and those with no qualifications at all.
4. The decline in mobilising agencies such as trade unions is also often used to explain why, in the United States in particular, voter turnout has declined in spite of increases in educational attainment (Inglehart, 1990).
5. However, no less than 50 per cent say they have stopped buying goods in protest against the actions of a particular company or country.

References

Almond, G.A. and Verba, S. (1963), *The Civic Culture: Political Attitudes and Democracy in Five Nations*, Princeton, NJ: Princeton University Press.

Barnes, S.H. and Kaase, M. (1979), *Political Action: Mass Participation in Five Western Democracies*, Beverly Hills, Calif. Sage.

Brody, R.A. (1978), 'The Puzzle of Political Participation in America', in King, A., (eds.), *The New American Political System*, Washington, DC: American Enterprise Institute.

Bromley, C., Curtice, J. and Seyd, B. (2001), 'Political engagement, trust and constitutional reform', in Park, A., Curtice, J., Thomson, K., Jarvis, L. and Bromley, C. (eds.), *British Social Attitudes – the 18th Report: Public Policy, Social Ties*, London: Sage.

Bromley, C. and Curtice, J. (2002), 'Where have all the voters gone?', in Park, A., Curtice, J., Thomson, K., Jarvis, L. and Bromley, C. (eds.), *British Social Attitudes – the 19th Report*, London: Sage.

Curtice, J. and Jowell, R. (1997), 'The Sceptical Electorate', in Jowell, R., Curtice, J., Park, A., Brook, L., Thomson, K. and Bryson, C. (eds.), *British Social Attitudes: the 14th Report: the end of Conservative values?* Aldershot: Ashgate.

Dalton, R.J. (2002), *Citizen Politics: Public Opinion and Political Parties in Advanced Industrial Democracies*, New York: Chatham House.

Franklin, M. (2002), 'The Dynamics of Electoral Participation', in LeDuc, L., Niemi, R. and Norris, P. (eds.), *Comparing Democracies 2: New Challenges in the Study of Elections and Voting*, London: Sage.

Heath, A.F. and Topf, R. (1986), 'Educational Expansion and Political Change in Britain, 1964–1983', *European Journal of Political Research*, **14**: 543–67

Heath, A.F. and Topf, R. (1987), 'Political Culture', in Jowell, R., Witherspoon, S. and Brook, L. (eds.), *British Social Attitudes: the 1987 Report*, Aldershot: Gower.

Heath, A.F. and Taylor, B. (1999), 'New Sources of Abstention?', in Evans, G. and Norris, P. (eds), *Critical Elections: British Parties and Voters in Long-Term Perspective*, London: Sage.

Inglehart, R. (1990), *Culture Shift in Advanced Industrial Democracies*, Princeton, NJ: Princeton University Press.

Inglehart, R. (1997), *Modernization and Postmodernization: Cultural, Economic and Political Change in 43 Societies*, Princeton, NJ: Princeton University Press.

Marsh, A. (1977), *Protest and Political Consciousness*, Beverly Hills, Calif.: Sage.

Marsh, A. and Kaase, M. (1979), 'Background of Political Action', in Barnes, S.H. and Kaase, M. *Political Action: Mass Participation in Five Western Democracies*, Beverly Hills, Calif.: Sage.

Norris, P. (2002), *Democratic Phoenix: Reinventing Political Activism*, New York: Cambridge University Press.

Parry, G., Moyser, G. and Day, N. (1992), *Political Participation and Democracy in Britain*, Cambridge: Cambridge University Press.

Pattie, C. and Johnston, R. (1998), 'Voter Turnout at the British General Election of 1992: Rational Choice, Social Standing or Political Efficacy?', *European Journal of Political Research*, **33**:, 263–283.

Pattie, C. and Johnston, R. (2001), 'Losing the Voters' Trust: Evaluations of the Political System and Voting at the 1997 British General Election' *British Journal of Politics and International Relations*, (**3:2**): 191–222.

Topf, R. (1999a), 'Electoral Participation', in Klingemann, H.D. and Fuchs, F. (eds.), *Citizens and the State*, Oxford: Oxford University Press.

Topf, R. (1999b), 'Beyond Electoral Participation', in Klingemann, H.D. and Fuchs, F. (eds.), *Citizens and the State*, Oxford: Oxford University Press.

Wolfinger, R.E and Rosenstone, S.J. (1980), *Who Votes?*, New Haven: Yale University Press.

Acknowledgements

The *National Centre for Social Research* would like to thank the Economic and Social Research Council (ESRC) for funding the questions reported in this chapter relating to the 2000 and 2002 surveys. These were asked as part of a research project on 'Legitimacy, Participation and Constitutional Change' funded as part of the ESRC's Democracy and Participation Programme (grant no. L215252032). The authors are grateful to Sarinder Hunjan of the Social Statistics Laboratory, University of Strathclyde, for assistance with data analysis.

6 Pass or fail? Perceptions of education

Ted Wragg and Lindsey Jarvis [*]

The transition from a Conservative to a Labour administration in 1997 produced surprisingly little change on a number of major educational issues, in England at least (as education is a devolved policy, important differences of approach exist between England, Scotland and Wales). Labour pledged there would be no more selection, but the existing grammar and secondary modern schools survived, and specialist schools were introduced which were allowed to select a small proportion of their pupils according to their aptitude in the school's chosen specialism. The national curriculum and national tests for 7, 11 and 14 year olds, introduced by the Conservatives in the 1988 Education Reform Act, were left intact, as were some features that accompanied them, such as school performance tables. The shift from local to central control continued, as the incoming Labour government introduced daily literacy and numeracy hours in primary schools, and the trend for more and more pupils to go to university accelerated, until the participation rate had almost trebled, from the 14 per cent it had been in 1983.

The 1960s had been a decade of major reports, with enquiries into every aspect of education, from primary schooling right up to university level. The 1980s and 1990s, by contrast, saw the enactment of a great deal of legislation. Substantial Acts of Parliament decreed what should be taught, how it should be examined, what form of organisation schools should adopt, parents' rights and responsibilities, the role and powers of school governors, the appraisal of teachers and a host of other matters. This was a very significant change in climate, as legislation had previously administered a light touch on the system, with most major decisions being left to schools and local education authorities.

The last twenty years have also witnessed a significant growth in the importance of formal qualifications. High levels of unemployment in the 1980s focused attention on the importance of the eleven compulsory years of

[*] Ted Wragg is Professor of Education at Exeter University. Lindsey Jarvis is a Research Director at the *National Centre for Social Research* and Co-Director of the *British Social Attitudes* survey series.

schooling. Jobs which at the beginning of the period required no written qualifications were, by the end of it, requiring newcomers to have taken the General Certificate of Secondary Education (GCSE). Employers once satisfied with the GCSE eventually wanted the Advanced level qualification taken by eighteen year olds. Meanwhile, traditional A level jobs began to recruit graduates, as a third of young people were finishing their education at degree level. It was a qualifications spiral that showed no signs of abating. Compared with 1983, the entry fee for young people into adult society in 2003 had simply gone up.

The findings of the *British Social Attitudes* series over the last twenty years offer several different insights into these substantial changes, and these form the basis of this chapter. In 1997, Prime Minister Tony Blair declared that "education, education, education" would be his three top priorities; we begin by considering whether this view is one shared with the public. We then turn to higher education, an area which has undergone massive changes since 1983, in terms of both its size and its range. In the 1980s, there was considerable public support for increased access to higher education. So we assess whether this enthusiasm has abated as the sector has expanded. We also consider how people would rather students' participation in higher education was funded.

Next we consider primary and secondary education. Do people feel that primary and secondary schools are meeting the many demands that society puts on them? What is thought to be the principal purpose in education: academic study or preparation for a job? And are the public enthusiastic about the ability of extensive testing programmes to improve educational standards? Finally, in recognition of a possible approaching crisis in the recruitment and retention of teachers, we consider how attractive teaching is seen to be as a career and how it is perceived to compare with other jobs in terms of overall interest, career prospects and pay.

Prioritising education?

We start by considering the importance attached to education as a beneficiary of extra government spending. As discussed in the chapters in this Report by Sefton, and by Appleby and Alvarez Rosete, education has consistently come second behind health care when respondents are asked to choose their top priorities for extra government spending from the ten areas shown in the next table. Although there has been some fluctuation, the level of support for more money for education has risen in the last twenty years. In 1983, a half made this a priority; by 2002, almost two-thirds did so. In both years, however, it remained in second place behind health.

Table 6.1 First or second priorities for extra government spending, 1983–2002

	1983	1987	1990	1993	1997	2000	2002
	%	%	%	%	%	%	%
Health	63	79	81	70	78	81	79
Education	50	56	63	57	70	64	63
Police and prisons	8	8	7	11	10	10	14
Public transport	3	1	6	4	6	10	13
Housing	21	24	20	22	11	11	10
Roads	5	3	4	4	3	6	6
Social security	12	12	13	13	9	7	5
Help for industry	29	12	6	14	8	5	4
Defence	8	4	2	3	3	3	3
Overseas aid	1	1	1	2	1	1	2
Base	*1761*	*2847*	*2698*	*2945*	*1355*	*3426*	*3435*

Note: As the table adds together first and second priorities for extra spending, columns sum to 200 per cent.

But if this extra government money *were* provided for education, on whom would the public like it to be spent? Here, opinion was divided across the five possible beneficiaries shown in Table 6.2. In 2002, around three in ten supported extra money being spent to benefit secondary schoolchildren, while a similar proportion opted for more money being spent on those with special needs. Meanwhile, two in ten chose primary schoolchildren and one in ten nursery or pre-school children.

Table 6.2 Highest priority for extra government spending on education, 1983–2002

	'83	'85	'87	'90	'93	'94	'95	'96	'98	'99	'00	'01	'02
	%	%	%	%	%	%	%	%	%	%	%	%	%
Secondary school	29	31	37	27	29	28	32	25	24	24	28	29	29
Special needs	32	34	29	29	34	28	19	21	21	25	26	22	27
Primary school	16	13	15	15	16	11	18	21	24	21	22	23	18
Nursery/pre-school	10	10	8	16	11	21	21	17	17	14	13	10	10
Students at university	9	9	9	9	7	9	9	11	9	12	9	13	14
Base	*1761*	*1804*	*2847*	*1400*	*1484*	*1167*	*1227*	*1221*	*1035*	*1052*	*1133*	*1107*	*3435*

Looking back to the 1983 figures, we see that, despite fluctuations in the interim, support for more spending on all four types of compulsory education were at a similar level in 2002 to twenty years ago. In fact, it is only students at colleges or universities who have received a boost in support – from nine per cent to 14 per cent in 2002. Given the radical expansion of higher education in the last twenty years, it may seem a little surprising that this has been accompanied by an *increase* in support for even more money for students. However, there was a great deal of publicity after 2000 about the level of debt that students were incurring since the abolition of grants, and how the introduction of tuition fees had made the position worse. Consequently, public concern may reflect a greater awareness of many students' personal financial problems because of the more severe financial pressures they, and their parents, have faced through changes to the funding of higher education during this time.

Higher education

In terms of its size and range, higher education is an area of education that has undergone massive changes since 1983. It has been expanded to create many more university and college places, so that by 2003 more than one pupil in three was entering the sector, compared with one in seven two decades earlier. In addition, the financing of these places has altered dramatically, with the burden passing from the state to the individual. There has been a huge shift from government funding via means-tested grants, to a system of student loans plus additional tuition fees of over £1,000 per annum, with the intention to increase this amount, possibly to £3,000 or more.

The expansion of higher education

We begin by considering whether public support for higher education has run in tandem with successive governments' policies of expansion in recent years. To assess this, we asked whether "opportunities for young people in Britain to go on to higher education – to a university or college – should be increased or reduced" or whether they were at about the right level now. Although roughly half were happy with the levels of higher education opportunities throughout the period, a similar proportion wanted further expansion. In the late 1980s and early 1990s, there was pressure for even further expansion, but overall the pattern has been fairly stable.

It is notable that, even though the proportion of young people entering university has soared, about half the population has consistently stated that the number should increase further still. So, among this group at least, there appears to be clear support for the government's aim that, by 2010, 50 per cent of young people should participate in higher education (DfES, 2003). Around half take a quite different view – that opportunities to participate in higher education are either about right or could actually be reduced somewhat although, as the next table shows, the size of this group has changed surprisingly little given the expansion of the sector.

Table 6.3 Attitudes towards the expansion of higher education, 1983–2002

Higher education should be ...	1983	1985	1987	1990	1993	1994	1995	1999	2000	2002
	%	%	%	%	%	%	%	%	%	%
Increased a lot	22	25	29	32	32	32	28	25	27	24
Increased a little	22	24	24	20	17	17	19	19	17	22
About right	49	43	42	43	46	46	48	48	49	45
Reduced a little/a lot	5	5	3	2	2	2	3	4	5	5
Base	*1761*	*1804*	*2847*	*1400*	*1484*	*1167*	*1227*	*1052*	*1133*	*3435*

Whether it is a reflection on the number of places perceived to be on offer at university or college, or just parental pride, the expectations of parents of school-aged children that their offspring will go on to university is very high. Three-quarters of parents thought it was "very" or "fairly likely" that one of their children would go to university. Only four per cent thought it was "not at all likely". This question was first asked in 2002 and so it is not possible to see how expectations have changed with the expansion of higher education. However, as would be expected, those parents who expect one of their children to go to university were keener than others on the further expansion of higher education. In fact, 38 per cent of parents who thought it "very likely" their child would go into higher education supported higher education being "increased a lot" compared with 29 per cent of those parents who thought it "not very" or "not at all likely" their child would go to university.

Despite this enthusiasm, there remains a perception that students from less advantaged backgrounds are under-represented in higher education. Our results suggest that this is a concern for the majority, with 75 per cent thinking it "very" or "fairly important" to encourage "more people from working-class backgrounds go to university". It is notable that support is strongest of all among those who expect their own children to enter higher education. Among this group, a half (50 per cent) consider encouraging more working-class students into higher education to be "very important", compared with only 21 per cent of those who do not think it likely their child would attend.

The view that there should be a greater number of working-class students within higher education partly reflects a belief that there is a current bias against this group. We asked:

Suppose two young people with the same A/A2-level (or Scottish Higher) grades apply to go university. One is from a very well-off background and the other is from a less well-off background. Which one do you think would be more likely to be offered a place?

Although four in ten (44 per cent) thought the two young people would be "equally likely to be offered a place", the same proportion (43 per cent) thought the young person from the well off background would be more likely to get a place. Only three per cent believed the person from a less well off background would be favoured. Since 2000, there has been considerable publicity about Oxford and Cambridge universities in particular taking large numbers of students from private schools, even though the universities themselves have emphasised the efforts they have been making to broaden the social base of their entry. This may well have had an impact on public opinion, since a wealthy background is clearly perceived by many to be an advantage to gaining entry to university when all else is equal. It is notable that this perception is particularly widely held among those who do *not* think their own children will go to college. Perhaps alarmingly, nearly six in ten (57 per cent) of this group think it likely the young person from the well off background would be favoured (compared with 42 per cent of those who think it very likely their child will attend).

Funding of higher education

One possible barrier to those from a less well off background entering higher education is the cost of further studying. Over the last twenty years, there have been sweeping changes to the ways in which higher education is funded, primarily the replacement of student grants with the student loans system and the introduction of student-paid tuition fees.

The *British Social Attitudes* survey has tracked public opinion on grants and loans for students but, as policy has changed, so too have the questions we have been able to ask. From 1983 to 1990, we asked:

> *When British students go to university or college, they generally get grants from the local authority. Do you think they should get <u>grants</u> as now, or <u>loans</u> which would have to be paid back when they start working?*

In 1983, the majority, 57 per cent, supported giving grants while 38 per cent were in favour of loans. The question was last asked in this format in 1990, when support for grants stood at 71 per cent. From 1995 to 2000, the question focused on the issue of loans:

> *Many full-time university students are now taking out government loans to help cover their living costs. They have to start repaying these loans when they begin working. Generally speaking, do you think that ...*
> *... students **should** be expected to take out loans to help cover their living costs,*

*or, students **should not** be expected to take out loans to help cover living costs?*

This question was last asked in 2000, when we found 59 per cent opposed loans while 28 per cent supported them.

Table 6.4   Attitudes towards student grants and loans, 1983–2000

	1983	1985	1987	1990	1995	1999	2000
	%	%	%	%	%	%	%
Grants/Not loans	57	60	65	71	64	58	59
Loans	38	34	31	24	26	30	28
Base	*1761*	*1804*	*2847*	*1400*	*1227*	*1052*	*1133*

Table 6.4 suggests that there has been very little change in the public's preference for some form of grant-based system, despite widespread changes in funding practices and, of course, in the proportion of young people attending higher education. However, support for grants is not quite as uniform as Table 6.4 implies. A question introduced in 1995 asks whether grants should be given to *all* students to help cover their living costs, *some* or *none*:

*And, at present, some full-time British university students get grants to help cover their **living** costs. Getting a grant depends upon the student's circumstances and those of their family. Do you think that ... READ OUT ...*
*... **all** students should get grants to help cover their living costs,*
***some** students should get grants to help cover their living costs, as now,*[1]
or, that no grants should be given to help cover students' living costs?

Table 6.5 Attitudes towards student grants, 1995–2000

	1995	1999	2000
	%	%	%
All students should get grants	30	29	27
Some students should get grants	65	64	67
No grants	2	3	2
Base	*1227*	*1052*	*1133*

True, the most recent figures in Table 6.5 (from 2000) show strong support for grants. But the majority position (67 per cent) is for *some* students to get grants (depending upon their circumstances), and not for all to do so (27 per cent).

   More recent still, of course, has been the proposal that students contribute towards their tuition costs, through the payment of tuition fees. To assess views about this, we asked:

> *I'm now going to ask you what you think about university or college students paying towards the costs of their tuition – either while they are studying or after they have finished. Firstly, students and their families paying towards the costs of their tuition **while they are studying**.*
> *Which of the views on this care come closest to what you think about that?*
> *All students or their families should pay towards their tuition costs while they are studying*
> *Some students or their families should pay towards their tuition costs while they are studying, depending on their circumstances*
> *No students or their families should pay towards their tuition costs while they are studying*

Responses to this question show that, while a third think that *no* students should contribute to their tuition costs while they are studying, the majority (58 per cent) accept that *some* students should do so, depending upon their circumstances. Only seven per cent thought that *all* students should pay these costs at that time. We followed this question with another which asked about paying tuition fees "after they have finished studying". This time there was slightly more support for fee-paying after graduation, but still only 16 per cent thought everyone should pay such fees. Half (47 per cent) thought some should pay tuition fees and a third (35 per cent) thought no students or their families should pay fees after graduation.

Table 6.6 Attitudes towards tuition fees, 2001

	While studying	After studying
	%	%
All students/families should pay towards tuition costs	7	16
Some students/families should pay towards tuition costs	58	47
No students/families should pay towards tuition costs	33	35
Base: 1107		

Of course, our question does not specify *how much* students and their families should contribute towards their tuition costs. That said, it is clear that, although large minorities oppose *any* such payments, a larger proportion considers it appropriate that students do contribute, so long as their circumstances are taken into account. However, it is notable that there was a small increase in those who opposed tuition fees completely between 2000 and 2001 (of three to four percentage points). This is a particularly important finding, because government proposals for top-up tuition fees since then proposed a maximum level nearly three times higher than the rate in existence at the time and some university vice-chancellors talked of fees that would be even higher. The public, it seems, has reservations about such moves, and it will be important to monitor future changes.

Tests and exams in schools

Improving primary and secondary education

One of the most obvious changes to have occurred within the education system since 1983 is the increase in examinations and tests, at both primary and secondary level. In the mid-1980s, the General Certificate of Secondary Education (GCSE) replaced two earlier examinations for 16 year olds: the former Ordinary level for the most able and the Certificate of Secondary Education (CSE) for the next ability tier. Meanwhile, national tests for 7, 11 and 14 year olds were introduced by the 1988 Education Reform Act. In addition, optional tests became available for most age groups, so in some schools children were taking a national test almost every year. Considerable problems in 2001 and 2002 showed that the examination system was no longer able to cope as easily as in the past because of the increased number of scripts it had to handle (a ten-fold increase to 25 million over the two decades to 2003), and in 2002 the government set up a committee, chaired by former chief inspector of schools Mike Tomlinson, to come up with recommendations.

We begin by considering the extent to which the public share the government's enthusiasm for an extensive testing programme as a means of improving standards in education. This is one of the options presented in a question which asks what would be the most effective way of improving the education of children in primary and secondary schools. When we look at the results for primary schools (in Table 6.7), we see that only one per cent actually wanted "more emphasis on exams and tests" throughout the period from 1995 to 2002. The clearly preferred solution to improving primary education, selected by two-fifths, was to have smaller class sizes. Better-quality teachers, more emphasis on skills and interests, and more resources were the next most popular choices, but exams hardly figured.

Table 6.7 Most effective measure to improve primary education, 1995–2002

	1995	1996	1998	1999	2000	2001	2002
	%	%	%	%	%	%	%
Smaller class sizes	36	35	37	36	39	41	41
Better-quality teachers	16	19	21	16	14	17	16
More emphasis on developing the child's skills and interests	16	12	12	13	14	13	15
More resources for buildings, books and equipment	19	21	15	19	17	14	14
More links with parents	9	6	8	8	9	8	8
Better leadership within individual schools	n/a	2	2	2	2	1	2
More information about individual schools	1	1	2	2	1	2	1
More emphasis on exams and tests	1	1	1	1	1	1	1
Other	1	1	0	1	2	1	1
Base	*1227*	*1221*	*1035*	*1052*	*1133*	*1107*	*3435*

n/a = not asked

Table 6.8 shows the options for *secondary schools* and we again find that greater emphasis on exams and tests was not seen by many as the most effective route to better secondary education. Four per cent made this choice, a slight decrease from the earliest results in 1995. Instead, mirroring our findings for primary education, smaller class sizes were the most commonly selected means of improving secondary education. Likewise, better-quality teachers, more emphasis on skills and interests, and more resources were the next most popular choices. The option of "more training and preparation for jobs" (which we only asked in relation to secondary education) was also selected by at least one in ten. For both primary and secondary schools, only one or two per cent have required "more information about individual schools" throughout the seven-year period; we return to this later when we discuss performance tables.

Table 6.8 Most effective measure to improve secondary education, 1995–2002

	1995	1996	1998	1999	2000	2001	2002
	%	%	%	%	%	%	%
Smaller class sizes	21	21	20	22	24	27	27
Better-quality teachers	19	21	23	20	18	24	18
More resources for buildings, books and equipment	18	21	17	18	17	15	14
More emphasis on developing the child's skills and interests	13	10	10	11	14	11	13
More training and preparation for jobs	15	13	12	12	11	10	12
More links with parents	4	3	5	5	6	4	6
More emphasis on exams and tests	6	5	8	4	6	3	4
Better leadership within individual schools	n/a	2	2	2	2	2	3
More information about individual schools	0	1	1	1	1	1	1
Other	1	0	0	1	2	1	1
Base	*1227*	*1221*	*1035*	*1052*	*1133*	*1107*	*3435*

n/a = not asked

This suggests that introducing more exams and tests is a long way down most people's lists of necessary improvements for primary and secondary education. Of course, this might not necessarily mean they are *unhappy* with the current level of testing, just that they do not want further additions (or there are other more significant problems facing schools). This does indeed appear to be the case, at least in relation to secondary schools. As the next table shows, when asked their views about the number of tests or exams that school pupils have to take, around half feel that there is currently the right level of testing in secondary schools, and a quarter that there is too much. For primary schools, there was an even split, two-fifths taking either view, between those happy with the *status quo* and those who think there are too many tests. So there is clearly greater concern about the amount of tests in primary schools than in secondary schools, where the majority supported current levels of assessment. There was no strong support for further increases at either level as only around one in ten thought there was too little testing.

Table 6.9 Number of tests and exams taken in schools

% who say the number of tests or exams that school pupils have to take are …	Primary schools	Secondary schools
	%	%
… too many	40	26
… too few	7	10
… or about the right number	39	53
Don't know	14	12
Base: 3435		

Unfortunately, the previous questions were first asked in 2002, meaning that we cannot use them to assess the extent to which views have changed over time. However, we can obtain clues about this by examining two attitude statements first introduced in 1987 and asked regularly since then. These show that in 2002 just under a half felt that "formal exams are the best way of judging the ability of pupils", a very similar view to that taken 15 years earlier in 1987. However, as the next table reveals, nearly two-thirds take the view that "a pupil's everyday classroom work counts for too little". This suggests that, despite increasing levels of continuous assessment and coursework within schools, large proportions of people continue to think that exam results are over-prioritised.

Table 6.10 Assessment by exams or through classroom work, 1987–2002

% who agree	1987	1990	1993	1994	2002
	%	%	%	%	%
Formal exams are the best way of judging the ability of pupils	45	48	53	54	47
So much attention is given to exam results that a pupil's everyday classroom work counts for too little	70	62	60	59	64
Base	*1243*	*1233*	*1306*	*984*	*2900*

Vocational versus academic qualifications

The problems faced by governments in trying to deal with unemployment over the last two decades have led to some substantial changes in vocational qualifications. In the past, vast numbers of qualifications have been on offer, leading to the vocational field often being called the "post-16 jungle", as bewildered students and their parents tried to pick a pathway through them. In an attempt to bring order and clarity, many of these disparate awards have been brought within a National Vocational Qualifications (NVQ) framework, and in 1997 the incoming Labour government created the Qualifications and Curriculum Authority (QCA) to deal with both school and post-school qualifications. During its second administration, after 2001, there was increasing emphasis on coherent pathways for students in the 14–19 age range.

An especially interesting question is whether these sorts of qualification are seen as more useful than academic examinations, or whether people believe the best preparation for the future is to leave school as soon as possible and gain training through a job. To examine this, we ask:

> *Suppose you were advising a 16 year old about their future. Would you say they should ...*
> *... stay on in full-time education to get their A levels/A2 levels (or Highers/Higher Stills),*
> *or, study full-time to get vocational, rather than academic, qualifications,*
> *or, leave school and get training though a job?*

The next table shows that, despite changes within the vocational qualification market, academic qualifications continue to be the most highly recommended route, just as was the case when we first asked this question in 1995. While half supported getting conventional A levels (now in two parts, the Advanced Supplementary (AS) and Advanced (A2) level) after the age of 16, only one in ten selected vocational qualifications, and the same level chose leaving school to get work training. This finding confirms the rigid class system which exists in the qualifications field in Britain, a system within which, in the public's eyes at least, vocational awards simply do not have parity with academic ones.

Table 6.11 Advice to a 16 year old about their future, 1995 and 2002

	1995	2002
	%	%
Stay on in full-time education to get A levels	53	51
Study full-time to get vocational, rather than academic, qualifications	12	11
Leave school and get training through a job	12	10
(Varies/depends on the person)	22	29
Base	*1227*	*3435*

By contrast, there is a pragmatic side to the public view, especially over the longer term. Newspaper stories that plumbers can earn more than graduates may have influenced these beliefs. So, despite their rejection of vocational qualifications as the best choice for a 16 year old, when asked "in the long-run, which do you think gives people more opportunities and choice in life" respondents were more likely to select "good practical skills and training" than "good academic results". The following table shows that there has been a fall from the 44 per cent who selected "good practical skills" in 1993 to the 38 per cent who did so ten years later, but these are still viewed more favourably than academic results.

Table 6.12 Options which give people more opportunities and choice in life, 1993–2002

	1993	1995	2002
	%	%	%
Good practical skills and training	44	43	38
Good academic results	30	32	32
(Mixture/depends)	25	25	30
Base	*1484*	*1227*	*3435*

Performance tables

Exam results have been fed into first unofficial and then official published performance tables for each school since national test scores were first published, from the early 1980s onwards. The earlier finding in Tables 6.7 and

6.8 showed that the public did not regard being given further information about a school to be the most effective means of improving education. However, when we ask explicitly about the publication of exam results, perhaps we get a different picture. Although we do not have findings on these in recent years, from 1983–1996 we asked:

> It is now compulsory for state **secondary schools** to publish their exam results. How useful do you think this information is for parents of present or future pupils?

This was followed in 1993–1996 by a question on the publication of "results of tests for 7 and 11 year olds at **primary schools**". In 1996, a third felt that secondary school performance tables were "very useful", a consistent finding since 1983, while a quarter supported publication of primary school tables. Two in ten saw tables as "not very useful" at secondary level and three in ten at primary level. There was very little change in views on these matters between 1983 and 1996.

Table 6.13 Publication of exam results, 1983–1996

Per cent who think it is useful for schools to publish their exam results	1983	1985	1993	1994	1996
	%	%	%	%	%
Secondary schools					
Very useful	32	30	33	34	34
Quite useful	35	37	39	44	40
Not very useful	24	25	24	20	21
Primary schools					
Very useful	n/a	n/a	24	24	27
Quite useful	n/a	n/a	39	38	39
Not very useful	n/a	n/a	32	35	29
Base	*1214*	*1769*	*1484*	*1167*	*1221*

n/a = not asked

The challenge to comprehensive education

Under the last Conservative government, a number of alternatives to the state comprehensive were introduced, such as specialist schools. The Labour government has continued (and indeed extended) the policy, and at one government press briefing journalists were told this marked the end of the "bog standard" comprehensive. But is this policy in tune with the public's views?

One relevant measure here is the level of support that exists for children going to the same kinds of secondary schools rather than a selective system. The question asked whether "children should go to a different kind of secondary school, according to how well they do at primary school" or whether "all children should go to the same kind of secondary school, no matter how well or badly they do at primary school". As the next table shows, opinion was divided evenly on this issue in 2002. Since 1984, around half have opted for selective schools, but there has also been a growth in support for children going to the same kind of secondary school, from four in ten in 1984 to five in ten in 2002. This growth is evident even among those middle–class groups who are most likely to benefit from a selective system (Wragg and Thomson, 2002).

Table 6.14 Support for selection in secondary schools, 1984–2002

	1984	1987	1990	1994	1998	2001	2002
	%	%	%	%	%	%	%
Selective	50	52	48	49	50	45	49
Non-selective	40	41	44	48	48	52	49
Base	*1675*	*2847*	*1400*	*1167*	*1035*	*1107*	*3435*

Given the growth in support for *non-selective* education since 1984, Labour's introduction of specialist schools appears to be going against the grain (with these schools being allowed to select a small number of pupils according to their aptitude in the specialism involved, such as science, technology, languages, the arts or sports). However, as most specialist schools have chosen *not* to exercise their right to select, they cannot be seen as illustrative of a major form of selection. But it is clear that the introduction of *more* selection would be contrary to the view of many members of the public, including the middle classes.

Quality of primary and secondary education

Earlier, Table 6.2 showed that secondary schoolchildren are the top priority (alongside special needs children) for extra government spending on education. The question then arises as to whether or not this is a reflection on the current quality of education provided by secondary schools. The series of questions shown in Tables 6.15–6.17 present findings on how well state secondary schools nowadays are seen to provide three different aspects of education: basic skills in reading, writing and maths; preparing young people for work; and "bringing out pupils' natural abilities".

Starting with basic skills first, seven in ten thought that schools did "very" or "quite well" at teaching young people reading, writing and maths. This is a notable advance on 15 years ago, when only 56 per cent held this view. Just under a half in 2002 also thought secondary schools did their jobs well in preparing young people for work and bringing out young people's natural abilities. Again, this is a marked improvement from 1987, when only about three in ten assessed schools positively on these two tasks. Conversely, however, it is clear that around a half of people think that schools are not doing well, either in preparing pupils for work or in bringing out their natural abilities.

Table 6.15 Success of state secondary schools teaching three Rs, 1987–2002

	1987	1990	1993	1995	1996	1998	1999	2000	2001	2002
	%	%	%	%	%	%	%	%	%	%
Very well	10	9	12	11	10	12	13	16	12	15
Quite well	46	48	53	49	46	53	55	59	61	56
Not very well	31	33	25	30	33	28	24	20	21	22
Not at all well	11	8	7	6	8	5	7	3	4	4
Base	1281	1233	1306	1058	1038	847	833	972	941	2900

Table 6.16 Success of state secondary schools preparing young people for work, 1987–2002

	1987	1990	1993	1995	1996	1998	1999	2000	2001	2002
	%	%	%	%	%	%	%	%	%	%
Very well	2	2	5	5	4	6	6	5	5	4
Quite well	27	35	38	35	34	40	43	50	45	44
Not very well	54	50	47	49	51	45	41	39	44	43
Not at all well	15	11	8	7	8	6	7	5	4	6
Base	1281	1233	1306	1058	1038	847	833	972	941	2900

Table 6.17 Success of state secondary schools bringing out pupils' natural abilities, 1987–2002

	1987	1990	1993	1995	1996	1998	1999	2000	2001	2002
	%	%	%	%	%	%	%	%	%	%
Very well	3	4	6	5	5	8	7	7	4	6
Quite well	32	32	40	37	35	43	42	44	44	41
Not very well	49	50	42	44	46	38	38	41	43	41
Not at all well	15	12	10	10	11	10	10	6	7	8
Base	1281	1233	1306	1058	1038	847	833	972	941	2900

A final overall assessment of schools' performance is given in the next table. When asked whether primary, and then secondary, schools in the area were getting better, worse or staying much the same, 31 per cent saw improvements in primary schools and 26 per cent in secondary schools. Around a third thought both primary and secondary schools were staying much the same. And only one in ten thought primary schools were getting worse, although one in five believed this about secondary schools. Press accounts may sometimes give the impression of great disaffection with schooling but amongst the public only a minority believe schools generally are getting worse.

Table 6.18 Standards of local schools

% who say schools in their area are …	Primary schools	Secondary schools
	%	%
… getting better	31	26
… getting worse	11	21
… or staying much the same	38	34
Don't know	21	19
Base: 3435		

The teaching profession

There is still thought to be some room for improvements in schools, more often in the secondary sector, though Tables 6.7 and 6.8 showed that more tests and exams were not seen as the key to better education and that smaller class sizes were of paramount concern. This can only be achieved with more resources and, in particular, more and better teachers. Indeed, it was "better-qualified teachers" that was selected as the second most popular recommendation for improving primary and secondary schools.

The Office for Standards in Education (Ofsted), which inspects teacher training institutions, reported in 2003 that standards among new recruits were high (Ofsted, 2003). However, although more people are currently entering teacher training than at any point in the last ten years there is, nonetheless, concern about the recruitment and retention of teachers. It is known that half the teaching profession will be over the age of fifty in the year 2006, which means large numbers of the 450,000 primary and secondary teachers in post are due to retire. In subjects like mathematics and the physical sciences there are major recruitment problems in secondary schools, especially in large cities. Many classes have had to be taken by non-specialists and, in an attempt both to make teaching more attractive and to reduce workloads, the government has begun to recruit new support staff. Support staff will work with teachers in the classroom and perform routine tasks, like collecting money and distributing resources.

In attracting new recruits, teaching has to compete with other fields of employment. So we turn now to examine what the public considers to be the most important characteristics of a first job, and how teaching compares with other careers in satisfying these characteristics. To assess this, we asked respondents which of a number of attributes they would consider the most important if they were "advising a young person who was looking for his or her first job". The results are shown in Table 6.19. This shows that "interesting work" and "a secure job for the future" are seen as the most important attributes, each selected in 2002 by approximately a third of the sample. This marks a notable change compared with earlier years, and suggests that the nature and content of a young person's first job has become more important than was the case previously. In particular, in 1986 and 1993, job security was seen as the most important attribute by double the proportion nominating "interesting work". Such changes may be the result of two factors: firstly, lower unemployment rates in 2002 (meaning that job security recedes somewhat as a primary concern); and, secondly, a change in people's expectations and patterns of work (with the idea of 'a job for life' having been lost in many occupations, especially those that employ part-timers, freelances, or face rapid change).

In 2002, half the sample were asked a slightly amended version of the question which included "a chance to help other people" as one of the options. The results were very similar to those in Table 6.19 as only two per cent chose "a chance to help other people" as the most important characteristic of a first job.

Table 6.19 Most important characteristics of a first job, 1986–2002

	1986	1987	1989	1993	2002
	%	%	%	%	%
Interesting work	26	30	35	26	37
A secure job for the future	57	51	46	56	36
Opportunities for promotion	9	12	9	8	12
Good working conditions	4	4	4	7	9
Good starting pay	3	2	5	3	6
Base	1548	1410	1513	2945	1749

Having established which attributes were seen as important, we then asked which, of a number of professions, would offer a young person the best (and the next best) starting pay, most interesting work, and chance of helping others. Earlier we saw that "interesting work" was commonly cited as an important attribute of a new job; so we turn now to consider how teaching compares with other professions in this respect.

The results are shown in Table 6.20. This shows that, when compared with the other professions in the table, very few indeed (only one in fifty) see teaching as offering the best starting pay. In fact, very few indeed think the pay on offer to a new teacher matches that available to doctors, police officers, lawyers or computer engineers. In practice, 97 per cent of experienced teachers were awarded an additional £2,000 merit award in 2001, but the public perception of poor salary prospects seems firmly established. Nor does teaching fare well when it comes to offering interesting work, with only eight per cent choosing it as their first choice (although a further 14 per cent selected teaching as their second choice). Once again, other professions are seen as more likely to offer this attribute, with journalism being seen as particularly good in this respect (even though it is perceived to be a very low paid profession). Only when it comes to offering a chance to help others, does teaching feature significantly, although it should be remembered that very few saw this as the most important attribute in a new job.

Table 6.20 Careers best suited to offering certain characteristics to a young person

% who select the following career:	Best starting pay	Most interesting work	Best chance of helping other people
	%	%	%
Nurse	1	6	37
Doctor	12	11	32
Schoolteacher	2	8	18
Police officer	10	18	8
Lawyer	32	14	3
Computer engineer	38	7	*
Journalist	1	32	*
(None of these)	*	1	*

Base:3435

Unfortunately, we did not ask which occupations offered the best job security (an attribute which was seen as equal to "interesting work" in its importance when choosing a new job). In this respect, teaching would be likely to win out over some of the other occupations mentioned.

Conclusions

One prominent feature of these two decades is how remarkably similar the policies of Conservative and Labour administrations were, the latter sometimes embracing one of its predecessor's policies with even more enthusiasm. Public attitudes to some of these policies, such as the proliferation of examinations, has been unenthusiastic. In other areas, however, it is clear that Labour policy has echoed public concerns, most notably in relation to class sizes and the quality of teaching.

Despite changes of government, and policy, public views about education have remained remarkably stable over the last two decades, give or take a wobble from one year to the next. Take, for instance, the extent to which the public prioritise education over other areas of public spending. Here we find that, despite Labour's headlining of education as its top priority, the public have consistently prioritised health over education (although the gap between these two has narrowed over the last two decades). Priorities within education have remained remarkably similar; with secondary schools and special needs remaining the top two priorities for additional spending. And, perhaps most dramatically, attitudes towards the expansion of higher education have barely changed, despite a massive increase in the proportion of young people going to college. The reasons for this immobility in attitudes are not clear. Perhaps they reflect an unwillingness on the part of the public to suggest that education or its expansion is not important. It is also likely that there is a lag between actual policy change and public awareness of it, particularly among those not affected by the changes.

Although opinion remains divided on the need to expand higher education further still, nearly half think that further expansion should take place, lending support to the government's desire to increase to 50 per cent the proportion of young people entering the tertiary sector. However, a similar proportion consider that opportunities to enter higher education are "about right", and it remains to be seen whether the size of this group will increase as expansion continues. But it is the issue of funding which is far more problematic. Here, higher education poses a number of problems for the government, especially as the public seems unenthusiastic about universal fee charges and the high cost nowadays of a university course. The desire to shift the burden of paying for higher education from the state to the individual remains a very contentious one, and shows no sign of disappearing, although there is clear recognition that the circumstances of students and their families should be taken into account when deciding who should and should not get help. Meanwhile, calls by government that higher education institutions should increase the proportion of students from less advantaged backgrounds have strong public support, with many being sceptical about the extent to which selection criteria currently ignore social background.

The job-getting function of higher education stands high in public esteem. In fact, one of the more curious findings of these surveys is the public's ambivalent view of vocational education, a rapidly expanding field. On the one hand, vocational qualifications are seen to lag well behind traditional academic education when people are asked what advice they would give to a 16 year old as to what to do next. Traditional snobberies about the horny-handed seem to persist. But, on the other hand, there is also the widespread belief that one is better off in the longer term with employable skills, rather than mere academic qualifications.

Overall, the public has become much more satisfied with schools than was the case in the 1980s, so there is some cause for congratulation. Unfortunately, this does not mean that all is thought to be well in primary and secondary schools. A significant minority believe pupils are over-examined (particularly at primary school level) and there is a perhaps surprisingly high degree of support for coursework and continuous assessment to be taken into account more than they are at present, so as to recognise more what children do in the classroom. Increased unemployment in the 1980s and 1990s made the examination structure a high stakes system, but the public does not have any appetite to see the volume increased.

There is a strong public belief that one of the most effective ways of improving both primary and secondary education is through smaller class sizes and better-quality teachers. Both these require a high-quality supply of teaching staff. However, the next few decades could see a shortage of teachers, making it critical that the profession continues to attract sufficient and suitable recruits. In so doing, it will have to battle hard against the perception that teaching offers less interesting or well-paid work than other professions. True, teaching *is* seen to score well as a job that involves helping others, but few appear to see this as key when choosing their career.

Notes

1. The words 'as now' in the second option were dropped in 2000.

References

Department for Education and Skills (DfES) (2003), *White Paper – The Future of Higher Education*, London: TSO.

Ofsted (2003), *Quality and Standards in Secondary Initial Teacher Training*, HMI 546, and *Quality and Standards in Primary Initial Teacher Training*, HMI 547, London: TSO.

Wragg, T. and Thomson, K. (2002), 'Education, education, education', in Park, A., Curtice, J., Thomson, K., Jarvis, L. and Bromley, C. (eds.), *British Social Attitudes: the 19th Report*, London: Sage.

Acknowledgements

The *National Centre for Social Research* is grateful to the Department for Education and Skills for their financial support which enabled us to ask the questions reported in this chapter.

7 Charting change in British values

Alison Park and Paula Surridge [*]

Various chapters in this Report look at attitudes towards some of the issues that have dominated British political and social life over the last twenty years – public spending, social welfare, the NHS, education, and Europe. By contrast, this chapter steps back from particular policy areas to examine two of the broader value systems that can play a crucial role in shaping people's attitudes towards more specific social, moral and political issues.

By a 'value system' we mean the enduring beliefs or philosophies that people hold about what is good or desirable (Converse, 1964; Alwin and Scott, 1996). These, in turn, underpin a person's attitudes towards a range of issues. Take, for example, a person with strongly held religious beliefs; such beliefs tend to be long-standing (and so will not be prone to rapid change over time) and inevitably play an important role in helping that person form views about a wide range of related issues – the way in which children are educated, for example, or the acceptability of different forms of sexuality. These religious beliefs can therefore be seen as a value system, and we can make assumptions about it actually *causing* attitudes to specific issues. Moreover, we should find that those with similar religious beliefs would tend to have similar views on these other issues (although to make such predictions on an individual level would clearly be foolhardy).

In this chapter, we focus on two broad value systems which influence, and therefore help us understand, people's views on a range of social, political and moral subjects: one concerned with 'left' and 'right', and the other with 'libertarianism' and 'authoritarianism'. We start by describing these value systems, and explaining how we measure them. We then explore the different values held by a range of social groups, identifying those whose values are particularly distinctive. Our main focus, however, will be on exploring the ways

[*] Alison Park is a Research Director at the *National Centre for Social Research* and a Co-director of the *British Social Attitudes* surveys series. Paula Surridge is a Lecturer in Sociology at the University of Bristol.

in which these values have changed over time, both overall and among specific groups. In so doing, we shall focus on three key areas. Firstly, we examine the impact that increasing access to higher education has had on libertarian/authoritarian values. Secondly, we assess the extent to which social changes have affected the left/right values of different classes. And, thirdly, we explore how the values of different party supporters (and, indeed, of those who support no party at all) have changed over the last two decades. Are, for instance, the left/right values of Labour and Conservative supporters as far apart now as was the case in the mid-1980s?

The value dimensions

'Left/right' values

Our first value dimension is concerned with *economic* issues, most notably the desirability of government intervention in the economy, income and wealth redistribution, and the relationship between workers and owners (or management). The range of possible beliefs about this can best be imagined as a continuum. At one end, we find those with 'right-wing' values emphasising individualism and the market; at the other, those with 'left-wing' values emphasising redistribution and the unequal relationship between workers and more privileged social groups (Heath *et al.*, 2001). Not surprisingly, this value dimension has been particularly closely associated with political attitudes and opinions.

'Libertarian/authoritarian' values

Our second value dimension is concerned with *authority*. At one end, are those who have an 'authoritarian' concern with conformity and obedience, and who are punitive in their views about dealing with those who break the law. At the other end, are 'libertarians' who stress the importance of individualism and are uncomfortable about imposing rigid conditions upon the way in which people live their lives (Ahrendt and Young, 1994).

Whose values?

These two value dimensions do *not* tend to go together with each other – it is not the case that someone who is 'left-wing' will necessarily tend to be 'libertarian', nor that someone who is 'right-wing' will necessarily tend to be 'authoritarian'.[1] The fact that the two dimensions tend to be cross-cutting add to the complexity of the ways in which they influence social and political attitudes in Britain and interact with the political party system. We shall explore this in more detail later on in the chapter.

Traditionally, the notion of 'left' and 'right' has been closely entwined with the British class system, with 'left-wing' approaches tending to favour working-class interests, and 'right-wing' ones the interests of the middle classes. However, some argue that the profound social changes of the last few decades (including a dramatic increase in service sector occupations, rising home ownership and increased access to higher education) have resulted in class becoming increasingly 'outmoded' as a social concept. Social class, it is said, is no longer as strong a predictor of a person's life chances as once it was, suggesting that our attention would be better focused upon other social divisions, most notably education and income, which might play a more important role in influencing people's behaviour, expectations and attitudes (Clark and Lipset, 1996; Pakulski and Waters, 1996). So one of our key tasks will be to explore what impact, if any, such social changes have had upon the distribution of left/right values. In particular, we shall focus on exploring whether or not there has been a blurring of the distinction between the values held by different classes – and, if so, whether other social divisions have opened up in their stead.

Although the concept of authoritarian/libertarian values is not as commonly used as that of left and right, it is by no means a new concern. There was considerable interest in what was called the 'authoritarian personality' in the years preceding and following the Second World War (Adorno et al., 1950), and many of our notions about what constitute libertarianism and authoritarianism continue to reflect these debates. What groups might we expect to have distinctive libertarian/authoritarian values? It will certainly be important to consider how these values vary by education, as one common finding has been that those who have been through higher education are far more likely to be libertarians than any other group (Lipset, 1981; Ahrendt and Young, 1994; Phelan et al., 1995; Evans, 2000). If we find such a relationship, we shall need to assess the impact of the recent expansion in higher education upon the distribution of these values. It will also be important to consider how these values vary by class, not least because one of the most contentious claims made by Adorno in *The Authoritarian Personality* was that authoritarianism is particularly prevalent among the working class (Adorno et al., 1950).

No discussion of left/right values can ignore the relationship that these values have with traditional British party politics, most obviously through the tendency of people with left-wing values to support the Labour Party while those with right-wing values tend to favour the Conservatives. This brings class back into the equation again, as Labour have tended to advocate left-wing policies favouring the interests of the working class, and the Conservatives more right-wing policies which favour the middle class (Sanders, 1999). And voters who perceive themselves to be one class rather than another will tend to opt for the party that represents that class. Of course, the strength of this relationship between class, party and left/right values is increasingly being questioned as the role of class changes in British society and as the main parties have apparently adopted less distinctive policies than in the past. For example, the resignation from government in 2000 by Peter Kilfoyle MP was interpreted by many commentators as a reflection of his view that insufficient attention was being paid by the Labour government to its working-class heartlands. So, we shall also examine the values held by different party supporters. Is there, for instance, a clear difference between the left/right values of Conservative and Labour supporters? Have supporters of the new Labour and Conservative parties the same values as those held by the supporters of their 1980s counterparts? And how distinctive are Liberal Democrats. We shall also assess the extent to which libertarian/authoritarian values cut across the more traditional party lines of left and right.

Of course, there has also been considerable concern expressed about rising political 'disengagement', not least as a result of very low turnouts at recent elections. The causes of this are disputed, as are the cures. However, as the earlier reference to Peter Kilfoyle makes clear, one commonly voiced concern is that, in its shift to capture more 'middle-class' voters, the Labour Party has left behind some of its most traditional supporters. So, we shall also explore any changes in the values held by those who do *not* identify with particular parties. In particular, we will consider whether there is any evidence that this group are becoming notably more left-wing, suggesting that there might be some truth to the notion that frustration with New Labour among some of its more traditional supporters has resulted in them abandoning politics altogether.

Measuring values

How do we go about measuring left/right and libertarian/authoritarian values? At first sight it might appear that we could simply ask people where they stand in relation to 'left' and 'right', but even if this were possible we could hardly ask people where they stand with regard to libertarianism and authoritarianism! Moreover, even with commonly used terms such as 'left' and 'right', there can be considerable confusion and disagreement about what they actually mean. This is aptly illustrated by the findings of a study carried out in the late 1980s which found that a substantial body of people took 'left' to mean extreme, and 'right' to mean moderate (Heath and Martin, 1997). Consequently, we are better off measuring these values indirectly – that is, by taking account of people's views on a range of issues that relate to that value dimension. We do this by presenting respondents with a series of statements, each of which taps a particular element of the value in question. We ask respondents whether they "agree" or "disagree" with each statement (and, if so, how strongly), or whether they "neither agree nor disagree". Their responses to all the questions can then be combined into a summary measure, or scale, which indicates where they stand on that value dimension. (Further details of these scales can be found in Appendix I to this Report.)

This approach is advantageous because it allows us to take account of a range of issues of relevance to the particular value dimension, rather than relying on responses to one question alone. It minimises the impact of a sudden change in view about one particular issue upon the scale. It also reduces the effect of an individual holding an idiosyncratic view on one particular issue (perhaps as a result of something that has happened to them in their life). As a result, our measure is likely to be more accurate overall.

The five statements that make up our left/right scale are shown in the next table, alongside the proportions who agree, disagree or neither agree nor disagree with each statement.

Table 7.1 Left/right values

		Agree	Neither	Disagree
Government should redistribute income from the better off to those who are less well off	%	39	25	34
Big business benefits owners at expense of workers	%	57	25	15
Ordinary working people do not get their fair share of the nation's wealth	%	63	23	12
There is one law for the rich and one for the poor	%	61	19	18
Management will always try to get the better of employees if it gets the chance	%	60	21	16

Base: 2900

As well as looking at responses to each of the five questions separately, we can also add them together to calculate a mean *scale score*. We have done this in such a way that the lowest possible score on the scale is -2, indicating someone who *agrees strongly* with all five of the statements (the most left-wing position possible); the highest is +2, indicating someone who *disagrees strongly* with all the statements (the most right-wing position). In summary, therefore, a negative value indicates a left of centre position, and a positive one a right of centre position. Overall, the mean score on the left/right scale in 2002 was -0.5.

Table 7.2 Libertarian and authoritarian values

		Agree	Neither	Disagree
Young people today don't have enough respect for traditional British values	%	68	20	10
People who break the law should be given stiffer sentences	%	76	15	6
For some crimes, the death penalty is the most appropriate sentence	%	55	13	28
Schools should teach children to obey authority	%	82	11	5
The law should always be obeyed, even if a particular law is wrong	%	39	31	28
Censorship of films and magazines is necessary to uphold moral standards	%	63	15	17

Base: 2900

The six questions which make up our libertarianism/authoritarianism scale are shown in Table 7.2. As before, we have added together people's answers to calculate a scale score (where negative values refer to libertarian values and positive values to authoritarian ones). This time, the mean score is +0.7.

How confident can we be that our two value scales do the job for which they were intended – that is, that they are tapping an important element of a person's beliefs? To assess this, we can consider how these two sets of values relate to other attitudes. After all, one defining feature of a belief system is that being aware of a person's beliefs should help us predict other ideas and attitudes that they might have (Converse, 1964). So, if our scales are doing their job, they should be closely linked to views on other issues that are 'left/right' or 'liberal-authoritarian' in character. To test this we now examine the relationship between our left/right scale and responses to the following statement:

> On the whole, do you think it should or should not be the government's responsibility to provide a job for everyone who wants one?

We also consider the relationship between our libertarian/authoritarian scale and responses to the statement:

> People who want children ought to get married

To best illustrate this relationship, we have allocated people into one of three groups according to their scores on our value scales – separating out the fifth or so at each end of the continuum from the three-fifths whose values lie more towards the middle.[2]

Table 7.3 Relationship between value scales and particular attitudes

	Left right scale		Libertarian authoritarian scale		
	% most right-wing	Mean scale score	% most libertarian	Mean scale score	Smaller base
Government responsibility to provide jobs					
Definitely should be	14	-0.72	13	0.83	628
Probably should be	18	-0.52	16	0.68	739
Probably should not be	34	-0.18	25	0.48	252
Definitely should not be	46	-0.05	14	0.66	127
People who want children should marry					
Strongly agree	20	-0.56	7	1.05	275
Agree	22	-0.46	12	0.75	703
Neither	18	-0.47	20	0.59	312
Disagree	23	-0.43	26	0.50	419
Strongly disagree	16	-0.67	34	0.41	146

Reassuringly, there is a strong relationship between responses to the two statements and 'their' value scales. Of those who think it "definitely should *not* be" the government's responsibility to provide jobs, nearly half are in our most right-wing category, compared with only one in seven of those who think it "definitely should be" the government's responsibility. And, when it comes to views about marriage preceding parenthood, of those who "strongly disagree" that people should get married first, a third are in our most libertarian category, compared with only one in fourteen of those who "strongly agree". Note also that the scales do not predict the 'other' attitude: for example, left/right attitudes are not related in any consistent way to views on whether people wanting children should marry.

So our two scales do appear to tap sets of values and beliefs which can help us predict and understand other social, political and moral attitudes. We turn now to examine how the values of various groups differ.

Left-wingers and right-wingers

Earlier we described the 'traditional' relationship between class and left/right values, partly mediated through British party politics. We shall return later to the question of whether or not this relationship has changed, and begin simply by considering what this relationship between class and values currently looks like. For the purposes of this chapter we use the 'Goldthorpe' class schema (Goldthorpe, 1987). We prefer this schema to other measures of social class because it is more theoretically based and separates out several groups who we might expect to hold distinctive attitudes and values, reflecting their different market position. In particular, those who own small businesses or are 'own account workers' are identified as a separate class (referred to as the 'petty bourgeoisie'), rather than being allocated to a range of different groups depending upon the work they do. The schema also distinguishes between the 'working class' (who are defined as skilled, semi-skilled and unskilled manual workers) and 'manual foremen' and technicians. (For more details of the Goldthorpe schema see Appendix I to this Report.)

The next table shows the proportion of people within each of our five broad social class groups who fall into the three different categories within our left/right scale, as well as their mean scores on the scale. It shows that there appears to be a strong relationship between class and left/right values, with those in the working class and manual foremen/technicians being especially likely to hold left-wing values (around a quarter doing so) and very unlikely to hold right-wing ones (fewer than one in ten). At the other end of the class spectrum, the 'salariat' (professional and managerial workers) and 'petty bourgeoisie' are more likely to have right-wing values (30 per cent do so) and less likely to hold left-wing ones (just over one in ten do so). Meanwhile, the views of those in routine non-manual occupations lie somewhere between the two.

Table 7.4 Left/right values by social class

		Most left-wing	Middle ground	Most right-wing	Mean scale score	Base
All	%	18	62	20	-0.50	2826
Salariat	%	12	58	30	-0.26	788
Routine non-manual	%	17	63	20	-0.49	557
Petty bourgeoisie	%	11	59	30	-0.31	155
Manual foremen/ technicians	%	27	66	8	-0.77	170
Working class	%	25	66	9	-0.79	672

A good illustration of these class differences can be seen when considering responses to one of the statements which makes up our left/right scale – that there is "one law for the rich and one law for the poor". Half (51 per cent) of the salariat agree with this view, rising to 60 per cent among routine non-manual workers, and 72 per cent of the working class.

But is class the whole picture? Could it not be that class is simply reflecting other social divisions that are even more closely linked to left/right values? As the next table shows, there certainly is a pattern in the values held by different social groups, very much along the lines that we would expect from what we have already seen.

Table 7.5 Left/right values by household income, education and tenure

		Most left-wing	Middle ground	Most right-wing	Mean scale score	Base
Education						
Degree	%	16	59	24	-0.37	455
Higher education, below degree	%	13	58	30	-0.28	413
A level (or equiv.)	%	16	57	27	-0.41	384
GCSE (or equiv.)	%	16	66	18	-0.51	502
No qualifications	%	26	63	11	-0.77	687
Household income						
£38,000 plus	%	11	56	33	-0.21	794
£23,000 to £37,999	%	14	65	21	-0.44	590
£12,000 to £22,999	%	21	62	17	-0.63	598
Less than £12,000	%	26	65	10	-0.74	591
Housing Tenure						
Owner-occupiers	%	15	61	24	-0.75	2054
Renter and others	%	26	63	11	-0.42	743

So, those in more advantaged socio-economic circumstances (for example, who have a degree, have household incomes in the higher income brackets or own their own home) are the most likely to have right-wing values. Most notably, graduates are over twice as likely to have right-wing views as those without qualifications, and those in the highest household income bracket are three times more likely than those in the lowest to have right-wing values.

These socio-economic factors are obviously intertwined with one another in complex ways. Graduates, for instance, will tend to predominate in more middle-class occupations, and will be more likely than non-graduates to own their own home. So, to assess which factors are of the *most* importance in predicting people's left/right values, we need to use multivariate analysis. This allows us to test the importance of particular characteristics, while taking other relationships into account.

Such analysis confirms that social class, income and housing tenure are all important influences on a person's left/right values in their own right (see model A in the appendix to this chapter). The two most important factors are class and income which emerge as of equal importance in explaining left/right attitudes, with little statistical difference between them.[3] The working class (including manual foremen and technicians), and those with lower incomes, are the most likely to have left-wing values. Once these factors are taken into account, education does not have any independent influence on left/right values.

So far, then, these values appear to be firmly grounded in socio-economic advantage and disadvantage. However, while social class is an important predictor of left/right values, it is notable that it only provides us with a part of the picture. Income is also an important factor that needs to be taken into account. This means that, within the middle class for instance, there will be important distinctions between the left/right values of richer and poorer groups.

In summary, therefore, there is a strong link between a person's socio-economic background and whether they tend more to left or right. Later we shall return to this relationship and assess whether it is the same now as it was in the mid-1980s. Before doing so, however, we consider our other value dimension: that of authoritarianism and libertarianism.

Authoritarians and libertarians

Earlier we drew attention to a commonly found relationship between education and libertarian/authoritarian values. This is substantiated by our findings. As the next table shows, the more highly educated are substantially more libertarian than those with lower levels of education. In fact, graduates are *five* times more likely than those with no qualifications to be in the most libertarian camp and those with no qualifications are *six* times more likely than graduates to be at the most authoritarian end of the spectrum.

To illustrate this, consider the response of graduates and those with no qualifications to a statement that the death penalty is "the most appropriate sentence" for some crimes (which forms one of the statements in our libertarian/authoritarian scale). Just over a quarter of graduates (27 per cent) agree with this view, compared with nearly two-thirds of those with no qualifications (64 per cent).

Table 7.6 Libertarian/authoritarian values by education

		Liber-tarians	Middle ground	Authori-tarians	Mean scale score	Base
All	%	17	64	19	0.70	2840
Degree	%	40	56	5	0.20	454
Higher education, below degree	%	15	67	18	0.67	417
A level (or equiv.)	%	22	63	15	0.60	384
GCSE (or equiv.)	%	9	69	21	0.82	504
No qualifications	%	8	63	29	0.93	696

Although the relationship between education and libertarianism is a strong one, the factors which underpin it are disputed. Some stress the role that higher education plays in allowing students to absorb more tolerant values, while others emphasise the ways in which education helps individuals to develop cognitive skills which enable them to process information, empathise with others and acknowledge viewpoints that are different to their own (Phelan *et al.*, 1995). Conversely, some argue that what we see is simply the ability of higher education to inculcate 'political correctness' among graduates, but it is notable that many of the questions which make up our libertarian/authoritarian scale do not have a socially acceptable answer.[4]

Education is not the only characteristic linked to distinctive libertarian/ authoritarian values. There are also notable social class and income differences, some of which are shown in the next table. The general pattern here is one whereby the most economically advantaged are the most likely to be libertarians, while the more disadvantaged are the most likely to be authoritarians. In class terms, the most libertarian of all are the salariat (that is, professional and managerial staff), nearly a quarter of whom can be classified in this way. Meanwhile, manual foremen and technicians are the most likely to be authoritarian, with over a quarter in this category.

The relationship with income follows a similar path, with those on very low incomes being the least likely to be libertarians and the most likely to be authoritarians. There is also a notable relationship with religion, with those who do not see themselves as belonging to a particular religion being the most likely libertarians (while Anglicans are the most likely to have views that place them at the authoritarian end of our value scale). The strength of the association between libertarian/authoritarian values and these characteristics is, however, considerably weaker than that found earlier with education.

Table 7.7 Libertarian/authoritarian values by class, income and religion

		Liber-tarians	Middle ground	Authori-tarians	Mean scale score	Base
Social class						
Salariat	%	24	62	15	0.75	793
Routine non-manual	%	17	65	19	0.72	557
Petty bourgeoisie	%	8	68	23	0.83	155
Manual foremen and technicians	%	7	64	29	0.96	173
Working class	%	11	65	23	0.81	677
Household income						
£38,000 plus	%	26	63	11	0.46	802
£23,000 to £37,999	%	16	66	18	0.67	592
£12,000 to £22,999	%	12	65	23	0.82	600
Less than £12,000	%	12	64	25	0.81	592
Religion						
Church of England	%	9	66	24	0.85	899
Roman Catholic	%	16	66	19	0.70	262
Other	%	15	66	19	0.72	486
No religion	%	23	61	16	0.56	1185

The primacy of education is confirmed by multivariate analysis (see model A in the appendix to this chapter). This shows that, when the influence of a range of socio-economic measures is assessed, education remains the most important influence on libertarian/authoritarian values. Such analysis also confirms that income and religion play a significant part. However, the class variation disappears once these other factors are taken into account.[5]

Overall, therefore, this leaves us with two very distinct patterns. When considering left/right values, those factors more closely associated with material advantage are the best predictors of a person's values (particularly social class and income). On left/right values, education is not an important factor, once other material advantages were taken into account. When considering liberterian/authoritarian values, however, there is an exceptionally strong relationship between education and a person's values, with graduates being markedly more liberal than anyone else. This time, however, there is no relationship with social class once education and other factors are taken into account. But there remains room for additional relationships between libertarian/authoritarianism and both religiosity and income.

Party values

Left/right issues have long been the bread and butter of mainstream British political debate, although many dispute the extent to which this is as true now as it has been in the past. So we turn now to consider the relationship between a person's left/right values and their party preferences, a relationship that remains very strong indeed. As seen in the next table, nearly a quarter of Labour identifiers have views that place them in our most left-wing group, three times the rate found among Conservatives. However, the most distinctive profile is found among the Conservatives, two-fifths of whom are at the most right-wing pole of our scale (compared with one in eight Labour identifiers).

Table 7.8 Left/right values by party identification

		Most left-wing	Middle ground	Most right-wing	Mean scale score	Base
Conservative	%	8	52	40	-0.09	712
Labour	%	24	64	12	-0.70	1159
Liberal Democrat	%	19	62	20	-0.54	330
None	%	19	63	17	-0.58	342

The relationship between left/right values and party position is confirmed by multivariate analysis (see model B in the appendix to this chapter). This shows that, when a range of socio-economic characteristics are taken into account, a person's left/right values are still the most important predictor of their being a Conservative identifier (as opposed to identifying with another party, or with no party at all). The same is true for Labour identifiers. However, for Liberal Democrats, and those with no party identification at all, left/right values are not significantly linked to their party choice (or lack of it). This means that there is no distinctive profile, at least in terms of left/right values, among those who do not identify with any mainstream political parties, and no evidence that they are made up of disaffected left-wingers who think New Labour has moved too far to the right.

   Although British party politics has tended to be seen as organised along left/right lines, there are also marked differences in the libertarian/authoritarian values of their supporters. As the next table shows, the most distinctive views of all are held by Liberal Democrat and Conservative identifiers. Conservatives are most likely to be authoritarians. Liberal Democrats are most likely to be libertarians – four times more so than Conservatives. This is, perhaps, not surprising. After all, some of the key components of our scale relate specifically to issues such as tradition and obedience, issues that might well strike a particular chord for Conservative identifiers, while the Liberal Democrats and their predecessors have traditionally stood for the opposite. Labour identifiers lie somewhere between these two groups and are notable in having a similar proportion of libertarians and authoritarians (rather than one group clearly outweighing the other).

Table 7.9 Libertarian/authoritarian values by party identification

		Liber-tarians	Middle ground	Authori-tarians	Mean scale score	Base
Conservative	%	7	69	24	0.86	716
Labour	%	20	62	18	0.65	1161
Liberal Democrat	%	28	56	16	0.50	331
None	%	13	67	20	0.76	346

The strong relationship between party choice and libertarian/authoritarian values is confirmed by multivariate analysis (see model B in the appendix to this chapter). Holding right-wing and authoritarian values play a roughly equal part in predicting Conservative identification. And among Liberal Democrats, it is their libertarian values which best predict their party preference. Among Labour identifiers, left/right values remain the single most important predictor of their party choice, but holding views towards the libertarian end of the spectrum also contributes. Finally, those with no party preference at all do not have a distinctive value profile, either in terms of their left/right or libertarian/authoritarian values.

Changing values?

We turn now to examine how these values may have changed since 1986, when the questions used to tap them were first introduced to the *British Social Attitudes* survey. We shall begin by reviewing what overall changes have taken place, and then move on to focus on the values held by particular groups.

As the next table shows, there have been only very small changes in left/right and libertarian/authoritarian values since 1986. In the case of left/right values, there has been a small shift towards the middle of the scale, away from the 'extremes' at either end. Meanwhile, the libertarian/authoritarian scale shows a small shift away from the most authoritarian position.

Perhaps the most remarkable feature of the table is the relative stability it shows over what is nearly a two-decade period. This is less surprising than it might at first appear; the very definition of value systems is that they are stable belief systems – and so should not be prone to the kind of fluctuation that we might expect if we were simply measuring attitudes towards key issues of the day.

Table 7.10 Left/right and libertarian/authoritarian values, 1986 and 2002

	1986	2002	Change 1986–2002
Left/right scale	%	%	
Left-wing	22	18	-4
Middle ground	54	61	+7
Right-wing	25	21	-4
Mean value	-0.46	-0.50	+0.04
Base	*1288*	*2826*	
Libertarian/authoritarian scale	%	%	
Libertarian	15	17	+2
Middle ground	60	64	+4
Authoritarian	25	19	-6
Mean value	0.76	0.70	-0.06
Base	*1298*	*2840*	

Libertarianism by degree?

Earlier we saw that graduates are distinctively 'libertarian' in their views. In 1986, however, there were relatively few of them compared to their numbers now. Then, only seven per cent of the *British Social Attitudes* sample had degrees. By 2002, this had more than doubled to 16 per cent. In the meantime, the proportion of people without any qualifications has almost halved, from 45 per cent in 1986 to 23 per cent now.

What might this mean for libertarian/authoritarian values? Given the strong link between libertarianism and education we might have expected the growth in higher education to have lead to a marked shift of beliefs among the population as a whole in a libertarian direction. But we have already seen that this is not the case. So we turn now to look at the extent to which some of the relationships we identified earlier between libertarian/authoritarian values and education have changed their complexion over time. Perhaps the expansion of higher education has reduced the distinctive nature of graduates (either because the social composition of graduates has changed or because of wider changes within higher education as a whole)? Meanwhile, we might envisage that the proportion of people with no qualifications might have become more distinctively authoritarian in their views as they become more and more of a minority.

The next table explores this by focusing upon the two educational groups most likely to have been affected by change: graduates and those with no academic qualifications whatsoever. Among graduates there does indeed seem to have been a move towards the middle ground, with the proportion of libertarians shrinking by six percentage points, although they remain the most libertarian group by far. More notable, however, is that the proportion of graduates whose views are at the more authoritarian end of the scale has fallen from an already small 16 per cent to a smaller still five per cent. As a result, over 50 per cent graduates now fall into our 'middle ground' category, a considerable increase on the 37 per cent who were there in 1986. The table also shows that, despite a dramatic shrinkage in the proportion of the population without qualifications, this group has not retreated to an authoritarian hardcore – if anything they have become slightly *less* authoritarian. Both groups are, in effect, following a nationwide trend away from authoritarianism.

The net effect of these changes is to reduce slightly the gap between those with a degree and those with no qualifications. It remains, however, a considerable one.

Table 7.11 Libertarianism/authoritarianism and education, 1986 and 2002

	Graduates		No qualifications		Graduate – No qualification difference	
	1986	2002	1986	2002	1986	2002
	%	%	%	%		
Libertarian	46	40	8	8	+38	+32
Middle ground	37	56	59	63	-22	-7
Authoritarian	16	5	33	29	-17	-22
Base	*99*	*454*	*562*	*696*		

That education continues to relate closely to a person's libertarian/authoritarian values is confirmed by multivariate analysis (see model A in the appendix to this chapter). This analysis also shows that income plays an important role; in both 1986 and 2002, it proves a significant predictor of a person's values, with lower income groups being more likely to be authoritarians than higher income ones. However, since 1986, one important predictor of libertarian/authoritarian values has disappeared: age. It is to this that we now turn.

There was a remarkable age gradient in libertarian/authoritarian values in 1986. Among 18–24 year olds, nearly a third (31 per cent) were in the most libertarian camp, and only seven per cent in the most authoritarian. By contrast, among the 65-plus age group, almost half (48 per cent) were in the most authoritarian camp, and only three per cent in the most libertarian. By 2002, however, this difference was less pronounced, to the point that age had ceased to be significantly linked to libertarian/authoritarian values once other factors, such as education, had been taken into account.[6]

The next table assesses how this change might have come about. It focuses upon cohorts of people born in particular years, and what their values were at two separate points of time, 1986 and 2002. Although we did not interview the same people on these separate occasions, this exercise allows us to trace whether a cohort's values have changed as they have aged (so called 'lifecycle' changes) or whether certain distinctive values are associated with particular cohorts and remain very stable over time (so called 'generational' changes).

The first row in the table shows us the overall change in the population as a whole, in this case the proportion with values which put them at the most authoritarian end of our scale. It shows a fall of six percentage points in this proportion over the period between 1986 and 2002. The subsequent rows show the comparable change among specific cohorts of people. The first of these rows shows the values of those born between 1977 and 1984. They were clearly not old enough to have participated in the 1986 survey, but in 2002 only 12 per cent of them fall into our most authoritarian group. The same is true of the next row, whereas the cohort after that, those born between 1961 and 1968, show a nine point *increase* in their proportion of authoritarians over the 16-year period.

Table 7.12 Authoritarianism, by birth cohort, 1986 and 2002

			% authoritarians				
			1986	**2002**	**Difference 1986–2002**	*Base 1986*	*Base 2002*
All			25	19	-6	*1298*	*2840*
Cohort	**Age in 1986**	**Age in 2002**					
1977–1984	0–6	18–25	-	12	-	-	*255*
1969–1976	10–17	26–33	-	12	-	-	*407*
1961–1968	18–25	34–41	8	17	+9	*219*	*515*
1953–1962	26–33	42–49	15	19	+4	*193*	*400*
1945–1952	34–41	50–57	17	20	+3	*211*	*353*
1937–1944	42–49	58–65	27	26	-1	*208*	*350*
1929–1936	50–57	66–73	35	22	-13	*153*	*256*
1921–1928	58–65	74–81	36	34	-1	*121*	*209*
1913–1920	66–73	82+	42	37	-5	*96*	*90*
Pre-1913	74+	-	54	-	-	*93*	-

What does this mean? Our starting point is the fact that the gradient between the most and least authoritarian age group has become less pronounced. This is illustrated in the table by the fact that the 'gap' between the most and least authoritarian age cohorts has halved over the period, from a massive 46 percentage points in 1986 (the difference between eight and 54 per cent) to 23 percentage points in 2002 (the difference between 12 and 35 per cent).

So our age cohorts are no longer as distinctive as they were in 1986. The main explanation for this change lies with the cohorts entering and leaving the population. In particular, note that the very high proportion of authoritarians in the two eldest cohorts in 1986 has not been 'replaced' by changes in the cohorts immediately coming along behind them. If we look, for instance, at our oldest cohort in 1986 (those born in 1912 or earlier), we see that over half had values that placed them at the most authoritarian end of our scale. But this is not apparent at all in people of a similar age in 2002 (those born between 1921 and 1928), only just over a third of whom have views that place them in this most authoritarian group. This points towards a degree of generational change whereby older generations (particularly those born before or during the First World War), with their distinctive social values, are dying out and, as a result, social values overall are changing. Consequently, although age differences remain between our cohorts, they are becoming less pronounced over time.

But this is not the whole story: intriguingly, younger cohorts (particularly those born in the decades after the end of the Second World War) have become *more* authoritarian as they have aged. Take, for instance, those born in 1961–1968 who were aged 18–25 in 1986 and 34–41 in 2002; among this cohort, the percentage in the most authoritarian group increased by nine percentage points (even though the change among the population as a whole was in the opposite direction). This pattern is typical of a life-cycle effect, affecting people as they move from their 20s and 30s towards their 40s and 50s. This is intuitively plausible, suggesting that views on these matters held in one's youth can be modified over time by lifetime experiences in the period up to middle age (the table suggests that this applies particularly to views held in one's 20s!), but remain fairly stable after that. This phenomenon helps explain why, if we focus on the cohorts for whom we have two readings, the 'gap' between their views has shrunk over time.

In summary, therefore, we have found that education continues to relate closely to a person's libertarian/authoritarian values, as does income. However, age (which was once very closely associated with these values) is no longer significant once other factors are taken into account. As a result of these, and other, changes there has been a slight shift within the population as a whole away from the authoritarian 'extreme'.

The end of class values?

As seen in the next table, there have been considerable changes in the social class composition of Britain over the last two decades. In particular, the proportion of people in 'middle-class' jobs has increased, with the increase in 'salariat' (that is, professional and managerial occupations) being particularly notable. Indeed, the salariat is now the single largest social class. There has been a concomitant shrinkage in the proportion in the 'working class'.

These, and other changes, have lead some commentators to assert that class is now less important in Britain than was once the case. So we turn now to examine whether or not this is true in relation to social attitudes and values. Earlier we saw that class remains a significant factor in understanding left/right values in Britain – but perhaps its influence now is weaker than was the case in 1986?

Table 7.13 Class composition, 1986 and 2002

	1986	2002
	%	%
Salariat	22	32
Routine non-manual	22	23
Petty bourgeoisie	6	7
Manual foremen and technicians	6	7
Working class	34	29
Base	*3100*	*3424*

We begin by examining whether the differences between the values of different classes have changed over time. As the next table shows, over the period in which we are interested, there has been a shift away from the 'extreme' ends of our left/right value scale towards the centre, although the pattern to this differs depending upon the class in question. Among the salariat (which contains the highest proportion with very right-wing values), there has been a pronounced decline in the proportion at this end, down ten percentage points to 30 per cent. Among routine non-manual workers there has been a similar shift away from the right-wing end, while among the working class there has been a move away from the left-wing end of the scale, down eight points to 25 per cent. Despite this shift to the centre, however, the left/right values of the different classes remain pronounced.

Table 7.14 Left/right values and class, 1986 and 2002

	Salariat		Routine non-manual		Working class	
	1986	2002	1986	2002	1986	2002
	%	%	%	%	%	%
Left-wing	10	12	14	17	33	25
Middle ground	51	58	56	63	53	66
Right-wing	40	30	30	20	14	9
Base	*296*	*788*	*292*	*557*	*432*	*672*

Earlier we saw that income is also a good predictor of a person's left/right values. The next table shows that this was as true in 1986 as it is now, although it is notable that there has been a marked shift away from the right-wing end of our scale among those with the highest household incomes. In 1986, nearly half were found at this end of the scale; by 2002, this had shrunk to a third.

Table 7.15 Left/right values and income, 1986 and 2002

	Lowest quartile		2nd lowest		2nd highest		Highest quartile	
	1986	2002	1986	2002	1986	2002	1986	2002
	%	%	%	%	%	%	%	%
Left-wing	34	26	27	21	17	14	8	11
Middle	53	65	56	62	57	56	47	56
Right-wing	13	10	18	17	27	33	46	33
Base	*282*	*591*	*375*	*598*	*237*	*590*	*259*	*794*

As we have already discussed, the relationships between values and different measures of material advantage are complex and can only be disentangled by using multivariate models. We have already seen that, in 2002, social class, income and housing tenure were all independently related to left/right attitudes. When we compare these results with those from 1986 we find that, if anything, the impact of social class on left/right values is *stronger* now than was the case in 1986 (see model A in the appendix to this chapter). In particular, routine non-manual workers are now significantly more left-wing than the salariat, something that was not the case in 1986. This possibly reflects the changing nature of routine non-manual occupations, suggesting that those within them now have more in common with manual workers than they did in 1986. In both years income and housing tenure are also important, but there is no evidence to suggest that their importance has grown in size at the expense of social class distinctiveness.

Party politics

The last two decades have been marked by a considerable change in the political world, both in terms of the parties themselves and the ways in which the population engages with them (this is explored in detail in the chapter by Fisher and Curtice in this Report). In 1986, Britain was in its second term of a Conservative government, with many wondering whether the Labour Party could ever recover from its damning 1983 defeat; by 2002, we were in our second term of a Labour government, and similar debates were taking place about the ability of the Conservatives ever to recover. At the same time, there has been considerable concern in some quarters about the extent to which the Labour Party now appeals to less advantaged groups, originally seen as part of its 'natural' constituency.

Against this changing political backdrop, decreasing proportions of people are readily identifying with specific political parties. To measure this we ask people whether they consider themselves a *supporter* of a particular party, as *closer* to one party than to others, or as more likely to *vote* for a particular party than another were there a general election (for further details, see Appendix I to this Report). In 1986, just eight per cent of respondents said there was no political party which they would opt for in any of these situations; by 2002 this had risen to 13 per cent. Meanwhile, the proportion of people who identify *very strongly* with a particular party has fallen, from 11 per cent in 1987 to just five per cent in 2002 (Bromley and Curtice, 2002).

We turn now to examine the impact these changes have had on the relationship between left/right values and party support. We begin by examining whether particular party supporters have different profiles to the ones they had in 1986 – for instance, are Labour identifiers less 'left-wing' or working class than they were in 1986, or are Conservatives less 'right-wing' or middle class? Are some parties' supporters closer to each other than was the case sixteen years ago?

The next table shows that, in left/right terms at least, the values of different party identifiers have indeed become less distinct over time. In the case of Labour and Conservative identifiers, the proportion with views at the 'natural' end of the spectrum (that is, left for Labour and right for Conservatives) has shrunk markedly, reducing the gap between them, although a gap undoubtedly remains. In 1986, well over a third of Labour identifiers fell into our most left-wing category. This now applies to just under a quarter. The net effect of this is to bring the profiles of Labour and Liberal Democrat identifiers much closer together than was the case in 1986.

Table 7.16 Left/right values by party identification, 1986 and 2002

	Conservative		Labour		Liberal/SDP/ Liberal Democrat	
	1986	2002	1986	2002	1986	2002
	%	%	%	%	%	%
Left-wing	7	8	37	24	19	19
Middle ground	44	52	57	64	59	62
Right-wing	48	40	7	12	22	20
Base	441	712	461	1159	222	330

The next table shows that there have also been intriguing changes in the relationship between party support and libertarian/authoritarian values. In 1986, it was Labour identifiers who were the most likely to be at the most libertarian end of our scale; by 2002, this position was clearly occupied by Liberal Democrat identifiers. Whereas in 1986 one in five of those who identified with the Liberal or the Social Democratic Party (SDP), or the Alliance, had views that put them in our most libertarian category, by 2002 this was true of well over a quarter (28 per cent).

Table 7.17 Libertarian/authoritarian values by party identification, 1986 and 2002

	Conservative		Labour		Liberal/SDP/ Liberal Democrat	
	1986	2002	1986	2002	1986	2002
	%	%	%	%	%	%
Libertarian	6	7	23	20	19	28
Middle ground	62	69	56	62	56	56
Authoritarian	32	24	22	18	25	16
Base	*446*	*716*	*462*	*1161*	*222*	*331*

In order to consider whether the relationship between these value systems and political identity has changed over time, we carried out multivariate analysis (see model B in the appendix to this chapter). As mentioned earlier in the chapter, left/right values and, to a lesser extent, libertarian/authoritarian values were found to be strongly related to party identification in 2002. Not surprisingly, this was even more so in 1986. Put simply, if we know a person's left/right values, we can make an educated guess as to their party loyalties. In 2002, however, our guess would be more error-prone than in 1986, as for both Labour supporters and Conservatives the link between left/right values and party support is less strong now than it once was. The same is also true for libertarian/authoritarian values – though Labour supporters have less authoritarian values than Conservatives, this relationship is weaker than it was in 1986. We have thus identified a weakened link between values and party choice for the two main parties.

For Liberal Democrats, the picture is different, and confirms the earlier observations we made about Tables 7.16 and 7.17. Among this group, left-wing views used to be associated with party allegiance, but this is no longer the case; now it is their libertarian values which are most significant.

Once values are taken into account, class either disappears altogether or plays a lesser role as a significant predictor of a person's party support. (This was already the case in 1986.) This should not, however, necessarily be taken as a sign that class does not matter; rather, as suggested earlier, class will exert an indirect influence, by shaping the left/right values people hold and which, in turn, shape their party loyalties.

What of those who do *not* identify with a particular party? We find no evidence that the values of this group are becoming more distinctive; rather, there has been little change in either the left/right or libertarian/authoritarian profile of this group. Then, as now, around one in five have the most left-wing views, while 17 per cent have right-wing ones (a slight increase on the 14 per cent who did so in 1986). The lack of a relationship between either set of values and not identifying with a party means we can rule out the suggestion that at least a part of the reason for the decline in party identification over time reflects a disenchantment with traditional politics, and that those with distinctively left-wing or right-wing values are 'dropping out'.

However, we can detect *other* factors which are associated with lack of party identification. In both 1986 and 2002, age is strongly associated with *not* identifying with a particular party (see model B in the appendix to this chapter). But the influence of age has not got stronger over time, so its importance is unlikely to be an explanation for the increasing disenchantment with politics among the young. Rather, the age differences are likely to reflect the fact that party identification and loyalty take time to coalesce, in much the same way as a brand loyalty. What has changed, however, between these years is that non-identifiers in 2002 are more readily predictable than they were in 1986. In 1986, beyond age, there was very little else that would help predict a non-identifier. But by 2002, the working class, non-graduates and those on lower incomes were all more likely not to identify with a political party than were, respectively, the salariat, graduates and those in the top income quartile. This does point towards a danger of certain less privileged social groups becoming disengaged from politics, perhaps reflecting the current nature of political competition and the battle for 'middle England'. There is a danger that social exclusion becomes compounded as no party makes a clear appeal to these less advantaged social groups, and they in turn give up any attempt to shape their future via the political system.

Conclusions

Different social groups continue to have very distinct values when it comes to matters to do with 'left' and 'right' or 'authoritarianism' and 'libertarianism'. In some cases, however, there are signs that these social differences are less pronounced than was once the case. Where changes have occurred, they have tended to involve movement towards the centre ground, with a slight fall in the proportions with the most 'extreme' views. In this sense, therefore, British society is less polarised and more consensual than was the case two decades ago.

On matters of left and right, there is no sign at all that class is disappearing in its importance. Indeed, there is now a stronger relationship between class and left/right values than was the case in 1986, most notably because of divisions that have opened up within the middle class (as the views of routine non-manual workers and the salariat increasingly diverge). And, if the middle class continues to expand, it is possible that these divisions will become larger still, reflecting the increasingly divergent market positions and statuses of different middle-class occupations. However, it is clear that class is by no means the only influence on a person's values; rather, a range of other signs of material advantage play a role, even when class is taken into account. The most notable of these are income and housing tenure. This is not a new phenomenon, as both these characteristics were also important in 1986.

Class does not play an important role in accounting for libertarian/authoritarian values, however. Here it is education that matters the most, though (again) income also plays a role. These relationships have not changed very much over time. However, age (which was strongly related to these values in 1986) is no longer important, perhaps explaining the slight decrease over time we found in the proportion with the most authoritarian views, and hinting towards a further reduction in the future.

It is notable that income emerges as significantly related to a person's left/right and libertarian/authoritarian values, even when class and education are taken into account. Those on lower incomes tend to have more left-wing, and authoritarian, values than those on higher incomes. So, although there is no sign of class 'dying out', to try to explain a person's left/right values by relying upon class alone and not taking into account these other measures of material advantage would be foolhardy. Equally, it would be misleading only to take account of educational background when considering libertarian/authoritarian values; here, too, income matters. The fact that, as outlined in the chapter by Bromley in this Report, the last two decades have been marked by a considerable increase in both affluence and income inequality might go some way to explaining why income exerts such a strong influence on a person's values – and why its influence might increase in the future.

When we consider the value profiles of different party supporters we find evidence of a slight move to the centre, particularly among Labour and Conservative identifiers. So, although knowing a person's left/right values still helps us predict which of these parties he or she supports, it does so less well than it did in 1986. Here then, we do find some evidence of the value profiles of supporters of these two parties drawing closer, undoubtedly reflecting the changing nature of British politics over the last two decades. It is also notable that, although left/right values might be the bread and butter of British party politics, libertarian/authoritarian values also have an important role to play. This is particularly true for Conservative identifiers (whose values tend to lie at the more authoritarian end of the spectrum) and Liberal Democrats (whose values tend to be more libertarian). Indeed, the distinctiveness of Liberal Democrats rests entirely in their libertarian/authoritarian profile; their left/right values are no longer distinctive enough to help explain their party support.

What changes might we expect to see in the values held by different party supporters? To some extent, this will depend upon the movements of the particular parties on left/right issues. In particular, if the Labour and Conservative parties shift further away from one another, we might expect to find their supporters' values diverging once again. Equally, parties could begin to try to appeal to the distinctive libertarian/authoritarian values of their potential supporters. This would bring a different set of issues to the forefront of British politics, but could prove very divisive because of the way in which opinion on these sorts of issues cuts across the left/right divide which has tended to characterise British political debate to date.

Reassuringly, perhaps, there is no sign that the decline in party identification is caused by people with distinctive value profiles abandoning the party system (for example, those who are left- or right-wing). On the other hand, they are becoming distinctive in their socio-economic background, with those from less advantaged backgrounds now being notably less likely than other groups not to identify with any party at all.

Left/right and libertarian/authoritarian values remain of key importance in helping form social, political and moral judgements. True, in some cases, the values held by different social groups have shifted in such a way as to bring them closer together rather than further apart. But it is unlikely that the distinctive values held by particular groups will disappear completely; whether a person tends more towards left or right, or towards libertarianism or authoritarianism is likely to continue playing a crucial role in shaping the way in which they respond to the social world around them.

Notes

1. For a full discussion of these scales and their stability and derivation see Heath *et al.*, 1994.
2. For the left/right scale, we focus on the 18 per cent in 2002 who *agree* with all or most of the statements shown in Table 7.1 (those with the most left-wing values) and on the 21 per cent who *disagree* with all or most of them (those with the most right-wing values). For the libertarian/authoritarian scale, we focus upon the 19 per cent in 2002 who *agree* with all or most of the statements in Table 7.2 (the most authoritarian) and the 17 per cent who *disagree* with all or most of them (the most libertarian). We deliberately defined these groups so that each represented approximately the fifth of the 2002 sample whose views placed them at the extreme ends of our scale. (Consequently, this should not be taken as implying that one-fifth of the British public is, for instance, left-wing and one fifth right-wing). In order to measure change in beliefs over time, we used the same scale value cut-offs to identify the 'extreme' groups in 1986. (Hence they do not necessarily make up a fifth of the population in 1986.)
3. The standardised coefficients for income and social class are of a similar magnitude in all years. However, for social class the key division is between manual and non-manual occupations, rather than a gradual shift across the social class spectrum. For income, the relationship is a more gradual move to the right of the scale as income increases.
4. The questions were also asked in the self-completion supplement, which should make respondents less vulnerable to social pressures when answering them.
5. It should be noted that one social group coefficient is significant in this model, that of manual foremen and technician who are significantly more likely to tend to the authoritarian end of the scale than the reference category (in this case, the salariat), while the rest of the working class are not.
6. Our regression models use two age bands only. However, separate analyses confirm that, even when more finely graded age bands are used, the importance of age as a predictor of libertarian/authoritarian values declined markedly between 1986 and 2002.

References

Adorno, T.W., Frenkel-Bunswick, E., Levinson, D. and Sanford, R.N. (1950), *The Authoritarian Personality*, New York: Harper.

Ahrendt, D. and Young, K. (1994), 'Authoritarianism updated', in Jowell, R., Curtice, J., Park, A., Brook, L. and Ahrendt, D. (eds.), *British Social Attitudes: the 11th Report*, Aldershot: Dartmouth.

Alwin, D. and Scott, J. (1996), 'Attitude change: its measurement and interpretation using longitudinal surveys', in Taylor, B. and Thomson, K. (eds.), *Understanding Change in Social Attitudes*, Aldershot: Dartmouth.

Bromley, C. and Curtice, J. (2002), 'Where have all the voters gone?', in Park, A., Curtice, J., Thomson, K., Jarvis, L. and Bromley, C. (eds.), *British Social Attitudes: the 19th Report*, London: Sage.

Clark, T. and Lipset, S. (1996), 'Are social classes dying?', in Lee, D. and Turner, B. (eds.), *Conflicts about Class*, London: Longman.

Converse, P. (1964), 'The nature of belief systems', in Apter, D. (ed.), *Ideology and Discontent*, NewYork: Free Press.

Evans, G. (2000), 'The working class and New Labour: a parting of the ways?', in Jowell, R., Park, A., Curtice, J., Thomson, K., Jarvis, L., Bromley, C. and Stratford, N. (eds.), *British Social Attitudes: the 17th Report – Focusing on Diversity*, London: Sage.

Goldthorpe, J. (1987), *Social Mobility and Class Structure in Britain*, 2nd edition, Oxford: Clarendon.

Heath, A., Evans, G., and Martin, J. (1994), 'The measurement of core beliefs and value', *British Journal of Political Science*, **24**.

Heath, A., Jowell, R. and Curtice, J. (2001), *The Rise of New Labour*, Oxford: Oxford University Press.

Heath, A. and Martin, J. (1997), 'Why are there so few formal measuring instruments in social and political research', CREST Working Paper, 58, www.crest.ox.ac.uk/papers.

Lipset, S. (1981), *Political Man: The Social Bases of Politics*, London: Heinemann.

Pakulski, J. and Waters, M. (1996), *The Death of Class*, London: Sage.

Phelan, J., Link, B., Stueve, A. and Moore, R. (1995), 'Education, Social Liberalism and Economic Conservatism' *American Sociological Review*, **60(1)**: 126–140

Sanders, D. (1999), 'The impact of left/right ideology', in Evans, G. and Norris, P. (eds.), *Critical Elections*, London: Sage.

Appendix

The models referred to in the chapter follow. In all cases we used multiple regression, a technique explained more fully in Appendix I to this Report. The following tables present the coefficients (or parameter estimates) for each model. These show whether a particular characteristic differs significantly from its 'comparison group'. For each characteristic included in the model, details of its comparison group are shown in brackets (so, for example, the comparison group for education is graduates). A positive coefficient indicates that those with the characteristic score more highly than the comparison group on the dependent variable (for example, left/right values) and a negative coefficient indicates that they are likely to have a lower score. Two asterisks indicate that the coefficient is statistically significant at a 99 per cent level, and one asterisk that it is significant at a 95 per cent level.

Model A Left/right and libertarian/authoritarian values, 1986 and 2002

The dependent variables for these models were a person's score on the two value dimensions. The scales are scored so that higher values denote more right-wing or authoritarian values, and lower values more left-wing or libertarian ones.

	Left/right values		Libertarian/ authoritarian values	
	1986	2002	1986	2002
Constant	-0.026	-0.479	3.077	3.023
Educational level (degree)				
Higher ed., below degree	0.108	0.109	0.424**	0.389**
A level	-0.027	0.082	0.282**	0.371**
O level/CSE	-0.097	0.060	0.501**	0.547**
No qualifications	-0.210	-0.067	0.552**	0.615**
Income quartile (highest quartile)				
Lowest quartile	-0.432**	-0.345**	0.173**	0.091*
Second quartile	-0.437**	-0.311**	0.138*	0.186**
Third quartile	-0.285**	-0.187**	0.102	0.080*
Social class (salariat)				
Routine non-manual	-0.091	-0.154**	0.092	-0.042
Petty bourgeoisie	0.070	0.074	0.142	0.096
Manual foremen	-0.382**	-0.390**	0.044	0.189**
Working class	-0.395**	-0.316**	0.027	0.034
Religion (no religion)				
Church of England	0.106	0.217**	0.290**	0.218**
Roman Catholic	-0.074	0.022	0.189**	0.109*
Other	-0.068	0.058	0.162**	0.166**
Housing tenure (non-owner)	0.141*	0.136**	0.079	0.053
Gender (male)	0.147**	0.117**	-0.025	-0.006
Age (over 35)	-0.102	0.178**	-0.259**	-0.030
Weighted base	*965*	*1875*	*965*	*1875*

Model B Party support, 1986 and 2002

The dependent variables in the first three models are whether a person identifies with the party in question (as opposed to not identifying with it). For the final model, the dependent variable is whether a person has *no* party identification at all (as opposed to having one).

	Conservative identity		Labour identity	
	1986	2002	1986	2002
Constant	-0.491	-1.898	-1.442	-0.122
Left/right values	1.365**	0.998**	-1.254**	-0.626**
Libertarian/authoritarian values	0.974**	0.826**	-0.830**	-0.257**
Educational level (degree)				
Higher ed., below degree	0.144	-0.136	0.010	0.026
A level	0.705	0.325	-0.156	-0.331
O level/CSE	0.588	0.043	-0.179	-0.270
No qualifications	0.235	-0.198	0.406	0.031
Income quartile (highest quartile)				
Lowest quartile	-0.351	-0.067	0.568*	0.034
Second quartile	-0.515*	-0.024	0.443	-0.212
Third quartile	-0.151	0.039	0.175	0.012
Social class (salariat)				
Routine non-manual	-0.220	-0.017	0.434	0.131
Petty bourgeoisie	0.288	0.294	0.439	-0.343
Manual foremen	-0.186	-0.304	1.006**	0.487
Working class	-0.388	-0.426*	0.613*	0.165
Religion (no religion)				
Church of England	0.212	0.748**	-0.047	-0.326
Roman Catholic	-0.210	0.011	0.389	0.537
Other	-0.122	0.475**	-0.278	-0.309
Housing tenure (non-owner)	0.185	0.794**	-0.213	-0.287
Gender (male)	-0.137	-0.040	-0.053	0.220
Age (over 35)	-0.255	-0.716**	0.201	0.182
Weighted base	*965*	*1875*	*965*	*1875*

	Liberal/Alliance identity		No party identity	
	1986	**2002**	**1986**	**2002**
Constant	-0.917	-1.127	-4.575	-3.375
Left/right values	-0.272*	-0.123	0.053	-0.132
Libertarian/authoritarian values	-0.156	-0.533**	0.139	0.043
Educational level (degree)				
Higher ed., below degree	-0.097	-0.486	0.232	1.249**
A level	-0.745	-0.216	1.050	0.897*
O level/CSE	-0.536	-0.332	1.027	1.385**
No qualifications	-0.930*	-0.363	1.160	1.329**
Income quartile (highest quartile)				
Lowest quartile	-0.324	-0.339	0.687	0.536*
Second quartile	0.020	0.293	0.690	0.346
Third quartile	-0.182	-0.450*	1.017*	0.578**
Social class (salariat)				
Routine non-manual	-0.076	-0.320	0.237	0.341
Petty bourgeoisie	-0.910	-0.137	0.342	0.305
Manual foremen	-1.357*	-0.537	0.684	0.189
Working class	-0.349	-0.157	0.621	0.490*
Religion (no religion)				
Church of England	0.279	0.394*	-1.157**	-0.942*
Roman Catholic	-0.093	-0.263	-0.258	-0.767*
Other	0.466	0.353	0.019	-0.214
Housing tenure (non-owner)	0.342	-0.001	-0.411	-0.230
Gender (male)	0.058	-0.118	0.391	-0.300
Age (Over 35)	-0.250	-0.066	0.706**	0.735**
Weighted base	*965*	*1875*	*965*	*1875*

8 A woman's place... Employment and family life for men and women

Rosemary Crompton, Michaela Brockmann and Richard D. Wiggins [*]

This chapter examines the impact of one of the most important social changes that has taken place over the last 20 years – the changes in the aspirations and economic behaviour of women, particularly mothers. In Britain, women's labour force participation rates have been rising since the 1950s and stood at 66 per cent in 1984. The rate then increased markedly during the 1980s to 71 per cent in 1990. During the 1990s, overall women's participation rates were rather more stable, reaching 72 per cent by 2001, but the participation rates of mothers with young children changed rapidly. In 1990, the economic activity rate amongst mothers with a child under 5 was 48 per cent but by 2001 this had risen to 57 per cent. In contrast, men's participation rates have been falling, from 88 per cent in the 1980s to 84 per cent by 2001 (Dench *et al.*, 2002).

It is not only employment levels amongst women that are changing, but their occupational location – that is, the kinds of jobs they do. Young women are now achieving the same (or better) educational qualifications as men. Among the over 55 age group, men are twice as likely to have a degree as women. In the years since this group left full-time education in the 1960s or earlier, qualification levels have risen rapidly among both men and women, but faster among women. In the 25–34 age group, there is practically no difference: 20 per cent of women, and 22 per cent of men, have a university degree (Dench *et al.*, 2002).

Changes in women's employment patterns are the outcome of a complex set of factors including technological advances (such as efficient contraception), changes in legislation (such as the Sex Discrimination and Equal Pay Acts, from 1976 onwards), and, as we have seen, rising levels of education and qualifications amongst women. These 'material' factors are closely intertwined

[*] Rosemary Crompton is Professor of Sociology at City University; Michaela Brockmann is a Research Officer at City University; and Richard D. Wiggins is Professor of Social Statistics at City University.

with normative changes – both in women's aspirations and in the attitudes to gender roles and gender relations which have been associated with second-wave feminism. In parallel with these social and cultural transformations, the changes in labour markets and the structure of employment – the relative decline of manufacturing jobs, the growth of service employment – have led to a substantial increase in the numbers and proportion of jobs conventionally carried out by women. For example, while the proportion of jobs in manufacturing fell from 23 per cent to 18 per cent between 1984 and 1999, the service sector expanded from 63 per cent to 73 per cent (TUC, 2000).

As many commentators have noted, changes in women's employment have progressively transformed the 'male breadwinner' model of employment and family life, where men were assumed to take the major responsibility for market work ('breadwinning') whilst women took the major responsibility for home and family life (i.e. unpaid care-giving) (Rubery, 1988; Lewis, 1992; Crompton, 1999). The male breadwinner model was associated with characteristic patterns of employment (for example, 'standard' employment was considered to be full-time employment), and underpinned a range of institutional arrangements, from school hours to pensions and the delivery of health and welfare services (Esping-Andersen, 1990). This gender/welfare arrangement has been described by Crouch as the "mid [20th] century social compromise" (1999: 53).

We may now anticipate a wide range of changes in institutions, as well as in the domestic sphere, as individuals and families, organisations and governments adjust to the realities of women's employment. In some important respects, however, the pattern of women's employment has not been transformed to the extent that might have been expected given the proportional and numerical increase of women in the labour force. Research on occupational segregation has documented a long history of direct and indirect discrimination against women within organisations (Crompton, 1997). Although such discrimination undoubtedly persists, there can also be little doubt that it is much less prevalent than it once was. More persistent, however – and probably more resistant to change – are the difficulties faced by women in combining employment with their conventionally assigned family responsibilities, particularly the care of children. Childcare and other domestic responsibilities are clearly reflected in the pattern of women's employment, which remains very different to that of men despite the increase in women's economic activity. Thus 44 per cent of British women work part-time, compared to only nine per cent of men.

In this chapter, we shall focus in particular on how changes in attitudes to gender roles, and related issues such as maternal employment, have run in parallel with changes in women's working patterns since 1989. We shall also examine the important issues of the extent to which there have been changes in the allocation between men and women of unpaid work in the home, and whether attitudinal changes vary between people in different age groups. Finally, we shall examine in greater depth evidence from the most recent *British Social Attitudes* survey on the important and contemporary issue of work–life 'balance', which has recently become the focus of considerable government attention (e.g. DTI 2000, 2003).

The data for this chapter are drawn from the *International Social Survey Programme* which, in Britain, forms part of the *British Social Attitudes* questionnaire. Questions on family and gender roles have been asked in 1989, 1994 and 2002. Some, but not all, of the questions have been repeated in each survey, allowing us to examine change over time. (See Appendix I to this Report for more information about the *International Social Survey Programme*.) In 2002, the British module was augmented by additional questions on career aspirations and workplace experiences.

The changing face of women's employment

Changes in the economic activity of mothers

From the 1970s, economic activity has gradually risen amongst mothers, including mothers of young children, so that "... by the end of the 1980s it had become the norm for working women to be economically active again within nine months of having a baby" (McRae, 1996: viii). Since the Employment Protection Act of 1979, this has been accompanied by improvements in entitlements to maternity leave (and rights). Research suggests that the proportion of mothers returning to work within a year of giving birth rose from about one-quarter in 1979 to around two-thirds in 1996 (Callender *et al.*, 1997).

These changes are clearly reflected in our data. The next table shows that the proportion of mothers reporting that they themselves had stayed at home with a pre-school child declined from over three-fifths in 1989 to under half in 2002. (These figures include older women whose child-rearing lies many years in the past.)

Table 8.1 Own working patterns when child(ren) were under school age, 1989–2002

	1989	1994	2002
	%	%	%
Full-time	8	15	14
Part-time	28	27	34
At home	62	52	48
Base	*430*	*408*	*811*

Base: women only.

Meanwhile the proportion of couples where the man was the sole breadwinner fell from a third (31 per cent) in 1989 to one in six (17 per cent) in 2002, with a corresponding rise in the proportion of households where both partners were economically active from a half (50 per cent) to three-fifths (61 per cent).

Changes in attitudes to working mothers

Changes in women's employment have run in parallel with changing attitudes to gender roles. As the employment of women (especially mothers) has been rising, the next table shows that there has been a steady decline, among both men and women, in the proportion of respondents who take the view that "a man's job is to earn money, a woman's is to look after the home and family". Whereas around a third of men took this view in 1989, this is now down to a fifth. The corresponding change among women has been from a quarter to one in seven. Note, however, that men still hold more traditional views than women.

Table 8.2 "A man's job is to earn money; a woman's job is to look after the home and family", 1989–2002

% who agree	1989	Base	1994	Base	2002	Base
Men	32	587	26	448	20	852
Women	26	720	21	536	15	1108
All	28	1307	24	984	17	1960

It is not unusual to find, however, that while general attitudes are changing, respondents confronted with specific situations fall back into a more traditional pattern of responses. We therefore need to check whether the pattern holds for specific questions linked to gender roles, such as attitudes to childcare. We look first at the question of whether mothers should stay at home when their children are under school age. As the next table shows, attitudes to this question show a pattern of change similar to attitudes on the male breadwinner model: the proportions of men and women who think mothers of young children should stay at home have declined substantially so that under half the population now take that view (down from almost two-thirds). Nevertheless, men still hold views that are more traditional than those of women.

Table 8.3 Women should stay at home when there is a child under school age, 1989–2002

% who think women should stay at home	1989	Base	1994	Base	2002	Base
Men	67	587	60	448	51	852
Women	61	720	51	536	46	1108
All	64	1307	55	984	48	1960

However, when looking at the proportion of respondents who think that a working mother can establish just as warm and secure a relationship with her child as a mother who does not work, the trend is much more muted – and there is no real change between 1994 and 2002. However, over half the population already thought in 1989 that working mothers were able to establish warm and secure relationships.

Table 8.4 "A working mother can establish just as warm and secure a relationship with her children as a mother who does not work", 1989–2002

% who agree	1989	Base	1994	Base	2002	Base
Men	51	587	57	448	58	852
Women	63	720	69	536	69	1108
All	58	1307	63	984	64	1960

Household tasks

It is commonplace to comment that although changes in women's employment behaviour have been considerable, changes in the responsibilities for household tasks have lagged behind – women are still responsible for, and carry out, a disproportionate amount of household work (Gershuny et al., 1994; Sullivan, 2000).

Unfortunately, our analysis is here limited by the absence of questions asked in all three years. Working with the data that we have got, the next table shows a substantial change in attitudes between 1989 and 1994: in 1989 over four-fifths of respondents said that, within their relationship, household duties were always or usually the responsibility of the woman. By 1994 this had fallen to less than three-quarters. Reported responsibilities for childcare had changed even more. It should be noted, however, that men were considerably more likely than women to report that household duties and childcare were 'shared', and in 1994, the discrepancies between men and women in the reporting of responsibilities for household tasks and childcare were much wider than in 1989.

Although we are forced to use a different set of questions to look at change over the period 1994 to 2002, the impression is that the pace of change has slowed. For example, the proportion of women who said that they usually did the laundry was not significantly different in the two years. Shopping for groceries actually showed a reverse trend – but it has to be said that the difference is not statistically significant.

Although we cannot be conclusive from this data about the extent of change over time in the division of household tasks between men and women, we can carry the analysis forward by looking at the patterning of domestic work. Not surprisingly, this is significantly shaped by the distribution of employment between men and women. Table 8.5 divides couples according to whether both partners are in employment or economically inactive, and also identifies couples where there is a 'male breadwinner' or 'female breadwinner'. On both of the household tasks examined, women are most likely to carry them out in male breadwinner households, less likely to have responsibility for them in dual earner households, and least likely either to do the laundry or to shop for groceries in female breadwinner households (although the number of couples where the woman is the breadwinner is rather too small to draw any firm conclusions). Given the decline over time in the number of 'male breadwinner' households, this pattern indicates the growth of a somewhat more equitable sharing of household tasks in the future.

Table 8.5 Distribution of household tasks within couples, 1989–2002

% saying always or usually the woman's responsibility …	1989	Base	1994	Base	2002	Base
Household duties						
Men	78	587	63	448	n/a	
Women	86	720	80	536	n/a	
All	82	1307	72	984	n/a	
Childcare						
Men	79	587	58	448	n/a	
Women	87	720	79	536	n/a	
All	83	1307	69	984	n/a	
Laundry						
Men	n/a		77	448	78	852
Women	n/a		84	536	82	1108
All	n/a		81	984	81	1960
Shopping for groceries						
Men	n/a		39	448	43	852
Women	n/a		45	536	49	1108
All	n/a		42	984	46	1960

Base: respondents who are married or living as married.
n/a = not asked

Our review of changes over time, therefore, shows a mixed picture. General attitudes to men's and women's roles in employment and domestic work appear to be changing in parallel with the actual changes in women's employment. As our data do not follow the same respondents over time, we cannot be certain whether changes in attitude are the result of changes in behaviour, rather than the other way round. But other analysis, drawing on the longitudinal *British Household Panel Study*, suggests that this is likely to be the case (Himmelweit and Sigala, 2003). However, our data on domestic work suggests that there has not been as much change here, and women are still much more likely to be responsible for household tasks – although less so if woman is economically active.

Table 8.6 Distribution of household tasks between men and women by economic status of household

	Both economi-cally active	Male bread-winner	Female bread-winner	Both economi-cally inactive	Total
% saying woman always or usually does the laundry	79	89	70	84	81
Base	*559*	*168*	*38*	*193*	*958*
% saying woman always or usually does the shopping for groceries	46	56	37	40	46
Base	*564*	*166*	*38*	*189*	*957*

Base: respondents who are married or living as married.

Attitudes to working mothers, particularly those with young children, are also changing – although here, the trend is less pronounced, and much of the change occurred between 1989 and 1994 with less change since then. As we have seen, women's participation rates increased very rapidly in the 1980s and stabilised somewhat during the 1990s, and it is likely that the apparent slowing down of the rate of attitudinal change reflects this fact. The next table reveals a similar slowing down or even reversal of changing attitudes towards the impact of women working on family life in general – perhaps as the pressures of women's employment on the family have begun to be experienced by an increasing number of people.

**Table 8.7 "All in all, family life suffers when the woman has a full-time job",
1989–2002**

% who agree	1989	*Base*	1994	*Base*	2002	*Base*
Men	45	*587*	32	*448*	36	*852*
Women	39	*720*	33	*536*	34	*1108*
All	42	*1307*	32	*984*	35	*1960*

Hence it would seem that the erosion of the male breadwinner model has resulted in continuing – perhaps even increasing – pressures on family life. Later on in this chapter we shall explore the topic of work–life articulation, but first we shall examine another important question: whether changes in attitudes to gender roles are likely to be permanent or not. In order to do this we must investigate the different rates of attitudinal change between different age groups.

Changes in economic behaviour between different age groups of women

We begin by examining the extent to which women of different ages have varied in their actual economic behaviour when their children were young. As we have seen in our previous discussion, women's employment rates have changed very rapidly. This is graphically illustrated in the next table by the proportion of mothers in different age groups reporting that they stayed at home when their children were under school age. The percentage of women up to the age of 30 'staying at home' has fallen dramatically (by more than 20 percentage points) between 1989 and 2002. But the reported behaviour of women aged 57 or over shows much less difference over the three surveys. This is to be expected as, in 2002, most women in this age group would have been looking after their pre-school children in the 1970s or before.

Table 8.8 Proportion of women reporting they "stayed at home" when their youngest child was under school age, 1989–2002

Age in survey year	1989	Base	1994	Base	2002	Base
18–30	59	48	33	54	36	59
31–43	51	146	45	118	34	244
44–56	69	132	56	90	47	193
57+	72	103	66	146	64	313
All	62	430	52	408	48	811

Changes in gender role attitudes – lifecycle, period or cohort effect?

As we shall see, there are (declining) attitudinal differences between different age groups, but the *causes* of differences in attitudes between age groups are rather complicated to disentangle. Older people tend, in general, to be rather more 'traditional' than younger people. This may in part be because of the effect of age itself and lifetime experiences. If so, we would expect individuals to become more 'traditional' as they become older. This is known as a *lifecycle effect*. Another factor contributing to the greater traditionalism of older people might be their primary socialisation during a more traditional era. Attitudes to gender roles (and related issues such as sexual behaviour) changed very rapidly, particularly amongst the young, in the 1960s and 1970s. However, older respondents would have initially been socialised in relation to gender and sexual roles and mores in the 1930s, 1940s, and 1950s, and we might expect them to carry these more traditional views with them throughout life, whereas the younger respondents might be expected to retain their more liberal views as they age. This is known as a *cohort effect*. Then again, there may be external events which change the views of people of all ages at the same time. These are known as *period effects*.

Either a lifecycle effect or a cohort effect would show up in the data as differences in attitudes between different age groups at any one particular point in time. However, if age differences in attitudes are primarily the result of a life-cycle effect, there is no particular reason for thinking that attitudes will grow more liberal over time: old people dying off are simply replaced by other people who become more traditional as they age. If, however, the age differences in attitudes are primarily the result of a cohort effect we would expect change in a more liberal direction to continue over time as more traditional groups of people die off and are replaced by more liberal groups.

Although these effects cannot be precisely disentangled in data of this sort, we can gain a good indication of the effects at work by a method called cohort analysis. This involves comparing change within each 'cohort' of respondents (born in particular years) with change across cohorts of respondents.[1] Tables 8.9 and 8.10, therefore, compare the attitudes of people with the same birth dates interviewed in the successive surveys – for example, someone aged 31 in 1989 would have been aged 36 if they had been interviewed in 1994, and 44 if interviewed in 2002. Reading across the table allows us to track the attitudes of the same 'cohort' over time. Total figures, indicating the broad trends in attitudinal change amongst the population over the three surveys, have also been given in the tables.

One question we need to examine is whether attitudes towards women's employment are shaped by respondents' own experiences. If so, we might expect to find two things:

- older women to be more traditional than younger women and

- attitudes to have changed more rapidly among younger women who are the ones with most experience of working while having young children.

Looking at the first of these hypotheses, there are, in fact, substantial differences in attitudes by age. For example, in Table 8.9 we can see that in 2002 over four-fifths of women aged 30 or under disagree with the male breadwinner model, while in the 70 or above age group, this falls to under a third. Similarly, in Table 8.10, we see that under a third of women aged 30 or below think that a woman should stay at home while she has pre-school children, but this rises to two-thirds among those aged 70 or above.

Table 8.9 "A man's job is to earn money; a woman's job is to look after the home and family", by age cohort, 1989–2002

% who disagree		1989		1994			2002		
Birth cohort	Age in 1989		Base	Age in 1994		Base	Age in 2002		Base
All		53	1307		58	984		63	1960
All men		47	587		56	448		58	852
1972–1984		n.a.			n.a.		18–30	77	149
1959–1971	18–30	68	150	23–35	73	140	31–43	67	224
1946–1958	31–43	63	130	36–48	69	99	44–56	64	189
1933–1945	44–56	47	123	49–61	46	87	57–69	40	158
Pre 1933	57+	15	184	62+	21	103	70+	26	132
All women		58	720		60	536		67	1108
1972–1984		n.a.			n.a.		18–30	83	187
1959–1971	18–30	79	177	23–35	75	155	31–43	77	316
1946–1958	31–43	76	192	36–48	72	120	44–56	73	224
1933–1945	44–56	48	144	49–61	42	96	57–69	51	210
Pre 1933	57+	28	204	62+	32	139	70+	32	168

n.a. = not applicable

The total figures in Tables 8.9 and 8.10 also confirm what we have already seen – namely that there has been considerable change over time in these attitudes among both men and women.

Tables 8.9 and 8.10 allow us to follow the attitudinal changes, in successive surveys, amongst people born at the same time. So, reading across the rows of Table 8.9 we see that there has been very little change within each age group – for example, among women born in 1959 to 1971, who were aged 18 to 30 in 1989, an overwhelming majority of 79 per cent already rejected the male breadwinner model in 1989. Among this group, the figure is virtually unchanged at 77 per cent in 2002. This combination of overall attitude change in the population at large combined with little or no change within particular cohorts is characteristic of a cohort effect. This suggests that attitudes across women in the population as a whole will continue to become more liberal as cohorts socialised in more recent years replace those socialised in the 1950s or earlier.

But this is not necessarily the end of the story. Although the differences are not statistically significant, Table 8.9 suggests that older women seem to have changed their views *more* than younger women and in a more *liberal* direction. For example, of women born before 1932, 28 per cent disagreed with traditional gender roles in 1989, but by 2002 this figure had *risen* to 32 per cent. Hence the age differences across the population have narrowed between 1989 and 2002.[2]

This is not what we would expect from our second hypothesis: if attitudes are changing as a result of personal experience, we would expect younger cohorts to have changed their attitudes more than older cohorts. Moreover, the same pattern can be observed for men, with older cohorts becoming more liberal while younger cohorts have unchanged views.[3] This may suggest a period effect, where all age groups are subject to changes in attitudes. Perhaps the change in economic activity by women is simply so pervasive that it affects attitudes of everyone in society, whether they are directly involved or not.

These trends are even more apparent in relation to the question of whether a woman should work when she has pre-school children (Table 8.10). Here, as indicated by the total figures, we see a substantial move in a more liberal direction among both men and women over the period 1989 to 2002, yet a much smaller change within each particular cohort, suggesting a cohort effect. Where there *is* a significant within-cohort change it is among the older age cohorts (men and women), who are uniformly becoming more liberal. For example, whereas in 1989 74 per cent of women born between 1933 and 1945 agreed that a woman should stay at home with her children when they were under school age, by 1994 this had declined to 63 per cent, and by 2002, to 58 per cent. Although age differences persist, they have narrowed since 1989.

Table 8.10 A woman should stay at home when there are children under school age, by age cohort, 1989–2002

% who agree		1989			1994			2002	
Birth cohort	**Age in 1989**		*Base*	**Age in 1994**		*Base*	**Age in 2002**		*Base*
All		64	*1307*		55	*984*		48	*1960*
All men		67	*587*		60	*448*		51	*852*
1972–1984		n.a			n.a		18–30	38	149
1959–1971	18–30	48	*150*	23–35	43	*140*	31–43	40	*224*
1946–1958	31–43	50	*130*	36–48	60	*99*	44–56	58	*189*
1933–1945	44–56	81	*123*	49–61	69	*87*	57–69	58	*158*
Pre 1933	57+	85	*184*	62+	77	*103*	70+	70	*132*
All women		61	*720*		51	*536*		46	*1108*
1972–1984		n.a			n.a		18–30	32	187
1959–1971	18–30	46	*177*	23–35	33	*155*	31–43	37	*316*
1946–1958	31–43	50	*192*	36–48	52	*120*	44–56	48	*224*
1933–1945	44–56	74	*144*	49–61	63	*96*	57–69	58	*210*
Pre 1933	57+	77	*204*	62+	63	*139*	70+	66	*168*

n.a. = not applicable

The evidence reviewed in Tables 8.8 to 8.10, therefore, indicates that changes in women's employment patterns are closely reflected in changing attitudes to working women and gender roles and that these changes are permeating society through several different mechanisms. To the extent that there is a cohort effect in operation, we would expect the change to continue as younger, more liberal, age cohorts replace older, more traditional, ones. To the extent that attitudes are changing most rapidly amongst older men and women – even though their own domestic arrangements when their children were young are likely to have been 'gender stereotypical' – we would expect the more liberal attitudes to both women's economic behaviour and gender role attitudes to be permanent features of society. Thus the necessity to address the topic of the next section of this paper – the articulation of work (i.e. employment) and family life – is becoming ever more urgent.

Work–life articulation

In this section, we shall examine more closely the important and contemporary topic of work–life balance or articulation. In policy discussions, the term usually employed is 'work–life balance'. However, we prefer the more neutral term, 'work–life articulation', not least because – as shall be seen – our evidence suggests that many women and men who combine employment and family life fail to achieve a 'balance'. Our discussion will demonstrate that, despite the recent 'official' recognition of this topic and its importance in recent policy developments, there remain significant issues that have yet to be resolved.

In 2002, the *International Social Survey Programme* included a series of direct questions on work–life stress. The extent of work–life stress varies with the extent of employment, and part-time employees are considerably less likely to report stress than full-time employees. For example, only just over two-fifths (43 per cent) of part-time women, but two-thirds (65 per cent) of those who worked full-time, said that they sometimes found it difficult to fulfil their family responsibilities because of the demands of their job. We shall focus, therefore, on full-time employees in our discussion since this is where the greatest problem seems to lie.

In particular, we shall be using two sets of questions to explore the topic of work–life 'balance'. In the first set 'home' and 'work' stress were addressed separately through a series of statements with which respondents were invited to agree or disagree:

> *There are so many things to do at home, I often run out of time before I get them all done*

> *My life at home is rarely stressful*

> *There are so many things to do at work, I often run out of time before I get them all done*

> *My job is rarely stressful*

In the second set of questions, 'work' and 'home' were directly juxtaposed – that is, the respondent was required to adjudicate between their own perceptions of the demands of the two spheres. They were asked how often each of the following things had happened in the last three months:

> *I have come home from work too tired to do the chores which need to be done*

> *It has been difficult for me to fulfil my family responsibilities because of the amount of time I spend on my job*

> *I have arrived at work too tired to function well because of the household work I had done*

> *I have found it difficult to concentrate at work because of my family responsibilities*

In general, respondents were more likely to find their working lives stressful than their home lives. For example, whereas almost half (47 per cent of men, and 43 per cent of women), agreed that their lives at home were rarely stressful, only around a fifth (22 per cent of men, and 19 percent of women) thought that their jobs were rarely stressful. However, in relation to work–life stress, women appeared to experience higher levels than men. The next table shows that whereas a fifth of men frequently arrived at home from work too tired to do chores, over a third of full-time women were in this position. This question showed the greatest difference between men and women of any of this set of questions – no doubt a reflection of continuing sex imbalances in the domestic division of labour.

Table 8.11 Proportion who have arrived home from work too tired to do the chores which needed to be done (in the last three months)

		Several times a week	Several times a month	Once or twice	Never	Base
Men	%	22	32	36	10	406
Women	%	35	29	32	4	334
All	%	28	30	34	8	740

Base: full-time employees.

Family 'spill over' into work seems to be less of a problem (over half of respondents saying that this had never happened in the last three months). But when it does happen, it seems to affect women more than men, as seen in the next table.

Table 8.12 Proportion who have found it difficult to concentrate at work because of family responsibilities (in the last three months)

		Several times a week	Several times a month	Once or twice	Never	Base
Men	%	1	4	35	57	393
Women	%	2	5	48	45	313
All	%	2	5	41	52	706

Base: full-time employees.

The remaining questions in this set (arriving too tired at work because of family responsibilities and difficulties in fulfilling family responsibilities because of the amount of time at work) show little difference in aggregate between the sexes. However, as we shall see later, there are interesting within-sample variations (by sex, class and individual aspirations) in the answers to these questions.

Difficulties in achieving work–life 'balance' will be the outcome of a number of factors. Workplace factors will obviously include long working hours. Some jobs will be more pressured than others, and some employers more understanding than others. People with children at home are more likely to experience problems than those who have no children, or whose children are grown up. Individuals who are seeking to develop careers may be more likely to feel a tension between home and family life, given that career development usually involves demonstrating a high level of workplace commitment. In the next sections of this chapter, we explore the relative impact of some of these factors.

Class, gender and work–life 'balance'

Men work longer hours than women – amongst all employees, almost three-quarters (70 per cent) of men said they worked 40 hours a week or more, as compared to around a third (36 per cent) of women. Hours worked, not surprisingly, has an impact on running out of time for household chores, although women are more likely than men to have problems at all levels of working hours. Over three-quarters (76 per cent) of women who work 40 hours a week or more said they ran out of time to do household chores, compared with just fewer than 60 per cent of men.

There is considerable variation in the hours worked by occupational class, particularly for women. Over half (55 per cent) of managerial and professional women work 40 hours a week or more, compared with a fifth (20 per cent) of women in routine/manual jobs. The comparable figures for men are four-fifths (81 per cent) of professional and managerial men working more than 40 hours per week and three-fifths (62 per cent) of routine/manual men. Managerial and professional employees, therefore, work longer hours. They are also more likely to perceive their jobs as stressful. As seen in the next table, three-quarters of professional and managerial employees found their jobs stressful as compared to just under half of routine and manual workers.

Table 8.13 "My job is rarely stressful" by occupational class and sex

% who disagree	Managerial and professional	Base	Inter-mediate	Base	Routine and manual	Base
Men	75	234	63	37	47	164
Women	76	234	55	110	47	166
All	75	468	57	147	47	330

Base: full-time employees.

However, in respect of other employment conditions that might contribute to work–life 'balance', managerial and professional men and women fare rather better than those in working-class jobs. Half of working-class respondents (46 per cent of men and 50 per cent of women) said they would lose money if they took time off work for family reasons, as compared to only a fifth to a quarter of professional and managerial employees (18 per cent of men and 24 per cent of women). We asked a number of questions relating to 'family-friendly' working conditions, including whether immediate supervisors were understanding about taking time off for family reasons, and whether respondents had to use holiday or flexi hours to cover family leave. By combining the answers to these questions, we identified those who had particularly 'family-friendly' working conditions.[4] As the next table shows, people in professional and managerial and 'intermediate' jobs generally have more 'family-friendly' working conditions than those in routine and manual jobs.

Table 8.14 Family-friendly working conditions by occupational class and sex

% who have 'good' family friendly working conditions	Managerial and professional	Base	Inter-mediate	Base	Routine and manual	Base
Men	67	243	68	41	40	195
Women	60	251	55	120	35	169
All	64	494	58	161	38	364

Base: full-time employees.

However, in general, family-friendly working conditions do not appear to have an impact on levels of job stress, with the possible exception of middle-class women: they are more likely to find their jobs stressful if their working conditions are not family-friendly. They are also less likely to say that they never found it difficult to concentrate on work because of family problems – a third (32 per cent) of middle-class women with family-friendly working conditions gave this response compared with over four-fifths (44 per cent) of those without family-friendly working conditions.

The presence of children is obviously a major factor impinging on the work–family situation. Women are more likely than men to be affected by the presence of children, but there were also interesting variations by occupational class. Over four-fifths (81 per cent) of managerial and professional women with children (who, it will be remembered, were also more likely to work longer hours) said that they ran out of time at home, as compared to two-thirds (65 per cent) of those without children. However, the presence of children did not have any impact on the proportions of routine and manual women who said that they ran out of time at home.

To summarise our argument so far: levels of work–family stress appear to be relatively high amongst the respondents, particularly those working more than 40 hours a week. Women – particularly managerial and professional women – are more likely to report stress than men, and domestic chores represent the major problem. Managerial and professional employees work longer hours, and are more likely to run out of time at home, than routine and manual employees. However, managerial and professional employees (on the whole) enjoy more family-friendly working conditions than routine and manual employees, particularly in respect of whether or not they lose money if they take time off work for family reasons. Nevertheless, better working conditions do not appear to have an impact on work–life stress, with the notable exception of managerial and professional women. Indeed, the group reporting the greatest level of domestic pressures are managerial and professional women with child(ren) at home.

This section has briefly explored the impact of a number of contextual factors likely to be significant in achieving work–life 'balance' – hours worked, job type, employment conditions and the presence or absence of children in the household. In the next section, we turn to what might be described as an individual level factor affecting work–life 'balance', that is, the significance of career aspirations.

Careers, jobs and work–life 'balance'

We have seen that, in general, men and women in routine and manual occupations tend to work shorter hours, and report a lower level of job stress, than men and women in managerial and professional occupations. These class differences are reflected in capacities to achieve work–life 'balance', as can be seen from the next table. Managerial and professional men and women are considerably more likely to report difficulties in balancing work and family life.[5]

Table 8.15 Work–life balance by occupational class

	Managerial and professional	Base	Routine and manual	Base
% who agree that "There are so many things to do at work, I often run out of time before I get them all done"				
Men	71	219	49	148
Women	67	194	52	72
All	69	413	50	220
% who have ever in the last 3 months found that "It has been difficult for me to fulfil my family responsibilities because of the amount of time I spend on my job"				
Men	75	208	51	144
Women	72	176	58	65
All	74	384	53	209

Base: full-time employees.

One factor that might be contributing to these class differences is the impact of career aspirations, which are likely to be more salient for managerial and professional employees. When asked a general question, most people indicated that they would put their family lives before their careers – two-thirds (66 per cent) of men, and three-quarters (77 per cent) of women disagreeing with the statement that "it is important to move up the career ladder at work, even if it gets in the way of family life". A further question focused more narrowly on individual aspirations for career development. Over a half of male respondents (53 per cent) and a third of the women, felt it was important for them to move up the job ladder at work. As we anticipated, there are important variations by class in individual aspirations: managerial and professional men and women were much more likely to aspire to a career than routine and manual employees. Other factors that we might have expected to affect career aspirations were age (people towards the end of their working lives being perhaps less concerned about career development than younger people), and the presence or absence of children – there is evidence that women tend to put their careers 'on hold' when they have children (Becker and Moen, 1999).

However, when we analysed all these factors together using a logistic regression we found that the presence of children did not have a significant impact on career aspirations, once other factors were taken into account. The important factors are class, sex and age. Men are more than twice as likely as women to think that moving up the career ladder is important. People in the managerial and professional class grouping are three times more likely to think that moving up the career ladder is important than people in routine and manual jobs. It should be remembered that career opportunities are, of course, more numerous in managerial and professional occupations than in routine and manual occupations. (Details of the logistic regression are given in the appendix to this chapter.)

What impact do career aspirations have on capacities to achieve work–life 'balance'? After all, people wanting to be promoted are likely to be under pressure to 'perform' at work – which might include, for example, working longer hours. As we have seen, managers and professionals experience more work–life stress, and are considerably more likely to want to move up the career ladder, than routine and manual employees. When we analysed all these factors together, however, we found that career aspirations had no impact on work–life stress in the case of managerial and professional men – both the aspiring and the non-aspiring men had the same level of stress. However, professional and managerial women who wished to be promoted were significantly more likely to express difficulties in combining work and family than those women who did not consider promotion important. Almost four-fifths (78 per cent) of the aspiring, but only two-thirds (67 per cent) of the non-aspiring women, said that it had been difficult for them to fulfil their family responsibilities because of the amount of time they spent on their jobs.

The other group for whom career aspirations were associated with work–life stress were working-class men. Almost two-thirds (63 per cent) of aspiring routine and manual men said that it had been difficult for them to fulfil their family responsibilities because of the amount of time they spent on their jobs, compared with only two-fifths (40 per cent) of routine and manual men who did not consider promotion important. Figure 8.1 describes the pattern of work–life stress, by gender, aspirations and occupational group, that we found in our sample.

Figure 8.1 Occupational class, sex, promotion aspirations and work–life stress

	Professional and managerial		Routine and manual	
	Wants promotion	Does not want promotion	Wants promotion	Does not want promotion
Men	–	–	+	–
Women	+	–	(–)	(–)

+ report higher levels of work–life stress than comparable sex/occupational group.
– report lower or the same levels of work–life stress as comparable sex/occupational group.
Bracketed symbols indicate small base.

Work–life 'balance' and career aspirations: the case of managerial and professional women

The finding that work–life stress for professional and managerial women is related to whether they think a career is important is supported by the responses to a number of questions, as seen in the next table. Even though the numbers of respondents in each group are small, the differences are statistically significant for the first two statements. (As expected, there were no similar differences for professional and managerial men.)

Table 8.16 Work–life balance by career aspirations among professional and managerial women

	Career not important	Base	Career important	Base
% who have ever found that it was difficult to fulfil family responsibilities because of the amount of time spent on job	67	92	78	84
% who have ever arrived at work too tired to function well because of the household work they had done	21	96	38	96
% who have come home at least several times a month too tired to do the chores which need doing	40	86	60	61

Base: full-time female professional/managerial employees.

We explored a range of factors which, independently of career aspirations, might have made work–life 'balance' more problematic for these women. It is true that those with career aspirations were on average younger than the women not interested in promotion and were rather more likely to have child(ren) in their households. They worked significantly longer hours than women who were not interested in promotion – but this is likely to be a consequence of the career aspirations, rather than a cause of them. However, the major difference between professional and managerial women who wished to be promoted, and professional and managerial men in the same position, is in the likelihood of having a partner who also works full-time. Of those who had a partner, almost all of the women in this group (92 per cent) had a partner who also worked full-time, whereas for the men the figure was less than half (47 per cent).

We would suggest, therefore, that a primary reason why professional and managerial women with career aspirations are more likely to experience work–life stress than similar men is because the women's partners are more likely to be in full-time work than men's partners.[6] When we put this together with the fact that women still carry out a disproportionate amount of domestic work, we can see that this is a group of women who receive relatively lower levels of domestic support compared with men in similar positions. For example, although less than a third (29 per cent) of aspirant men with full-time working partners said that they had arrived at work too tired because of household chores, two-fifths (41 per cent) of aspirant women with full-time partners did so. In a similar vein, three-quarters (74 per cent) of aspirant women with partners in full-time employment said they had so much to do at work they ran out of time, compared with two-thirds (66 per cent) of aspirant men with full-time partners.

Work–life 'balance' and career aspirations: the case of routine and manual men

A similar argument cannot, however, be made in the case of routine and manual men hoping to move up the career ladder. As already suggested, routine and manual men who wish to move up the career ladder are significantly more likely to have problems with work–life 'balance' than those who do not, and this is confirmed by the next table. As with the professional and managerial women, the numbers of respondents in each group are rather small but the differences are nevertheless statistically significant for the first two statements.

Table 8.17 Work–life balance by career aspirations among routine and manual men

	Career not important	Base	Career important	Base
% who have ever found that it was difficult to fulfil family responsibilities because of the amount of time spent on job	40	85	63	58
% who have ever arrived at work too tired to function well because of the household work they had done	17	89	39	59
% who have ever found that there are so many things to do at work they run out of time before they get them all done	40	86	60	61

Base: full-time male routine/manual employees.

Like managerial and professional women, aspirant routine and manual men are younger, and less likely to be married, than men who were not interested in promotion. They were also more likely to work longer hours, and are more likely to think that they would have to be prepared to move (geographically) if they wanted to achieve promotion. However, why should routine and manual men who want to move up the job ladder, unlike managerial and professional men, express higher levels of work–life stress than those who are not interested in promotion? Unlike the case of the managerial and professional women, there is no distinct factor, such as being more likely to have a partner who does not do their share of domestic work, that would seem to be contributing to these levels of stress.

Rather, we would suggest that the reason for the greater level of work–life stress articulated by working-class men rests in the nature of contemporary working-class careers (although we cannot demonstrate this on the basis of the available data). Grimshaw *et al.* (2001, 2002) have argued that a significant effect of recent changes in service sector organisations (and it is in such organisations that employment has been increasing most rapidly) has been to open up the 'gap' in the job ladder between lower grade employees and the first step on the promotional ladder "... the most direct effect of the flattened jobs hierarchy has been to remove the architecture necessary for career progression" (2001: 38). Making the transition to the first rung of the managerial ladder had become increasingly dependent on individual appraisals, and Grimshaw *et al.* argue that: "... staff with ambitions to 'move up' the organisation ... know that they face an *'all-or-nothing' effort in time and energy to make the transition to a mid-level post.*" (2002:109, our emphasis).

In a similar vein, Crompton's (2003) research on careers and work–life articulation in a major supermarket chain demonstrated that, although the organisation had high profile 'family-friendly' policies, managers above the basic employee level worked long hours and complex shifts, often to the detriment of their family lives. Thus, although promotion opportunities were available, and enthusiastically promoted by the company, many employees did not want to take advantage of them, because they anticipated (correctly) that gaining promotion would mean long hours working (on relatively low wages), together with work intensification. Case study evidence, therefore, suggests that men in routine and manual occupations with career aspirations will face considerable pressure and effort in order to achieve them – and of course, they may not be successful. It is these kinds of pressures, we would suggest, that contribute to the higher levels of work–life stress amongst routine and manual men who wish to be promoted.

Conclusions

In this chapter, we have explored the impact of changes both in women's employment behaviour (particularly that of mothers) and in women's aspirations associated with this increase. In 2002, only a minority (17 per cent) of those interviewed in the *British Social Attitudes* survey were living in 'male breadwinner' households and in over three-fifths of two-person households, both people were in employment of some kind. Changes in women's behaviour have been accompanied by changes in attitudes, and in 2002 only a fifth (20 per cent) of men, and one in seven (15 per cent) of women, thought that it was the "woman's job" to look after the home and family. Attitudes to working mothers have also become more positive. Indeed, the last few decades of the twentieth century saw a fundamental shift in gender role attitudes, together with a remarkable convergence in the attitudes of older and younger men and between older and younger women.

One thing that has not changed, however, are the persisting attitudinal differences between men and women. Women are more gender 'liberal' than men in respect of both gender roles and attitudes to working mothers. This and other evidence[7] suggests that women are unlikely voluntarily to revert to traditional gender stereotypes in respect of either attitudes or behaviour. The civil and social rights that were finally achieved by second-wave feminism in the decades after the 1950s appear to have been associated with permanent transformations in attitudes and behaviour amongst women in general.

However, another feature of the relations between men and women that appears to have changed less than might have been anticipated is the gender division of domestic labour. Women still carry out a disproportionate amount of domestic tasks and childcare. Men, however, tend to claim that they have assumed a greater share in domestic labour than is reported by women.

The 'male breadwinner' model of the articulation of employment and family life assumed that men specialised in 'breadwinning' – market work – and women specialised in the unpaid work of caring and nurturing. As far as women were concerned, this gender division of labour may not have been 'fair', but it did ensure the process of social reproduction (Folbre, 1994). Although we have not addressed this issue directly in this chapter, a number of recent commentators on the 'crisis' of the modern family (associated with declining fertility, increasing rates of family breakdown, etc.) have suggested that this crisis can only be resolved if women can 'rediscover' their nurturing roles, and men can be persuaded to re-assume their 'breadwinning' roles (Kristol, 1998; Fukuyama, 1999). Our evidence, however, suggests that there would be no great enthusiasm amongst respondents of either sex for this solution. Nevertheless, our data also suggests that contemporary family life is characterised by considerable strains and pressures.

Changes in the economic behaviour and aspirations of women, therefore, have served to re-focus attention on the articulation of employment and family life, given that the problem is no longer 'solved' by the domestication of women. Work–life 'balance' has increasingly emerged as a major policy issue at the European level, as well as for national governments (COM, 2001). The data we have summarised in this chapter suggests that despite this increasing policy attention, there are many issues that remain to be resolved.

Our evidence suggests that work–life stress is experienced most acutely by men and women in professional and managerial occupations, even though, in terms of 'family-friendliness', their working conditions are better than those in routine and manual occupations. On average, men and women in routine and manual occupations express lower levels of work–life stress. However, the explanation for this probably lies in the shorter hours worked and the greater incidence of part-time employment – particularly amongst routine and manual women. Lower levels of work–life stress, therefore, are achieved at some economic cost, and this will be one of the factors contributing to the increasing gap in household incomes between those at the bottom and those at the top of the occupational hierarchy.[8] Indeed, as Blossfeld and Drobnic have argued, "the decrease in gender inequality in terms of labour-force participation is accompanied by an increase in social class inequalities" (2001: 381).

The longer reported hours of work of professional and managerial respondents are an important factor contributing to their reported levels of work–life stress. These longer hours no doubt reflect the greater workplace pressures to be found in these kinds of jobs, but will also be a consequence of individual aspirations. Many social theorists have argued that contemporary societies are characterised by an increase in levels of 'individuation', as, in the growing absence of 'traditional' normative prescriptions and roles, people are faced with the necessity of 'working on' their own biographies in order to construct their 'reflexive selves' (Giddens, 1991; Beck, 1992). Developing an employment career will be an important aspect of this construction of the self. However, employment careers have themselves become increasingly 'individualised' as organisations have been restructured and 'delayered', and the stable career paths that once characterised formal bureaucratic hierarchies have been increasingly eroded (Handy, 1994). Thus the individual wanting to move up the occupational ladder will be faced with the necessity of demonstrating their personal promotable worth to their superiors.

Not surprisingly, individual aspirations for moving up the job ladder vary by both sex and class. Men are twice as likely to want to move up the career ladder as women, and professional and managerial employees are three times as likely to want to move up the job ladder as routine and manual employees. However, the impact of aspirations on hours worked varied importantly by sex within occupational class categories. Our data suggests that aspirations for promotion do not have an impact on the hours worked by professional and managerial men (39 per cent of those wishing to move up the ladder worked more than 50 hours a week, compared with 40 per cent of those who did not). But the wish for promotion did have a significant impact on the hours worked by professional and managerial women. In the case of routine and manual workers, it was the men who wished to move up the job ladder, who worked longer hours, and expressed more work–life stress than similar men who did not wish to be promoted.

For two groups within our sample, therefore, promotion aspirations were associated with higher levels of work–life stress – professional and managerial women and routine and manual men. We have argued that the greater levels of stress experienced by professional and managerial women might be a consequence of their relative lack of domestic supports (as compared to similar men). The greater levels of stress experienced by routine and manual men might be a consequence of the level of work intensity required for promotion from lower level (service) jobs.

In conclusion, we would draw attention to the broader implications of our findings. Work–life articulation has become a 'problem' because of fundamental shifts in gender roles and attitudes, together with changes in the economic behaviour of women. At the same time as these shifts have been taking place, British governments have, increasingly, embraced neo-liberal economic and labour market policies, have promoted flexible employment, and have sought to enhance individual and organisational competitiveness. Together with these changes, 'high commitment' management policies (of which individualised promotion opportunities are but one aspect) are increasing workplace pressures on employees. This increasing 'marketisation' of economic and social life has been achieved at some cost. Material inequalities have been widening. It has also been demonstrated that contemporary policies of workplace management have increased the tensions between employment and family life (Hochschild, 1997). Our data suggest that these tensions are greatest for two groups who have responded 'positively' to these competitive changes, and seek advancement within increasingly individualised career structures, that is, aspirant managerial and professional women, and men in routine and manual occupations who want to move up the job ladder. At the national level, policies are beginning to be developed in response to growing problems of work–life articulation. Not only do such national policies need to be further developed and improved, but also, it would seem that employers need, increasingly, to become more sensitive to the work–life tensions experienced by their employees.

Notes

1. For a more thorough discussion of cohort analysis see Park, 2000 and Heath and Martin, 1996.
2. By the time we have limited ourselves to women only in particular age groups, we do not have very large numbers in each group. Smallish differences in percentages will therefore struggle to reach statistical significance – we might well have found statistically significant differences if we had had a bigger sample.
3. It should be noted, however, that the difference between 1989 and 2002 in the oldest (pre-1933) cohort will have been artificially inflated by cohort replacement within the reported cohort. i.e. many of the older men born before 1933 who were available for interview in 1989 will have died, stopped living in a private household or otherwise become incapable of being interviewed by 2002.
4. Working conditions are coded as 'family-friendly' if a respondent does not lose money if they have to take time off, their supervisor is 'very understanding' if they do take time off, and they put in extra hours or extra effort to cover absence, rather than using holiday or flexi hours.
5. Although it should be noted that full-time routine and manual women were ten percentage points more likely to say that they arrived at work too tired to function properly.
6. Professional and managerial women who wanted promotion were less likely to be in a partnership than those who did not want promotion (they were younger). However, partnership as such did not seem to have a significant impact on work–life stress.
7. For example, the received psephological wisdom of the 1960s was that women were more politically conservative than men, and indeed, women were more likely to vote for right-leaning political parties than men up to the end of the 1960s. However, by the end of the 20th century, this pattern had been transformed and young women, in particular, were more likely to vote for left-leaning parties than men (see Norris, 1999).

8. In 2002, 61 per cent of employees in managerial and professional occupations reported an annual household income of £32,000 and above, compared with 22 per cent of those in routine and manual occupations.

References

Beck, U. (1992), *Risk Society,* London: Sage.

Becker, P.E. and Moen, P. (1999), 'Scaling Back: Dual-Earner Couples' Work-Family Strategies' in *Journal of Marriage and the Family* **61**: 995-1007.

Blossfeld, H.-P. and Drobnic, S. (eds.) (2001), *Careers of Couples in Contemporary Societies*, Oxford: Oxford University Press.

Callender, C., Millward, N., Lissenburgh, S. and Forth, J. (1997), *Maternity Rights and Benefits in Britain 1996*, Department of Social Security Research Report No. 67, Norwich: The Stationery Office.

COM (2001) 313 'Employment and social policies: a framework for investing in quality', Brussels, 20.6.2001.

Crompton, R. (1997), *Women and Work in Modern Britain*, Oxford: Oxford University Press

Crompton, R. (ed) (1999), *Restructuring Gender Relations and Employment* Oxford: Oxford University Press.

Crompton, R. (2003 forthcoming), *Organisations, Careers and Caring*, Bristol: Policy Press.

Crouch, C. (1999), *Social change in Western Europe*, Oxford: Oxford University Press.

Dench, S. *et al.* (2002), 'Key indicators of women's position in Britain', London: Department of Trade and Industry.

Department for Trade and Industry (2000), *Work & Parents: Competitiveness and Choice*, London: The Stationery Office.

Department for Trade and Industry/HM Treasury (2003), *Balancing work and family life: enhancing choice and support for parents*, London: The Stationery Office.

Esping-Anderson, G. (1990), *The Three Worlds of Welfare Capitalism*, Cambridge: Polity Press.

Folbre, N. (1994), *Who Pays for the Kids? Gender and the Structures of Constraint*, London: Routledge.

Fukuyama, F. (1999), *The Great Disruption*, London: Profile Books.

Gershuny, J., Godwin, M. and Jones, S. (1994), 'The Domestic Labour Revolution: a Process of Lagged Adaptation,' in Anderson, M., Bechhofer, F. and Gershuny, J. (eds.), *The Social and Political Economy of the Household*, Oxford: Oxford University Press.

Giddens, A. (1991), *Modernity and Self Identity*, Cambridge: Polity.

Grimshaw, D., Ward, K.G., Rubery, J. and Beynon, H. (2001) 'Organisations and the transformation of the internal labour market in the UK' *Work, Employment and Society*, **15(1)**: 25–54.

Grimshaw, D., Beynon, H, Rubery, J. and Ward, K. (2002) 'The restructuring of career paths in large service sector organisations: "delayering" upskilling and polarisation, *Sociological Review* **50(1)**: 89–115

Handy, C. (1994), *The Empty Raincoat*, London: Hutchinson.

Heath, A. and Martin, J. (1996), 'Changing attitudes towards abortion: life-cycle, period and cohort effects', in Taylor, B. and Thomson, K. (eds.), *Understanding Change in Social Attitudes*, Aldershot: Dartmouth.

Himmelweit, S. and Sigala, M. (2003), 'Internal and External Constraints on Mothers' Employment: Some Implications for Policy', ESRC Future of Work, Working paper no. 27.

Hochschild, A. (1997), *The Time Bind*, New York: Metropolitan Books.

Kristol, W. (1998), 'A Conservative perspective on public policy and the family', in Wolfe, C. (ed.), *The Family, Civil Society, and the State*, Oxford: Rowman and Littlefield.

Lewis, J. (1992), 'Gender and the Development of Welfare Regimes' in *Journal of European Social Policy*, **2(3)**: 159–173.

McRae, S. (1996), *Maternity Rights in Britain*, London: Policy Studies Institute.

Norris, P. (1999), 'Gender: a gender-generation gap?', in Evans, G. and Norris, P. (eds.), *Critical Elections*, London: Sage.

Park, A. (2000), 'The generation game' in Jowell, R., Curtice, J., Park, A., Thomson, K., Jarvis, L., Bromley, C. and Stratford, N. (eds.), *British Social Attitudes: the 17th Report – Focusing on Diversity*, London: Sage.

Rubery, J. (ed.) (1988), *Women and Recession*, London: Routledge and Kegan Paul.

Sullivan, O. (2000), 'The Division of Domestic Labour' *Sociology*, **34(3)**: 437–456.

Trades Union Congress (2000), *The Future of Work*, London: TUC.

Acknowledgements

The *National Centre for Social Research* and the authors would like to thank the Economic and Social Research Council (ESRC) for its funding of the *International Social Survey Programme*, through its funding of the *Centre for Research into Elections and Social Trends* (grant reference M543285002). We would also like to thank the ESRC for the additional funding of the 'Employment and the Family' project (grant reference R000239727). The ESRC project also involves co-operation with colleagues in Portugal, France, Norway, Finland, the Czech Republic and Hungary.

Appendix

Logistic regression: Important to move up the career ladder at work

	Odds ratio
Respondent's sex: male	2.430 ***
Age	.918 ***
Child in household	1.026
Occupational class	
(Reference category: routine and manual)	
Professional/managerial	3.070 ***
Intermediate	.580 *
Constant	7.850 ***
Base	*1085*

*   sig at 5%
**   sig at 1%
***   sig at 0.1%

9 Trends in racial prejudice

Catherine Rothon and Anthony Heath [*]

There are strong grounds for anticipating that levels of racial prejudice and views about racial discrimination will have changed over the last two decades. The make-up of the British population has changed considerably; in the last decade Britain's minority ethnic population grew by 53 per cent from 3 million in 1991 to 4.6 million in 2001, and now represents 7.9 per cent of the total UK population.[1] Awareness of racial prejudice, and a commitment to tackle it, is far higher now than in the past. Indeed, the Labour government has emphasised the centrality of racial harmony and equality in its vision of "New Britain". In key areas – including politics, the media, and sport – ethnic minorities are now more visible than ever before. We might also anticipate a greater tolerance of 'difference' resulting from the fact that Britain is now a more educated society than it was (Hyman and Wright, 1979). Not surprisingly then, we might expect younger groups, who have grown up in a more multicultural Britain, to have very different views on these matters to those held by their parents and grandparents.

Despite these changes, serious doubts remain about the success of race relations in modern Britain. Concern about "institutional racism", as expressed in the Macpherson Report (1999) on the investigation by the police of the murder of Stephen Lawrence, shows no sign of abating. Widespread evidence exists of intolerance towards immigrants and asylum seekers, and the United Nations Committee on Racial Discrimination has severely criticised race-relations in Britain, expressing deep concern about continuing racial attacks and the harassment of ethnic minority groups (United Nations International Convention on the Elimination of all Forms of Racial Discrimination, 2001).

This chapter begins by exploring how racial prejudice has changed over the last two decades. Where we find change, we assess how it might best be explained and speculate as to what this might mean for the future. It might be, for instance, that people's views on these issues are indelibly shaped by the

---

[*] Catherine Rothon is a Research Officer for the Centre for Research into Elections and Social Trends (CREST) at the University of Oxford. Anthony Heath is Professor of Sociology at the University of Oxford and Co-director of CREST.

world in which they grew up, and then remain fairly consistent throughout their lives. If this is the case, we might expect that prejudice will decline over time, as those socialised in a less 'tolerant' era die out. Alternatively, we might find that people's views change as they age – meaning that an ageing population could have an increasingly powerful influence on social values overall. We also consider how strongly education is linked to tolerance and an opposition to discrimination.

We also explore the relationship between external 'reality' and levels of prejudice. In particular, we consider what impact changing levels of immigration might have on views about ethnic minorities. We also assess whether the changing nature of immigration (and in particular, the 'new' immigration from the Middle East, Eastern Europe and Africa) has had an effect on public attitudes. It has been suggested, for instance, that while the British may have become relatively more tolerant of their established ethnic minority population from the New Commonwealth, they are far from passionate about the recent arrival of immigrants from other countries of origin. If this is found to be the case, we might expect prejudice to have increased over recent years.

The question of how prejudice affects support for practical policy measures is also important. Some researchers have found that, while people are willing to support *principles* of anti-discrimination, they are less keen to accept the more *practical* policy measures that implement these beliefs (Jackman, 1978, Jackman and Muha, 1984, Jackman 1994). So we examine the extent to which views about anti-discrimination policies match people's self-expressed prejudice.

To answer these questions we use data from three sources: the *British Social Attitudes* surveys; the *British General Election Study, 1997*; and the *European Social Survey* of 2002.[2]

How prejudiced are you?

We begin by considering a long-standing question included on most *British Social Attitudes* surveys since 1983:

> *How would you describe yourself ... as very prejudiced against people of other races, a little prejudiced, or not prejudiced at all?*

The percentage of respondents who claim to be prejudiced in any way varies considerably, from a high of 39 per cent in 1987 to a low of 25 per cent in 2000 and 2001. However, it is notable that, prior to 1996, the proportion of people describing themselves as prejudiced consistently lay between 30 and 40 per cent. From 1996, however, the proportions in this group range between 20 and 30 per cent (with the exception of 2002, where the number of people who see themselves as prejudiced rises to 31 per cent). On this evidence, then, the British are slowly but steadily becoming less prejudiced over time.

Table 9.1 Self-reported racial prejudice, 1983–2002

	1983	1985	1987	1990	1994	1996	1998	2000	2001	2002
	%	%	%	%	%	%	%	%	%	%
Very prejudiced	4	5	5	4	2	2	2	2	2	2
A little prejudiced	31	29	34	32	34	27	24	23	23	29
Not prejudiced at all	64	65	60	64	63	70	73	73	73	67
Base	*1719*	*1769*	*2766*	*1397*	*2332*	*2399*	*1035*	*2293*	*2188*	*3435*

Although Table 9.1 shows a gradual downward trend in prejudice, it is not a simple linear one. As Figure 9.1 shows, there are some striking deviations from the general pattern, with marked increases in prejudice in 1986–1987, 1994 and 2002. The rise is particularly marked in 2002, with an increase of six percentage points. So we need to examine not only why there is a gradual long-term decline in self-reported prejudice, but also why this trend is not wholly linear.

Figure 9.1 Self-reported racial prejudice: percentage who see themselves as "very prejudiced" or "a little prejudiced", 1983–2002

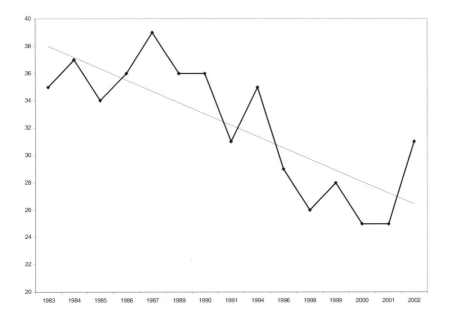

One concern that has been frequently raised about measuring attitudes towards ethnic minorities in this way is that the views expressed might represent little more than a superficial verbalisation of socially approved norms (Evans, 2002).

So, if it has become less tolerable over the past half century to express negative attitudes towards minority ethnic groups, perhaps we are simply measuring how people *think* they should report feeling, rather than how they actually do? Others argue that the context within which people express their views is important, and that in certain situations (unlikely to be duplicated during an interview) it will be more acceptable to display negative attitudes towards ethnic minorities than in others (Schuman *et al.*, [1985] 1997). However, although these are important concerns, they do not invalidate our findings. Firstly, self-expressed racial prejudice is, in fact, a very good predictor of people's views on related, but less direct, issues (Evans, 2002). And, secondly, expressed attitudes are often powerful determinants of the way in which people act.

Understanding changing attitudes

There are three common reasons as to why the attitudes of a population might change over time. The first relates to *generational* (or cohort) differences between people of different ages. These lead to change within society as a whole as older people die and are replaced by younger people holding different attitudes. For example, children born in South Africa after the end of apartheid might be expected to hold quite different political opinions to their parents and grandparents. A second possible reason relates to the way in which people's views change as they get older, whether for physiological, psychological or social reasons (Sears, 1983). The supposed increase in authoritarianism as a person ages is one example of such a *lifecycle* effect. Often, these changes will *not* lead to change within society as a whole (as the impact of one group getting older is counter-balanced by changes within the age groups above and below them). However, if the proportion of people within a particular age group increases, such explanations can be helpful in explaining change within society overall. Our third possible explanation of change concerns what are called *period effects*. These are changes that affect everyone within a society. Often, they reflect important events, a topical example being the impact that September 11th has had upon people's views about a range of issues (from their willingness to tolerate stringent security checks at airports to attitudes towards the relationship between the West and Islam). Period effects can also be more gradual in their impact on social attitudes, but will always have an impact upon all social groups.

  It can be very difficult to disentangle these three competing explanations for change, particularly as they rarely occur in isolation from one another. In fact, when all three contribute to overall changes in attitudes, they become confounded in a manner that makes them almost impossible to separate (Glenn; 1976, 1989, Fienberg and Mason; 1985; Rodgers, 1990; Heath and Martin, 1996; Schuman *et al.* [1985], 1997). So we need to remember that all three processes may be operating simultaneously, and take stock of this before reaching any conclusions.

A generation gap?

'Generation replacement' theories argue that attitudes are developed when people are young and remain fairly stable as they grow older. They are shaped by a person's early socialisation which, in turn, is a product of the historical period in which they grew up. Different generations, therefore, would be expected to develop quite different attitudes on a range of issues. People who are now aged 70-plus, for example, grew up in a time of great economic instability during which the prospect of war was a pressing concern. As Inglehart (1971, 1990) has argued, this group would be likely to have significantly different values to the "baby-boomers" of the immediate post-war period, who grew up in a time of relative optimism and affluence. So, if these values remain constant throughout a person's life, as younger generations replace older ones, we would expect to see values change in society as a whole. In particular, in the case of racial prejudice, we might expect younger respondents who have grown up in a more multicultural Britain to be less prejudiced than older generations who had little knowledge of or contact with ethnic minorities. In fact, it might be the case that 'period effects' (such as changing levels of immigration or the changing ethnic make-up of Britain's population) have a particularly strong impact on younger age groups. After all, younger people, whose opinions are still forming, may be more open to the influence of period effects than older groups whose views are more firmly embedded (Mannheim, [1928] 1952; Alwin and Krosnick, 1991).

The next table assesses the extent to which generational change helps explain this overall downward trend we have found in racial prejudice. It does so by showing, for a range of survey years, the proportion within specific generations (or 'cohorts') who describe themselves as either "very" or "a little" prejudiced. If generational factors are responsible for a decline in levels of prejudice, we should expect to see two clear patterns in the table. Firstly, we should find that, within a single cohort, levels of prejudice across the years are fairly consistent. And, secondly, we should expect to find higher prejudice among older cohorts than among younger ones. If both these conditions are true, the dying out of older, more prejudiced, generations and their replacement by younger, less prejudiced ones, is likely to underpin the changes we have seen in society as a whole.

In fact, neither of these conditions is met in Table 9.2. Within any single cohort, levels of prejudice vary from one year to the next. True, this may well indicate only that all cohorts are affected by the sorts of period changes discussed earlier. But, even if we focus on 1984 and 2001 (two years which fall close to the overall trend line shown in Figure 9.1), we *still* find that many of the cohorts have become markedly less prejudiced over time. In fact, only one of the six cohorts (those born in the 1930s) can be said to exhibit stable attitudes between 1984 and 2001. Table 9.2 also shows that, within any single survey year, it is not the case that older generations are more prejudiced than younger ones. Indeed, the pre-1920 and 1920–1929 cohorts report the highest levels of prejudice in only two survey years. Nor is there any consistency as to which cohort reports the greatest intolerance (although the 1930–1939 and 1940–1949 cohorts achieve this position more often than the youngest and oldest groups).

Table 9.2 Percentage in each cohort who see themselves as "very prejudiced" or "a little prejudiced", 1983–2002

Cohort	1984	1985	1987	1990	1994	1996	1998	2000	2001	2002	Base (smallest)
	%	%	%	%	%	%	%	%	%	%	
Pre-1920	29	23	36	32	35	36	21	18	35		62
1920s	37	38	38	35	37	33	37	33	30	35	98
1930s	33	38	41	39	39	29	30	31	35	33	132
1940s	40	34	44	39	42	36	21	29	28	42	166
1950s	42	35	36	37	34	26	29	24	20	30	160
1960s	41	38	38	33	34	27	26	23	23	30	175
1970s				34	36	25	18	22	26	27	78
1980s								23	13	31	64
Average	37	34	39	36	36	29	26	26	25	32	

Note: Cells with no respondents, or fewer than 50, have been left blank

These patterns do not fit well with theories of generational replacement, making it unlikely that this explains changing levels of prejudice over time. They also throw up the question as to whether different age groups attach different meanings to the word "prejudice". Perhaps, in other words, older people report low levels of prejudice because they were socialised at a time when it was more acceptable to hold views that by modern standards would be deemed intolerant? We discuss this possibility in more detail later, but turn now to examine whether there is an alternative relationship between age and prejudice.

Age and prejudice

A lifecycle explanation of attitude change is based on the assertion that individuals change their views as they get older. One common assumption, for instance, is that as people grow older, they will inevitably become more authoritarian. They may have narrower social circles than younger people, and be less likely to mix with the wider range of people that the more youthful population are able to access through education, work, or social gatherings. Consequently, they may have less access to new ideas and be less tolerant of alternative viewpoints. Alternatively, their views might change as a result of major life-events, such as buying property or having children.

If lifecycle processes are related to racial prejudice, an ageing population might be expected to lead to increasing levels of intolerance. Over the last 50 years, the population of the UK has aged considerably, with the proportion of people aged over 60 increasing from 16 to 21 per cent. There has been a particularly dramatic increase in the number of people aged 85 and over. In 1951, 0.2 million people in the UK (0.4 per cent of the population) were aged over 85; by the time of the 2001 Census, this group numbered some 1.1 million, and accounted for 1.9 per cent of the population (Office for National Statistics, 2002a).

Ideally, we would use panel survey data to assess the importance of different lifecycle stages on racial prejudice, as these are based upon repeated contact with the same people over time. Such data is not, however, readily available. But, as we saw earlier in Table 9.2, we can use data from the *British Social Attitudes* series to track the views of particular cohorts over different survey years. Although we are not interviewing the same *individuals* on each occasion, every survey will include a cohort born in, say, the 1950s – allowing us to compare the views of this cohort across a range of survey years. Since the surveys cover the period from 1983 to 2002, this gives us a reasonable life-span over which we can study the ageing process.[3]

We saw earlier in Table 9.2 that the prejudice expressed by each of our cohorts did change as we moved from earlier survey years to later ones. We turn now to explore this in more detail, focusing on whether there is any evidence to support either of two hypotheses which link lifecycle changes with decreased tolerance. The first argues that, as cohorts reach late middle age (their fifties), a range of physiological, psychological and social changes result in their becoming less liberal in their views about ethnic minorities (Sears, 1983). If this explanation is correct, we should expect to see a significant rise in self-reported prejudice in late middle age. The second explanation, less widely accepted, sees the key changes occurring somewhat earlier, in early middle age. Thus, the liberalism associated with youth gives way by early middle age to more conservative and less tolerant views as a result of the pressures caused by marriage, becoming a parent, and work. If this explanation is correct, we should expect to see a rise in prejudice as people move into their 30s and 40s.

Table 9.3 shows how much a particular cohort deviates in any given survey year from the overall level of prejudice found that year. If the members of a particular cohort have become more intolerant as they age, we would expect to see a pattern emerge whereby they are *below* the average when they are younger (that is, the proportion who are prejudiced is *lower* than the proportion overall, a minus figure) and *above* the average when they are older (that is, the proportion who are prejudiced is higher than the proportion overall, a positive figure). In reality, the only group that displays a clear trend towards increased prejudice over their lifecycle is the cohort born before the 1920s. Between 1983 and 1985 (when they would have been in their 60s or over), this group reported levels of prejudice significantly lower than the average; indeed, they are the group reporting the lowest levels of prejudice overall at this point. Between 1986 and

1994 they move closer to the average; and, by 1996, they are reporting levels of prejudice significantly above the average.

For the rest of the cohorts, the process is less clear-cut. The 1920s cohort, and perhaps the 1930s and 1940s cohorts too, appear to be becoming slightly more prejudiced in the more recent surveys. But the younger cohorts do not exhibit any clear pattern of increase in levels of prejudice over the 20-year period. One possible explanation for this is that increased intolerance towards other races only occurs in very late life and is not, therefore, linked to life events such as marriage, childbirth and home ownership. If this is the case, we would not expect to see a great deal of change among younger cohorts until a later survey point.

Table 9.3 Distance from average level of self-reported prejudice for each cohort, in percentage points, 1983–2002

	1983	1985	1987	1990	1994	1996	1998	2000	2001	2002	Base (smallest)
	%	%	%	%	%	%	%	%	%	%	
Pre-1920	-8	-11	-3	-4	-1	7	-5	-8	10		62
1920s	1	4	-1	-1	1	4	11	7	5	3	98
1930s	5	4	2	3	3	0	4	5	10	1	132
1940s	2	0	5	3	6	7	-5	3	3	10	166
1950s	-1	1	-3	1	-2	-3	3	-2	-5	-2	160
1960s	4	4	-1	-3	-2	-2	0	-3	-2	-2	175
1970s				-2	0	-4	-8	-4	1	-5	78
1980s								-3	-12	-1	64
Average	36	34	39	36	36	29	26	26	25	32	

Note: Cells with no respondents, or fewer than 50, have been left blank

These findings suggest that the lifecycle hypothesis might have some merits, particularly when it comes to changing views among the elderly (that is, those aged over 70). Lifecycle hypotheses may be correct to assert that changes occur in racial attitudes as people age, but wrong in their prediction of the stage of the ageing process at which this happens. However, these forces do not seem clear or strong enough to lead to a leveling off in rates of prejudice among the general population.

The impact of changing levels of immigration on racial prejudice

So far we have not found a convincing explanation as to why racial prejudice has gradually declined over the last two decades. So we turn now to consider whether period effects might best explain the changes we have seen. One obvious example of a period effect that might relate to racial prejudice concerns immigration. The relationship between the two is explored in the next table, which examines whether the percentage change in self-reported prejudice varies in tandem with the change in the numbers of immigrants accepted for settlement in Britain. If there is a connection between the two, we might expect to see that, when the numbers accepted for settlement drop, so too does the percentage of respondents who describe themselves as prejudiced. This exercise is not very fruitful. Changes in prejudice levels do *not* appear to match the movement in numbers accepted for settlement. In fact, in 2000 (when there is a 29 per cent rise in those accepted for settlement), the level of self-rated prejudice actually decreases. There is a similar pattern in other years of high immigration, such as 1998 and 2001. Overall, there is only one year in which the changes move together in the direction we might expect.

Table 9.4 Movement of self-reported prejudice and percentage change in numbers accepted for settlement, 1983–2002

	1983	1985	1987	1990	1994	1996	1998	2000	2001	2002
% increase in those who see themselves as prejudiced		-3	15	-8	0	-19	-10	-4	0	24
Base		*1719*	*1769*	*2766*	*1397*	*2332*	*2399*	*1035*	*2293*	*2188*	*3435*
% increase from previous year in numbers accepted for settlement (1000s of persons)	-1	9	4	7	-1	11	19	29	-15	

Source: Home Office, 2001, 2002

Of course, we should consider the possibility of time lags: it might take some time for an increase in immigration to affect the public's attitudes. However, even allowing for such lags, Table 9.4 does not suggest that there is any clear relationship between racial prejudice and immigration levels.

Another possibility is that it is not *actual* immigration levels that matter, but the degree of attention given to them by the media. After all, many people's awareness of immigration will be crucially shaped by the newspapers they read and the television they watch. Certainly, in recent years, immigration has become a key political focus point for many newspapers. In a single week, official statistics on asylum and immigration can produce headlines such as "Magnet for refugees: Labour accused as new figures show Britain is 'asylum capital of Europe'" (*Daily Mail,* 9th May 2003) and "Bill for asylum seekers soars to GBP 900m a year" (*The Times,* 11th May 2003). That same month, *The Guardian* reported that the "Asylum backlog could be cut" (12th May 2003) and, on 14th August 2003, the *Daily Express* conveyed on its front page "Outrage as Britain tops the WORLD asylum league".

To assess the importance of the media as an influence on levels of prejudice, we used the *Index to The Times* to look at the number of articles that appeared in *The Times* newspaper for relevant years.[4] Given its relatively small circulation, *The Times* is not an ideal paper for our purposes, but unfortunately no comparable index exists for a newspaper with a wider circulation. That said, it is likely that the coverage in *The Times* will give us a reasonable idea of the amount of public discussion and interest in questions of immigration.

The next table shows no consistent correlation between the number of articles published in *The Times* and the changes in the level of prejudice reported by respondents in any given year. However, there are certainly more ticks than there were in Table 9.4 (which looked at the relationship between prejudice and changes in levels of immigration). It is also noticeable that there was a huge increase in articles relating to immigration from 2000 onwards, and this could well be linked with the reversal in 2002 of what had until then been a downward trend in levels of prejudice. So, while these data are far from conclusive, they do suggest that the relationship between self-reported prejudice and hostile newspaper coverage of immigration merits further investigation. In particular, this might help explain fluctuating levels of prejudice from one year to the next.

Table 9.5 Movement of self-reported prejudice and percentage change in numbers of articles in *The Times*, 1983–2002

	1983	1985	1987	1990	1994	1996	1998	2000	2001	2002
% increase in self-defined prejudice		-8	8	0	16	-19	-10	-10	0	24
Base	*1719*	*1769*	*2766*	*1397*	*2332*	*2399*	*1035*	*2293*	*2188*	*3435*
Number of articles	57	35	131	40	82	121	121	350	371	403
% increase in number of articles		-39	274	-69	105	48	0	189	6	9
Correlation between the measures		√	√		√	✗		✗		√

Source: *The Times Index*

Another period effect that may be responsible for the rise in prejudice between 2001 and 2002 concerns the events of 11th September 2001. A report published by the European Monitoring Centre on Racism and Xenophobia states that a rise in "Islamophobia" following the attacks was identifiable throughout many parts of the European Union (Commission for Racial Equality, 2002). Indeed, many such attacks were targeted specifically at some of the more 'visible' elements of Islamic culture, and included vandalism and arson attacks on Mosques. At the same time, Muslim women, many of whom wear headscarves, reported becoming increasingly subject to abuse and attacks in public.

Certain views expressed by public figures and the media may not have helped in this respect. For example, Lady Thatcher's comment that she "had not heard enough condemnation from Muslim priests" against the attacks is cited in the report. And, while a number of newspapers carried editorials urging their readers not to automatically link Islam and terrorism, the report also contains numerous examples of articles expressly making this link.

In summary, therefore, we have still not found a clear explanation as to why Britain has gradually become less racially prejudiced over the last two decades. True, we have found hints that changing levels of prejudice might be linked to patterns of immigration and their coverage in the press. But these hints can only help us account for some of the fluctuations we have seen from one year to the next, rather than the general downward trend in racial prejudice.

Education

We turn now to investigate the importance of one of the major differences between Britain now and Britain as it was in the 1980s; rising educational standards. As outlined in Chapter 8 (the chapter in this Report by Wragg and Jarvis), the proportion of graduates in Britain has increased substantially over the last two decades, and the proportion without any formal qualifications has shrunk dramatically.

As described in Chapter 7 (the chapter by Park and Surridge), education has been strongly linked to increased tolerance, although the reasons for this are unclear (Evans, 2002). This link is confirmed by the table below which shows that those with no qualifications are nearly twice as likely as graduates to be prejudiced. So might this link, combined with the increasing proportion of graduates in the population, explain the gradual decline in prejudice we have seen over the last two decades?

The next table explores this by showing, for a selection of years, the proportion within one of four educational groups who define themselves as prejudiced. In every case, graduates are the least likely to report any prejudice. However, levels of prejudice do not increase systematically as we move down the educational spectrum. For example, only in a few years do those with the lowest level of, or no, qualifications exhibit the highest levels of prejudice. In fact, self-reported prejudice is more likely to be found in the group with

intermediate qualifications (that is, those whose highest qualifications are
GCSE/O levels).

Table 9.6 "Very prejudiced" or "a bit prejudiced", by education, 1985–2002

	1985	1987	1990	1994	1996	1998	2000	2001	2002	Base (smallest)
	%	%	%	%	%	%	%	%	%	
Degree	23	26	31	29	23	20	22	20	18	102
Higher, below degree/ A level	42	43	37	38	29	25	22	23	31	292
O level	32	39	37	43	30	25	29	26	38	176
Below O level/ none	33	38	35	34	31	29	27	29	35	408

The spread of higher education may not only increase the tolerance of the
highly educated but may also influence the attitudes of those they come into
contact with. Geoffrey Evans (2002) has suggested that the general decline in
levels of prejudice can be explained by a "diffusion process" whereby the
already tolerant views of the degree-level group are adopted over time by lower
level groups. Figure 9.2 suggests that something of this sort may have been
happening in the first part of our period of interest. Thus, until 1991, the self-
reported prejudice of those without a degree appeared to be moving towards the
stance adopted by those who have attained a degree. This is certainly consistent
with a diffusion process. However, there has been no further convergence
between the educational groups since 1991 and, now that we have the benefit of
the most recent data, we can see that the trend from 2000 onwards follows the
opposite pattern. Rather than following the declining levels of prejudice among
those with degrees, the non-degree group now displays a significant increase in
levels of prejudice. Diffusion alone, therefore, will not reduce racial prejudice
among non-graduates.

So, in seeking to explain why racial prejudice has declined gradually over the
last two decades, rising educational levels appear to offer the most plausible
explanation. This does not, however, mean that prejudice will continue to
decline at a similar rate. In fact, even if the numbers entering higher education
were to double in the future, the expected decline in racial prejudice would
amount to less than two percentage points.

Figure 9.2 Self-reported racial prejudice, by education, 1985–2002

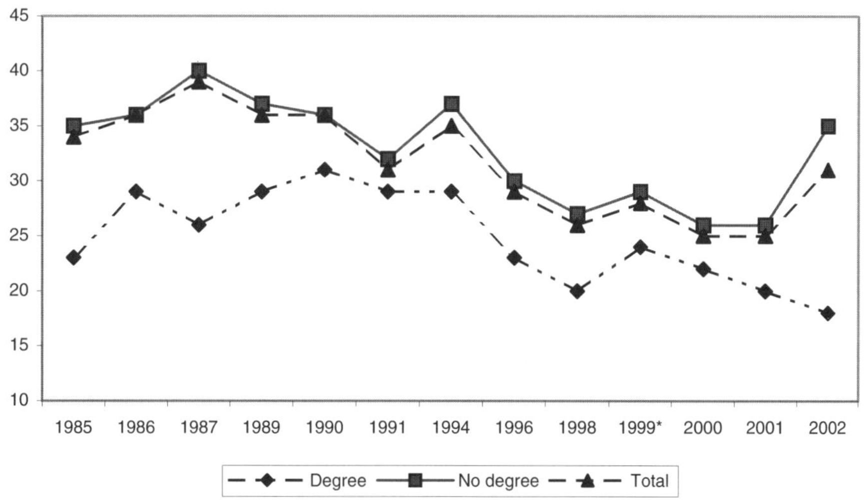

* Asked in England only

Defining prejudice

"General" and "applied" tolerance

Earlier we found some trends in racial prejudice which were contrary to our expectations. Two in particular stand out. Firstly, we had expected to find that prejudice would be highest among older cohorts, who grew up at a time when there were fewer ethnic minorities in Britain and less concern with issues such as discrimination and multiculturalism. Instead, we found that the self-reported prejudice of our two oldest cohorts, born before 1920 or between 1920 and 1929, was *lower* than that found among the 1930–1939 and 1940–1949 cohorts. Indeed, the reported levels of prejudice among these very elderly groups were much closer to those expressed by the younger cohorts. For this reason, we ruled out the suggestion that generational change might best explain changing levels of prejudice over time. Secondly, we found that the highest levels of prejudice were found among those with middle-range qualifications (GCSE/O levels), rather than among those with lower, or no, qualifications. This is counter to our expectation that the relationship between education and tolerance would operate along a continuum, with those with degrees having the most tolerant attitudes, and those with the lowest level of educational qualifications the most intolerant ones. Earlier, we suggested that a part of the explanation for these unexpected results may lie in the understandings that different groups have as to what the word "prejudice" actually means. It is to this that we now turn.

One way of examining this is to consider the extent to which measures of self-reported prejudice are related to support for practical policy measures. A number of researchers have found that, while people will support the principle of equality, they find it less easy to accept the implications of their beliefs. Schuman *et al.* ([1985], 1997) have called this phenomenon the "principle implementation gap". Mary Jackman (1978) and Jackman and Muha (1984) argue that it is through thorough examination of the relationship between "general" and "applied" measures of tolerance that we can assess the *strength* of commitment to the norm of tolerance. To do this, we examine the relationship between self-reported prejudice (a "general" attitude) and commitment to equal opportunities policy (an "applied" attitude):

> There is a law in Britain against racial discrimination, that is against giving unfair preference to a particular race in housing, jobs and so on. Do **you** generally support or oppose the idea of a law for this purpose?

The time-series for the *British Social Attitudes* surveys ends in 1996, but we can use data from the 1997 *British General Election Study* to extend the series. Unfortunately, from 1997 onwards this question has not been asked but, as we shall see, the pattern which emerges is a strong one and is not likely to have changed over the last five years.

We begin by considering the extent to which the overall trend in levels of prejudice is reflected in support for a law against racial discrimination. As the next table shows, since the early 1990s, around three-quarters of people have supported a law against racial discrimination. So far, then, there seems to be a fairly strong commitment to what Jackman calls the norm of tolerance.

Table 9.7 Prejudice and support for law against discrimination, 1986–1997

	1986	1989	1990	1991	1994	1996	1997*	Base (smallest)
% not prejudiced at all	63	63	64	68	63	70	72	*1383*
% support law	65	68	68	76	73	75	75	*1397*

* Source: *British General Election Study*, 1997

However, Jackman (1978) has suggested that the relationship between the general and applied tolerance (or what we might call theory and practice) can be complicated when we focus on specific groups of people. Certain sectors of the population, she argues, may express a high degree of tolerance when asked about prejudice in abstract terms, but will not show similarly high levels of commitment to related policies. To test this theory, we now look at the degree to which support for equal opportunities legislation is matched by self-rated prejudice within a range of birth cohorts and educational groups. If there is a disjuncture between the two measures in a particular group, we might suspect that the concept of "prejudice" is being variously interpreted by different sectors of the population.

Birth cohorts

We start by looking at different birth cohorts. Table 9.8 shows that cohorts do indeed differ when it comes to the relationship between self-rated prejudice and support for equal opportunities legislation. In particular, among the two oldest cohorts the proportion who claim not to be prejudiced *always* exceeds the proportion who support equal opportunities legislation. In 1997, for instance, nearly two-thirds of the cohorts born before the 1920s say that they are not racially prejudiced, and 56 per cent support legislation against discrimination. Among younger cohorts, however, support for legislation tends to be greater than the proportion claiming not to be prejudiced.

To make comparisons easier, the table also shows the 'average' level of prejudice and support for equal opportunities legislation shown by each cohort over the period between 1986 and 1997. It also shows the 'gap' between these figures. This shows that, among all cohorts born before 1940, there is a lower level of support for equal opportunities policy than we might expect from the same cohorts' self-rated prejudice, with the gap being largest of all among the two oldest cohorts. By the time we reach the 1930s cohort, the general and applied variables for racial prejudice almost match each other. For the cohorts born from 1940 onwards, there is a similarly linear trend in the gap between the measures, but in the opposite direction. Now the proportion supporting equal opportunities legislation exceeds the proportion saying that they are not prejudiced. The younger the cohort, the higher the degree to which they support equal opportunities legislation as compared to their self-reported prejudice.

These findings support Jackman's assertion that the strength of commitment to tolerance varies across the population. This could reflect a tendency for people to have a rather relative view as to what actually constitutes prejudice. Thus, at the beginning of the twentieth century it was far more acceptable to articulate what would now be considered racist viewpoints; perhaps those born before 1930 who claim to be "not prejudiced at all" simply see themselves as unprejudiced in the context of their upbringing during that time. When faced with more modern policy measures, however, their strength of commitment to *contemporary* notions of equality appears to be rather wobbly.

It is also notable from Table 9.8 that, while self-expressed racial prejudice does not vary consistently from one cohort to the next, views about equal opportunities legislation clearly do. In all years, the lowest levels of support are found among the older cohorts, and the highest among younger ones. Here, then, we might well anticipate clear generational differences to result in change over time, as older, less supportive cohorts die out and are replaced by younger, more supportive ones.

Table 9.8 Prejudice and support for law against discrimination, by year of birth, 1986–1997

	1986	1989	1990	1991	1994	1996	1997*	Avg.	'Gap'	Base (smallest)
Pre-1920s										
% not prejudiced	69	65	68	72	65	64	65	67		145
% support law	54	57	62	71	53	47	46	56	-11	149
1920s										
% not prejudiced	64	63	65	65	63	67	68	65		190
% support law	63	62	54	64	60	63	63	61	-4	193
1930s										
% not prejudiced	59	64	61	60	61	71	71	64		206
% support law	58	60	60	65	63	68	70	63	-1	207
1940s										
% not prejudiced	64	60	61	73	58	64	65	64		244
% support law	64	73	69	80	71	68	67	70	6	244
1950s										
% not prejudiced	65	62	63	72	66	74	76	68		253
% support law	69	73	77	84	84	81	80	78	10	254
1960s										
% not prejudiced	65	66	67	71	66	73	73	69		226
% support law	74	75	78	85	81	83	81	80	11	227
1970s										
% not prejudiced		69	66	65	65	75	76	69		70
% support law		87	74	77	84	85	84	82	13	47
1980s										
% not prejudiced							69	69		28
% support law							83	83	14	28

* Source: *British General Election Study*, 1997

Education

When Jackman (1978) examined commitment to race-related policy measures in the United States, she found that, although education is related strongly to endorsements of integration, it is related more weakly to support for the implementation of policies to promote racial integration. The highly qualified, she argues, have "a greater familiarity with the appropriate democratic principle of racial integration" but this does not necessarily result in greater support for policy measures (Jackman, 1978: 322). This does not mean that the well educated lie to interviewers, but that they are more likely to have "learned" abstract principles, to know what the socially acceptable answers are, and to actually believe in those answers. Their learning, however, is relatively superficial. Their professed principles are not deeply embedded, which means that in an "applied" situation, they are no more likely to be influenced by such principles than the uneducated (Jackman, 1978 see also Jackman; 1972).

We have already seen that more educated groups, particularly those with degrees, express lower levels of racial prejudice than less educated ones. However, if Jackman's theory is correct, we should also expect to find that more educated groups answer more positively on general questions than on applied ones, and that the relationship between education and general attitudes is stronger than that between education and views on applied measures.

These issues are explored in the next table. It shows that, when we examine differences in levels of "general" and "applied" tolerance, the least educated respondents do indeed appear to have a slightly different definition of prejudice to that held by those with more education. Thus, in every year surveyed, the group with no, or very low, qualifications shows a lower level of support for equal opportunities policy than we might expect from their expression of tolerance. For the rest of the educational groups, the opposite relationship applies. There is a slight narrowing of the gap between the "general" and "applied" measures as we move from those with degrees, to those with a higher qualification or A levels, to those with O levels. When we reach those with lower, or no, qualifications the direction of the relationship changes direction altogether. This lends no support to Jackman's thesis that there is a stronger link between education and general attitudes than between education and support for practical policies. If anything, the reverse is the case.

Table 9.9 Prejudice and support for law against discrimination, by education, 1986–1997

	1986	1989	1990	1991	1994	1996	1997*	Avg.	'Gap'	Base (smallest)
Degree										
% not prejudiced	71	71	69	72	70	77	76	72		107
% support law	81	89	82	95	92	93	93	89	17	88
Higher, below degree/A level										
% not prejudiced	63	61	62	67	61	71	74	66		334
% support law	72	78	75	82	78	85	84	79	13	309
O level										
% not prejudiced	63	57	62	64	57	70	72	64		249
% support law	66	72	73	79	77	74	74	74	10	249
Below O level/ none										
% not prejudiced	64	66	65	70	66	68	69	67		673
% support law	59	59	61	68	64	64	65	63	-4	673

* Source: *British General Election Study*, 1997

Contrary to Jackman's theory, those with high levels of formal education also display the most support for related policy measures. In addition, the distance between the views of graduates and those without a university education is far greater on the "applied" measure of equal opportunities legislation than on the more "general" measure of prejudice. So, when it comes to rejecting racial prejudice and being committed to equal opportunities legislation, education does appear to have a significant impact upon people's views. Moreover, the suggestion that different educational groups define prejudice in different ways might also help explain the lack of a clear gradient in the levels of self-expressed prejudice found among different educational groups. Then we found that the most prejudiced were *not* those with the lowest levels of qualifications; when it comes to support for putting anti-discrimination sentiment into practice, however, support is lowest of all among this group.

Support for race-related policy measures

We have found that both education and age are strongly related to attitudes towards views about equal opportunities legislation. Both factors are, of course, closely related to one another (as younger groups will contain a far higher proportion of graduates than older ones), making it difficult to establish whether it is age or education that plays the more important role. To overcome this problem we used multivariate analysis techniques (in this case, logistic regression) to untangle the key factors linked to support for the implementation of race-related policy. Further details of multivariate analysis can be found in Appendix I to this Report.

The explanatory variables we included in our model are our measures of educational level, self-rated prejudice, age, and the libertarian–authoritarian scale developed by researchers at the *National Centre for Social Research* (described in detail in Chapter 7 – the chapter by Park and Surridge). Just in case opposition to a law against racial discrimination simply reflects a general opposition to government intervention (rather than opposition to this policy in particular), we also included a measure of support for government intervention as well.

Figure 9.3 summarises the results. Bars to the right of the *x*-axis indicate a *higher* level of support for the policy among the group in question than among a defined comparison group, and bars to the left a *lower* level of support. Bars shaded black denote cases where the relationship is statistically significant. The group against which the different educational levels are compared is that with low, or few, qualifications (defined as having qualifications below O level/GCSE or no qualifications); while, for our different age groups, the comparison group is those born before 1920. For attitudes towards government intervention, those that are most pro-intervention are the comparison group. Informally, we can say that the longer the bar, the more difference there is between those in a given group compared with those in the comparison category.

Figure 9.3 Logistic regression model of support for law against racial discrimination

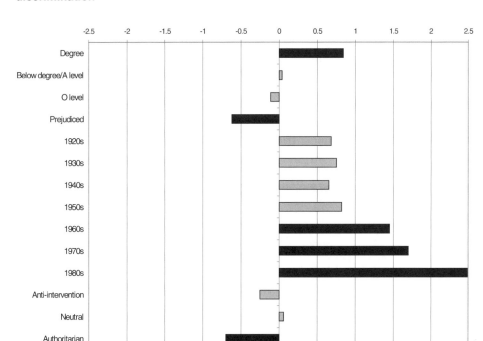

This analysis confirms that there is a clear pattern of rising support for a law against racial discrimination as we move from older to younger cohorts, even when we take account of their differing educational levels. The 'effect' of age is significant and substantial for the cohorts born in the 1960s, 1970s and 1980s. Similarly, our suggestion that it is having a degree that makes the difference in terms of support for such a law is confirmed as correct; among our different educational groups, only graduates emerge as being significantly more likely than those with no, or few, qualifications to support a law. The model also shows that those who describe themselves as racially prejudiced are significantly more likely than those who do not to oppose the race-related policy measure, although the size of the effect is relatively small. This may well reflect the fact that, as discussed earlier, the 'meaning' of prejudice to respondents of different ages might vary. There is also a strong relationship between authoritarian values (which stress issues such as obedience and conformity) and opposition to a law against racial discrimination.

Immigration and the future

How might we expect patterns of prejudice among the British to develop in the future? Until 2002, the *British Social Attitudes* surveys indicated a general decline in levels of self-rated prejudice. However, in 2002 there is a significant reversal in this trend. How might this be explained? Earlier we saw that, although there has been a general downward trend in racial prejudice, there has also been considerable fluctuation from one year to the next, most likely reflecting period effects. It is likely that the upturn in prejudice found in 2002 conforms to this pattern. One possibility is that this change reflects the changing nature of debates about immigration. These debates are now more likely than before to focus upon 'asylum seekers' and 'newer' immigration from Eastern Europe, the Middle East and Africa.

Table 9.10 Acceptances for settlement in Britain, by area, 1991–2000

	1991–1992	1993–1994	1995–1996	1997–1998	1999–2000	% incr. 1991–2000
Eur. Economic Area	4190	2050	340	380		-91*
Remainder of Europe	6010	7610	11400	14940	31080	417
Americas	14460	15530	16650	18570	20040	39
Africa	18600	22780	24970	29290	71480	284
Indian sub-continent	29360	28160	28040	29500	44170	50
Middle East	5700	5420	7670	8340	12680	122
Remainder of Asia	15720	18130	18290	17890	30780	96
Oceania	4780	5500	6970	6790	9020	89
Other	7650	5480	2870	2820	2940	-62
Total	106470	110650	117200	128520	222190	109

Source: Home Office, 2001
A full definition of the countries included in the areas shown in the table can be found in the appendix to this chapter.
* Figure for 1991–1998.

As Table 9.10 shows, immigration from non-EU European nations (predominantly Eastern Europe) has witnessed a particularly large expansion, with a percentage increase of 417 between 1991–1992 and 1999–2000. There has also been a significant rise in "new" immigrants from Africa and the Middle East. So, it is possible that, while the British have become more tolerant of their established ethnic minority population, this tolerance might not extend to more recent immigrants.

There is, however, little evidence that the British are more tolerant of immigration from the countries of origin of the more established British ethnic minorities than they are of immigration from 'newer' source countries. We last assessed this in 1996 by asking, for a range of countries, whether the respondent would like to see more, less or about the same level of immigration from it. Then we found that the largest level of opposition was to further immigration from India and Pakistan (which 53 per cent opposed). By comparison, opposition to further immigration from Eastern Europe stood at 45 per cent, 39 per cent opposed more immigration from European Union countries, and 29 per cent opposed more arrivals from Australia and New Zealand. This suggests that, in the mid-1990s at least, the issue was more one of skin colour and economic resources than country of origin. However, it will clearly be important to update these questions over the next few years to establish whether changing patterns of immigration have had an impact on people's views.

To explore this issue further, we can use British data from the 2002 *European Social Survey* (*ESS*). It asked:

> *To what extent do you think Britain should allow people of the same race or ethnic group as most British people to come and live here? ... And how about people of a different race or ethnic group from most British people?*

While 63 per cent of respondents answer that they would allow "many" or "some" immigrants of the same ethnic group as most British people to come and live in Britain, when asked about those of a different ethnic group the figure fell to only 50 per cent.

Table 9.11 Support for immigration for the same and different ethnic groups to the majority population

		Allow many	Allow some	Allow a few	Allow none
Same ethnic group	%	11	52	27	8
Different ethnic group	%	8	42	34	15
Base (smallest)		*147*	*867*	*553*	*173*

Source: *European Social Survey*, 2002, Britain only

Questions relating specifically to country of origin show a weaker pattern. When asked about the extent to which Britain should allow people from the richer countries in Europe, the poorer countries in Europe, the richer countries outside Europe and the poorer countries outside Europe to come and live here, there were only small differences in responses.

Table 9.12 Proportion supporting immigration by type of country

		Allow many	Allow some	Allow a few	Allow none
Richer countries in Europe	%	11	45	31	12
Poorer countries in Europe	%	8	44	34	13
Richer countries outside Europe	%	8	43	34	14
Poorer countries outside Europe	%	8	40	36	15
Base (smallest)		144	831	627	256

Source: *European Social Survey*, 2002, Britain only

Overall, the pattern of responses suggests that we are unlikely to see a significant rise in levels of prejudice as a specific response to "new" immigration from Eastern Europe and the Middle East.

Conclusions

It is important to be circumspect when interpreting our data on attitudes towards ethnic minorities in Britain. We have provided quite compelling evidence that the meaning of the question on self-reported prejudice may well be different for older and younger respondents and for better- and less- educated individuals. That said, the *British Social Attitudes* series suggests that there has been a slow decline in racial prejudice over the last twenty years, accompanied by a gradual increase in support for anti-discrimination measures. However, this has been something of a bumpy ride, and there has been an increase in self-reported prejudice in 2002. We believe the hypothesis that this increase is related to the increased media focus on immigration is worthy of detailed further investigation.

Explaining the downward trend in prejudice has not proved easy. Perhaps the clearest finding is that people with degrees are less likely to describe themselves as prejudiced than are other educational groups. Since the proportion of British adults with degrees is increasing, this could in part explain the growth of tolerance, albeit to a modest extent. However, there are also factors working in the opposite direction. In particular, there are hints in the data that at older ages people do have some tendency to become more prejudiced. As society ages, this could gradually result in increased overall levels of prejudice, but the net effect is likely to be very small.

The picture is somewhat clearer when accounting for increased commitment to equal opportunities legislation. In this case, there are clear generational differences. This means that, as older (less enthusiastic) cohorts die out and are replaced by subsequent (more enthusiastic) ones, we should expect commitment to these sorts of legislative measures to increase.

Finally, the evidence from the *European Social Study* also encourages us to conclude that new patterns of immigration from other European countries should not provide a long-term source of intolerance. However, we would emphasise the risks posed by a media-led campaign against immigration. Our best guess, then, is that the 'bumpy ride' will continue in the short term but that in the medium term a continued decline in prejudice and intolerance is the most likely scenario.

Notes

1. Census data taken from www.statistics.gov.uk/census2001/. Note that the ethnicity question was more detailed in the 2001 Census than it had been in 1991 and that this could account for a small part of the increase reported here.
2. The *European Social Survey* is a new, academically driven social survey designed to chart and explain the interaction between Europe's changing institutions and the attitudes, beliefs and behaviour patterns of its diverse populations. The first round took place in 2002 and further rounds are intended every two years. Further details can be found at: www.europeansocialsurvey.org
3. The major limitation to this form of analysis is the fact that, in any given survey year, a particular cohort may have a different demographic make-up to that in other survey years, mostly usually due to migration or illness. This type of selection bias is likely to be a particular problem in older cohorts.
4. There is likely to be a degree of measurement error in the figures quoted due to the difficulty of judging exactly what constitutes an "article".

References

Alwin, D.F. and Krosnick, J.A. (1991), 'Aging, cohorts, and the stability of socio-political orientations over the life span', *American Journal of Sociology*, **97**: 169–195.

Commission for Racial Equality (2002), *Anti-Islamic Reactions in the EU After the Terrorist Acts Against the USA: A Collection of Country Reports from RAXN National Focal Points (NFPs) 12th September to 31st December 2001 United Kingdom*, Vienna: European Monitoring Centre on Racism and Xenophobia.

Evans, G. (2002), 'In search of tolerance', in Park, A., Curtice, J., Thomson, K., Jarvis, L. and Bromley, C. (eds.), *British Social Attitudes: The 19th Report*, London: Sage.

Fienberg, S.E. and Mason, W.M. (1985), 'Specification and implementation of age, period and cohort models', in Mason, W.M. and Fienberg, S.E. (eds.), *Cohort Analysis in Social Research: Beyond the Identification problem*, New York: Springer-Verlag.

Glenn, R.D. (1976), 'Cohort analysts' futile quest: statistical attempts to separate age, period and cohort effects', *American Sociological Review*, **41**: 900–904.

Glenn, R.D. (1989), 'A caution about mechanical solutions to the identification problem in cohort analysis: comments on Sasaki and Suzuki', *American Journal of Sociology*, **95**: 754–761.

Heath, A. and Martin, J. (1996), 'Changing attitudes towards abortion: life-cycle, period and cohort effects', in Taylor, B. and Thomson, K. (eds.), *Understanding Change in Social Attitudes*, Aldershot, Dartmouth.

Home Office (2001), *Control of Immigration: Statistics United Kingdom 2000*, London: The Stationary Office.

Home Office (2002), *Control of Immigration: Statistics United Kingdom 2001*, London: The Stationary Office.

Hyman, H. and Wright, C. (1979), *Education's Lasting Influence on Values*, Chicago: University of Chicago Press.

Inglehart, R. (1971), 'The silent revolution in Europe: intergenerational change in post-industrial societies', *American Political Science Review*, **65**: 991-1017.

Inglehart, R. (1990), *Culture Shift in Advanced Industrial Society*, Princeton: Princeton University Press.

Jackman, M. (1978), 'General and applied tolerance: does education increase commitment to racial integration?', *American Journal of Political Science*, **22**: 302–324.

Jackman, M. (1994), *The Velvet Glove: Paternalism and Conflict in Gender, Class and Race*, Berkeley: University of California Press.

Jackman, M. and Muha, M. (1984), 'Education and intergroup attitudes: moral enlightenment, superficial democratic commitment, or ideological refinement?', *American Sociological Review*, **49**: 751–769.

Jackman, R.W. (1972), 'Political elites, mass publics, and support for democratic principles', *Journal of Politics,* **34**: 753-773.

Mannheim, K. ([1928] 1952), 'The problem of generations', *Essays on the Sociology of Knowledge*, London: RKP.

Macpherson, W. (1999), *The Stephen Lawrence Inquiry: Report of an inquiry by Sir William Macpherson of Cluny*, Cmnd 4262-I, London: The Stationery Office.

Office for National Statistics (2002a), *Census 2001: First Results on Population for England and Wales*, London: The Stationery Office.

Rodgers, W.L. (1990), 'Interpreting the components of time trends', in Clogg, C.C. (ed.), *Sociological Methodology 1990*, volume 20, Cambridge: Basil Blackwell.

Schuman, H., Steeh, C., Bobo, L. and Krysan, M. ([1985] 1997), *Racial Attitudes in America*, Cambridge, MA: Harvard University Press.

Sears, D.O. (1983), 'The persistence of early political predisposition: the roles of attitude object and life stage', in Wheeler, L. (ed.), *Review of personality and Social Psychology*, volume 4, Beverly Hills: Sage.

The Times Index (1983, 1984, 1985, 1986, 1987, 1989, 1990, 1991, 1994, 1996, 1998, 1999, 2000, 2001, 2002), Reading: Newspaper Archive Developments Ltd.

United Nations International Convention on the Elimination of all Forms of Racial Discrimination (2001), *Concluding Observations of the Committee on the Elimination of Racial Discrimination: United Kingdom of Great Britain and Northern Ireland.* 57th Session, 31st July to 25th August 2000.

Appendix

Acceptances for settlement: areas defined

European Economic Area	Austria, Belgium, Denmark, Finland, France, Germany, Greece, Iceland, Italy, Luxembourg, Netherlands, Norway, Portugal, Spain, Sweden
Remainder of Europe	Bulgaria, Cyprus, former Czechoslovakia, Hungary, Malta, Poland, Romania, Switzerland, Turkey, former USSR, former Yugoslavia
Americas	Argentina, Barbados, Brazil, Canada, Chile, Colombia, Guyana, Jamaica, Mexico, Peru, Trinidad and Tobago, USA, Venezuela
Africa	Algeria, Angola, Congo, Egypt, Ethiopia, Ghana, Kenya, Libya, Mauritius, Morocco, Nigeria, Sierra Leone, Somalia, South Africa, Sudan, Tanzania, Tunisia, Uganda, Zambia, Zimbabwe
Indian sub-continent	Bangladesh, India, Pakistan
Middle East	Iran, Iraq, Israel, Jordan, Kuwait, Lebanon, Saudi Arabia, Syria, Yemen
Remainder of Asia	China, Hong Kong, Indonesia, Japan, Malaysia, Philippines, Singapore, South Korea, Sri Lanka, Taiwan, Thailand
Oceania	Australia, New Zealand
Other	British Overseas Citizens, Stateless

Logistic regression model of support for law against racial discrimination, *British General Election Survey*, 1997

The model reports the parameter estimates for each of the characteristics specified on the left-hand side of the table. These parameter estimates tell us about the natural logarithm of the odds of someone in a particular category supporting a law against racial discrimination compared with the odds of someone in the reference category (shown in brackets). Informally we can say that the bigger the estimate, the bigger the difference in support between the people in that category and those in the reference category. Negative figures denote a lower level of support for the policy, and positive figures a higher level. Because this is a multivariate analysis, the parameter estimates tell us about the net effects of a particular variable, controlling for other variables in the model. For example, the parameters for education estimate the effect of education among those who share similar levels of prejudice.

Variable (comparison group in brackets)	Parameter estimate
Education (below O level/none)	
Degree	0.84 (0.43)*
Below degree/A level	0.04 (0.23)
O level	-0.11 (0.26)
Self-rated prejudice (not prejudiced)	
Prejudiced	-0.62 (0.19)***
Cohort (Pre-1920)	
1920s	0.68 (0.53)
1930s	0.75 (0.51)
1940s	0.65 (0.50)
1950s	0.82 (0.49)
1960s	1.45 (0.52)**
1970s	1.70 (0.54)**
1980s	2.49 (1.03)*
Pro-intervention scale (pro-intervention)	
Anti-intervention	-0.25 (0.23)
Neutral	0.06 (0.22)
Libertarian–authoritarian scale (libertarian)	
Authoritarian	-0.70 (0.34)*
Constant	1.14 (0.57)
Base	*3662*

* = significant at 5% level ** = significant at 1% level *** = significant at 0.1% level

10 Will we ever vote for the Euro?

Geoffrey Evans [*]

Five years ago I concluded a chapter on Britain's relationship with the European Union (EU) with the observation that "the only absolute certainty is that this story will run and run" (Evans, 1998:187). And five years later so it does. In the last few months alone, the Chancellor and the Prime Minister have been at loggerheads over Britain's entry into the Euro; Giscard D'Estaing's proposed European constitution has led to outcry and calls for a referendum from the Conservatives; and the government has signalled that it too wants to examine the possibility of a referendum before the next election – this one on the Euro. This latter aspiration assumes, of course, that the Chancellor's famous five tests of convergence have been satisfied in one way or another. Yet the most important test of all remains the unstated 'sixth test' – do *the people* want to join the Euro? And, implicitly, does the British public want closer links with the EU, or do they prefer to maintain some distance?

   The importance of these questions is incontestable. The economic and political significance of integration makes joining the Euro arguably the most important public policy decision facing the government. Yet Britain's persistent reluctance to embrace European integration to the extent that most of its fellow members of the EU have done has been one of the striking and important features of the country's public opinion over the last two decades – as indeed has been the persistent ability of the issue to divide governments internally. Relations with the EU have had a profound effect on British politics and with the prospect of a referendum on the Euro, possibly even before the next general election, the disputes both within and between parties are sure to become still more intense. The final decision, however – unusually in a representative democracy – will be made by the electorate as the government has promised that there will be a referendum before entry. Ultimately, it is the public's preferences that will

---

[*] Geoffrey Evans is a Professor and Official Fellow in Politics at Nuffield College, Oxford.

count.

To provide an understanding of public attitudes towards the Euro and the EU, this chapter examines how attitudes have changed since the 1980s. This involves examining levels of support and opposition, the evolution of more established and meaningful attitudes towards the EU, the role of political partisanship in attitudes, and the growing salience of the European Monetary Union (EMU) as a central issue conditioning responses to the EU more generally. The chapter then characterises the nature of current attitudes towards the EU, and the bearing the nature of these attitudes might have of any attempts by the government to move Britain into closer alignment with its sister powers in the EU by way of a referendum. Along with a consideration of the various sources of stability and direction in attitudes towards the EU and the Euro, this section will include an examination of knowledge about the European currency system and how it relates to the attitudes people have on the Euro and an evaluation of the partisan character of attitudes and the bearing this might have on a referendum outcome.

The main theme of this year's *British Social Attitudes Report* is how public attitudes in Britain have changed over the last 20 years. However, this is not the easiest task to do for attitudes towards Europe as there are only two indicators of Britain's relationship with Europe that have been maintained across the period and both of these – on membership of the EU and the single currency – have had major changes in the wording of the questions. In some years, however, both old and new forms of the question wording were asked, so that we can compare the pattern of responses to the two versions and take this into account when extending the time-series.

Attitudes towards European integration

The following question was asked on each *British Social Attitudes* survey from the start of the series in 1983 until 1991, and finally in 1997. We can supplement this with a reading from the *British General Election Study* in 1992 (when the *British Social Attitudes* survey was not conducted):

> *Do you think Britain should continue to be a member of the European Union or should it withdraw?*[1]

Table 10.1 Should Britain stay in the EU or withdraw – two categories, 1983–1997

	1983	1984	1985	1986	1987	1989	1990	1991	1992	1997
	%	%	%	%	%	%	%	%	%	%
Continue	53	48	56	61	63	68	76	77	72	55
Withdraw	42	45	38	33	31	26	19	16	22	28
Don't know	5	6	6	6	6	6	5	6	6	17
Base	*1719*	*1645*	*1769*	*3066*	*2766*	*2930*	*2698*	*1422*	*2834*	*1355*

1992 figure is from the *British General Election Study*.

This question, which presents a stark choice between Britain's either staying in the EU or leaving it, was replaced in 1993 by a question which gives people a fuller set of options that more closely reflect the changing terms of the debate about *degrees* of integration and the strength of the links rather than about the pros and cons of departure from the EU:

> *Do you think Britain's long-term policy should be to ...*
> *... leave the European Union,*
> *stay in the EU and try to reduce the EU's powers,*
> *leave things as they are,*
> *stay in the EU and try to increase the EU's powers,*
> *or, work for the formation of a single European government?*

The new question has been asked on *British Social Attitudes* surveys in every year since 1993, and, again, the time-series can be supplemented with a reading from the *British General Election Study* in 1992.

Table 10.2 Should Britain stay in the EU or withdraw – five categories, 1992–2002

	1992	1993	1994	1995	1996	1997	1998	1999	2000	2001	2002
	%	%	%	%	%	%	%	%	%	%	%
Leave EU	10	11	11	14	19	17	14	14	17	14	15
Reduce EU power	30	25	25	23	39	29	36	43	38	38	35
Leave as is	16	23	21	20	19	18	23	20	20	21	23
Increase EU power	28	24	28	28	8	16	9	11	10	11	12
Single Eur. government	10	9	8	8	6	7	8	6	7	7	8
Don't know	7	8	7	6	9	13	10	7	8	9	8
Base	*2834*	*1461*	*1165*	*1227*	*1180*	*1355*	*1035*	*1060*	*2293*	*1099*	*3455*

1992 figure is from the *British General Election Study*.

We can combine the information from these two series to assess the picture for the full period. First, we can see that from the early 1980s until 1991 there was a steady increase in the public's acceptance of EU membership, from less than half supporting continued membership in 1984 to over three-quarters by 1991. The impression during that period was of a population slowly becoming accustomed to, and even perhaps comfortable with, being part of the European Community. However, in 1992 there was a small but significant fall in acceptance and, still looking at the question reported in Table 10.1, it would appear that by 1997 the secular upward trend had reversed. This interpretation is confirmed by the answers to the more recent series of questions reported in Table 10.2. Here we see evidence of a downward trend during the mid 1990s, when the proportion favouring closer links with the EU fell from almost two-fifths (38 per cent) in 1992 to just one in seven (14 per cent) in 1996, before recovering somewhat to almost a quarter (23 per cent) a year later and stabilising around the one in six mark from then on. Conversely, those seeking to weaken EU influence or to leave the EU increased dramatically (from just under two-fifths in the early 1990s) to a high point of 59 per cent in 1996, and then stabilised at just over half of the population for the rest of the period.

  Overall, we can conclude that during the 1990s the proportion of respondents seeking to leave the EU grew considerably, as did the proportion of respondents who wanted to weaken the EU's influence, while the proportion seeking closer links fell. Since then, however, the level of support has shown no evidence of a trend. This indicates that the early 1990s may well have marked the high point for British support for European integration. After that point there was a reaction against it, probably as a consequence of events that dominated news coverage of the EU at the time – the Exchange Rate Mechanism (ERM) fiasco of 1992, serious Conservative Party splits on the issue, the rise (and fall) of the Referendum Party, the BSE crisis[2] and an increasing focus on monetary union as *the* European issue.

Attitudes towards monetary union and a Euro referendum vote

British adoption of the Euro is clearly a major issue on the contemporary political agenda. For some years now it has been the hot topic in disputes about integration and is the defining question around which parliamentary divisions on integration polarise. Public opinion on this question is therefore in some respects more immediately consequential than are attitudes towards the somewhat vaguer notion of European integration. It also provides a more concrete and therefore more reliable topic on which to elicit the public's attitudes – as evidenced by the smaller proportion of 'don't know' responses typically evoked by questions asking about attitudes towards keeping or replacing the pound compared with those enquiring about Britain's long-term policy on integration.

  Again we have a problem with the continuity of questions. A question on the adoption of a common currency was asked from 1992 to 1999:

> *Here are three statements about the future of the pound in the European Union. Which one comes closest to your view?*
> * *Replace the pound by a single currency*
> * *Use both the pound and a new European currency in Britain*
> * *Keep the pound as the only currency for Britain*

Table 10.3 Should Britain use the Euro, the pound or both, 1992–1999

	1992	1993	1994	1995	1995	1997	1998	1999
Should Britain ...	%	%	%	%	%	%	%	%
Replace the pound with the Euro	21	15	17	18	13	17	20	17
Use both pound and Euro	21	16	18	18	16	17	22	22
Keep pound only	54	66	62	62	68	61	53	58
Don't know	4	3	4	4	3	6	4	3
Base	*2834*	*1461*	*1165*	*1227*	*1180*	*1355*	*1035*	*1060*

1992 figure is from the *British General Election Study*.

By 2000, it was so apparent that the middle option was not likely to be on offer in reality, that it no longer made sense to ask this question, and it was replaced by a question asking people how they would vote in a referendum on the Euro. Fortunately, the two questions were asked alongside each other in 1999.

Table 10.4 Likely vote in a Euro referendum, 1999–2002

	1999	2000	2001	2002
Would vote	%	%	%	%
To join the Euro	28	27	30	35
Not to join the Euro	65	64	59	58
Don't know	7	9	11	7
Base	*1060*	*2293*	*1099*	*3435*

As we can see in Tables 10.3 and 10.4, there is no evidence of a clear trend in responses to the keep/replace the pound question. Throughout the 1990s only a small minority (around 17 per cent) of the public were content to lose the pound as their currency, and a fifth or so were prepared to see a new European currency phased in alongside the pound. There are a couple of high-points of opposition – notably in 1993 following the ERM crisis of the previous autumn and in 1996 when, as we have seen above, attitudes towards Europe generally took a pronounced negative turn.

Unlike the keep/replace question, the question on the referendum vote has no middle option, which increases the proportion of responses for both 'join' and 'not join' positions – though this is more pronounced with the 'join' responses which were 11 percentage points higher in 1999 than with the keep/replace the pound question, compared with a seven percentage point difference in the 'not join' responses. Despite the fact that we saw earlier that attitudes towards the EU as a whole have remained fairly steady in the last few years, there is arguably slight evidence of a growth in 'join' responses to the referendum vote question over the period 1999 to 2002.

The overwhelming impression to be taken from the over-time survey responses, however, is that the public has remained solidly anti-Euro for as long as these sentiments have been measured in the *British Social Attitudes* series. Throughout the ten-year series the proportion wishing to keep the pound as the only currency for Britain has never dipped below half. Even with the presumed weight of a government campaign behind the proposition, a referendum victory on Britain's adoption of the Euro will be no easy task.

Evidence for the malleability of public attitudes?

Given the lack of any long-term trend towards acceptance of EU integration and the Euro itself, any prospects the government might have to swing public opinion towards a 'yes' response on the question of adopting the Euro must rely on attitudes being relatively mutable in the short term. This is a tall order, though it is not impossible: in 1975, opposition to joining the Common Market turned to endorsement in a relatively short space of time in the heat of a strong pro-join government campaign. Is this a likely scenario with respect to a Euro referendum?

One indication of such a possibility would be provided if there was evidence of high levels of instability in aggregate public opinion on the Euro over relatively short time periods, which might be taken to suggest that the public does not have a settled view on the matter. Quite how much fluctuation would indicate a consequential level of instability is not easy to assess of course. Tables 10.1 to 10.4 would seem to imply a fair amount of stability in such attitudes, but it is probably more useful to compare the over-time stability of attitudes towards the Euro with those on other important political issues that the *British Social Attitudes* survey has enquired about over the years. Attitudes towards redistribution and law and order, for example, are generally thought to be stable, core aspects of British political beliefs (Heath, Evans and Martin, 1994; Evans, Heath and Lalljee, 1996) and thus give us a yardstick against which to compare attitudes towards the Euro. In contrast, attitudes on questions such as whether benefits for the unemployed are too high or too low show substantial year-on-year variations and reversals in the majority view (see Figure 1.3 in the chapter by Sefton in this Report). In comparison, the public's views on EU-related issues are not wildly fluctuating. Unlike in 1975, when the majority against joining the Common Market was transformed into a pro-join majority, public opinion on the Euro has not displayed marked volatility.

Sources of support for the Euro

Part of the reason for the stability in attitudes on Europe lies in their roots in social groups. Certainly, the heartland of support for European integration is to be found among the professional, educated 'chattering classes', with opposition being clear-cut among the working class, the self-employed and those with less schooling. Opposition to the Euro also is far higher among the less highly educated, the working class and the self-employed (differences by age and gender are less clear-cut and consistent). These social bases of attitudes towards aspects of European integration have remained relatively constant throughout the last two decades (Evans, 1995; Evans, 1999). Indeed, class differences in attitudes towards the Euro are stronger than those for traditional divisions over issues concerning inequality and redistribution: opposition towards the Euro is what most distinguishes the attitudes of working-class people from those in the middle class (Evans, 2000). In the next table we display the most important social divisions on the Euro. [3]

Table 10.5 Attitudes towards the Euro by class and education

		Join	Not join	Don't know	Base
Class					
Managerial & professional	%	47	48	6	1202
Intermediate occupations	%	30	63	7	418
Small employers/ own account workers	%	36	57	7	261
Lower supervisory & technical	%	26	67	7	399
Semi- & routine occupations	%	25	67	8	1057
Education					
Degree	%	56	37	7	519
Higher education below degree	%	41	54	5	496
A level or equivalent	%	36	60	4	441
O level or equivalent	%	30	65	5	589
CSE or equivalent	%	26	66	9	390
No qualification	%	23	67	10	895

The reasons for the persistence of such divisions are too complex to be unpacked in this context, but there are various aspects of lifestyles and beliefs that can help account for and reinforce the social structuring of EU beliefs. One such candidate is likely to be patterns of newspaper consumption. Broadsheets and tabloids tend to give somewhat different takes on the EU and the Euro, with the broadsheets presenting perhaps a more reasoned approach (whether pro or against). To some degree their readers might be expected to be influenced by the presentation of news on these questions. Certainly, over half (56 per cent) of tabloid readers say that if "there is an argument between Britain and the EU", their paper would usually side with Britain, while much the same proportion of broadsheet readers thought that their paper would usually give "equal weight to both sides" (Evans, 1998).

As the next table shows, broadsheet readers are markedly more pro-Euro than tabloid readers – a difference which exists despite the fact that broadsheets vary in their attitude to the Euro. It also withstands multivariate tests, controlling among other things for the varying level of education of broadsheet and tabloid readers. Indeed, along with degree holders, broadsheet readers are just about the only social category in which there is a majority in favour of adopting the Euro. To infer from this evidence that the type of newspaper read *causes* views on the Euro is, of course, not without its problems – the newspapers would doubtless argue that they tend to give their readers what they want. However, it is unlikely that position on the Euro *per se* is the reason for choosing to read a broadsheet versus a tabloid. Clearly, cause and effect are difficult to separate, but it is at least likely that influence runs both ways, and the differences in attitudes between broadsheet and tabloid are substantial. Needless to say, however, only a small minority of the electorate read broadsheets, thus heavily restricting any pro-Euro impact they might have.

Table 10.6 Attitudes towards the Euro by newspaper readership

		Join	Not join	Don't know	Base
Broadsheet	%	52	42	6	385
Tabloid	%	28	67	6	1235

A further source of stability in attitudes towards the EU and the Euro lies in the sorts of reasons people have for supporting or, more particularly, opposing it. Although expectations about economic costs and benefits undoubtedly have a part to play in influencing attitudes towards integration and the adoption of the Euro – and thus it is possible that people can change their minds in one way or the other in response to the Chancellor's pronouncements about the five economic tests – there are also other, less economically instrumental, motives also.[4] It would simply be wrong to characterise the divisions over the Euro as ones relating only to dispassionate economic interests. An alternative type of explanation of support for, or opposition to, the EU is concerns about the preservation of cultural and national identity (see Deflem and Pampel, 1996) and national pride. The *British Social Attitudes* data do reveal some associations, albeit rather modest, between feelings of national identity and opposition to European integration. In 1997 some 45 per cent of respondents agreed with the proposition that "in a united Europe, the various nations will lose their culture and individuality" (Evans, 1998).

More substantial, however, is the finding shown in the next table (using questions from the 2000 survey), that national pride is quite strongly related to opposition to the Euro. There is an 18 percentage point gap in opposition to the Euro between the admittedly rather small group who are "not at all proud" to be British and those who are "very proud". National pride militates quite strongly against endorsement of the Euro – a relationship that survives multivariate analysis controlling for other factors. Significantly, however, even among people who profess no pride at all in being British, there was a majority opposed to the Euro!

Table 10.7 Attitudes towards the Euro by whether proud to be British, 2000

		Join	Not join	Don't know	Base
Very proud	%	22	71	7	997
Somewhat proud	%	29	63	9	784
Not very proud	%	33	57	11	195
Not at all proud	%	39	53	9	59

Clearly, if the government is going to influence public opinion so as to change clear opposition into majority support for the Euro in the space of a year or two, it has its work cut out. Concerns about national pride and a sense of cultural tradition are not easy to overcome – as the continuing arguments about the new EU constitution have illustrated. So what sorts of factors might play a role in facilitating such a dramatic and unlikely short-term change in opinion? We shall consider two: knowledge and political partisanship.

The knowledge basis of opinions on the Euro

Research has shown that the more knowledge-based are one's attitudes, the more likely they are to be robust (Ajzen and Fishbein, 1980; Bartle, 2000; Delli Carpini and Keeter, 1996). In other words, informed citizens tend to be surer of their opinions than are uninformed citizens and are less easily won over by counter campaigns. Conversely, the less informed might be persuaded to change their minds if given appropriate information. This was found to be the case in a highly publicised 'Deliberative Poll' on the EU carried out in 1995, in which a national sample of adults (whose prior views on the EU had been elicited) took part in a weekend of discussion, debate and information, at the end of which they were asked for their views again. A marked increase in public support for the EU resulted amongst this sample – presumably at least in part as a result of their greater knowledge (Curtice and Gray, 1995), suggesting that more information about the Euro might also provide a basis for greater popular endorsement.

Knowledge about such a complex topic as European monetary union is not easy to assess in the context of a general social survey such as the *British Social Attitudes*. However, the 2002 questionnaire includes a short quiz specifically designed to tap respondents' knowledge of the Euro that gives a rough indication of differences in basic levels of knowledge amongst the population. Respondents were asked to say which of the statements shown in the next table were true and which false.

Table 10.8 Knowledge about the Euro

		Correct	Incorrect	Don't know
One Euro is worth less than one British pound (T)	%	68	11	19
Britain is the only member of the EU that is not a member of the single European currency (F)	%	57	21	21
The headquarters of the European Central Bank are in Germany (T)	%	36	21	42
The countries that have introduced the Euro are still using their own currencies as well (F)	%	60	21	18

Base: 3435

The average of number of correct answers across the four items was 56 per cent. Only 15 per cent of respondents got all four questions right, and only 12 per cent got none right. Clearly, some questions were easier than others: the high level of knowledge on the item about the value of the Euro probably reflects respondents' experience in dealing with the currency, while by far the hardest question was that on the location of the European Central Bank, which had an extremely high proportion of 'don't know' responses. Whether one should regard these responses as showing high levels or low levels of public knowledge is a matter of opinion, but they do not indicate complete ignorance.

They also show that people vary considerably in their level of knowledge. The relationship between knowledge and attitudes towards the EU and the Euro is shown in the next table. We can see that the relationship between knowledge and Euroscepticism is by no means a straightforward one. Those for and against the EU have similar (higher) levels of knowledge – it is those who give "leave things as they are" responses (which would appear to be effectively equivalent to 'don't know' answers) who have least knowledge. The 'informed Eurosceptics' are likely to take some convincing of the merits of further integration.

However, when we look at voting intentions in a Euro referendum, the picture is somewhat more straightforward. According to our quiz scores, people who intend to vote 'no' in a referendum are less knowledgeable about the Euro than those who would vote 'yes' – a finding that remains significant even when we take differences in other factors, such as educational levels and interest in politics, into account. It might be argued, therefore, that public antipathy towards the Euro reflects a continued ignorance of the facts and a corresponding susceptibility to anti-European 'scare stories'. Those who do not know which way they will vote are even less knowledgeable than the no voters. However, it is not true to say that opposition to the Euro is mainly confined to the ill-informed: even among people with high levels of knowledge – a score of 3 or above in the quiz – only a minority (43 per cent) endorse the Euro.

Table 10.9 Knowledge about the Euro by attitudes to the Euro and EU

	Average quiz score	Base
All	2.2	3435
Britain's long-term policy should be ...		
... to leave the EU	2.1	525
... to reduce the EU's power	2.6	1226
... to leave things as they are	1.9	779
... to increase EU power	2.6	367
... to work for a single European government	2.3	253
Don't know	1.2	276
How would vote in Euro referendum		
To join	2.5	1150
Not to join	2.1	2020
Don't know	1.8	256

The relative lack of information about the Euro among the no voters can be interpreted in two rather different ways: ignorance of the facts might reduce support for the Euro, or their negative opinion on the adoption of the Euro leads to a corresponding lack of interest in facts relating to it. Whichever way the relationship goes, however – and it probably goes in both directions – we would expect a lack of knowledge to be associated with the possession of less firmly based and stable opinions. Possibly therefore, opponents of the Euro might be open to having their opinions changed by the government (and other interested parties) proselytising in favour of Euro-entry. Note, however, that this is a high risk strategy which has already spectacularly misfired in the Swedish case.

The British government might prove more successful, but, for a message to impact on opinions, it needs to come from credible sources. Trust becomes the issue, and perhaps as never before in British politics we would appear to be undergoing a crisis of trust in government. Moreover, even before Iraq and the Hutton Inquiry, Eurosceptics were far more distrustful of politicians and their motives than were pro-Euro respondents. Over a third (37 per cent) of those planning to vote yes to the Euro said that they trust politicians to tell the truth "just about always" or at least "most of the time" when they are in a tight corner. This fell to a fifth (20 per cent) among those who were planning to vote no. Almost a third (30 per cent) of this group trust politicians "almost never", compared with 16 per cent of those who were planning to vote yes.

Ironically, this scepticism about politicians' trustworthiness might well be why even most opponents of the Euro believe that Britain will probably be joining Euroland in the not too distant future, as seen in the next table: some four-fifths of Euro opponents think that Britain is "very" or "fairly likely" to adopt the Euro. Regardless of what the electorate wants, the electorate expects the government to do as *it* wants. This would appear to be a classic domestic example of the sort of 'democratic deficit' that has so often been attributed to the EU and its institutions.

Table 10.10 How likely Britain is to join the Euro by attitudes towards the Euro

How likely Britain is to join Euro in the next ten years	Intended Euro referendum vote		
	Join	Not join	Don't know
	%	%	%
Very likely	67	46	41
Fairly likely	26	35	34
Not very likely	5	12	2
Not at all likely	1	4	*
Don't know	2	3	22
Base	*1150*	*2020*	*253*

The EU and political partisanship

The second route through which the government might swing support on the Euro is *loyalty*. To use loyalty as a weapon for passing referendums is hardly a new idea for the government – the Welsh Devolution referendum of 1997 obtained an incredibly close yes result, partly on the basis of mobilising loyalty among traditional Labour supporters who might not otherwise have supported devolution (Evans and Trystan, 1999).[5] Any attempts by the government to use a referendum to bring in the Euro will likewise involve considerations of how to mobilise their political supporters.

In this respect the government has been doing its work. One of the key long-term changes in public opinion on matters European has been the reversal of traditional Euroscepticism among Labour voters. The Labour Party itself shifted from advocating withdrawal from the European Economic Community without a referendum in 1983, to strong support by 1989 (George and Rosamund, 1992; Heath and Jowell, 1994), and has since then become the political force behind the adoption of the Euro. The Conservatives, in contrast, who were the main pro-European party of the 1970s, have become markedly more Eurosceptical ever since. Correspondingly, what we have seen over the long haul is that partisan differences in attitudes towards the EU reversed their direction, during the period from the late 1980s through to the late 1990s.

From responses to the *British General Election Studies* we find that in 1987 no less than 40 per cent of Labour voters wanted to leave the EU compared with only 23 per cent of Conservatives. By 1997, these figures had almost reversed, dropping to 25 per cent among Labour voters and jumping to 37 per cent among Conservatives (Evans, 1999). For Labour, this change took place very clearly between 1987 and 1992 – by which time only 24 per cent wanted to leave the EU, effectively the same as in 1997. For the Conservatives, however, the proportion wanting to leave the EU in 1992 (21 per cent) was still as low in 1992 as in 1987. For them, the change in attitudes occurred only after the 1992 election, when at least some of the Conservative Party expressed their Euroscepticism with increasing fervour (Sowemimo, 1996; Berrington and Hague, 1998) – though in part this reflected the more hard-core character of the much reduced Conservative vote in 1997.[6]

Table 10.11 Attitudes to the EU by general election vote, 1997 and 2001

	1997 election			2001 election		
	Cons	Lab	Lib Dem	Cons	Lab	Lib Dem
	%	%	%	%	%	%
Leave EU	17	16	14	17	10	13
Reduce EU's power	59	39	41	55	36	47
Leave things as they are	11	16	16	17	21	19
Increase EU's power	5	13	15	4	14	8
Single European government	4	9	6	3	8	7
Don't know	5	8	7	4	11	6
Base	*637*	*1096*	*387*	*178*	*334*	*131*

1997 figure is from the *British General Election Study*

Since 1997, the new Labour government has managed to prevent a hardening of views towards European integration among its supporters: as seen in Table

10.11, the proportion wanting closer ties with the EU has stayed steady at just over a fifth, while the proportion wanting weaker ties or a complete exit has fallen from over half (55 per cent) to under half (45 per cent). Meanwhile, the views of Conservative voters have stayed fairly stable, causing a slight widening of the gap between the views of the supporters of the two main parties.

In part this polarisation reflects the tendency for Europe-related issues to have been the reason for some voters switching their allegiance during the 1992–1997 (Evans, 1999) and 1997–2001 (Evans, 2001) electoral cycles. An analysis of vote switching between 1997 and 2001 using the *British Election Panel Study* shows that Eurosceptics were five times more likely than pro-EU respondents to have switched to the Conservatives than not to have switched, with a similar though more muted impact of pro-European attitudes on switches to Labour. Nevertheless, the number of voters who made these switches was still relatively small, so it is also likely that the increasing polarisation between the parties derives from the influence of party positions on supporters' attitudes. In any case, the result of both processes is that Labour has extended and consolidated its pro-Euro support base. We can see the resulting pattern of a likely Euro referendum vote by party identification in the next table.

Table 10.12 Likely vote in a Euro referendum by party identification

	Conservative	Labour	Liberal Democrat
Would vote	%	%	%
To join the Euro	21	44	41
Not to join the Euro	74	49	52
Don't know	5	6	6
Base	*856*	*1400*	*383*

However, before Labour politicians decide that this is an adequate basis on which to fight a referendum, they should reflect on the fact that only 44 per cent of their own supporters say they would vote yes in a referendum. Admittedly, this compares with only 21 per cent of Conservatives, but almost half (49 per cent) of Labour supporters say they would vote no. It would need far more pronounced evidence of a party impact on voters' attitudes than we have found to produce a ready majority in favour of the Euro.

Conclusions

In some ways, attitudes towards European integration and a European currency have remained remarkably steady in the last two decades. The most notable swings are the ones in attitudes towards the European project as a whole.

During the 1980s, even under Mrs Thatcher's stridently sceptical leadership, approval for the EU grew. After 1992 there was clear evidence of declining support for integration, but attitudes then stabilised, albeit at a lower level than the late 1980s. Nevertheless, the stabilisation suggests that support for European integration is by no means in inexorable decline. It also remains the case that only a small proportion of people favour actual British withdrawal from the EU.

European integration has traditionally been an issue with low political salience, only occasionally emerging as a topic that moved British public opinion in the 1970s and 1980s (Janssen, 1991; Evans, 1995; Rasmussen 1997). In the 1990s, however, the increasing prominence and proximity of integration has promoted Europe to a more central political position. Since the period of the Maastricht Treaty, various European electorates have become increasingly aware of – and sceptical about – the integration agenda (Franklin *et al.*, 1994).

In Britain, the partisan nature of integration has transformed. This change has not only been one where pre-existing Labour supporters have changed their minds, but also reflects the migration of Eurosceptics from Labour to the Conservatives since 1997. Europe is probably the only issue that has lead to people switching from Labour to the Conservatives during that period, thus consolidating the relatively pro-Europe nature of Labour's support base. This represents a clear change since the chapter on Europe in *The 15th Report*, written in 1998, which concluded that in the main "it is politicians themselves who are most in dispute over the EU" (Evans, 1998: 186).

So, European integration and its currently most emotive aspect, monetary union, are now politicised to a greater degree than for many years, if ever. The bland assumption that characterised earlier academic interpretations of the role of public opinion in the process of European integration (Lindberg and Scheingold, 1970), that of a 'permissive consensus' obtained from a disinterested electorate, is finished. This increasingly partisan nature of EU attitudes is, however, likely to dampen any attempts by the Labour Party to change opinions across the population as a whole.

Whether the asymmetry in knowledge about the Euro between the relatively informed 'yes' voters and the less well-informed 'no' and 'don't know' respondents might make it easier to increase rather than undermine support for the Euro is doubtful. It is not simply a case of a need for education about the EU: as we have seen, the most informed can equally well want European influence to be limited as want it extended. Indeed, increases in attention to European issues in the 1990s were probably related to the *drop* in support for integration at that time (Evans, 1998). Moreover, for pro-Euro messages to be persuasive they need to come from a trusted source. Trust in politicians – especially government politicians – is clearly in rather short supply generally nowadays, and especially among those who might be the very target of such messages: Eurosceptics and those who simply don't know.

Given this divided state of public opinion, how might the issue unfold over the next few years? The government has both committed itself to a referendum and given its support to Britain joining Euroland. And the public appears to be (in the main) resigned to this outcome, whether they want it or not. Labour Party strategists will be aware, however, that the way people are likely to vote in a referendum on joining the Euro will not turn solely on attitudes to Britain's future role in the EU. Even if it did, we have seen that the public's ambivalence about the EU suggests that the result is far from certain. Added to this problem is the likelihood that for many voters – those for whom national pride is of some significance – the issue at stake will not simply be Britain's role in the EU or the relative economic costs and benefits of the Euro, but the much more salient one, perhaps, of a fear of a loss of national control over the economy and a threat to a potent cultural symbol – the British pound.

Notes

1. The wording of questions about the EU has altered over the years to fit common usage. This question referred to 'the EEC – the Common Market' until 1989; to 'the EC – the Common Market' in 1990; to 'the European Community' in 1991 and 1992; and to 'the European Union' in 1997. This chapter refers to 'the EU' throughout.
2. The BSE crisis broke in the spring of 1996 and the controversy about British beef would seem to be the most likely reason why public support for the EU was so low in that year (see Evans, 1998).
3. Evidence on these divisions with respect to the EU as a whole has been presented in previous *British Social Attitudes* Report chapters; see Evans, 1995 and 1998. For the same reason this focus on the Euro will apply also to most of the tables that follow.
4. There is a substantial body of research into attitudes towards European integration that has focused on economic motivations for supporting or opposing EU integration across the EU: Eichenberg and Dalton, 1993; Gabel and Palmer, 1995; Anderson and Reichert, 1996. In the British case such motives are examined in Evans (1998) and Curtice (2003).
5. The significance of positive or negative cues from parties for support or opposition to the EU is also argued by both Flickinger (1994) and Anderson (1998).
6. That the electorate registered this change in party positions can be seen from answers to a question asked in the *British Election Panel Study* in both 1992 and 1997 which enquired about respondents' views on where the parties stood on Europe. In 1992 only 36 per cent saw the Conservatives as being anti-integration. By 1997 this figure had risen to 53 per cent. In contrast, both Labour and the Liberal Democrats were perceived to have become more pro-integration over the same period.

References

Ajzen, I. and Fishbein, M. (1980), *Understanding Attitudes and Predicting Social Behavior*, Englewood Cliffs, NJ: Prentice-Hall.

Anderson, C.J. (1998), 'When in doubt use proxies: attitudes towards domestic politics and support for European integration', *Comparative Political Studies*, **31**: 569–601.

Anderson, C.J. and Reichert, M.S. (1996), 'Economic benefits and support for membership in the EU: a cross-national analysis', *Journal of Public Policy*, **15**: 231–249.

Bartle, J. (2000), 'Political Awareness, Opinion Constraint and the Stability of Ideological Positions', *Political Studies*, **48**: 467–484.

Berrington, H. and Hague, R. (1998), 'Europe, Thatcherism and traditionalism: opinion, rebellion and the Maastricht treaty in the backbench Conservative Party, 1992–94', in Berrington, H., (ed.) *Britain in the Nineties: The Politics of Paradox*, London: Frank Cass.

Curtice, J. (2003), 'It's not just the economics stupid! UK public opinion and the Euro', *New Economy*, **10**: 113–118.

Curtice, J. and Gray, R. (1995), 'Deliberative poll shows voters keen on Europe when fully informed', *New Statesman and Society*, 16th June.

Deflem, M. and Pampel, F.C. (1996), 'The myth of postnational identity: popular support for European unification', *Social Forces*, **75**: 119–143.

Delli Carpini, M. and Keeter S. (1996), *What Americans Know About Politics and Why it Matters*, New Haven, C: Yale University Press.

Eichenberg, R.C. and Dalton, R.J. (1993), 'Europeans and the European Community: the dynamics of public support for European integration', *International Organization*, **47**: 507–534.

Evans, G. (1995), 'The state of the Union: attitudes towards Europe', in Jowell R., Brook L., and Ahrendt D., (eds.), *British Social Attitudes*: the 12th Report, Aldershot: Dartmouth.

Evans, G. (1998), 'How Britain views the EU', in Jowell R., Curtice J., Park A., Brook L., Thomson K., and Bryson C.,(eds.), *British – and European– Social Attitudes: the 15th Report*, Aldershot: Ashgate.

Evans, G. (1999), 'Europe: A New Electoral Cleavage?', in Evans, G. and Norris, P. (eds.), *Critical Elections: The 1997 British Election in Long-term Perspective*, London: Sage.

Evans, G. (2000), 'The Working Class and New Labour: A parting of the ways?', in Jowell, R., Curtice, J., Park, A., Thomson, K., Bromley, C., Jarvis, L. and Stratford, N. (eds.), *British Social Attitudes, the 17th Report – Focusing on Diversity*, London: Sage.

Evans, G (2001), 'The Conservatives and Europe: waving or drowning?, in Jowell R., Curtice J., Park A., Thomson K., Bromley C., Jarvis L., and Stratford N. (eds.), *British Social Attitudes: the 18th Report – Public Policy, Social Ties*, London: Sage.

Evans, G.A., Heath, A.F. and Lalljee, M.G. (1996), 'Measuring left–right and libertarian–authoritarian values in the British electorate, *British Journal of Sociology*, **47**: 93-112.

Evans, G. and Trystan, D. (1999), 'Why was 1997 different? A comparative analysis of voting behaviour in the 1979 and 1997 Welsh referendums', in Taylor, B. and Thomson, K. (eds.), *Scotland and Wales, Nations Again?*, Cardiff: University of Wales Press.

Flickinger, R.S. (1994), 'British political parties and public attitudes towards the European Community: leading, following or getting out of the way?', in Broughton, D., Farrell, D.M., Denver, D. and Rallings, C. (eds.), *British Elections and Parties Yearbook 1994*, London: Frank Cass.

Franklin, M., Marsh, M. and McLaren, M. (1994), 'Uncorking the Bottle: popular opposition to European unification in the wake of Maastricht', *Journal of Common Market Studies*, **32**: 455–472.

Gabel, M. and Palmer, H.D. (1995), 'Understanding variation in public support for European integration', *European Journal of Political Research*, **27**: 3–19.

George, S. and Rosamund, B. (1992), 'The European Community', in Smith, M.J. and Spear, J. (eds.), *The Changing Labour Party*, London: Routledge.

Heath, A. and Jowell, R. (1994), 'Labour's policy review', in Heath, A., Jowell, R. and Curtice, J. (eds.), *Labour's Last Chance?*, Aldershot: Dartmouth.

Heath, A.F., Evans, G.A. and Martin, J. (1994), 'The measurement of core beliefs and values: the development of balanced socialist/laissez-faire and libertarian/authoritarian scales', *British Journal of Political Science*, **24**: 115–132.

Janssen, J.I.H. (1991), 'Postmaterialism, cognitive mobilization and public support for European integration', *British Journal of Political Science*, **21**: 443–468.

Lindberg L.N. and Scheingold, S.A. (1970), *Europe's Would-be Polity,* Englewood Cliffs, NJ: Prentice-Hall.

Rasmussen, J. (1997), 'What kind of vision is that? British public attitudes towards the European Community during the Thatcher era', *British Journal of Political Science*, **27**: 111–118.

Sowemimo, M. (1996), 'The Conservative Party and European integration 1989–95', *Party Politics*, **2**: 77–97.

Acknowledgements

The author is grateful to Sarah Butt for her research assistance with this chapter.

11 The power to persuade? A tale of two Prime Ministers

John Curtice and Stephen Fisher[*]

Britain has had just three Prime Ministers over the last twenty years. Yet no less than two of them, Mrs Thatcher and Mr Blair, are widely considered to have been unusually radical in their approach to political leadership. Both, in their different ways, wanted to change public attitudes and thereby change British politics fundamentally.

But the kind of change they desired was very different. Mrs Thatcher wanted to change people's attitudes towards what it is that governments should do. She believed that the role of government should be reduced, but appreciated that any reduction she might manage to achieve while in office could soon be reversed unless the public also came to believe in less government. So she both tried to persuade the public of her views and to change the structure of society (through such policies as the selling off of council houses) in a way that made it likely that more people would come to accept her approach (Dunleavy and Husbands, 1985; Crewe, 1988; Heath *et al*, 1991; Thatcher, 1993: 618; Curtice, 1994). And, of course, if she were successful in this aim her party, the Conservatives, could hope that its chances of being able to continue winning elections would be boosted.

In contrast, Mr Blair did not attempt to change people's views about what government should do. Instead, he set out to change people's perceptions of his party (Gould, 1998; Seyd, 1998; Heath *et al.*, 2001). He wanted to persuade people that Labour had changed its views and was now in tune with public opinion, whatever may have been the case previously. So he persuaded his party to accept policies that might previously have been thought to be the preserve of those of a Thatcherite persuasion and, once in office, pursued the same approach. He required his party to ditch Clause IV and, in government,

[*] John Curtice is Research Consultant at the *National Centre for Social Research*, Scotland, Deputy Director of the *Centre for Research into Elections and Social Trends*, and Professor of Politics and Director of the Social Statistics Laboratory at Strathclyde University. Stephen Fisher is Lecturer in Political Sociology and Fellow of Trinity College, University of Oxford.

implemented further limited privatisation. At the 1997 election he promised not to increase income tax rates and to keep to the spending plans of the outgoing Conservative administration for the first two years in office; once in power, that promise was kept. He promised a policy of 'welfare to work', and in office Labour has made it more difficult for people to continue to receive welfare benefits if they are unavailable for work or training. He hoped these moves would persuade the public that Labour now shared the existing values of 'middle England' and that this would enhance the electoral prospects of his party.

In this chapter we assess which, if either, of these two Prime Ministers succeeded in achieving their objective. Did Mrs Thatcher persuade people of her views? Did this mean that her party reached out to sections of society that it had not previously touched? And what has happened to Mr Blair? Did he simply move his party in line with existing public opinion? And, if so, does this mean that people from social backgrounds traditionally unsympathetic to Labour found it increasingly acceptable to support the party?

We address these questions by looking at some of the long-term time trends in public attitudes and party support provided by the last twenty years of *British Social Attitudes* surveys. Our interpretation of our findings will also be assisted by looking at some results from two *British Election Panel Study* surveys conducted between 1992 and 1997, and between 1997 and 2001. We look at three particular key sets of trends. First, we examine how attitudes towards a number of key policy areas, and especially the role of the government in the economy, have or have not changed over the last twenty years. After all, if Mrs Thatcher achieved her aim then attitudes towards the role of the government should have changed under her premiership and not reverted back once her premiership had ended. Second, we consider whether at any time over the last twenty years there has been a change in the social background of those who vote Conservative or Labour, this being a goal for both Mrs Thatcher and Mr Blair. Finally, we look at whether there has been any change in the attitudes of those who vote Labour. For, if Mr Blair has achieved his aim, he should have persuaded those who are disinclined to think that the government should have a large role in society that they could now support the Labour Party with ease.

Changing attitudes

Our first question is whether Mrs Thatcher persuaded Britain to adopt her views, thereby causing a permanent change in the pattern of public opinion in Britain. In the next table we look at three measures that are available for all or most *British Social Attitudes* surveys conducted over the last twenty years. The first looks at attitudes towards one of the key means by which the state helps to cushion people from adverse economic circumstances – namely, the provision of unemployment benefits. Here respondents are asked which of two statements comes closest to their views:

*Benefits for unemployed people are **too low** and cause hardship,
or, benefits for unemployed people are **too high** and discourage them
from finding jobs?*

Table 11.1 shows the proportion who say that benefits are too low. Our second measure taps very directly into the role that government should play in society, by asking people whether they agree or disagree that:

*Government should redistribute income from the better off to those
who are less well off*

Table 11.1 shows the proportions over time who said that they agreed or strongly agreed with this proposition. Finally, the table shows the proportion of people whose views put them to the 'left' of the middle position on a left–right value scale (the full details of which can be found in Appendix I of this Report).

What might we expect to see in the table? If Mrs Thatcher *did* shift political attitudes in Britain so that they were closer to her own, we would expect to find over her term in office a drop in the proportion who think that unemployment benefit is "too low", a fall in support for redistribution, and a decline in the number of people on the left-hand side of our left–right value scale. In fact, although each measure in Table 11.1 tells the same story, it is not the story that we were expecting to hear. Far from being a period during which more and more people adopted Mrs Thatcher's view of the world, according to these measures the later stages of her premiership (which ended in 1990) were marked by something of a *decline* in the number of people with views sympathetic to her own. Thus, in 1983 only 46 per cent thought that unemployment benefit was too low, but in the three readings taken between 1989 and 1991 that figure had risen to 52–54 per cent. Similarly, while only 43 per cent in 1986 backed redistribution, by 1990, 51 per cent did so. And, over the same period the proportion of people on the left of our scale grew from 53 per cent to 59 per cent. Moreover, this drift away from support for Mrs Thatcher's views appeared if anything to continue further during the early years of her successor as Prime Minister, John Major.

But this clash with our expectations does not end there. Table 11.1 shows that Mr Blair's tenure as Prime Minister has also been marked by a shift in opinion – towards views more similar to those held by Mrs Thatcher. Indeed, on two of our three measures (attitudes towards redistribution and views on benefit levels), Britain now looks like more of a Thatcherite country than it did at any time when Mrs Thatcher herself was Prime Minister. For example, support for government redistribution has consistently been below 40 per cent over the last five years, whereas previously it had never been lower than the 43 per cent figure obtained in 1986. In both cases, the decisive change in attitudes occurred after the election of Labour to office in 1997.[1] In the case of our left–right scale, however, the decline in the proportion of the left appears to have begun as soon as Mr Blair became Labour leader in the summer of 1994, but at the same time it has only been sufficient to return opinion to where it was in the mid-1990s.

Table 11.1 How Britain moved to the right, 1983–2002

	% unemployment benefits are too low	% government should redistribute from rich to poor	% left of centre	*Base (smallest)*
1983	46	n/a	n/a	*1761*
1984	49	n/a	n/a	*1675*
1985	44	n/a	53	*1493*
1986	44	43	52	*1321*
1987	51	45	55	*2493*
1989	53	51	58	*3384*
1990	52	51	59	*3202*
1991	54	50	54	*3540*
1993	58	48	59	*1306*
1994	53	51	64	*2929*
1995	51	47	61	*1234*
1996	48	44	58	*3085*
1997	46	n/a	51	*1080*
1998	29	39	52	*2531*
1999	33	36	50	*2450*
2000	40	39	52	*2980*
2001	37	38	49	*2795*
2002	29	39	53	*2900*

n/a = not asked

So it appears we have an unexpected irony. Mrs Thatcher's hopes of changing public opinion were not fulfilled during her own premiership but show signs of having been during Mr Blair's tenure in office. Of course, so far we have only looked at three indicators of public attitudes. So we turn now to see how far responses to other questions asked throughout the lifetime of the *British Social Attitudes* survey corroborate our story.

In many respects they do. We illustrate this in the next table which shows the readings that have been obtained over the last two decades on four further questions. Three of our measures further tap attitudes towards various aspects of the welfare state. First of all we ask respondents whether they agree or disagree that:

*Large numbers of people these days **falsely** claim benefits.*

And then whether:

*Large numbers of people who are eligible for benefits these days **fail** to claim them.*

In the case of the first of these statements, Table 11.2 shows the proportion who said that they *disagreed* with the statement (whether strongly or not); on the second, we show the proportion who *strongly agreed*. Meanwhile we also show the trends in attitudes towards the role and scope of the NHS. Respondents were asked:

*It has been suggested that the National Health Service should be available **only to those with lower incomes**. This would mean that contributions and taxes could be lower and most people would then take out medical insurance or pay for health care. Do you support or oppose this idea?*

Table 11.2 shows the proportion who *oppose* this idea. Finally, our fourth measure provides another indication of attitudes towards income inequality. Respondents were asked:

Thinking of income levels generally in Britain today, would you say that the gap between those with high incomes and those with low incomes is too large, about right or, too small?

In this case, we show the proportion who say that the gap is *too large*.

So, as in Table 11.1, the figures in this next table should give us an indication of the extent to which public opinion is at odds with Mrs Thatcher's point of view. Two patterns can be discerned. First of all, so far as attitudes towards benefits are concerned, there appears to have been little change during Mrs Thatcher's premiership. However, attitudes have subsequently become more negative during Mr Blair's tenure. For example, 49 per cent in 1983 strongly agreed that large numbers of people fail to claim benefits, very similar to the 47 per cent who agreed in 1990. Now, however, just 39 per cent agree (and all the readings since 1997 are lower than those obtained in any year while Mrs Thatcher was Prime Minister). Meanwhile, a second pattern applies when it comes to attitudes towards the NHS and income inequality. Here, opinion moved *away* from Mrs Thatcher during her premiership and has largely remained unchanged during Mr Blair's term in office. For example, the proportion who feel that the gap in incomes is "too large" rose from 72 per cent in 1983 to 81 per cent in 1990, and our most recent reading is much the same, at 82 per cent (see also the chapter by Bromley in this Report). This latter pattern is also evident if we examine attitudes towards taxation and spending. For instance, the proportion favouring more spending on health, education and social benefits doubled from 32 per cent in 1983 to 65 per cent in 1991, while at present 63 per cent are still in favour (see Figure 1.1 in Chapter 1 for further details). So, taken individually, none of the measures in Table 11.2 show *both* a move away from Mrs Thatcher's point of view during her premiership and a move in the opposite direction while Mr Blair has been in power. But in combination they do provide further evidence that overall this is what has happened (see also Curtice, 1986; Crewe, 1988; Rentoul, 1989; Heath *et al.*, 2001).

Table 11.2 Trends in attitudes towards the welfare state and income inequality, 1983–2002

	1983	1985	1987	1990	1994	1996	1998	2000	2002
% disagree large numbers falsely claim benefits	25	22	25	24	23	n/a	12	20	14
% strongly agree many fail to claim benefits	49	50	48	47	44	n/a	37	45	39
% who say gap between high and low incomes is too large	72	77	79	81	85	n/a	81	82	82
% who oppose restricting the NHS to those with low incomes	64	n/a	68	72	78	77	72	74	73
Base(smallest)	*1761*	*1804*	*2847*	*3693*	*1167*	*3620*	*3146*	*2292*	*1148*

n/a = not asked

Our evidence so far, then, indicates that not only did Mrs Thatcher fail to persuade the public of her views, but that, in many respects, public opinion drifted in the opposite direction while she held office. On the other hand, since Mr Blair has been Prime Minister, public opinion has apparently moved rather closer to that of the position of the former premier.

Changing supporters?

Earlier we argued that one aim shared by both Mrs Thatcher and Mr Blair was the desire to extend their party's appeal amongst those sections of the electorate that traditionally were less likely to support them. We turn now to assess whether either of them succeeded in this aim. To do this, we use a measure of support for a party known as 'party identification'. A party identifier is someone who forms an emotional bond with a political party, a bond that is expected to help ensure they remain loyal to that party in the ballot box even if they are currently dissatisfied with its performance (Campbell *et al.* 1960). So, party identification is intended to be a measure of a *long-term* loyalty rather than an immediate short-term preference, although people will, of course, sometimes change the party with which they identify. We measure party identification by asking, firstly:

> *Generally speaking, do you think of yourself as a supporter of any one political party? IF YES: Which one?*

If a respondent says that they do not support a party, they are then asked:

> *Do you think of yourself as a little closer to one of the parties than to the others? IF YES: Which one?*

And, finally, those who respond in the negative to this question are asked:

> *If there were a general election tomorrow, which party do you think you would be most likely to support?*

Table 11.3 Party identification, 1983–2002

	1983	1985	1987	1989	1991	1993	1995	1997	2000	2002
	%	%	%	%	%	%	%	%	%	%
Conservative	39	31	38	39	35	30	26	28	28	25
Labour	33	36	29	34	35	39	44	42	40	41
Liberal Democrat*	15	18	19	11	12	12	12	10	10	11
Other	1	1	1	3	4	6	3	4	3	4
None	8	9	8	7	7	7	9	10	13	13
Base	1761	1804	2847	2797	2797	2945	3633	1355	3426	3434

* Or Liberal/Social Democratic Party (SDP)/Alliance.

Table 11.3 shows the proportion of people who name a party in response to any of these questions, and the proportion who did not name a party at all. This confirms that, despite this supposedly being a measure of long-term party loyalty, short-term shifts in party popularity do occur. For example, in 1987 the proportion of Labour identifiers dipped to 29 per cent, only then to return to the *status quo ante* immediately after. But a more decisive and permanent shift occurred between 1991 and 1995. Over that period the proportion of Conservative identifiers fell from 35 per cent to 26 per cent, and has never reached 30 per cent again since. Over the same period, the proportion of Labour identifiers rose from 35 per cent to 44 per cent, and has not fallen below 40 per cent since. During this same period, of course, Mr Blair had not only become the new leader of the Labour Party, but also the Conservative government had presided over 'Black Wednesday' when the pound was forced out of the European Exchange Rate Mechanism. This latter event is widely thought to have done serious damage to the credibility of the Conservative Party in the eyes of the electorate (Butler and Kavanagh, 1997).

Our interest, however, is not in whether there has been a rise or fall in the level of support for a particular party, but rather whether there has been a change in the *character* of that support. We assess this in the next table, which shows the proportion of people in two key occupational classes, the salariat and the working class, who identified with the Conservative and Labour parties. The salariat comprise those in relatively secure occupations who have a degree of authority over others in the workplace and/or autonomy in how they undertake their work. The working class comprise those whose employment is largely devoid of all three of these characteristics. (Further details of the construction of these classes can be found in Appendix I to this Report.) We also show for each party the difference between its level of support in the salariat and its level of support in the working class.

Table 11.4 Class and party identification, 1986–2002

	% Conservative identifiers			% Labour identifiers				
	Salariat	Working class	Salariat working-class gap	Salariat	Working class	Salariat working-class gap	Base salariat	Base working class
1986	47	23	+25	20	48	-27	694	1062
1987	49	26	+23	19	42	-23	675	1026
1989	51	23	+28	21	49	-28	716	1046
1990	45	21	+24	30	52	-22	679	936
1991	48	20	+28	22	51	-29	747	1000
1993	40	17	+23	25	56	-31	715	917
1994	37	17	+21	32	55	-23	1007	1023
1995	35	13	+22	36	59	-23	1032	1062
1996	34	17	+17	37	54	-17	1036	1068
1997	33	17	+16	36	51	-16	374	410
1998	33	16	+18	39	52	-13	986	907
1999	33	15	+18	36	53	-16	907	984
2000	33	19	+14	37	47	-10	1046	1008
2001	26	15	+11	42	52	-9	867	904
2002	31	15	+17	36	48	-12	912	863

Two points immediately stand out. The first is that there was little change in the social character of Conservative and Labour support between 1986 and 1995. For example, although the proportion of the salariat who identified with the Conservatives fell over this period, so too did the proportion of those in the working class. Thus, in 1995 there was still a 22 percentage point difference between the proportion of the salariat who identified with the Conservatives and the proportion who did so in the working class, just three points lower than was the case in 1986. The equivalent figures for Labour were 23 points and 27 points respectively. Since then, however, the relationship between class and party identification has become much weaker. For example, the difference between the level of Conservative identification in the salariat and that among the working class fell to 17 points in 1996 and has hovered at or below that figure ever since. Meanwhile, the equivalent difference for Labour support also fell to 17 points in 1996 and has been even lower ever since, with a reading of just 12 points in our most recent survey. (For details of formal statistical tests of the claim that the relationship between class and party identification has been weaker since Mr Blair became leader see the appendix to this chapter.)

So it appears that Mr Blair has succeeded where Mrs Thatcher did not, in changing the kind of person who supports his party. The change appears to have taken place in 1995 around the time that Mr Blair persuaded Labour to remove from its constitution Clause IV, the clause that committed it to the 'common ownership of the means of production'. It seems that this change may well have fundamentally altered the image of the party in the minds of some voters. Certainly, since that change the proportion of those in the salariat who identify with Labour has remained at or above 36 per cent. At the same time the proportion of those in the working class who identify with Labour has fallen markedly, and is now as much as 11 points below what it was in 1995.

Changing the link between attitudes and supporters

But has this change in the social character of Labour supporters also been accompanied by a change in the *attitudes* held by the kind of person who supports Labour? Is Labour proving more adept at winning the support of those who might be characterised as more 'right of centre' in their views, while perhaps at the same time being relatively less successful in garnering support amongst those who might be described as 'left of centre'?

The next table provides an initial analysis of that possibility. It is based on the three measures we introduced in Table 11.1, all of which exhibited a movement away from Mrs Thatcher's viewpoint during her premiership but a switch back during that of Mr Blair's. For each measure we show the difference in the level of Conservative and Labour identification between those who take one stance on the question and those who take the opposite stance. For example, the first column of the table shows the difference between the proportion of Conservative identifiers among those who *favour* income redistribution (which stood at 14 per cent in 2002) and the proportion of Conservative identifiers among those who *oppose* redistribution (42 per cent in 2002). As higher levels

of Conservative identification are found among those who oppose income
redistribution than those who favour it, all of the entries in this first column are
negative (-28 per cent in 2002). Then in the second column we show the
equivalent figures for Labour support. However, as the level of Labour
identification is higher among those who *support* redistribution, all these entries
are positive. But irrespective of whether the figure is positive or negative, the
bigger it is, the more it shows that views on these issues make a difference to
whether someone supports Labour or the Conservatives. The subsequent
columns are calculated in the same way but are based on views upon
unemployment benefit levels and where people stand on our left–right scale.
(Readers interested in more formal statistical analysis of the results in the table
should refer to the appendix to this chapter.)

Table 11.5 The relationship between attitudes and party support, 1983–2002

	% [party] support among pro-redistribution minus % [party] support among anti- redistribution		% [party] support among 'benefits too low' minus % [party] support among 'benefits too high'		% [party] support among left of centre minus % [party] support among right of centre	
	Cons	Labour	Cons	Labour	Cons	Labour
1983	n/a	n/a	-30	+24	n/a	n/a
1984	n/a	n/a	-28	+22	n/a	n/a
1985	n/a	n/a	-33	+33	-20	+22
1986	-40	+38	-33	+29	-32	+35
1987	-49	+35	-32	+26	-43	+33
1989	-45	+35	-34	+29	-43	+36
1990	-46	+40	-31	+30	-39	+33
1991	-38	+30	-33	+28	-35	+30
1993	-38	+28	-30	+27	-34	+26
1994	-41	+37	-27	+25	-35	+31
1995	-32	+30	-25	+31	-30	+26
1996	-38	+33	-26	+26	-30	+31
1997	n/a	n/a	-25	+28	-30	+34
1998	-26	+22	-21	+20	-20	+20
1999	-25	+18	-14	+10	-19	+17
2000	-26	+22	-23	+21	-20	+18
2001	-24	+18	-15	+12	-18	+16
2002	-28	+24	-17	+15	-20	+17

Note: the bases for this table are shown in the appendix to this chapter.
n/a = not asked

The table shows there was no consistent trend during Mrs Thatcher's premiership in the relative propensity of those with differing views on these issues to support either the Conservative Party or the Labour Party. For example, throughout the period between 1983 and 1990, attitudes towards unemployment benefit levels consistently made more or less a 30 percentage point difference to the chances that someone identified with the Conservative party, and just under a 30 percentage point difference to the chances of someone supporting Labour. There are some signs of a small change during John Major's premiership, but nothing dramatic. A substantial change did occur, however, once Mr Blair came to power. For instance, just before Labour's 1997 election victory, the difference between the proportion of those with left of centre and with right of centre views who supported Labour was, at +34 points, similar to that which existed 10 years earlier. But, by 1998, this difference had fallen to just 20 points, and thereafter it has consistently been a little lower still. Indeed, the figures in the last four rows of our table are for the most part lower than those found in any year prior to 1998. So, just as the social characteristics of Labour and Conservative identifiers have become less distinctive over time, so too have their attitudes.

These are far from being the only measures where this pattern can be found. It is also evident if we consider attitudes towards welfare benefits and views about taxation and spending. True, these attitudes have never distinguished between Conservative and Labour supporters to the same extent as those shown in Table 11.5; even so, the extent to which they do has still declined over recent years. For example, over the last four years there has been less than a ten percentage point gap between the proportion of Conservative identifiers found among those who support higher taxes and the proportion among those who oppose them, a gap that was previously always well above ten points. Meanwhile, such differences as there ever were between those with different views on unemployment benefits in their level of support for the parties appear to have almost disappeared. So it seems that, here too, Mr Blair's premiership has had an impact. The degree to which people's attitudes make a difference to their party support has weakened during his tenure in office, which is precisely what we would expect if he was to succeed in his aim of enhancing the ability of the Labour Party to secure support amongst sections of the electorate that it had previously found difficult to reach.

But how has this weakening come about? In particular, is it primarily the result of changes in the kind of person who supports the Labour Party rather than changes in the character of support for the Conservatives? To answer this question we look at the evidence a different way. Hitherto we have asked how much difference there is in the party pattern of support between those with different views. Now we look at the attitudes of those who support the Conservatives and Labour, and ask how have they changed over time. The relevant evidence is to be found in Tables 11.6 and 11.7.

Table 11.6 considers attitudes towards redistribution and left–right values. Here there is a clear and consistent picture. The views of Conservative supporters have changed little during Mr Blair's term in office, but those of Labour identifiers have changed considerably. So, for example, the proportion of Conservative supporters currently on the left of our left–right value scale is, at 33 per cent, much the same as it has been over the last twenty years. In contrast, not only is the current proportion of Labour identifiers on the left, 62 per cent, some 20 points *lower* than it was at various points in the 1980s, but every single reading since 1998 has been below every single reading obtained before then. A similar generalisation applies to attitudes towards the redistribution of income.

Table 11.6 Attitudes towards redistribution and position on the left–right scale amongst Conservative and Labour supporters, 1985–2002

	% support redistribution		% left of centre			
	Conservative identifiers	Labour identifiers	Conservative identifiers	Labour identifiers	*Base Cons*	*Base Labour*
1985	n/a	n/a	37	68	*485*	*533*
1986	22	64	29	76	*452*	*471*
1987	21	69	28	84	*986*	*699*
1989	29	72	32	83	*1069*	*848*
1990	26	70	31	78	*866*	*931*
1991	27	66	29	74	*985*	*937*
1993	10	30	31	75	*425*	*494*
1994	26	68	37	81	*860*	*1181*
1995	25	60	36	74	*837*	*1371*
1996	22	58	33	75	*859*	*1324*
1997	n/a	n/a	24	71	*305*	*448*
1998	23	48	34	63	*657*	*1122*
1999	21	44	32	60	*638*	*1024*
2000	22	50	35	63	*840*	*1220*
2001	22	46	31	58	*646*	*1262*
2002	21	49	33	62	*728*	*1187*

n/a = not asked

In Table 11.7 we see a not dissimilar pattern, this time in relation to attitudes towards unemployment benefits. Although there has been some drop in the proportion of Conservative identifiers who think that unemployment benefits are too low (a drop that, on its own, would have increased the difference between the two parties' sets of supporters) there has been an even sharper drop amongst Labour identifiers. Indeed, of all the time-series that we have examined, the only one on which there is any evidence that it is primarily the character of *Conservative* supporters that has changed is the series on attitudes towards taxation and spending. Between 1995 and now, the proportion of Conservatives supporting tax increases has increased by ten points, while there has been only a one percentage point drop amongst Labour supporters over the same period. The most recent 2002 figures may be misleading, however. Between 1999 and 2001, the proportion of Conservative identifiers in favour of higher taxes was, at 41–52 per cent, relatively typical of readings in previous years. In contrast, the Labour figures between 1999 and 2001 (57–64 per cent) were rather *below* other recent readings. So even here the evidence that it is a change in the attitudes of Conservatives that has been responsible for a narrowing of party division is at best ambiguous.

Table 11.7   Attitudes towards taxation and unemployment benefits amongst Conservative and Labour supporters, 1983–2002

	% unemployment benefits are too low		% taxes should be increased			
	Conservative identifiers	**Labour identifiers**	**Conservative identifiers**	**Labour identifiers**	*Base Cons*	*Base Labour*
1983	30	64	24	42	676	584
1984	33	65	25	53	640	595
1985	22	65	33	56	564	649
1986	24	63	36	55	1054	1080
1987	32	72	35	64	1095	824
1989	33	71	48	68	1198	1017
1990	30	68	42	65	986	1074
1991	34	70	56	73	1053	1010
1993	39	73	56	73	964	1101
1994	34	67	45	70	1009	1404
1995	30	66	45	70	319	561
1996	29	62	49	68	1012	1528
1997	30	58	54	66	378	560
1998	15	37	51	70	818	1398
1999	23	38	52	62	785	1333
2000	25	52	41	57	937	1394
2001	25	43	50	64	743	1481
2002	17	36	55	69	856	1400

How have attitudes been changed?

It appears then that Mr Blair's tenure as party leader has been marked by a change in the ideological as well as the social character of those who support the Labour Party. Labour appears to have reached parts of the electorate that it previously could not, thereby transforming its electoral prospects. Yet, in truth, we need to exercise some care before accepting this conclusion. First of all we should note that the rise in the proportion of Labour identifiers amongst the electorate (which occurred between 1991 and 1995) largely predates the change in the social or attitudinal character of the party's support (which appears to have occurred since 1995) (see also Crewe and Thomson, 1999). So if Labour is now reaching parts of the electorate that it previously could not reach, such gains must have been counterbalanced by losses amongst its more traditional supporters. Meanwhile, we should bear in mind that, rather than there having been a change in the kind of people willing to support Labour, what may have happened is a change in the attitudes of those who were supporting Labour already. After all, such a process could also help explain why under Mr Blair's leadership Britain as a whole has apparently moved closer to Mrs Thatcher's point of view. Perhaps Mr Blair has made Britain as a whole appear a more Thatcherite country because, in changing his party, he succeeded in changing the views of his party's supporters.

Unfortunately, we cannot tell from the kind of data we have been examining so far whether Mr Blair changed the kinds of people who voted for his party or changed the attitudes of those who were already Labour supporters. To be able to do so, we need to use data from 'panel' studies in which exactly the same individuals have been interviewed at intervals over an extended period of time (rather than, as is the case with the *British Social Attitudes* survey, data collected from different people each year). We can then see how distinctive were the attitudes of those who became Labour identifiers during Mr Blair's leadership, and equally whether there were any changes in the attitudes of those who had always been Labour identifiers. Fortunately we do have access to such data. The *British Election Panel Study* interviewed a representative sample of the public in 1992 and then on repeated occasions up to, and immediately after, the 1997 general election. It then repeated the same exercise on a new sample that was first interviewed in 1997 and thereafter on occasions up to and immediately after the 2001 general election. These studies carried a similar left–right scale to that included on the *British Social Attitudes* survey (Heath *et al.*, 1994) as well as a measure of party identification.

One way of looking at the results of these panel data is demonstrated in Table 11.8. It shows what proportion of new, old and consistent Labour identifiers had views that placed them on the left of our left–right value scale, with separate figures for 1992–1997 and 1997–2001. 'Old Labour identifiers' are those who were Labour identifiers in 1992 but not in 1997 (or who were in 1997 but not in 2001). 'New Labour identifiers' are those who were *not* Labour identifiers in 1992 but were in 1997 (or were not in 1997 but were in 2001), while 'consistent Labour identifiers' are those who were Labour identifiers at both the beginning and the end of the relevant period. We also show in the table the attitudes of those who were *never* Labour identifiers, together with those of the sample as a whole.

Table 11.8 Changing attitudes of new, old and consistent Labour identifiers, 1992–2001

	% left of centre			
1992–1997			**Change**	
	1992	**1997**	**1992–1997**	*Base*
New Labour identifier (1997 only)	52	61	+9	*199*
Old Labour identifier (1992 only)	79	54	-25	*34*
Consistent Labour identifier (1992 and1997)	79	69	-10	*470*
Never Labour identifier (Neither 1992 nor 1997)	20	26	+6	*889*
All	42	43	+1	*1592*
	% left of centre			
1997–2001			**Change**	
	1997	**2001**	**1997–2001**	*Base*
New Labour identifier (2001 only)	54	49	-5	*170*
Old Labour identifier (1997 only)	72	61	-11	*128*
Consistent Labour identifier (1997 and2001)	72	64	-8	*786*
Never Labour identifier (Neither 1997 nor 2001)	33	34	+1	*989*
All	52	48	-4	*2073*

Source: *British Election Panel Studies* 1992–1997 and 1997–2001. Analysis based on those who responded to both the 1992 and 1997 and the 1997 and 2001 waves respectively.

Three key points clearly emerge from Table 11.8. First, in neither period is there any evidence of those who were *never* Labour identifiers moving any further to the right. This suggests that the recent slight shift to the right among the public as a whole is the result of a change amongst Labour identifiers. Second, in both periods new Labour identifiers were less likely to start off on the left than either consistent or old Labour identifiers. Even so, between 1992 and 1997 at least the attitudes of these new Labour identifiers moved to the left over the course of the election cycle, so that by 1997 they were less distinctive than they had been five years earlier. Finally, in both periods the attitudes of those who remained

Labour identifiers throughout changed. Between 1992 and 1997 there was a ten percentage point drop in the proportion of consistent Labour identifiers who were on the left of our scale while there was a similar eight percentage point drop between 1997 and 2001.

So it seems that while changing his party may have helped Mr Blair acquire the support of those who, on average, were further to the right than many existing Labour identifiers, it also helped persuade those already backing the party to change their views. But which of these processes was the more important? We attempt to establish this in the next table, which breaks down the shift to the right amongst Labour identifiers as a whole into the proportion that can be accounted for, firstly, by changes in the attitudes of those people who backed Labour already, and, secondly, by changes in who supports Labour. In the first row of the table we show the proportion of those Labour identifiers in 1992 (1997 in the lower half of the table) who were on the left of our scale in 1992 (1997). Then in the second row we show the proportion of this group that was on the left in 1997 (2001). As we are looking at exactly the same people in these two rows, any change in the percentage of people on the left must be the result of changing attitudes rather than changes in who supports Labour. In short, the difference between these two rows gives us a measure of 'ideological conversion' amongst existing Labour identifiers. We then turn to measuring the impact of changes in *who* supports Labour on the ideological character of Labour support. To do this, we first of all recalculate in the third row of the table the percentage of Labour identifiers on the left in 1997 (2001) after we have excluded old Labour identifiers – that is, those people who stopped being Labour identifiers between 1992 and 1997 (1997 and 2001). In the fourth row, we add in new Labour identifiers – that is, those people who were recruited into Labour's ranks between 1992 and 1997 (1997 and 2001). The difference between the second row and the third row of the table therefore shows the impact on the attitudinal character of Labour support of the decision of some people to stop supporting Labour (that is the impact of 'desertion'), while the difference between the third and the fourth row shows the impact of those who decided to join Labour's ranks ('recruitment').

In both halves of Table 11.9, the impact of desertion and recruitment is clearly smaller than the impact of ideological conversion.[2] For example, there was a nine percentage point decline between 1997 and 2001 in the proportion of all 1997 Labour identifiers with views to the left of centre. Removing old Labour identifiers from this group makes little difference; after all, we have already seen that the views of Labour deserters were little different from those of consistent Labour voters. Meanwhile, adding *new* Labour identifiers to consistent Labour identifiers results in a further three percentage point drop in the proportion of Labour identifiers on the left, but this figure is just one-third of that in the first row. In short, it appears that Mr Blair's leadership did far more to change the attitudes of his party's existing supporters than it did to change the kind of people who supported Labour. And it is this process that also seems to hold the key as to why Britain has moved closer to Mrs Thatcher's views in recent years in a manner that did not happen during her premiership itself.

Table 11.9 Decomposing Labour identifiers' move to the right

1992–1997	% left of centre	Difference	Base	Process
1992 Labour identifiers' views in 1992	79			
1992 Labour identifiers' views in 1997	68	-11	*504*	'Ideological conversion'
As above, *minus* those no longer Labour identifiers in 1997	69	+1	*470*	'Desertion'
As above, *plus* those who became Labour identifiers by 1997	67	-2	*677*	'Recruitment'
Net change overall		**-12**	*703*	

1997–2001	% left of centre	Difference	Base	Process
1997 Labour identifiers' views in 1997	72			
1997 Labour identifiers' views in 2001	63	-9	*914*	'Ideological conversion'
As above, *minus* those no longer Labour identifiers in 2001	64	+1	*786*	'Desertion'
As above, *plus* those who became Labour identifiers by 2001	61	-3	*956*	'Recruitment'
Net change overall		**-11**	*1084*	

Source: *British Election Panel Studies* 1992–1997 and 1997–2001. Analysis based on those who responded to both the 1992 and 1997 and the 1997 and 2001 waves respectively.

Conclusions

It seems that Mr Blair has achieved what Mrs Thatcher failed to do; to move public opinion somewhat closer to the views espoused by the former Prime Minister. He has done so, it appears, primarily by changing the attitudes of those who were already Labour supporters and this, in turn, has helped narrow some of the differences between Conservative and Labour supporters. At the same time, however, our analysis has cast some doubt on the extent to which his party's electoral success rests on Mr Blair's ability to change the kind of people who were willing to support Labour. The rise in Labour identification largely predated the change in the social and ideological character in Labour support, while the change in the ideological character of Labour support appears to be more the product of the change in the attitudes of Labour supporters than it is of change in the kind of person willing to support Labour. In short, Mr Blair appears to have been more successful in achieving Mrs Thatcher's objective of moving the country towards her views than he has been in enhancing Labour's electoral prospects by persuading a different kind of person to support Labour.

Still, Mr Blair has demonstrated that Prime Ministers and party leaders can sometimes bring about changes in public attitudes and perhaps even ideology. But it appears from the experience of the last twenty years that they may be most influential when they adopt a stance that is to a considerable degree at variance with their party's traditional position. The truly radical leader is the one who changes the character of their party rather than one who merely reinforces it. There is, however, an obvious danger with such radicalism. In helping move the centre ground of public opinion to the right, Mr Blair has, of course, also moved it closer to the ideological territory of the Conservative Party. And, to that degree at least, he may have just made the Conservatives' chances of recapturing power that little bit easier if and when the public tires of his administration.

Notes

1. The 1997 survey took place immediately before the general election.
2. This remains the case, albeit less sharply so, if we focus upon Labour *voters* rather than Labour *identifiers*. Thus, there was a seven percentage point drop between 1992 and 1997 in the proportion of 1992 Labour voters who were on the left in 1997. The views of those who voted Labour in 1997 after not having done so in 1992 added a further five points to this drop, while the drop was then lessened by one point thanks to the slightly more right-wing views of those who deserted Labour between 1992 and 1997.

References

Butler, D. and Kavanagh, D. (1997), *The British General Election of 1997*, Basingstoke: Macmillan.

Campbell, A., Converse, P., Miller, W. and Stokes, D. (1960), *The American Voter*, New York: Wiley.

Crewe, I. (1988), 'Has the electorate become Thatcherite?', in Skidelsky, R. (ed.), *Thatcherism*, London: Chatto & Windus.

Crewe, I. and Thomson, K. (1999), 'Party loyalties: dealignment or realignment?', in Evans, G. and Norris, P. (eds.), *Critical Elections: British Parties and Voters in Long-Term Perspective*, London: Sage.

Curtice, J. (1986), 'Political partisanship', in Jowell, R., Witherspoon, S. and Brook, L. (eds.), *British Social Attitudes: the 1986 Report*, Aldershot: Gower.

Curtice, J. (1994), 'Why do the Conservatives keep on winning?', in Margetts, H. and Smyth, G. (eds.), *Turning Japanese? Britain with a Permanent Party of Government*, London: Lawrence & Wishart.

Dunleavy, P. and Husbands, C. (1985), *British Democracy at the Crossroads*, London: Allen & Unwin.

Gould, P. (1998), *The Unfinished Revolution: How the Modernisers Saved the Labour Party*, London: Little, Brown & Co.

Heath, A., Jowell, R., Curtice, J., Evans, G., Field, J. and Witherspoon, S. (1991), *Understanding Political Change: The British Voter 1964–87*, Oxford: Pergamon.

Heath, A., Evans, G. and Martin, J. (1994), 'The measurement of core beliefs and values: the development of balanced socialist/laissez-faire and libertarian/authoritarian scales', *British Journal of Political Science*, 24: 115–58.

Heath, A., Jowell, R. and Curtice, J. (2001), *The Rise of New Labour*, Oxford: Oxford University Press.

Rentoul, J. (1989), *Me and Mine*, Unwin Hyman.

Seyd, P. (1998), 'Tony Blair and New Labour', in King, A., Denver, D., McLean, I., Norris, P., Norton, P., Sanders, D. and Seyd, P. (eds.), *New Labour Triumphs: Britain at the Polls*, Chatham, NJ: Chatham House.

Thatcher, M. (1993), *The Downing Street Years*, London: HarperCollins.

Appendix

Bases for Table 11.5

	% [party] support among pro-redistribution minus % [party] support among anti- redistribution	% [party] support among 'benefits too low' minus % [party] support among 'benefits too high'	% [party] support among left of centre minus % [party] support among right of centre
1983	n/a	1415	n/a
1984	n/a	1291	n/a
1985	n/a	1418	1493
1986	977	2404	1308
1987	1940	2275	2459
1989	2051	2375	2580
1990	1928	2211	2407
1991	2088	2302	2643
1993	1014	2305	1292
1994	2211	2636	2886
1995	2384	993	3070
1996	2245	2862	3037
1997	n/a	1012	1080
1998	1762	2348	2476
1999	1747	2353	2403
2000	2255	2593	2947
2001	1976	2442	2756
2002	2070	2600	2825

n/a = not asked

Logistic regression

This section presents statistical models of the relationship between social class and attitudes on the one hand, and identifying with the Labour Party on the other. The following table presents the results of four logistic regressions of identifying with Labour versus not doing so (for details of logistic regression see Appendix of this Report). In the first column we model the relationship between social class and Labour identification, while in the remaining columns we model separately the relationship between the three measures we introduced in Table 11.1 and Labour identification. In each case, positive numbers indicate an increased chance of identifying with Labour and negative numbers the opposite.

The first row of each model gives the impact of having the characteristic stated in the column heading on the chances of supporting Labour during the Thatcher years that are covered by the *British Social Attitudes* surveys (1983–1990). Notice that all four characteristics (being working class, being in favour of redistribution, thinking that the unemployment benefit is too low, and being left of centre on our socialist–laissez-faire scale) are positively associated with Labour Party identification. The next three rows of the table show how the relationship between the relevant characteristic and Labour support changed since 1990. For this purpose we have divided the post-Thatcher period into three: that before Mr Blair became Labour leader (1991–1994); the period during which Mr Blair was leader of the opposition (1995–1997); and the period during which Mr Blair has been Prime Minister (1998–2002). For each period, the table shows the difference in the strength of the relationship in that period as compared with 1983–1990. A positive number indicates a strengthening of the relationship, a negative number a weakening.

The remaining rows of the table contain equivalent terms that measure the difference between the level of party identification in the period indicated and the level between 1983 and 1990, as well as the constant term.

Logistic regressions of Labour Party identification

x is ...	Working class		In favour of redistribution		Thinks unemployment benefits too low		Left of centre	
x	1.03	**	1.24	**	1.14	**	1.48	**
x * 91–94	0.03		-0.17	*	-0.12	*	-0.16	
x * 95–97	-0.20	*	-0.21	**	-0.12		-0.20	*
x * 98–02	-0.53	**	-0.56	**	-0.56	**	-0.75	**
91–94	0.29	**	0.39	**	0.22	**	0.32	**
95–97	0.86	**	0.87	**	0.66	**	0.77	**
98–02	0.92	**	1.07	**	0.95	**	1.15	**
Constant	-1.32		-1.57		-1.37		-1.77	
Base	26,786		35,693		46,641		38,198	

* = significant at 5% level; ** = significant at 1% level

Notes : Figures are logistic regression coefficients. Each column represents a single model with the x variable being defined by the column heading. The different time periods and x are all indicator (0,1) variables in the model. The variables x*time period are all simply the product of the x variable and the relevant indicator time period variable. The base for the models is all respondents with a non-missing answer to the item(s) from which x is derived, except for the first column which includes respondents in the working class and the salariat only.

The first column shows that there was no significant change from the Thatcher years to the pre-Blair–Major years in the strength of the class-partisanship relationship. A decline started after Mr. Blair became Labour leader and continued when he became Prime Minister. A similar decline in the strength of the relationship between political attitudes and Labour identification can be seen in the other three columns, though it occurs more gradually. There is already some evidence of a weakening of the relationship between the three attitudinal characteristics and Labour Party support in the 1991–1994 period, although this was not statistically significant for our left–right ideological scale. There was then little if any further weakening of the relationships before the 1997 election, but thereafter there was a substantial decline when Mr Blair became Prime Minister. The relationships between all four of the characteristics in the table and party identification have been between two-thirds and half as strong under Blair's premiership as they were in the Thatcher years.

Conclusion

As we noted in the Introduction, Britain has experienced considerable social change over the last twenty years. The country is much richer, and better educated. More people are engaged in middle-class occupations, and fewer in working-class ones. Many more women, including those with young children, go out to work. And Britain as a whole has had to respond to globalisation, whether this is reflected in increasing foreign travel, the rapid flow of information across the Internet, or the ease with which capital and business activity can be switched from one country to another.

There are very good reasons to believe that such changes will have affected social attitudes and values. A richer society is one in which people can be expected to feel able to look after themselves; consequently, we might expect to find a growing reluctance to rely on collective welfare provision, such as health care or social security benefits, and declining enthusiasm about paying the taxes needed to fund them. Equally, the growth of white collar occupations, combined with increased affluence, might well be expected to weaken the impact of social class on people's life chances, and thus the social and political differences between those in different classes (Clark and Lipset, 2001). In short, as we become increasingly middle class in the way in which we live our lives, so we can be expected to look increasingly middle class in our social outlook as well.

We might expect the growth of educational attainment to have made a difference too (Inglehart, 1997; Giddens, 1998; Beck and Beck-Gernsheim, 2001). In particular, it has been argued that better-educated people feel more able to express themselves and challenge authority – for example, by getting involved politically. The better educated are also seen as wanting to make more 'individual' choices about their lives and lifestyles, rather than obediently following tradition and authority. So we should expect to find that increasing access to higher levels of education will result in an increasingly liberal outlook on social and moral issues, and a reluctance to embrace 'tradition'. In addition, some argue that increasing education and affluence will lead to a growth in concern with protecting the environment, rather than the continual pursuit of more and more economic growth (Inglehart, 1997). A better-educated society should, therefore, be a greener one.

Globalisation could also be expected to have made its contribution. A more globalised world is one in which national differences might be thought to matter less and national identities should no longer seem so important. This is especially so in a highly educated society, where traditional 'ascribed' identities are seen to be less important than achieved ones. At the same time, however, globalisation might also be expected to encourage the feeling that there are limits to what the state can and should deliver to its citizens. So we might expect to find a decline in people's commitment to collective welfare provision, perhaps because of an increasing awareness that Britain must remain economically competitive.

If these social changes have indeed affected attitudes and values there is one way in particular that we might anticipate this has happened – through a process of generational replacement whereby younger generations gradually replace older ones. After all, it is those who have entered adulthood during the last twenty years who have profited most from the rise in educational attainment. It is younger women who have been going out to work while their children are still at school. And it is younger adults for whom a globalised world is the only world they know. Consequently, if some of the expectations we have outlined are correct, we might expect to see that social attitudes have changed largely because new generations of adults have very different views to those held by older generations.

But how far do the 50,000 interviews that form the basis of this report suggest that the social changes of the last twenty years have made a real difference to the social attitudes and values held by British society? Have the expectations we have outlined been fulfilled? Or have we discovered that social change has a far less predictable influence on what people think, and that a society's attitudes and values are rather more enduring than we had expected?

In truth, increasing material affluence and a changing occupational structure have had *less* impact than we might have expected. Support for better public services such as health and education is as high now as it has ever been. The public continues to believe that access to publicly funded health care should be based on need rather than income. It continues to believe as well that financial support for university students should be in the form of grants rather than loans (albeit coupled with an acceptance that these should not be available to all). Meanwhile, although income inequality may have grown, there is no evidence that it is tolerated to any greater extent now than was the case twenty years ago.

Equally, we have also uncovered little evidence to suggest that growing material affluence has reduced class differences in social attitudes and values. True, on left/right values we have found some evidence that the gap between the values held by the working class and those held by professional and managerial groups has narrowed slightly. But this appears to have been matched by a growing divergence between different groups *within* the middle class. The result is a society where social class still seems to make a difference to the attitudes and values of its citizens.

We have, however, uncovered one change along the lines we may have expected. Public support for those aspects of the welfare state that are targeted at the poor (such as unemployment benefits) has indeed declined over recent years, assisted perhaps by a fall in the level of unemployment itself. Support for the welfare state, it seems, is increasingly confined to those parts of the welfare state from which *all* benefit. However, we will return later to consider whether this change in attitudes is really the product of social change or whether other developments have been responsible.

So most of the expectations we might have had about the consequences of greater material affluence have not been fulfilled. But many of those that might be thought to flow from increasing educational attainment have taken place. There has been an increase in many forms of political participation (such as signing petitions and attending demonstrations) on more or less the scale one would expect given the rise in educational attainment (even if this growth has been too small to produce any radical change in levels of political participation and has not been able to stop a fall in the numbers willing to vote). Support for traditional gender roles, such as the notion that men are 'breadwinners' and women 'homemakers', has declined, even if the gender division of labour within the home is still marked. We have also seen a decline in racial prejudice, although this cannot be entirely accounted for by rising educational attainment. Meanwhile, as our *19th Report* has previously demonstrated, there has been a general increase in tolerance on many social and moral issues over the last twenty years (Evans, 2002).

However, our expectations about the impact of rising educational attainment in combination with increased affluence have not been realised. Our love affair with the car shows no sign of ending, despite the damage that car use is known to do to the environment and to people's health. Collectively provided public transport continues to struggle to match the benefits that are thought to derive from the individualised convenience of the car, despite its acknowledged negative effect upon the world in which we live. There is also little sign that rising education levels in tandem with globalisation have encouraged people in Britain to disregard their distinctive sense of national pride and identity and become more accommodating in their attitudes towards the European Union. True, pro-European attitudes did increase in the 1980s, but this trend was largely reversed in the subsequent decade. Meanwhile, Britain remains very doubtful about the merits of joining the single European currency, not least because doing so appears to offend some people's sense of national pride.

But where attitudes have changed in the direction we might have anticipated, our expectation that the attitudes of the young would be key has sometimes been fulfilled. Certainly, younger generations appear less likely than older ones to support traditional gender roles. And the decline in support for redistribution and welfare benefits for the poor has been most marked amongst younger people. But social attitudes have not changed over the last two decades simply because younger generations with one set of views have replaced older generations with a different set of views. For instance, those in older generations have changed their attitudes towards gender roles during the course of their adult lives. Meanwhile, a process of generational replacement does not help account for the decline in racial prejudice at all. Evidently social change is not something that only affects the young; it can also affect the attitudes and values of older people too. Indeed, if social change only influenced younger people, its impact on the overall distribution of public opinion over time would always be very slow indeed

Of course, the fact that people's views can change during their lifetime draws attention to another possible explanation for shifts in attitudes and values over time. This is that they might be occasioned by changes in the positions adopted by the political parties rather than changes in the structure of British society. After all, we have seen that the switch of the Conservative Party to a more Eurosceptic position, and of the Labour Party towards a more pro-European one, has been matched by similar switches of attitudes amongst their supporters. Moreover, it also seems that the repositioning of the Labour Party towards the centre of British politics has moved attitudes on some issues towards the right. This explanation can, for instance, help explain the recent decline in support for redistribution and welfare benefits for the poor to which we referred earlier.

So social change is not the only force that can shape social attitudes. Even so, it is striking that many of the changes that we might have expected to flow from the growth in educational attainment have occurred while most of those that we might have anticipated to reflect growing material affluence have not. This suggests we need to re-examine the reasoning behind our expectations about the consequences of growing material affluence. Perhaps in doing so we will be able to generate better-founded expectations as to what we might expect to happen over the next twenty years.

Why might an increasingly affluent, and middle class, society still value collective provision, remain concerned about inequality, and be characterised by marked variations in the attitudes and values of different social classes? One possible explanation is that the most popular parts of the welfare state, notably health and education, are the parts from which middle-class people benefit at least as much as working-class people (Le Grand, 1982). Certainly, over the last two decades, support for higher spending on health and education has consistently been at least as high – *or higher* – amongst those in middle-class professional and managerial positions (the salariat) as it has been amongst the working class. A middle-class society still clearly feels the need for some forms of collective welfare.

Table 12.1 Attitudes to welfare spending by class, 1986–2002

	1986	1993	2002
% in favour of increasing taxes and spending more on health, education and social benefits			
Salariat	48	62	67
Base	*694*	*1007*	*912*
Working class	44	56	62
Base	*1062*	*1023*	*864*

We also need to bear in mind that increasing levels of material affluence will not necessarily eradicate inequalities of income and wealth. Nor will it remove differences in people's working circumstances or, indeed, the extent to which social class affects their life chances. That the rising material affluence of the last twenty years has been accompanied by growing inequality is testament to this. In short, so far as it is *differences* in circumstances that underpin the varying views held by different social classes, we should not be surprised if there is little evidence of a decline in class differences over the last twenty years.

An important consequence of this argument is that increasing material affluence over the next twenty years will not necessarily undermine public support for the welfare state or reduce class differences in attitudes and values. But this does not mean that future public support for the welfare state can be taken for granted, especially if it fails to meet public expectations or if significant sections of the country's politicians decide it is a luxury that Britain can no longer afford. To a large extent, therefore, the future direction of support for the welfare state will depend on political decisions rather than social change.

On the other hand, further social change in the form of rising educational attainment would seem likely to have predictable consequences. We would certainly expect Britain to become yet more liberal on social and moral issues, and increasingly unwilling to accept traditional gender roles. Even so, expectations as to what rising educational attainment might bring should not be inflated. We have, for instance, already seen that, despite rising educational levels, our attitudes to Europe continue to be marked by a distinct sense of national pride and identity. And there seems to be no guarantee that racial prejudice could not increase in the future, perhaps in response to world events. Indeed if continued globalisation is to be *the* big social change of the next twenty years, then at the moment at least it is far from clear whether it is a change to which Britain will readily adapt or one to which it will offer significant resistance.

References

Beck, U. and Beck-Gernsheim, E. (2001), *Individualization*, London: Sage.

Clark, T. and Lipset, S. (eds.) (2001) , *The Breakdown of Class Politics*, Baltimore: Johns Hopkins University Press.

Evans, G. (2002), 'In search of tolerance', in Park, A., Curtice, J., Thomson, K., Jarvis, L. and Bromley, C. (eds.), *British Social Attitudes: the 19th report*, London: Sage.

Giddens, A. (1998), *The Third Way: The Renewal of Social Democracy*, Cambridge: Polity Press.

Inglehart, R. (1997), *Modernization and Postmodernization*, Princeton, NJ: Princeton University Press.

Le Grand, J., (1982), *The Strategy of Equality: Redistribution and the Social Services*, London: Allen and Unwin.

Appendix I
Technical details of the survey

In 2002, three versions of the *British Social Attitudes* questionnaire were fielded. Each 'module' of questions is asked either of the full sample (3,435 respondents) or of a random two-thirds or one-third of the sample. The structure of the questionnaire (versions A, B and C) is shown at the beginning of Appendix III.

Sample design

The *British Social Attitudes* survey is designed to yield a representative sample of adults aged 18 or over. Since 1993, the sampling frame for the survey has been the Postcode Address File (PAF), a list of addresses (or postal delivery points) compiled by the Post Office.[1]

For practical reasons, the sample is confined to those living in private households. People living in institutions (though not in private households at such institutions) are excluded, as are households whose addresses were not on the PAF.

The sampling method involved a multi-stage design, with three separate stages of selection.

Selection of sectors

At the first stage, postcode sectors were selected systematically from a list of all postal sectors in Great Britain. Before selection, any sectors with fewer than 500 addresses were identified and grouped together with an adjacent sector; in Scotland all sectors north of the Caledonian Canal were excluded (because of the prohibitive costs of interviewing there). Sectors were then stratified on the basis of:

- 37 sub-regions
- population density with variable banding used, in order to create three equal-sized strata per sub-region
- ranking by percentage of homes that were owner-occupied in England and Wales and percentage of homes where the head of household was non-manual in Scotland.

Two hundred postcode sectors were selected, with probability proportional to the number of addresses in each sector.

Selection of addresses

Thirty-one addresses were selected in each of the 200 sectors. The sample was therefore 200 x 31 = 6,200 addresses, selected by starting from a random point on the list of addresses for each sector, and choosing each address at a fixed interval. The fixed interval was calculated for each sector in order to generate the correct number of addresses.

The Multiple-Output Indicator (MOI) available through PAF was used when selecting addresses in Scotland. The MOI shows the number of accommodation spaces sharing one address. Thus, if the MOI indicates more than one accommodation space at a given address, the chances of the given address being selected from the list of addresses would increase so that it matched the total number of accommodation spaces. The MOI is largely irrelevant in England and Wales as separate dwelling units generally appear as separate entries on PAF. In Scotland, tenements with many flats tend to appear as one entry on PAF. However, even in Scotland, the vast majority of MOIs had a value of one. The remainder, which ranged between three and 12, were incorporated into the weighting procedures (described below).

Selection of individuals

Interviewers called at each address selected from PAF and listed all those eligible for inclusion in the sample – that is, all persons currently aged 18 or over and resident at the selected address. The interviewer then selected one respondent using a computer-generated random selection procedure. Where there were two or more households or 'dwelling units' at the selected address, interviewers first had to select one household or dwelling unit using the same random procedure. They then followed the same procedure to select a person for interview.

Weighting

Data were weighted to take account of the fact that not all the units covered in the survey had the same probability of selection. The weighting reflected the relative selection probabilities of the individual at the three main stages of selection: address, household and individual.

First, because addresses in Scotland were selected using the MOI, weights had to be applied to compensate for the greater probability of an address with an MOI of more than one being selected, compared to an address with an MOI of one. (This stage was omitted for the English and Welsh data.) Secondly, data were weighted to compensate for the fact that dwelling units at an address which contained a large number of dwelling units were less likely to be selected for inclusion in the survey than ones which did not share an address. (We use this procedure because in most cases of MOIs greater than one, the two stages will cancel each other out, resulting in more efficient weights.) Thirdly, data

Table A.1 Distribution of unscaled and scaled weights

Unscaled weight	Number	%	Scaled weight
0.08	1	0.0	0.0457
0.11	4	0.1	0.0609
0.13	4	0.1	0.0685
0.14	2	0.1	0.0783
0.17	3	0.1	0.0914
0.22	1	0.0	0.1218
0.25	1	0.0	0.1371
0.29	1	0.0	0.1566
0.33	5	0.1	0.1827
0.40	1	0.0	0.2193
0.67	1	0.0	0.3655
0.75	1	0.0	0.4112
0.83	1	0.0	0.4569
1.00	1188	34.6	0.5482
1.25	1	0.0	0.6853
1.50	1	0.0	0.8223
2.00	1782	51.9	1.0965
3.00	292	8.5	1.6447
4.00	120	3.5	2.1929
5.00	12	0.3	2.7411
6.00	7	0.2	3.2894
7.00	2	0.1	3.8376
8.00	4	0.1	4.3858

Base: 3435

were weighted to compensate for the lower selection probabilities of adults living in large households compared with those living in small households. The weights were capped at 8.0 (causing three cases to have their weights reduced). The resulting weight is called 'WtFactor' and the distribution of weights is shown in Table A1.

The mean weight was 1.82. The weights were then scaled down to make the number of weighted productive cases exactly equal to the number of unweighted productive cases (n = 3,435).

All the percentages presented in this Report are based on weighted data.

Questionnaire versions

Each address in each sector (sampling point) was allocated to either the A, B or C third of the sample. If one serial number was version A, the next was version B and the next after that version C. Thus each interviewer was allocated 10 or 11 cases from each version and each version was assigned to 2,066 or 2,067 addresses.

Fieldwork

Interviewing was mainly carried out between June and September 2002, with a small number of interviews taking place in October and November.

Table A.2 Response rate on *British Social Attitudes*, 2002

	Number	%
Addresses issued	6,200	
Vacant, derelict and other out of scope	556	
In scope	5,644	100.0
Interview achieved	3,435	60.9
Interview not achieved	2,209	39.1
Refused[1]	1,612	28.6
Non-contacted[2]	266	4.7
Other non-response	331	5.9

1 'Refused' comprises refusals before selection of an individual at the address, refusals to the office, refusal by the selected person, 'proxy' refusals (on behalf of the selected respondent) and broken appointments after which the selected person could not be recontacted.

2 'Non-contacted' comprises households where no one was contacted and those where the selected person could not be contacted.

Fieldwork was conducted by interviewers drawn from the *National Centre for Social Research*'s regular panel and conducted using face-to-face computer-assisted interviewing.[2] Interviewers attended a one-day briefing conference to familiarise them with the selection procedures and questionnaires.

The mean interview length was 49 minutes for version A of the questionnaire, 51 minutes for version B and 44 minutes for version C.[3] Interviewers achieved an overall response rate of 61 per cent. Details are shown in table A2.

As in earlier rounds of the series, the respondent was asked to fill in a self-completion questionnaire which, whenever possible, was collected by the interviewer. Otherwise, the respondent was asked to post it to the *National Centre for Social Research*. If necessary, up to three postal reminders were sent to obtain the self-completion supplement.

A total of 535 respondents (16 per cent of those interviewed) did not return their self-completion questionnaire. Version A of the self-completion questionnaire was returned by 84 per cent of respondents to the face-to-face interview, version B by 83 per cent and version C by 86 per cent. As in previous rounds, we judged that it was not necessary to apply additional weights to correct for non-response.

Advance letter

Interviewers were supplied with letters describing the purpose of the survey and the coverage of the questionnaire, which they posted to sampled addresses before making any calls.[4]

Analysis variables

A number of standard analyses have been used in the tables that appear in this report. The analysis groups requiring further definition are set out below. For further details see Exley *et al.* (2003).

Region

The dataset is classified by the 12 Government Office Regions.

Standard Occupational Classification

Respondents are classified according to their own occupation, not that of the 'head of household'. Each respondent was asked about their current or last job, so that all respondents except those who had never worked were coded. Additionally, if the respondent was not working but their spouse or partner *was* working, their spouse or partner is similarly classified.

With the 2001 survey, we began coding occupation to the new Standard Occupational Classification 2000 (SOC 2000) instead of the Standard Occupational Classification 1990 (SOC 90). The main socio-economic grouping based on SOC 2000 is the National Statistics Socio-Economic Classification (NS-SEC). However, to maintain time series, some analysis has continued to use the older schemes based on SOC 90 – Registrar General's Social Class, Socio-Economic Group and the Goldthorpe schema.

National Statistics Socio-Economic Classification (NS-SEC)

The combination of SOC 2000 and employment status for current or last job generates the following NS-SEC analytic classes:

- Employers in large organisations, higher managerial and professional
- Lower professional and managerial; higher technical and supervisory
- Intermediate occupations
- Small employers and own account workers
- Lower supervisory and technical occupations
- Semi-routine occupations
- Routine occupations

The remaining respondents are grouped as "never had a job" or "not classifiable". For some analyses, it may be more appropriate to classify respondents according to their current socio-economic status, which takes into account only their present economic position. In this case, in addition to the seven classes listed above, the remaining respondents not currently in paid work fall into one of the following categories: "not classifiable", "retired", "looking after the home", "unemployed" or "others not in paid occupations".

Registrar General's Social Class

As with NS-SEC , each respondent's Social Class is based on his or her current or last occupation. The combination of SOC 90 with employment status for current or last job generates the following six Social Classes:

I	Professional etc. occupations	
II	Managerial and technical occupations	'Non-manual'
III (Non-manual)	Skilled occupations	
III (Manual)	Skilled occupations	
IV	Partly skilled occupations	'Manual'
V	Unskilled occupations	

They are usually collapsed into four groups: I & II, III Non-manual, III Manual, and IV & V.

Socio-Economic Group

As with NS-SEC, each respondent's Socio-economic Group (SEG) is based on his or her current or last occupation. SEG aims to bring together people with jobs of similar social and economic status, and is derived from a combination of employment status and occupation. The full SEG classification identifies 18 categories, but these are usually condensed into six groups:

- Professionals, employers and managers
- Intermediate non-manual workers
- Junior non-manual workers
- Skilled manual workers
- Semi-skilled manual workers
- Unskilled manual workers

As with NS-SEC, the remaining respondents are grouped as "never had a job" or "not classifiable".

Goldthorpe schema

The Goldthorpe schema classifies occupations by their 'general comparability', considering such factors as sources and levels of income, economic security, promotion prospects, and level of job autonomy and authority. The Goldthorpe schema was derived from the SOC 90 codes combined with employment status. Two versions of the schema are coded: the full schema has 11 categories; the 'compressed schema' combines these into the five classes shown below.

- Salariat (professional and managerial)
- Routine non-manual workers (office and sales)
- Petty bourgeoisie (the self-employed, including farmers, with and without employees)
- Manual foremen and supervisors
- Working class (skilled, semi-skilled and unskilled manual workers, personal service and agricultural workers)

There is a residual category comprising those who have never had a job or who gave insufficient information for classification purposes.

Industry

All respondents whose occupation could be coded were allocated a Standard Industrial Classification 1992 (SIC 92). Two-digit class codes are used. As with Social Class, SIC may be generated on the basis of the respondent's current occupation only, or on his or her most recently classifiable occupation.

Party identification

Respondents can be classified as identifying with a particular political party on one of three counts: if they consider themselves supporters of that party, as closer to it than to others, or as more likely to support it in the event of a general election (responses are derived from Qs.151–153). The three groups are generally described respectively as *partisans, sympathisers* and *residual identifiers*. In combination, the three groups are referred to as 'identifiers'.

Attitude scales

Since 1986, the *British Social Attitudes* surveys have included two attitude scales which aim to measure where respondents stand on certain underlying value dimensions – left–right and libertarian–authoritarian. Since 1987 (except 1990), a similar scale on 'welfarism' has been asked.[5]

A useful way of summarising the information from a number of questions of this sort is to construct an additive index (DeVellis, 1991; Spector, 1992). This approach rests on the assumption that there is an underlying – 'latent' – attitudinal dimension which characterises the answers to all the questions within each scale. If so, scores on the index are likely to be a more reliable indication of the underlying attitude than the answers to any one question.

Each of these scales consists of a number of statements to which the respondent is invited to "agree strongly", "agree", "neither agree nor disagree", "disagree", or "disagree strongly".

The items are:

Left–right scale

>   Government should redistribute income from the better-off to those who are less well off. *[Redistrb]*

>   Big business benefits owners at the expense of workers. *[BigBusnN]*

>   Ordinary working people do not get their fair share of the nation's wealth. *[Wealth]*[6]

>   There is one law for the rich and one for the poor. *[RichLaw]*

>   Management will always try to get the better of employees if it gets the chance. *[Indust4]*

Libertarian–authoritarian scale

>   Young people today don't have enough respect for traditional British values. *[TradVals]*

>   People who break the law should be given stiffer sentences. *[StifSent]*

>   For some crimes, the death penalty is the most appropriate sentence. *[DeathApp]*

Schools should teach children to obey authority. *[Obey]*

The law should always be obeyed, even if a particular law is wrong. *[WrongLaw]*

Censorship of films and magazines is necessary to uphold moral standards. *[Censor]*

Welfarism scale

The welfare state encourages people to stop helping each other. *[WelfHelp]*

The government should spend more money on welfare benefits for the poor, even if it leads to higher taxes. *[MoreWelf]*

Around here, most unemployed people could find a job if they really wanted one. *[UnempJob]*

Many people who get social security don't really deserve any help. *[SocHelp]*

Most people on the dole are fiddling in one way or another. *[DoleFidl]*

If welfare benefits weren't so generous, people would learn to stand on their own two feet. *[WelfFeet]*

Cutting welfare benefits would damage too many people's lives. *[DamLives]*

The creation of the welfare state is one of Britain's proudest achievements. *[ProudWlf]*

The indices for the three scales are formed by scoring the leftmost, most libertarian or most pro-welfare position, as 1 and the rightmost, most authoritarian or most anti-welfarist position, as 5. The "neither agree nor disagree" option is scored as 3. The scores to all the questions in each scale are added and then divided by the number of items in the scale giving indices ranging from 1 (leftmost, most libertarian, most pro-welfare) to 5 (rightmost, most authoritarian, most anti-welfare). The scores on the three indices have been placed on the dataset.[7]

The scales have been tested for reliability (as measured by Cronbach's alpha). The Cronbach's alpha (unstandardized items) for the scales in 2002 are 0.83 for the left–right scale, 0.80 for the 'welfarism' scale and 0.73 for the libertarian–authoritarian scale. This level of reliability can be considered "very good" for the left–right scale and welfarism scales and "respectable" for the libertarian–authoritarian scale (DeVellis, 1991: 85).

Other analysis variables

These are taken directly from the questionnaire and to that extent are self-explanatory. The principal ones are:

Sex (Q.36)   Highest educational qualification
Age (Q.37)   obtained (Q.588)
Household income (Q.778)   Marital status (Q.130)
Economic position (Q.257)   Benefits received (Qs.750–767)
Religion (Q.485)

Sampling errors

No sample precisely reflects the characteristics of the population it represents because of both sampling and non-sampling errors. If a sample were designed as a random sample (if every adult had an equal and independent chance of inclusion in the sample) then we could calculate the sampling error of any percentage, p, using the formula:

$$s.e.\ (p) = \sqrt{\frac{p(100\text{-}p)}{n}}$$

where n is the number of respondents on which the percentage is based. Once the sampling error had been calculated, it would be a straightforward exercise to calculate a confidence interval for the true population percentage. For example, a 95 per cent confidence interval would be given by the formula:

$$p \pm 1.96 \text{ x } s.e.(p)$$

Clearly, for a simple random sample (srs), the sampling error depends only on the values of p and n. However, simple random sampling is almost never used in practice because of its inefficiency in terms of time and cost.

As noted above, the *British Social Attitudes* sample, like that drawn for most large-scale surveys, was clustered according to a stratified multi-stage design into 200 postcode sectors (or combinations of sectors). With a complex design like this, the sampling error of a percentage giving a particular response is not simply a function of the number of respondents in the sample and the size of the percentage; it also depends on how that percentage response is spread within and between sample points.

The complex design may be assessed relative to simple random sampling by calculating a range of design factors (DEFTs) associated with it, where

$$\text{DEFT} = \sqrt{\frac{\text{Variance of estimator with complex design, sample size n}}{\text{Variance of estimator with srs design, sample size n}}}$$

and represents the multiplying factor to be applied to the simple random sampling error to produce its complex equivalent. A design factor of one means that the complex sample has achieved the same precision as a simple random sample of the same size. A design factor greater than one means the complex sample is less precise than its simple random sample equivalent. If the DEFT for a particular characteristic is known, a 95 per cent confidence interval for a percentage may be calculated using the formula:

$$p \pm 1.96 \times complex\ sampling\ error\ (p)$$

$$= p \pm 1.96 \times DEFT \times \sqrt{\frac{p(100\text{-}p)}{n}}$$

Calculations of sampling errors and design effects were made using the statistical analysis package STATA.

The following table gives examples of the confidence intervals and DEFTs calculated for a range of different questions: some fielded on all three versions of the questionnaire and some on one only; some asked on the interview questionnaire and some on the self-completion supplement. It shows that most of the questions asked of all sample members have a confidence interval of around plus or minus two to three per cent of the survey proportion. This means that we can be 95 per cent certain that the true population proportion is within two to three per cent (in either direction) of the proportion we report. Variables with much larger variation are, as might be expected, those closely related to the geographic location of the respondent (e.g. whether living in a big city, a small town or a village). Here the variation may be as large as six or seven per cent either way around the percentage found on the survey.

It should be noted that the design effects for certain variables (notably those most associated with the area a person lives in) are greater than those for other variables. For example, the question about benefit levels for the unemployed has high design effects, which may reflect differing rates of unemployment across the country. Another case in point is housing tenure, as different kinds of tenures (such as council housing, or owner-occupied properties) tend to be concentrated in certain areas; consequently the design effects calculated for these variables in a clustered sample are greater than the design effects calculated for variables less strongly associated with area, such as attitudinal variables.

These calculations are based on the 3,435 respondents to the main questionnaire and 2,900 returning self-completion questionnaires; on the A version respondents (1,123 for the main questionnaire and 940 for the self-completion); on the B version respondents (1,164 and 971 respectively); or on the C version respondents (1,148 and 989 respectively). As the examples show, sampling errors for proportions based only on respondents to just one of the three versions of the questionnaire, or on subgroups within the sample, are somewhat larger than they would have been had the questions been asked of everyone.

Table A.3 Complex standard errors and confidence intervals of selected variables

		% (p)	Complex standard error of p	95% confidence interval	DEFT	Base
	Classification variables					
Q165	**Party identification**					3435
	Conservative	24.7	1.3	22.1 – 27.3	1.79	
	Labour	40.9	1.5	38.0 – 43.8	1.74	
	Liberal Democrat	11.3	0.8	9.8 – 12.8	1.40	
Q476	**Housing tenure**					3435
	Owns	73.7	1.2	71.3 – 76.0	1.57	
	Rents from local authority	11.4	0.9	9.6 – 13.2	1.68	
	Rents privately/HA	13.4	0.9	11.6 – 15.1	1.53	
Q485	**Religion**					3435
	No religion	41.1	1.2	38.8 – 43.4	1.40	
	Church of England	30.7	1.5	27.7 – 33.7	1.94	
	Roman Catholic	9.1	0.8	7.6 – 10.6	1.56	
Q528	**Age of completing continuous full-time education**					3435
	16 or under	58.2	1.6	55.1 – 61.4	1.88	
	17 or 18	18.5	0.8	16.9 – 20.1	1.20	
	19 or over	22.3	1.3	19.8 – 24.9	1.78	
Q650	**Home internet access**					3435
	Yes	51.9	1.2	49.5 – 54.3	1.43	
	No	47.7	1.2	45.3 – 50.0	1.40	
Q479	**Urban or rural residence (1 version)**					1148
	A big city	35.2	3.4	28.4 – 42.0	2.44	
	A small city/town	44.2	3.1	38.1 – 50.3	2.09	
	Village/countryside	20.0	2.6	14.8 – 25.2	2.22	
	Attitudinal variables (face-to-face interview)					
Q183	**Benefits for the unemployed are ... (3 versions)**					3435
	... too low	29.3	1.1	27.2 – 31.4	1.38	
	... too high	47.2	0.9	45.3 – 49.0	1.11	
Q211	**NHS should be available to those with lower incomes (2 versions)**					2287
	Support a lot	7.4	0.7	6.1 – 8.7	1.19	
	Support a little	16.5	0.9	14.7 – 18.3	1.16	
	Oppose a little	14.6	1.0	12.7 – 16.5	1.30	
	Oppose a lot	58.5	1.4	55.8 – 61.2	1.32	
Q366	**How important is monarchy for Britain (1 version)**					1123
	Very important	35.5	1.5	32.5 – 38.5	1.06	
	Quite important	32.5	1.6	29.3 – 35.8	1.17	
	Not very/not at all important	21.8	1.7	18.5 – 25.1	1.36	
	Should be abolished	8.3	1.0	6.3 – 10.3	1.23	

	% (p)	Complex standard error of p	95% confidence interval	DEFT
				Base

Attitudinal variables (self-completion)

A2.30a B2.59a C2.59a	Government should redistribute income from the better off to those who are less well off (3 versions)				*2900*
	Agree strongly	10.9	0.7	9.5 – 12.2	1.18
	Agree	27.6	1.0	25.6 – 29.7	1.22
	Neither agree nor disagree	25.2	1.1	23.2 – 27.3	1.30
	Disagree	26.6	1.1	24.5 – 28.7	1.28
	Disagree strongly	7.1	0.6	6.0 – 8.2	1.18

B2.2b C2.2b	A man's job is to earn money; a woman's job is to look after the home and family (2 versions)				*1960*
	Agree strongly	3.9	0.4	3.1 – 4.7	0.93
	Agree	13.5	0.9	11.7 – 15.2	1.14
	Neither agree nor disagree	17.5	0.9	15.7 – 19.3	1.04
	Disagree	43.6	1.2	41.1 – 46.0	1.10
	Disagree strongly	19.6	1.1	17.5 – 21.7	1.20

C2.49a	How important to cut down on the number of cars (1 version)				*989*
	Very important	26.9	1.5	24.0 – 29.8	1.03
	Fairly important	47.6	1.6	44.5 – 50.7	0.99
	Not very/not at all important	17.7	1.4	15.0 – 20.5	1.13

Analysis techniques

Regression

Regression analysis aims to summarise the relationship between a 'dependent' variable and one or more 'independent' variables. It shows how well we can estimate a respondent's score on the dependent variable from knowledge of their scores on the independent variables. It is often undertaken to support a claim that the phenomena measured by the independent variables cause the phenomenon measured by the dependent variable. However, the causal ordering, if any, between the variables cannot be verified or falsified by the technique. Causality can only be inferred through special experimental designs or through assumptions made by the analyst.

All regression analysis assumes that the relationship between the dependent and each of the independent variables takes a particular form. In *linear regression*, it is assumed that the relationship can be adequately summarised by a straight line. This means that a one percentage point increase in the value of an independent variable is assumed to have the same impact on the value of the dependent variable on average irrespective of the previous values of those variables.

Strictly speaking the technique assumes that both the dependent and the independent variables are measured on an interval level scale, although it may sometimes still be applied even where this is not the case. For example, one can use an ordinal variable (e.g. a Likert scale) as a *dependent* variable if one is willing to assume that there is an underlying interval level scale and the difference between the observed ordinal scale and the underlying interval scale is due to random measurement error. Categorical or nominal data can be used as *independent* variables by converting them into dummy or binary variables; these are variables where the only valid scores are 0 and 1, with 1 signifying membership of a particular category and 0 otherwise.

The assumptions of linear regression cause particular difficulties where the *dependent* variable is binary. The assumption that the relationship between the dependent and the independent variables is a straight line means that it can produce estimated values for the dependent variable of less than 0 or greater than 1. In this case it may be more appropriate to assume that the relationship between the dependent and the independent variables takes the form of an S-curve, where the impact on the dependent variable of a one-point increase in an independent variable becomes progressively less the closer the value of the dependent variable approaches 0 or 1. *Logistic regression* is an alternative form of regression which fits such an S-curve rather than a straight line. The technique can also be adapted to analyse multinomial non-interval level dependent variables, that is, variables which classify respondents into more than two categories.

The two statistical scores most commonly reported from the results of regression analyses are:

A measure of variance explained: This summarises how well all the independent variables combined can account for the variation in respondent's scores in the dependent variable. The higher the measure, the more accurately we are able in general to estimate the correct value of each respondent's score on the dependent variable from knowledge of their scores on the independent variables.

A parameter estimate: This shows how much the dependent variable will change on average, given a one unit change in the independent variable (while holding all other independent variables in the model constant). The parameter estimate has a positive sign if an increase in the value of the independent variable results in an increase in the value of the dependent variable. It has a negative sign if an increase in the value of the independent variable results in a decrease in the value of the dependent variable. If the parameter estimates are standardised, it is possible to compare the relative impact of different independent variables; those variables with the largest standardised estimates can be said to have the biggest impact on the value of the dependent variable.

Regression also tests for the statistical significance of parameter estimates. A parameter estimate is said to be significant at the five per cent level, if the range of the values encompassed by its 95 per cent confidence interval (see also section on sampling errors) are either all positive or all negative. This means that there is less than a five per cent chance that the association we have found between the dependent variable and the independent variable is simply the result of sampling error and does not reflect a relationship that actually exists in the general population.

Factor analysis

Factor analysis is a statistical technique which aims to identify whether there are one or more apparent sources of commonality to the answers given by respondents to a set of questions. It ascertains the smallest number of *factors* (or dimensions) which can most economically summarise all of the variation found in the set of questions being analysed. Factors are established where respondents who give a particular answer to one question in the set, tend to give the same answer as each other to one or more of the other questions in the set. The technique is most useful when a relatively small number of factors is able to account for a relatively large proportion of the variance in all of the questions in the set.

The technique produces a *factor loading* for each question (or variable) on each factor. Where questions have a high loading on the same factor then it will be the case that respondents who give a particular answer to one of these questions tend to give a similar answer to the other questions. The technique is most commonly used in attitudinal research to try to identify the underlying ideological dimensions which apparently structure attitudes towards the subject in question.

International Social Survey Programme

The *International Social Survey Programme (ISSP)* is run by a group of research organisations, each of which undertakes to field annually an agreed module of questions on a chosen topic area. Since 1985, an *International Social Survey Programme* module has been included in one of the *British Social Attitudes* self-completion questionnaires. Each module is chosen for repetition at intervals to allow comparisons both between countries (membership is currently standing at 40) and over time. In 2002, the chosen subject was Family and Changing Gender Roles, and the module was carried on the B and C versions of the self-completion questionnaire (Qs.1–24). In 2002, the *ISSP* module was supplemented by a module of questions on Employment and the Family asked in Britain, Portugal, France, Norway, Finland, the Czech Republic and Hungary.

Notes

1. Until 1991 all *British Social Attitudes* samples were drawn from the Electoral Register (ER). However, following concern that this sampling frame might be deficient in its coverage of certain population subgroups, a 'splicing' experiment was conducted in 1991. We are grateful to the Market Research Development Fund

for contributing towards the costs of this experiment. Its purpose was to investigate whether a switch to PAF would disrupt the time-series − for instance, by lowering response rates or affecting the distribution of responses to particular questions. In the event, it was concluded that the change from ER to PAF was unlikely to affect time trends in any noticeable ways, and that no adjustment factors were necessary. Since significant differences in efficiency exist between PAF and ER, and because we considered it untenable to continue to use a frame that is known to be biased, we decided to adopt PAF as the sampling frame for future *British Social Attitudes* surveys. For details of the PAF/ER 'splicing' experiment, see Lynn and Taylor (1995).

2. In 1993 it was decided to mount a split-sample experiment designed to test the applicability of Computer-Assisted Personal Interviewing (CAPI) to the *British Social Attitudes* survey series. CAPI has been used increasingly over the past decade as an alternative to traditional interviewing techniques. As the name implies, CAPI involves the use of lap-top computers during the interview, with interviewers entering responses directly into the computer. One of the advantages of CAPI is that it significantly reduces both the amount of time spent on data processing and the number of coding and editing errors. Over a longer period, there could also be significant cost savings. There was, however, concern that a different interviewing technique might alter the distribution of responses and so affect the year-on-year consistency of *British Social Attitudes* data.

   Following the experiment, it was decided to change over to CAPI completely in 1994 (the self-completion questionnaire still being administered in the conventional way). The results of the experiment are discussed in *The 11ᵗʰ Report* (Lynn and Purdon, 1994).

3. Interview times of less than 20 and more than 150 minutes were excluded as these were likely to be errors.

4. An experiment was conducted on the 1991 *British Social Attitudes* survey (Jowell *et al.*, 1992), which showed that sending advance letters to sampled addresses before fieldwork begins has very little impact on response rates. However, interviewers do find that an advance letter helps them to introduce the survey on the doorstep, and a majority of respondents have said that they preferred some advance notice. For these reasons, advance letters have been used on the *British Social Attitudes* surveys since 1991.

5. Because of methodological experiments on scale development, the exact items detailed in this section have not been asked on all versions of the questionnaire each year.

6. In 1994 only, this item was replaced by: Ordinary people get their fair share of the nation's wealth. *[Wealth1]*

7. In constructing the scale, a decision had to be taken on how to treat missing values ('Don't knows' and 'Refused'/Not answered). Respondents who had more than two missing values on the left–right scale and more than three missing values on the libertarian–authoritarian and welfare scale were excluded from that scale. For respondents with just a few missing values, 'Don't knows' were recoded to the midpoint of the scale and Not answered or 'Refused' were recoded to the scale mean for that respondent on their valid items.

References

DeVellis, R.F. (1991), 'Scale development: theory and applications', *Applied Social Research Methods Series*, **26**, Newbury Park: Sage.

Exley, S., Bromley, C., Jarvis, L., Park, A., Stratford, N. and Thomson, K. (2003), *British Social Attitudes 2000 survey: Technical Report*, London: *National Centre for Social Research*.

Jowell, R., Brook, L., Prior, G. and Taylor, B. (1992), *British Social Attitudes: the 9th Report*, Aldershot: Dartmouth.

Lynn, P. and Purdon, S. (1994), 'Time-series and lap-tops: the change to computer-assisted interviewing', in Jowell, R., Curtice, J., Brook, L. and Ahrendt, D. (eds.), *British Social Attitudes: the 11th Report*, Aldershot: Dartmouth.

Lynn, P. and Taylor, B. (1995), 'On the bias and variance of samples of individuals: a comparison of the Electoral Registers and Postcode Address File as sampling frames', *The Statistician*, **44**: 173–194.

Spector, P.E. (1992), 'Summated rating scale construction: an introduction', *Quantitative Applications in the Social Sciences*, **82**, Newbury Park: Sage.

Appendix II
Notes on the tabulations in chapters

1. Figures in the tables are from the 2002 *British Social Attitudes* survey unless otherwise indicated.
2. Tables are percentaged as indicated.
3. In tables, '*' indicates less than 0.5 per cent but greater than zero, and '–' indicates zero.
4. When findings based on the responses of fewer than 100 respondents are reported in the text, reference is generally made to the small base size.
5. Percentages equal to or greater than 0.5 have been rounded up (e.g. 0.5 per cent = one per cent; 36.5 per cent = 37 per cent).
6. In many tables the proportions of respondents answering "Don't know" or not giving an answer are omitted. This, together with the effects of rounding and weighting, means that percentages will not always add to 100 per cent.
7. The self-completion questionnaire was not completed by all respondents to the main questionnaire (see Appendix I). Percentage responses to the self-completion questionnaire are based on all those who completed it.
8. The bases shown in the tables (the number of respondents who answered the question) are printed in small italics. The bases are unweighted, unless otherwise stated.

Appendix III
The questionnaires

As explained in Appendix I, three different versions of the questionnaire (A, B and C) were administered, each with its own self-completion supplement. The diagram that follows shows the structure of the questionnaires and the topics covered (not all of which are reported on in this volume).

The three interview questionnaires reproduced on the following pages are derived from the Blaise computer program in which they were written. For ease of reference, each item has been allocated a question number. Gaps in the numbering system indicate items that are essential components of the Blaise program but which are not themselves questions, and so have been omitted. In addition, we have removed the keying codes and inserted instead the percentage distribution of answers to each question. We have also included the SPSS variable name, in square brackets, beside each question. Above the questions we have included filter instructions. A filter instruction should be considered as staying in force until the next filter instruction. Percentages for the core questions are based on the total weighted sample, while those for questions in versions A, B or C are based on the appropriate weighted sub-samples. We reproduce first version A of the interview questionnaire in full; then those parts of version B and version C that differ. The three versions of the self-completion questionnaire follow, with those parts fielded in more than one version reproduced in one version only.

The percentage distributions do not necessarily add up to 100 because of weighting and rounding, or for one or more of the following reasons:

(i)   Some sub-questions are filtered – that is, they are asked of only a proportion of respondents. In these cases the percentages add up (approximately) to the proportions who were asked them. Where, however, a series of questions is filtered, we have indicated the weighted base at the beginning of that series (for example, all employees), and throughout have derived percentages from that base.

(ii) At a few questions, respondents were invited to give more than one answer and so percentages may add to well over 100 per cent. These are clearly marked by interviewer instructions on the questionnaires.

As reported in Appendix I, the 2002 *British Social Attitudes* self-completion questionnaire was not completed by 16 per cent of respondents who were successfully interviewed. The answers in the supplement have been percentaged on the base of those respondents who returned it. This means that the distribution of responses to questions asked in earlier years are comparable with those given in Appendix III of all earlier reports in this series except in *The 1984 Report*, where the percentages for the self-completion questionnaire need to be recalculated if comparisons are to be made.

BRITISH SOCIAL ATTITUDES: 2002 SURVEY
Main questionnaire plan

Version A	**Version B**	**Version C**

Version A	Version B	Version C
Household grid		
Newspaper readership		
Party identification		
Public spending and social welfare		
Health care		Transport
Employment		
—	Employment and caring	
Education		
Democracy and participation (long)		Democracy and participation (short)
Classification		

Self-completion questionnaire plan

—	ISSP (Family and changing gender roles)	
—	Employment and caring	
Public spending and social welfare		
Health care		Transport
Education		
Democracy and participation		—
Scales		

BRITISH SOCIAL ATTITUDES 2002

FACE-TO-FACE QUESTIONNAIRE

Contents

Version A

Introduction

ASK ALL

Q1   [SerialNo] **(NOT ON SCREEN)**   N=3435
Serial Number
Range: 140001 ... 149999

Q16   [GOR] **(NOT ON SCREEN)**
%   Government office region 2002 version
5.9   North East
10.5   North West
8.6   Yorkshire and Humberside
7.5   East Midlands
9.2   West Midlands
9.9   SW
8.6   Eastern
3.9   Inner London
7.5   Outer London
13.6   South East
5.7   Wales
8.9   Scotland

Q26   [ABCVer] **(NOT ON SCREEN)**
%   A, B or C?
32.6   A
34.0   B
33.5   C

Household grid

ASK ALL

Q34   [HouseHld]
(You have just been telling me about the adults that
live in this household. Thinking now of **everyone**
living in this household, **including children**:)
Including yourself, how many people live here
regularly as members of this household?
CHECK INTERVIEWER MANUAL FOR DEFINITION OF HOUSEHOLD
IF NECESSARY.
IF YOU DISCOVER THAT YOU WERE GIVEN THE WRONG
INFORMATION FOR THE RESPONDENT SELECTION ON THE ARF:
*DO **NOT** REDO THE ARF SELECTION PRODECURE
*DO ENTER THE CORRECT INFORMATION HERE
*DO USE <CTRL + M> TO MAKE A NOTE OF WHAT HAPPENED.
%   **Median: 2 people**
-   (Don't know)
-   (Refusal/Not answered)

FOR EACH PERSON AT [HouseHld]
[Name] **(NOT ON DATA FILE)**
FOR RESPONDENT: (Can I just check what is your first
name?)
PLEASE TYPE IN THE FIRST NAME (OR INITIALS) OF
RESPONDENT
FOR OTHER HOUSEHOLD MEMBERS: PLEASE TYPE IN THE FIRST
NAME (OR INITIALS) OF PERSON NUMBER *(number)*

[RSex], [P2Sex]-[P12Sex] *(Figures refer to respondent)*
%   PLEASE CODE SEX OF *(name)*
47.0   Male
53.0   Female
-   (Don't know)
-   (Refusal/Not answered)

[RAge]-[P12Age] (Figures refer to respondent)
FOR RESPONDENT, IF ONLY ONE PERSON IN HOUSEHOLD: I would like to ask you a few details about yourself.
What was your **age** last birthday?
FOR RESPONDENT, IF SEVERAL PERSONS IN HOUSEHOLD: I would like to ask you a few details about each person in your household. Starting with yourself, what was your **age** last birthday?
FOR OTHER PERSONS IN HOUSEHOLD: What was (name)'s age last birthday?
FOR 97+, CODE 97.
Median: 44 years

%
0.0 (Don't know)
0.0 (Refusal/Not answered)

FOR PEOPLE IN THE HOUSEHOLD OTHER THAN THE RESPONDENT
[P2Rel3] (Figures refer to respondent)
PLEASE ENTER RELATIONSHIP OF (name) TO RESPONDENT

%
63.0 Partner/spouse/cohabitee
7.2 Son/daughter (inc. step/adopted)
0.1 Grandson/daughter (inc. step/adopted)
7.2 Parent/parent-in-law
0.2 Grand-parent
1.9 Brother/sister (inc. in-law)
0.5 Other relative
3.0 Other non-relative
- (Don't know)
- (Refusal/Not answered)

Q130

ASK ALL
[MarStat2]
CARD A1
Can I just check, which of these applies to you at present?
CODE FIRST TO APPLY

%
54.2 Married
9.3 Living as married
2.4 Separated (after being married)
5.9 Divorced
7.8 Widowed
20.3 Single (never married)
- (Don't know)
0.0 (Refusal/Not answered)

Q145-
Q150

CARD A2
Can I just check which, if any, of these types of relatives do you yourself have alive at the moment.
Please include adoptive and step-relatives.
PROBE: Which others?
DO NOT INCLUDE FOSTER RELATIVES
CODE ALL THAT APPLY
Multicoded (Maximum of 6 codes)

%
62.9 Brother   [RelBroth]
63.5 Sister   [RelSist]
52.9 Son   [RelSon]
51.0 Daughter   [RelDaugh]
20.0 Grandchild (daughter's child)   [RelGrChD]
16.8 Grandchild (son's child)   [RelGrChS]
3.0 None of these   [RelNone2]
0.0 (Don't know)
- (Refusal/Not answered)

Newspaper readership

Q158 **ASK ALL**
[Readpap]
Do you normally read any daily **morning** newspaper at least 3 times a week?   N=3435
%
54.4 Yes
45.6 No
- (Don't know)
- (Refusal/Not answered)

Q159 **IF 'yes' AT [ReadPap]**
[WhPaper]
Which one do you normally read?
IF MORE THAN ONE:
Which one do you read **most** frequently?
%
3.2 (Scottish) Daily Express
10.8 (Scottish) Daily Mail
9.4 Daily Mirror (/Daily Record)
1.9 Daily Star
12.0 The Sun
3.9 Daily Telegraph
0.7 Financial Times
3.0 The Guardian
0.9 The Independent
3.2 The Times
0.1 Morning Star
4.7 Other Irish/Northern Irish/Scottish regional or local **daily morning** paper (WRITE IN)
0.3 Other (WRITE IN)
0.3 **EDIT ONLY:** MORE THAN ONE PAPER READ WITH EQUAL FREQUENCY
- (Don't know)
- (Refusal/Not answered)

Party identification

Q162 **ASK ALL**
[SupParty]
Generally speaking, do you think of yourself as a supporter of any one political party?
%
35.7 Yes
64.2 No
- (Don't know)
- (Refusal/Not answered)

Q163 **IF 'no' OR DON'T KNOW AT [SupParty]**
[ClosePty]
Do you think of yourself as a little closer to one political party than to the others?
%
26.6 Yes
37.5 No
0.1 (Don't know)
0.0 (Refusal/Not answered)

Q165 **IF 'yes' AT [SupParty] OR 'yes'/'no'/DON'T KNOW AT [ClosePty]**
[PartyID]
IF 'yes' AT [SupParty] OR AT [ClosePty]: Which one?
IF 'no'/DON'T KNOW AT [ClosePty]: If there were a general election tomorrow, which political party do you think you would be most likely to support?
DO NOT PROMPT
%
24.7 Conservative
40.9 Labour
11.3 Liberal Democrat
1.3 Scottish National Party
0.7 Plaid Cymru
0.7 Other party
1.5 Other answer
13.0 None
1.3 Green Party
2.9 (Don't know)
1.7 (Refusal/Not answered)

Public spending and social welfare

Q173   **ASK ALL**
       [Spend1]   N=3435
       CARD A3
       Here are some items of government spending. Which of
       them, if any, would be your highest priority for **extra**
       spending?
       Please read through the whole list before deciding.
       ENTER ONE CODE ONLY FOR HIGHEST PRIORITY

Q174   **IF NOT 'none'/DON'T KNOW/REFUSAL AT [Spend1]**
       [Spend2]
       CARD A3 AGAIN
       And which next?
       ENTER ONE CODE ONLY FOR NEXT HIGHEST

	[Spend1]	[Spend2]
	%	%
Education	25.8	37.6
Defence	1.2	1.9
Health	52.8	25.7
Housing	3.3	6.4
Public transport	5.0	7.6
Roads	2.3	3.7
Police and prisons	4.7	8.8
Social security benefits	1.5	3.9
Help for industry	1.4	2.1
Overseas aid	1.0	0.8
(None of these)	0.5	0.3
(Don't know)	0.4	0.2
(Refusal/Not answered)	-	-

Q170   **IF PARTY GIVEN AT [PartyID]**
       [Idstrng]
       Would you call yourself very strong *(party)*,
       fairly strong, or not very strong?
       %
5.2   Very strong *(party)*
27.1   Fairly strong
48.4   Not very strong
0.1   (Don't know)
6.2   (Refusal/Not answered)

Q171   **VERSION A AND B: ASK ALL**
       [Politics]   N=2285
       How much interest do you generally have in what is
       going on in politics
       READ OUT ...
7.5   ... a great deal,
21.4   quite a lot,
35.4   some,
24.3   not very much,
11.3   or, none at all?
0.1   (Don't know)
-      (Refusal/Not answered)

ASK ALL

Q175   [SocSpnd1]
CARD A4
Some people think that there should be more government spending on social security, while other people disagree. For each of the groups I read out please say whether you would like to see **more** or **less** government spending on them than now. Bear in mind that if you want more spending, this would probably mean that you would have to pay more taxes. If you want less spending, this would probably mean paying less taxes.

Firstly, ... READ OUT ...
benefits for unemployed people: would you like to see more or less government spending than now

Q176   [SocSpnd2]
CARD A4 AGAIN
(Would you like to see more or less government spending than now on ...)
... benefits for disabled people who cannot work?

Q177   [SocSpnd3]
CARD A4 AGAIN
(Would you like to see more or less government spending than now on ...)
... benefits for parents who work on very low incomes?

Q178   [SocSpnd4]
CARD A4 AGAIN
(Would you like to see more or less government spending than now on ...)
... benefits for single parents?

Q179   [SocSpnd5]
CARD A4 AGAIN
(Would you like to see more or less government spending than now on ...)
... benefits for retired people?

Q180   [SocSpnd6]
CARD A4 AGAIN
(Would you like to see more or less government spending than now on ...)
... benefits for people who care for those who are sick or disabled?

	[SocSpnd1]	[SocSpnd2]	[SocSpnd3]
	%	%	%
Spend much more	2.1	10.6	9.3
Spend more	18.9	58.6	60.2
Spend the same as now	39.4	24.2	24.1
Spend less	30.5	2.1	3.6
Spend much less	5.7	0.1	0.2
(Don't know)	3.3	4.3	2.6
(Refusal/Not answered)	0.0	0.1	0.0

	[SocSpnd4]	[SocSpnd5]	[SocSpnd6]
	%	%	%
Spend much more	5.7	18.6	19.6
Spend more	33.1	54.1	62.0
Spend the same as now	39.3	23.0	15.0
Spend less	14.2	1.9	0.7
Spend much less	3.4	0.2	0.1
(Don't know)	4.2	2.2	2.5
(Refusal/Not answered)	0.0	0.0	0.0

Q181   [FalseClm]
I will read two statements. For each one please say whether you agree or disagree. Firstly ...
Large numbers of people these days **falsely** claim benefits.
IF AGREE OR DISAGREE: Strongly or slightly?

Q182   [FailClm]
(And do you agree or disagree that ...)
Large numbers of people who are eligible for benefits
these days **fail** to claim them.
IF AGREE OR DISAGREE: Strongly or slightly?

	[FalseClm]	[FailClm]
	%	%
Agree strongly	57.7	39.0
Agree slightly	23.5	41.2
Disagree slightly	8.3	10.3
Disagree strongly	5.3	2.9
(Don't know)	5.1	6.6
(Refusal/Not answered)	0.0	0.0

Q183   [Dole]
Opinions differ about the level of benefits for
unemployed people.
Which of these two statements comes closest to your
own view ...
READ OUT ...

%
29.3   ... benefits for unemployed people are **too low** and
cause hardship,

47.2   or, benefits for unemployed people are **too high** and
discourage them from finding jobs?

16.6   (Neither)

-   EDIT ONLY: BOTH: UNEMPLOYMENT BENEFIT CAUSES HARDSHIP
BUT CAN'T BE HIGHER OR THERE WOULD BE NO INCENTIVE TO
WORK

1.3   EDIT ONLY: BOTH: UNEMPLOYMENT BENEFIT CAUSES HARDSHIP
TO SOME, WHILE OTHERS DO WELL OUT OF IT

0.7   EDIT ONLY: ABOUT RIGHT/IN-BETWEEN

1.9   Other answer (WRITE IN)

3.2   (Don't know)

-   (Refusal/Not answered)

Q185   [TaxSpend]
CARD A5
Suppose the government had to choose between the three
options on this card. Which do you think it should
choose?

%
3.2   Reduce taxes and spend **less** on health, education and
social benefits

31.4   Keep taxes and spending on these services at the **same**
level as now

62.5   Increase taxes and spend **more** on health, education and
social benefits

2.1   (None)

0.7   (Don't know)

0.0   (Refusal/Not answered)

VERSIONS A AND C: ASK ALL   N=2269

Q186   [LonePaWk]
Suppose a lone parent on benefits was asked to visit
the job centre every year or so to talk about ways in
which they might find work. Which of the following
comes closest to what you think should happen to their
benefits if they did not go ...
READ OUT ...

%
16.4   ... their benefits should not be affected,

44.2   their benefits should be reduced a little,

14.7   their benefits should be reduced a lot,

21.3   or, their benefits should be stopped?

2.2   (Other (PLEASE WRITE IN))

1.0   (Don't know)

0.1   (Refusal/Not answered)

Q192

VERSION B: ASK ALL　　　　　　　　　N=1166

[LonPaWk2]

CARD A6

Suppose a lone parent on benefits was asked to visit the job centre every year or so to talk about ways in which they might find work. Which of the statements on this card comes closest to what you think should happen to their benefits if they did not go?

%
18.9　Their benefits should not be affected
37.4　Their benefits should be reduced a little
16.1　Their benefits should be reduced a lot
24.7　Their benefits should be stopped
1.4　(Other (PLEASE WRITE IN))
1.4　(Don't know)
0.1　(Refusal/Not answered)

Q188

VERSION A: ASK ALL　　　　　　　　　N=1119

[SickWk]

Now think about someone on long-term sickness or disability benefits. Which of the following comes closest to what you think should happen to their benefits if they did not go to the job centre to talk about ways in which they might find work ...

READ OUT ...

%
38.8　... their benefits should not be affected,
33.5　their benefits should be reduced a little,
9.8　their benefits should be reduced a lot,
10.6　or, their benefits should be stopped?
5.8　(Other (PLEASE WRITE IN))
1.4　(Don't know)
-　(Refusal/Not answered)

Q193

VERSION B: ASK ALL　　　　　　　　　N=1166

[SickWk2]

CARD A6 AGAIN

Now think about someone on long-term sickness or disability benefits. Which of these statements comes closest to what you think should happen to their benefits if they did not go to the job centre every year or so to talk about ways in which they might find work?

%
42.3　Their benefits should not be affected
30.9　Their benefits should be reduced a little
10.6　Their benefits should be reduced a lot
10.9　Their benefits should be stopped
3.7　(Other (PLEASE WRITE IN))
1.6　(Don't know)
-　(Refusal/Not answered)

Q195

VERSION C: ASK ALL　　　　　　　　　N=1150

[SickWk3]

Now think about someone on long-term sickness or disability benefits. Which of the following comes closest to what you think should happen to their benefits if they did not go to the job centre every year or so to talk about ways in which they might find work ...

READ OUT ...

%
39.6　... their benefits should not be affected,
36.6　their benefits should be reduced a little,
7.3　their benefits should be reduced a lot,
11.0　or, their benefits should be stopped?
4.3　(Other (PLEASE WRITE IN))
1.1　(Don't know)
0.1　(Refusal/Not answered)

Q190

VERSION A AND C: ASK ALL   N=2269

[CarerWk]
And suppose a carer on benefits was asked to visit the job centre every year or so to talk about ways in which they might find work. Which of the following comes closest to what you think should happen to their benefits if they did not go ...
READ OUT ...

%
48.7   ... their benefits should not be affected,
31.9   their benefits should be reduced a little,
5.4   their benefits should be reduced a lot,
9.6   or, their benefits should be stopped?
2.8   (Other (PLEASE WRITE IN))
1.6   (Don't know)
0.0   (Refusal/Not answered)

Q194

VERSION B: ASK ALL   N=1166

[CarerWk2]
CARD A6 AGAIN
And suppose a carer on benefits was asked to visit the job centre every year or so to talk about ways in which they might find work. Which of these statements comes closest to what you think should happen to their benefits if they did not go?

%
50.8   Their benefits should not be affected
27.8   Their benefits should be reduced a little
7.1   Their benefits should be reduced a lot
10.8   Their benefits should be stopped
1.8   (Other (PLEASE WRITE IN))
1.7   (Don't know)
-      (Refusal/Not answered)

Q196

VERSION C: ASK ALL   N=1150

[IncomGap]
Thinking of income levels generally in Britain today, would you say that the **gap** between those with high incomes and those with low incomes is
... READ OUT ...

%
82.2   ... too large,
13.3   about right,
1.2   or, too small?
3.2   (Don't know)
0.1   (Refusal/Not answered)

Q197

[SRInc]
Among which group would you place yourself ...
READ OUT ...

%
5.0   ... high income,
52.2   middle income,
41.8   or, low income?
0.8   (Don't know)
0.3   (Refusal/Not answered)

Q198

[HIncDiff]
CARD A6
Which of the phrases on this card would you say comes closest to your feelings about your household's income these days?

%
39.0   Living comfortably on present income
44.5   Coping on present income
13.1   Finding it difficult on present income
3.2   Finding it very difficult on present income
0.1   (Other answer (WRITE IN))
-      (Don't know)
-      (Refusal/Not answered)

Health

VERSION A AND B: ASK ALL

Q201 [NHSSat]   N=2285
CARD B1
All in all, how satisfied or dissatisfied would you say you are with the way in which the National Health Service runs nowadays?
Choose a phrase from this card.

Q202 [GPSat]
CARD B1 AGAIN
From your own experience, or from what you have heard, please say how satisfied or dissatisfied you are with the way in which each of these parts of the National Health Service runs nowadays:
First, local doctors or GPs?

Q203 [DentSat]
CARD B1 AGAIN
(And how satisfied or dissatisfied are you with the NHS as regards ...)
... National Health Service dentists?

Q204 [InpatSat]
CARD B1 AGAIN
(And how satisfied or dissatisfied are you with the NHS as regards ...)
... being in hospital as an in-patient?

Q205 [OutpaSat]
CARD B1 AGAIN
(And how satisfied or dissatisfied are you with the NHS as regards ...)
... attending hospital as an out-patient?

Q206 [AESat]
CARD B1 AGAIN
(And how satisfied or dissatisfied are you with the NHS as regards...)
... Accident and Emergency departments?

VERSIONS A AND B: IN ENGLAND AND WALES: ASK ALL
N=2078

Q207 [NDirSat]
CARD B1 AGAIN
(And how satisfied or dissatisfied are you with the NHS as regards ...)
... NHS Direct, the telephone or internet advice service?

	[NHSSat]	[GPSat]	[DentSat]
	%	%	%
Very satisfied	8.0	28.2	15.2
Quite satisfied	32.2	43.7	38.4
Neither satisfied nor dissatisfied	18.2	9.5	17.7
Quite dissatisfied	26.3	13.0	12.5
Very dissatisfied	14.5	5.1	9.5
(Don't know)	0.7	0.6	6.7
(Refusal/Not answered)	–	–	–

	[InpatSat]	[OutpaSat]	[AESat]
	%	%	%
Very satisfied	17.0	14.1	13.0
Quite satisfied	33.7	37.8	29.6
Neither satisfied nor dissatisfied	17.9	16.6	17.4
Quite dissatisfied	15.0	18.5	19.0
Very dissatisfied	7.5	7.7	13.0
(Don't know)	8.9	5.3	8.1
(Refusal/Not answered)	–	–	–

	[NDirSat]
	%
Very satisfied	7.6
Quite satisfied	17.7
Neither satisfied nor dissatisfied	28.1
Quite dissatisfied	4.3
Very dissatisfied	3.0
(Don't know)	39.4
(Refusal/Not answered)	–

Q208 **VERSIONS A AND B: ASK ALL**
[PrivMed]   *N=2285*
Are **you yourself** covered by a private health insurance scheme, that is an insurance scheme that allows you to get private medical **treatment**?
ADD IF NECESSARY: 'For example, BUPA or PPP'.
IF INSURANCE COVERS DENTISTRY **ONLY**, CODE 'No'

Q209 **IF 'yes' AT [Privmed]**
[PrivPaid]
Does your employer (or your partner's employer) pay the majority of the cost of membership of this scheme?

Q210 **VERSIONS A AND B: ASK ALL**
[PayAdhoc]
(Apart from any private medical treatment paid for by your insurance scheme, have/Have) you paid for any medical consultation, diagnosis or treatment in the last five years or so? - this could have been from a private health doctor or other private health professional.
IF ASKED, MEDICAL TREATMENT IS WHAT THE RESPONDENT THINKS OF AS MEDICAL TREATMENT.
IF PAID FOR DENTISTRY **ONLY**, CODE 'No'

	[PrivMed]	[PrivPaid]	[PayAdhoc]
	%	%	%
Yes	20.7	11.5	19.5
No	79.2	9.0	80.5
(Don't know)	0.1	0.1	0.0
(Refusal/Not answered)	-	0.2	-

Q211 [NHSLimit]
It has been suggested that the National Health Service should be available **only to those with lower incomes.** This would mean that contributions and taxes could be lower and most people would then take out medical insurance or pay for health care.
Do you support or oppose this idea?
IF 'SUPPORT' OR 'OPPOSE': A lot or a little?

%
Support a lot   7.4
Support a little   16.5
Oppose a little   14.6
Oppose a lot   58.5
(Don't know)   3.0
(Refusal/Not answered)   0.0

Q212 [OutPat1]
CARD B2
Now suppose you had a back problem and your GP referred you to a hospital out-patients' department. From what you know or have heard, please say whether you think ...
... you would get an appointment within three months?

Q213 [OutPat2]
CARD B2 AGAIN
(And please say whether you think ...)
... when you arrived, the doctor would see you within half an hour of your appointment time?

Q214 [OutPat3]
CARD B2 AGAIN
(And please say whether you think ...)
... if you wanted to complain about the treatment you received, you would be able to without any fuss or bother?

Q215   [WhchHosp]
CARD B2 AGAIN
Now suppose you needed to go into hospital for an operation.
Do you think you would have a say about which hospital you went to?

	[OutPat1]	[OutPat2]	[OutPat3]
	%	%	%
Definitely would	8.8	6.8	13.7
Probably would	33.0	31.3	41.5
Probably would not	35.3	38.9	26.9
Definitely would not	19.2	20.2	10.3
(Don't know)	3.6	2.8	7.6
(Refusal/Not answered)	0.0	-	0.0

	[WhchHosp]
	%
Definitely would	7.0
Probably would	18.7
Probably would not	43.0
Definitely would not	25.7
(Don't know)	5.6
(Refusal/Not answered)	-

Q216   [GPChange]
Suppose you wanted to change your GP and go to a different practice, how difficult or easy do you think this would be to arrange?
Would it be ... READ OUT ...

%	
10.9	... very difficult,
24.4	fairly difficult,
33.0	not very difficult,
22.3	or, not at all difficult?
9.4	(Don't know)
-	(Refusal/Not answered)

Q217   [NHSTrus2]
CARD B3
From what you know or have heard, in general, how much do you trust **NHS hospital doctors** to put the interests of their patients above the convenience of the hospital?

Q218   [HspNTrus]
CARD B3 AGAIN
And in general, how much do you trust **hospital nurses** to put the interests of their patients above the convenience of the hospital?

Q219   [NHMgTrus]
CARD B3 AGAIN
(In general, how much do you trust)... **NHS hospital managers** to put the interests of their patients above the convenience of the hospital?

Q220   [PrMgTrus]
CARD B3 AGAIN
From what you know or have heard, in general, how much do you trust **private hospital managers** to put the interests of their patients above the convenience of the hospital?

Q221   [GPTrust]
CARD B3 AGAIN
(In general, how much do you trust)... **GPs** to put the interests of their patients above the convenience of their practice?

Q222   [GPNTrust]
CARD B3 AGAIN
(In general, how much do you trust) ... **nurses at GP surgeries or health centres** to put the interests of their patients above the convenience of their practice?

	[NHSTrus2]	[HspNTrus]	[NHMgTrus]
	%	%	%
Just about always	16.8	29.8	2.8
Most of the time	49.4	47.4	18.0
Some of the time	26.1	18.1	44.6
Just about never	5.3	2.5	26.6
(Don't know)	2.4	2.2	8.0
(Refusal/Not answered)	-	-	-

	[PrMgTrus]	[GPTrus]	[GPNTrust]
	%	%	%
Just about always	14.2	26.8	30.6
Most of the time	28.5	47.2	49.7
Some of the time	28.0	20.5	15.5
Just about never	11.0	4.0	2.0
(Don't know)	18.2	1.4	2.2
(Refusal/Not answered)	-	-	-

Q223   [SRHealth]
How is your health in general for someone of your age? Would you say that it is ... READ OUT ...
%
39.2   ... very good,
41.1   fairly good,
14.6   fair,
3.9   bad,
1.1   or, very bad?
0.1   (Don't know)
0.0   (Refusal/Not answered)

Economic activity

Q257   ASK ALL
[REconAc=]   N=3435
CARD C1
Which of these descriptions applied to what you were doing last week, that is the seven days ending last Sunday?
PROBE: Which others? CODE ALL THAT APPLY
Multicoded (Maximum of 11 codes)
%
2.9   In full-time education (not paid for by employer, including on vacation)
0.4   On government training/employment programme
58.5   In paid work (or away temporarily) for at least 10 hours in week
0.5   Waiting to take up paid work already accepted
2.4   Unemployed and registered at a benefit office
1.4   Unemployed, **not** registered, but actively looking for a job (of at least 10 hrs a week)
0.4   Unemployed, wanting a job (of at least 10 hrs a week) but **not** actively looking for a job
5.1   Permanently sick or disabled
19.7   Wholly retired from work
8.0   Looking after the home
0.7   (Doing something else) (WRITE IN)
-       (Don't know)
0.1   (Refusal/Not answered)

Q258   ASK ALL NOT WORKING OR WAITING TO TAKE UP WORK
[RLastJcb]   N=1408
How long ago did you last have a paid job of at least 10 hours a week?
GOVERNMENT PROGRAMS/SCHEMES DO NOT COUNT AS `PAID JOBS'.
%
17.1   Within past 12 months
21.9   Over 1, up to 5 years ago
17.0   Over 5, up to 10 years ago
22.0   Over 10, up to 20 years ago
15.6   Over 20 years ago
6.1   Never had a paid job of 10+ hours a week
0.2   (Don't know)
0.2   (Refusal/Not answered)

Q259   **ASK ALL WHO HAVE EVER WORKED**
        [Title] **(NOT ON DATAFILE)**   *N=3349*
        Now I want to ask you about your *(present/future/last)* job.
        IF IN WORK: Now I want to ask you about your present job. What is your job?
        IF WAITING TO TAKE UP WORK: Now I want to ask you about your future job. What will that job be?
        IF WORKED IN THE PAST: Now I want to ask you about your last job. What was your job?
        PROBE IF NECESSARY: What *(is/was)* the name or title of the job?

Q260   [Typewk] **(NOT ON DATAFILE)**
        What kind of work *(do/will/did)* you do most of the time?
        IF RELEVANT: What materials/machinery *(do/will/did)* you use?

Q261   [Train] **(NOT ON DATAFILE)**
        What training or qualifications *(are/were)* needed for that job?

Q262   [REmployee]
        In your (main) job *(are/will/were)* you *(be)*
        ... READ OUT ...
        ... an employee,
        or self-employed?
        (Don't know)
        (Refusal/Not answered)

        %
        89.7
        10.1
        0.0
        0.2

Q264   [RSuperv]
        In your job, *(do/will/did)* you have any formal responsibility for supervising the work of other *(employees/people)*?
        DO NOT INCLUDE PEOPLE WHO ONLY SUPERVISE:
        - CHILDREN, E.G. TEACHERS, NANNIES, CHILDMINDERS
        - ANIMALS
        - SECURITY OR BUILDINGS, E.G. CARETAKERS, SECURITY GUARDS
        Yes
        No
        (Don't know)
        (Refusal/Not answered)

        %
        38.3
        61.5
        0.0
        0.2

Q265   **IF 'yes' AT [Supervise]**
        [RMany]
        How many?
        Median: 6 (Of those supervising any)
        (Don't know)
        (Refusal/Not answered)

        %
        0.1
        0.2

Q267   **ASK ALL EMPLOYEES IN CURRENT/LAST JOB**   *N=3009*
        [RSupman2]
        Can I just check, *(are/will/were)* you *(be)*
        ... READ OUT ...
        ... a manager,
        a foreman or supervisor,
        or not?
        (Don't know)
        (Refusal/Not answered)

        %
        20.1
        13.6
        66.1
        -
        0.2

Q268   [ROCSect2]
CARD C2
Which of the types of organisation on this card (do you work/will you be working/did you work) for?

67.5	PRIVATE SECTOR FIRM OR COMPANY Including, for example, limited companies and PLCs
2.3	NATIONALISED INDUSTRY OR PUBLIC CORPORATION Including, for example, the Post Office and the BBC
26.8	OTHER PUBLIC SECTOR EMPLOYER Incl. e.g.: - Central govt/Civil Service/Govt Agency - Local authority/Local Educ Auth (incl. 'opted out' schools) - Universities - Health Authority/NHS hospitals/NHS Trusts/GP surgeries - Police/Armed forces
2.5	CHARITY/VOLUNTARY SECTOR Including, for example, charitable companies, churches, trade unions
0.5	Other answer (WRITE IN)
0.1	(Don't know)
0.2	(Refusal/Not answered)

ASK ALL WHO HAVE EVER WORKED

Q270   [EmpMake] (NOT ON DATAFILE)   N=3349
IF EMPLOYEE: What (does/did) your employer make or do at the place where you (will) usually work(ed) (from)?
IF SELF-EMPLOYED: What (do/will/did) you make or do at the place where you (will) usually work(ed) (from)?

ASK ALL WHO HAVE EVER WORKED (FOR SELF-EMPLOYED, DERIVED FROM [SEmpNum]

Q271   [REmpWrk]
Including yourself, how many people (are/were) employed at the place where you usually (work/will work/worked) (from)?
PROBE FOR CORRECT PRECODE.

%
19.3	Under 10
14.4	10-24
22.6	25-99
19.9	100-499
16.3	500 or more
1.1	(Don't know)
0.2	(Refusal/Not answered)

ASK ALL SELF-EMPLOYED IN CURRENT/LAST JOB

Q272   [SEmpNum]   N=346
In your work or business, (do/will/did) you have any employees, or not?
IF YES: How many?
IF 'NO EMPLOYEES', CODE 0.
FOR 500+ EMPLOYEES, CODE 500.
NOTE: FAMILY MEMBERS MAY BE EMPLOYEES ONLY IF THEY RECEIVE A REGULAR WAGE OR SALARY.

%
Range: 0 ... 500
Median: 0 employees
- (Don't know)
1.9 (Refusal/Not answered)

ASK ALL IN PAID WORK

Q276   [WkJbTim]   N=2013
In your present job, are you working ... READ OUT ...
RESPONDENT'S OWN DEFINITION

%
78.5	... full-time,
21.2	or, part-time?
0.1	(Don't know)
0.2	(Refusal/Not answered)

Q279 [WkJbHrsI]
How many hours do you normally work a week in your main job - **including** any paid or unpaid overtime?
ROUND TO NEAREST HOUR.
IF RESPONDENT CANNOT ANSWER, ASK ABOUT LAST WEEK.
IF RESPONDENT DOES NOT KNOW EXACTLY, ACCEPT AN ESTIMATE.
FOR 95+ HOURS, CODE 95.
FOR 'VARIES TOO MUCH TO SAY', CODE 96.
Median: 40 hours
(Varies too much to say)
(Don't know)
(Refusal/Not answered)

%
1.0
0.1
0.2

Q280 [EJbHrsX]
ASK ALL CURRENT EMPLOYEES   N=1760
What are your **basic or contractual hours** each week in your main job - **excluding** any paid and unpaid overtime?
ROUND TO NEAREST HOUR.
IF RESPONDENT CANNOT ANSWER, ASK ABOUT LAST WEEK.
IF RESPONDENT DOES NOT KNOW EXACTLY, ACCEPT AN ESTIMATE.
FOR 95+ HOURS, CODE 95.
FOR 'VARIES TOO MUCH TO SAY', CODE 96.
Median: 37 hours
(Varies too much to say)
(Don't know)
(Refusal/Not answered)

%
2.5
2.2
0.2

Q281 [ExPrtFul]
ASK ALL WHO HAVE EVER WORKED BUT ARE NOT CURRENTLY WORKING   N=1322
(Is/Will/Was) the job (be) ... READ OUT ...
... full-time - that is, 30 or more hours per week,
or, part-time?
(Don't know)
(Refusal/Not answered)

%
66.8
32.5
0.2
0.4

Q298 [UnionSA]
ASK ALL WHO HAVE EVER WORKED   N=3349
(May I just check) are you **now** a member of a trade union or staff association?
CODE FIRST TO APPLY
Yes, trade union
Yes, staff association
No
(Don't know)
(Refusal/Not answered)

%
18.6
3.3
77.9
0.1
0.2

Q299 [TUSAEver]
IF 'no'/DON'T KNOW AT [UnionSA]
Have you **ever** been a member of a trade union or staff association?
CODE FIRST TO APPLY
Yes, trade union
Yes, staff association
No
(Don't know)
(Refusal/Not answered)

%
25.0
2.6
50.3
0.1
0.2

Q313 [EmploydT]
VERSIONS B AND C: ASK ALL CURRENT EMPLOYEES   N=1182
For how long have you been continuously employed by your present employer?
ENTER NUMBER. THEN SPECIFY MONTHS OR YEARS
Median: 60 months
(Don't know)
(Refusal/Not answered)

%
0.1
0.2

Q314 [NPWork10]
ASK ALL NOT IN PAID WORK   N=1424
In the seven days ending last Sunday, did you have any paid work of less than 10 hours a week?
Yes
No
(Don't know)
(Refusal/Not answered)

%
5.0
94.8
-
0.2

ASK ALL CURRENT EMPLOYEES

Q315 [WpUnions]   N=1760
At your place of work are there unions, staff
associations, or groups of unions recognised by the
management for negotiating pay and conditions of
employment?
IF YES, PROBE FOR UNION OR STAFF ASSOCIATION
IF 'BOTH', CODE '1'
%
43.7   Yes: trade union(s)
4.9   Yes: staff association
46.9   No, none
4.3   (Don't know)
0.1   (Refusal/Not answered)

        IF 'yes, trade unions' OR 'yes, staff association' AT
        [WpUnions]
Q316 [WpUnsure]
Can I just check: does management **recognise** these
unions or staff associations for the purposes of
negotiating **pay and conditions of employment?**
%
46.0   Yes
1.5   No
1.2   (Don't know)
4.4   (Refusal/Not answered)

Q317 [WpUnionW]
On the whole, do you think (unions/this staff
association)(do their/ does its) job well or not?
%
29.1   Yes
14.8   No
4.8   (Don't know)
4.4   (Refusal/Not answered)

Q318 [TUShould]
CARD C3
Listed on the card are a number of things trade unions
or staff associations can do. Which, if any, do you
think is the **most important** thing they should try to
do **at your workplace?**
UNIONS OR STAFF ASSOCIATIONS SHOULD TRY TO:
%
15.3   Improve working conditions
10.8   Improve pay
11.4   Protect existing jobs
2.4   Have more say over how work is done day-to-day
3.1   Have more say over management's long-term plans
1.0   Work for equal opportunities for women
0.4   Work for equal opportunities for ethnic minorities
2.7   Reduce pay differences at the workplace
1.2   (None of these)
0.3   (Don't know)
4.4   (Refusal/Not answered)

        ASK ALL CURRENT EMPLOYEES
Q319 [IndRel]
In general how would you describe relations between
management and other employees at your workplace ...
READ OUT ...
%
35.7   ... very good,
43.1   quite good,
11.6   not very good,
4.7   or, not at all good?
0.5   (Don't know)
4.5   (Refusal/Not answered)

Q320 [WorkRun]
And in general, would you say your workplace was ...
READ OUT ...
%
29.5   ... very well managed,
50.3   quite well managed,
15.4   or, not well managed?
0.4   (Don't know)
4.4   (Refusal/Not answered)

Q321

VERSIONS B AND C: ASK ALL EXCEPT THOSE WHOLLY RETIRED
OR PERMANENTLY SICK OR DISABLED　　　N=1727
[NwEmpErn]

IF IN PAID WORK: Now for some more general questions
about your work. For some people their job is simply
something they do in order to earn a living. For
others it means much more than that. On balance, is
your present job ... READ OUT ...
IF NOT IN PAID WORK: For some people work is simply
something they do in order to earn a living. For
others it means much more than that. In general, do
you think of work as ... READ OUT ...

%
31.3　　... just a means of earning a living,
67.4　　or, does it mean much more to you than that?
1.1　　　(Don't know)
0.2　　　(Refusal/Not answered)

Q322

If 'just a means of earning a living' AT [NwEmpErn]
[NwEmpLiv]
Is that because ... READ OUT ...
%
6.4　　... there are no (better/good) jobs around here,
8.0　　you don't have the right skills to get a (better/good)
　　　job,
13.7　　or, because you would feel the same about **any** job you
　　　had?
3.1　　　(Don't know)
1.4　　　(Refusal/Not answered)

Q323

ASK ALL CURRENT EMPLOYEES
[SayJob]　　　N=1760
Suppose there was going to be some decision made at
your place of work that changed the way you do your
job. Do you think that you **personally** would have any
say in the decision about the change, or not?
IF 'DEPENDS': Code as 'Don't know' <CTRL+K+Enter>
%
58.5　　Yes
38.5　　No
2.9　　　(Don't know)
0.2　　　(Refusal/Not answered)

Q324

IF 'yes' AT [MuchSay]
[MuchSay]
How much say or chance to influence the decision do
you think you would have ... READ OUT ...
%
16.0　　... a great deal,
24.5　　quite a lot,
17.8　　or, just a little?
0.1　　　(Don't know)
3.1　　　(Refusal/Not answered)

Q325

ASK ALL CURRENT EMPLOYEES
[MoreSay]
Do you think you should have **more** say in decisions
affecting your work, or are you satisfied with the way
things are?
%
42.9　　Should have more say
56.3　　Satisfied with way things are
0.7　　　(Don't know)
0.2　　　(Refusal/Not answered)

Q326

VERSION B AND C: ASK ALL IN PAID WORK　　　N=1372
[WkPrefJb]
If without having to work, you had what you would
regard as a reasonable living income, do you think you
would still prefer to (have a paid job/do paid work)
or wouldn't you bother?
%
67.3　　Still prefer paid (job/work)
28.4　　Wouldn't bother
3.5　　　Other answer (WRITE IN)
0.6　　　(Don't know)
0.2　　　(Refusal/Not answered)

ASK ALL CURRENT EMPLOYEES

Q328   [PrefHour]   N=1760
Thinking about the number of hours you work each week
including regular overtime, would you prefer a job
where you worked ... READ OUT ...

%
3.4   ... more hours per week,
38.5   fewer hours per week,
57.5   or, are you happy with the number of hours you work at present?
0.4   (Don't know)
0.2   (Refusal/Not answered)

IF 'more' AT [PrefHour]

Q329   [MoreHour]
Is the reason why you don't work more hours because
... READ OUT ...

%
2.3   ... your employer can't offer you more hours,
0.7   or, your personal circumstances don't allow it?
0.2   (Both)
0.2   Other answer (WRITE IN)
\-   (Don't know)
0.6   (Refusal/Not answered)

IF 'fewer' AT [PrefHour]

Q331   [FewHour]
In which of these ways would you like your working
hours to be shortened ... READ OUT ...

%
12.8   ... shorter hours each day,
24.1   or, fewer days each week?
1.6   Other answer (WRITE IN)
\-   (Don't know)
0.6   (Refusal/Not answered)

IF 'fewer' AT [PrefHour]

Q333   [EarnHour]
Would you still like to work fewer hours, if it meant
earning less money as a result?

%
10.5   Yes
25.5   No
2.4   It depends
\-   (Don't know)
0.6   (Refusal/Not answered)

VERSIONS B AND C: ASK ALL IN PAID WORK

Q334   [WkWorkHd]   N=1372
CARD C4
Which of these statements best describes your feelings
about your job?

%
8.3   I only work as hard as I have to
43.2   I work hard, but not so that it interferes with the rest of my life
48.2   I make a point of doing the best I can, even if it sometimes does interfere with the rest of my life
0.2   (Don't know)
0.2   (Refusal/Not answered)

ASK ALL

Q335   [PatLeav1]   N=3435
CARD C5
Taking your answers from this card, do you think
fathers should **have the right** to take at least two
extra weeks off work after their baby is born?

Q336   [PatLeav2]
CARD C5 AGAIN
And do you think fathers should **have the right** to take
a longer period of time off work, say, three months, in
the first year after their baby is born?

	[PatLeav1]	[PatLeav2]
	%	%
Definitely should	63.6	20.1
Probably should	20.5	22.9
Probably should not	7.1	25.4
Definitely should not	7.8	30.1
(Don't know)	1.0	1.5
(Refusal/Not answered)	-	-

Q337
ASK ALL WITH ODD SERIAL NUMBER
[FrstJob1]
N=1751
CARD C6
Suppose you were advising a young person who was looking for his or her first job. Which **one** of these would you say is **most** important?

Q338
IF ANSWER GIVEN AT [FrstJob1]
[FrstJob2]
CARD C6 AGAIN
(Still supposing you were advising a young person looking for his or her first job.)
And which **next**?

	[FrstJob1]	[FrstJob2]
	%	%
Good starting pay	5.6	13.7
A secure job for the future	36.2	15.8
Opportunities for promotion	11.9	24.3
Interesting work	36.8	20.5
Good working conditions	9.1	25.2
(Don't know)	0.4	0.1
(Refusal/Not answered)	-	0.4

Q339
ASK ALL WITH EVEN SERIAL NUMBERS
[FrstJb1b]
CARD C7
N=1684
Suppose you were advising a young person who was looking for his or her first job. Which **one** of these would you say is **most** important?

Q340
IF ANSWER GIVEN AT [FrstJb2b]
[FrstJb2b]
CARD C7 AGAIN
(Still supposing you were advising a young person looking for his or her first job.)
And which **next**?

	[FrstJb1b]	[FrstJb2b]
	%	%
Good starting pay	4.4	13.2
A secure job for the future	40.2	16.6
Opportunities for promotion	10.4	20.5
Interesting work	35.8	20.0
Good working conditions	7.0	25.0
A chance to help other people	1.9	4.3
(Don't know)	0.3	0.0
(Refusal/Not answered)	-	0.3

Q341
ASK ALL
[JobBSPy1]
CARD C8   N=3435
Suppose this young person had the ability to go into any of **these** careers. From what you know or have heard, which one of these careers would offer him or her the **best starting pay**?

Q342
IF ANSWER GIVEN AT [JobBSPy1]
[JobBSPy2]
CARD C8 AGAIN
And which would offer him or her the **next best** starting pay?

Q343
ASK ALL
[JobMInt1]
CARD C8 AGAIN
Again, from what you know or have heard, which one of these careers would offer him or her the **most interesting work**?

Q344
IF ANSWER GIVEN AT [JobMInt1]
[JobMInt2]
CARD C8 AGAIN
And which would offer him or her the **next most** interesting work?

ASK ALL

Q345 [JobBHel1]
CARD C8 AGAIN
Again, from what you know or have heard, which one of these careers would offer him or her the **best chance** of helping other people?

IF ANSWER GIVEN AT [JobBHel1]

Q346 [JobBHel2]
CARD C8 AGAIN
And which would offer him or her the **next best** chance of helping other people?

	[JobBSPy1]	[JobBSPy2]	[JobMInt1]
	%	%	%
Nurse	1.2	1.9	6.1
Computer engineer	38.4	19.7	6.8
School teacher	2.2	4.9	7.6
Lawyer	32.2	27.8	14.0
Police officer	10.1	11.8	18.1
Journalist	1.4	6.6	32.1
Doctor	11.7	23.6	11.3
(None of these)	0.2	0.3	0.8
(Don't know)	2.6	0.7	3.1
(Refusal/Not answered)	-	2.6	0.0

	[JobMInt2]	[JobBHel1]	[JobBHel2]
	%	%	%
Nurse	9.1	36.8	28.1
Computer engineer	5.2	0.4	0.3
School teacher	13.6	18.0	22.3
Lawyer	15.5	2.6	3.5
Police officer	16.5	8.3	16.0
Journalist	20.4	0.3	0.7
Doctor	15.3	32.0	27.0
(None of these)	0.3	0.1	0.1
(Don't know)	1.0	1.5	0.3
(Refusal/Not answered)	3.2	-	1.5

ASK ALL IN FULL-TIME EDUCATION　　　　N=101

Q347 [Digs]
Do you normally live at the same address during term-time as during the holidays?

	%
Same address	72.2
Different addresses	24.0
(Varies too much to say)	1.6
(Don't know)	-
(Refusal/Not answered)	2.2

IF 'different address' AT [Digs]

Q348 [DigsPare]
Can I just check, is **this** address your main term-time address or your main out-of-term address or neither?
INTERVIEWER: 'THIS ADDRESS' = SAMPLE ADDRESS

	%
Main term-time address	4.9
Main out-of-term address	19.1
Neither	-
(Don't know)	-
(Refusal/Not answered)	2.2

Q349 [KeepDigs]
Thinking now of the period from mid June to mid July this year, (are/were) you keeping on your main term-time home for all or part of this period?
PROBE FOR CORRECT PRECODE

	%
All	7.6
Part	3.8
No	12.5
(Don't know)	-
(Refusal/Not answered)	2.2

IF 'all' OR 'part' AT [KeepDigs]

Q350 [DigsWks]
How many weeks (do you plan/did you) spend in your **main term-time home** from mid June to mid July this year?
Median: 1 week

	%
(Don't know)	-
(Refusal/Not answered)	2.2

Democracy and participation

Q365   **VERSION A AND B: ASK ALL**
        [Lords00]   *N=2285*
        CARD E1
        Which of the statements on this card comes
        closest to your view about what should happen
        to the House of Lords.
%
4.8   All or most of its members should be appointed
30.9   All or most of its members should be elected
35.0   It should contain roughly an equal number of appointed
        and elected members
18.3   It should be abolished
10.8   (Don't know)
0.2   (Refusal/Not answered)

Q366   **VERSION A: ASK ALL**
        [Monarchy]   *N=1119*
        How important or unimportant do you think it is for
        Britain to continue to have a monarchy ...
        READ OUT ...
%
35.5   ...very important,
32.5   quite important,
16.3   not very important,
5.5   not at all important,
8.3   or, do you think the monarchy should be abolished?
1.8   (Don't know)
0.1   (Refused/Not answered)

Q351   [PareWks]
        How many weeks (do you plan/did you) spend in your
        main out-of-term home from mid June to mid July this
        year?
%   **Median: 3 weeks**
-       (Don't know)
2.2   (Refusal/Not answered)

Q367 VERSIONS A AND B: ASK ALL
[VoteSyst]   N=2285
Some people say we should change the voting system for general elections to the (UK) House of Commons to allow smaller political parties to get a fairer share of MPs.
Others say we should keep the voting system for the House of Commons as it is, to produce effective government.
Which view comes **closer** to your own ... READ OUT ...
IF ASKED YOU CAN SAY, 'This refers to proportional representation.'

%
33.5   ... that we should change the voting system for the (UK) House of Commons,
60.8   or, keep it as it is?
5.6   (Don't know)
0.1   (Refusal/Not answered)

Q368 [GovNoSay]
CARD E2
Please choose a phrase from this card to say how much you agree or disagree with the following statements.
People like me have no say in what the government does.

Q369 [LoseTch]
CARD E2 AGAIN
(Please choose a phrase from this card to say how much you agree or disagree with this statement)
Generally speaking those we elect as MPs lose touch with people pretty quickly.

Q370 [VoteIntr]
CARD E2 AGAIN
(Please choose a phrase from this card to say how much you agree or disagree with this statement)
Parties are only interested in people's votes, not in their opinions.

Q371 [VoteOnly]
CARD E2 AGAIN
(Please choose a phrase from this card to say how much you agree or disagree with this statement)
Voting is the only way people like me can have any say about how the government runs things.

Q372 [GovComp]
CARD E2 AGAIN
(Please choose a phrase from this card to say how much you agree or disagree with this statement)
Sometimes politics and government seem so complicated that a person like me cannot really understand what is going on.

	[GovNoSay]	[LoseTch]	[VoteIntr]
	%	%	%
Agree strongly	25.7	28.1	28.9
Agree	40.1	44.7	46.2
Neither agree nor disagree	12.0	12.2	11.4
Disagree	19.1	11.9	11.6
Disagree strongly	2.0	0.8	0.4
(Don't know)	1.0	2.2	1.4
(Refusal/Not answered)	0.1	0.1	0.1

	[VoteOnly]	[GovComp]
	%	%
Agree strongly	17.4	17.3
Agree	51.0	44.0
Neither agree nor disagree	9.9	10.0
Disagree	17.3	22.3
Disagree strongly	2.6	5.4
(Don't know)	1.6	0.8
(Refusal/Not answered)	0.1	0.1

Q373 [PtyNMat2]
CARD E2 AGAIN
(Please choose a phrase from this card to say how much you agree or disagree with this statement)
It doesn't really matter which party is in power, in the end things go on much the same.

%
22.4 Agree strongly
46.6 Agree
5.0 Neither agree nor disagree
22.1 Disagree
2.8 Disagree strongly
0.2 (It depends on the level of government)
0.9 (Don't know)
0.1 (Refusal/Not answered)

Q374 [GovtWork]
CARD E3
Which of these statements best describes your opinion on the present system of governing in Britain?

%
1.9 Works extremely well and could not be improved
35.9 Could be improved in small ways but mainly works well
42.3 Could be improved quite a lot
17.0 Needs a great deal of improvement
2.7 (Don't know)
0.1 (Refusal/Not answered)

Q375 [ImpGHoL]
CARD E4
Do you think that so far reforming the House of Lords has improved the way Britain as a whole is governed, made it worse, or has it made no difference?

Q376 [ImpGFOI]
CARD E4 AGAIN
And how about introducing freedom of information?
(Has this improved the way Britain as a whole is governed, made it worse, or made no difference ...)

Q377 [ImpGSctP]
CARD E4 AGAIN
And how about creating the Scottish Parliament?
(Has this improved the way Britain as a whole is governed, made it worse, or made no difference ...)

	[ImpGHoL]	[ImpGFOI]	[ImpGSctP]
	%	%	%
Improved it a lot	0.7	1.6	3.3
Improved it a little	9.0	20.7	17.5
Made no difference	72.0	60.2	53.0
Made it a little worse	4.2	2.8	6.9
Made it a lot worse	2.5	1.1	3.7
(It is too early to tell)	1.6	2.1	2.5
(Don't know)	9.7	11.5	13.0
(Refusal/Not answered)	0.1	0.1	0.2

Q378- CARD E5
Q385 Suppose a law was being considered by parliament which you thought was really unjust and harmful. Which, if any, of the things on this card do you think you would do?
PROBE Which others?
CODE ALL THAT APPLY
Multicoded (Maximum of 8 codes)

%
50.5 Contact my MP or MSP   [DoMP]
18.7 Speak to an influential person   [DoSpk]
15.7 Contact a government department   [DoGov]
26.7 Contact radio, TV or a newspaper   [DoTV]
62.9 Sign a petition   [DoSign]
10.5 Raise the issue in an organisation I already belong to   [DoRais]
18.0 Go on a protest or demonstration   [DoProt]
8.3 Form a group of like-minded people   [DoGrp]
7.2 (None of these)   [DoNone]
1.3 (Don't know)
0.1 (Refusal/Not answered)

Q395-
Q396
CARD E6
And do you think you would do either of the things on this card about a law being considered by parliament which you thought was really unjust and harmful?
CODE ALL THAT APPLY
Multicoded (Maximum of 2 codes)

%
30.3 Give money to a campaigning organisation [DoCash]
37.9 Get involved in a campaigning organisation [DoInv]
40.2 (Would do neither of these) [DoNeit]
1.3 (Don't know)
0.2 (Refusal/Not answered)

Q399-
Q406
CARD E7
And have you ever done any of the things on this card about a government action which you thought was unjust and harmful? Which ones? Any others?
CODE ALL THAT APPLY
Multicoded (Maximum of 8 codes)

%
16.5 Contact my MP or MSP [DoneMP]
6.2 Speak to an influential person [DoneSpk]
5.4 Contact a government department [DoneGov]
6.5 Contact radio, TV or a newspaper [DoneTV]
42.8 Sign a petition [DoneSign]
6.4 Raise the issue in an organisation I already belong to [DoneRais]
11.8 Go on a protest or demonstration [DoneProt]
2.0 Form a group of like-minded people [DoneGrp]
46.3 (None of these) [DoneNone]
0.6 (Don't know)
0.2 (Refusal/Not answered)

Q416-
Q417
CARD E8
And have you ever done either of the things on this card about a government action which you thought was unjust and harmful?
CODE ALL THAT APPLY
Multicoded (Maximum of 2 codes)

%
15.9 Give money to a campaigning organisation [DoneCash]
14.2 Get involved in a campaigning organisation [DoneInv]
74.3 (Would do neither of these) [DoneNeit]
1.0 (Don't know)
0.2 (Refusal/Not answered)

Q420
[DoneBoyc]
And **have** you ever stopped buying certain goods or products as a protest against something a company or country has done?

%
49.5 Yes
49.9 No
0.4 (Don't know)
0.2 (Refusal/Not answered)

Q421
[Voted01]
Talking to people about the last general election to the (UK) House of Commons in 2001, we have found that a lot of people did not manage to vote. How about you - did you manage to vote in the 2001 general election?
IF NECESSARY, SAY: The election last year where Tony Blair won against William Hague
DO NOT PROMPT

%
69.5 Yes
25.0 No
1.1 Too young to vote
3.0 Not eligible/Not on register
1.2 Can't remember/Don't know
0.2 (Refusal/Not answered)

Q422 [ScotPar2]
CARD E9
Which of these statements comes closest to your view?
%
7.4 Scotland should become independent, separate from the UK and the European Union
12.0 Scotland should become independent, separate from the UK but part of the European Union
42.7 Scotland should remain part of the UK, with its own elected parliament which has **some** taxation powers
9.7 Scotland should remain part of the UK, with its own elected parliament which has **no** taxation powers
15.1 Scotland should remain part of the UK **without** an elected parliament
12.6 (Don't know)
0.5 (Refusal/Not answered)

VERSION A: ASK ALL
Q423 [NIreland]   N=1119
Do you think the long-term policy for Northern Ireland should be for it ... READ OUT ...
%
27.1 ... to remain part of the United Kingdom
48.7 or, to unify with the rest of Ireland?
0.9 **EDIT ONLY:** NORTHERN IRELAND SHOULD BE AN INDEPENDENT STATE
- **EDIT ONLY:** NORTHERN IRELAND SHOULD BE SPLIT UP INTO TWO
5.6 **EDIT ONLY:** IT SHOULD BE UP TO THE IRISH TO DECIDE
2.8 Other answer (WRITE IN)
14.5 (Don't know)
0.3 (Refusal/Not answered)

ASK ALL
Q425 [ECPolicy]
CARD (E10/E1)   N=3435
Do you think Britain's long-term policy should be ... READ OUT ...
%
14.6 ... to leave the European Union,
35.1 to stay in the EU and try to reduce the EU's powers,
23.0 to leave things as they are,
11.7 to stay in the EU and try to increase the EU's powers,
7.5 or, to work for the formation of a single European government?
7.9 (Don't know)
0.3 (Refusal/Not answered)

Q426 [EuroRef]
If there were a referendum on whether Britain should join the single European currency, the Euro, how do you think you would vote? Would you vote to join the Euro, or not to join the Euro?
IF 'would not vote', PROBE: If you did vote, how would you vote?
IF RESPONDENT INSISTS THEY WOULD NOT VOTE, CODE DON'T KNOW
%
34.5 To join the Euro
58.3 Not to join the Euro
7.0 (Don't know)
0.3 (Refusal/Not answered)

Q427 [EURLikel]
(Can I just check, how/How) likely do you think that you would be to vote in such a referendum?
Would you be ... READ OUT ...
%
66.0 ... very likely,
20.0 fairly likely,
6.7 not very likely,
5.7 or, not at all likely?
1.4 (Don't know)
0.2 (Refusal/Not answered)

Q428 [EuroLkly]
And how likely do you think it is that Britain **will** join the single European currency in the next ten years ... READ OUT ...
%
53.0 ... very likely,
31.6 fairly likely,
8.6 not very likely,
2.6 or, not at all likely?
4.1 (Don't know)
0.2 (Refusal/Not answered)

Q429 [EurQuiz1]
For each of the following statements, please tell me whether you think it is true or false. If you don't know, please just say so and we'll go on to the next one.
So - true, false or don't know.
One Euro is worth less than one British pound.

Q430 [EurQuiz2]
Britain is the only member of the EU that is not a member of the single European currency.
(True, false or don't know?)

Q431 [EurQuiz3]
The headquarters of the European Central Bank are in Germany.
(True, false or don't know?)

Q432 [EurQuiz4]
The countries that have introduced the Euro are still using their own currencies as well.
(True, false or don't know?)

	[EurQuiz1]	[EurQuiz2]	[EurQuiz3]	[EurQuiz4]
	%	%	%	%
True	68.4	20.9	35.6	20.6
False	11.0	56.6	21.1	60.2
Don't know	20.4	22.3	43.1	19.0
(Refusal/Not answered)	0.2	0.2	0.2	0.2

VERSION A AND B: ASK ALL   N=2285

Q433 [GovTrust]
CARD E11
How much do you trust British governments of any party to place the needs of the nation above the interests of their own political party?
Please choose a phrase from this card.

Q434 [MpsTrust]
CARD E11 AGAIN
And how much do you trust politicians of any party in Britain to tell the truth when they are in a tight corner?

	[GovTrust]	[MpsTrust]
	%	%
Just about always	2.4	0.5
Most of the time	23.2	6.2
Only some of the time	47.4	36.8
Almost never	24.5	54.8
(Don't know)	2.2	1.4
(Refusal/Not answered)	0.3	0.3

Q435 [SocTrust]
Generally speaking, would you say that most people can be trusted, or that you can't be too careful in dealing with people?
%
39.1 Most people can be trusted
58.9 Can't be too careful in dealing with people
1.7 (Don't know)
0.3 (Refusal/Not answered)

Q436 [WWEcon]
In today's worldwide economy, how much influence do you think British governments of any party have on Britain's economy ... READ OUT ...
%
12.3 ... a great deal,
41.6 quite a lot,
32.1 not very much,
5.5 or, hardly any?
8.2 (Don't know)
0.3 (Refusal/Not answered)

VERSION A: ASK ALL

Q437 [PrejNow]   *N=1119*

Do you think there is generally more racial prejudice in Britain now than there was 5 years ago, less, or about the same amount?

%
42.8 More now
20.9 Less now
33.7 About the same
0.7 Other (WRITE IN)
1.8 (Don't know)
0.1 (Refusal/Not answered)

Q439 [PrejFut]

Do you think there will be more, less, or about the same amount of racial prejudice in Britain in 5 years time compared with now?

%
46.3 More now
22.8 Less now
26.1 About the same
1.7 Other (WRITE IN)
3.0 (Don't know)
0.1 (Refusal/Not answered)

Q441 [SRPrej]

How would you describe yourself ... READ OUT ...

%
1.4 ... as very prejudiced against people of other races,
29.8 a little prejudiced,
66.9 or, not prejudiced at all?
0.6 Other (WRITE IN)
0.8 (Don't know)
0.4 (Refusal/Not answered)

Q443 **ASK ALL**

[SEBenGB]   *N=3435*

On the whole, do you think that England's economy benefits more from having Scotland in the UK, or that Scotland's economy benefits more from being part of the UK, or is it about equal?

%
7.9 England benefits more
38.6 Scotland benefits more
37.2 Equal
2.1 (Neither/both lose)
13.9 (Don't know)
0.2 (Refusal/Not answered)

Q444 [UKSpenGB]

CARD (E12/E2)

Would you say that compared with other parts of the United Kingdom, Scotland gets **pretty much** its fair share of government spending, **more** than its fair share, or **less** than its fair share of government spending?

Please choose your answer from this card.

%
8.4 Much more than its fair share of government spending
14.1 A little more than its fair share of government spending
43.8 Pretty much its fair share of government spending
10.4 A little less than its fair share of government spending
2.3 Much less than its fair share of government spending
20.8 (Don't know)
0.2 (Refusal/Not answered)

IN ENGLAND: ASK ALL   N=2931

Q445 [RegPridE]
CARD (E13/E3)
How much pride do you have in being someone who lives
in (government office region) or do you not think of
yourself in that way at all?

%
24.1 Very proud
20.0 Somewhat proud
2.3   Not very proud
0.9   Not at all proud
52.0 Don't think of themselves in that way
0.5   (Don't know)
0.2   (Refusal/Not answered)

Q446 [EngParl]
CARD (E14/E4)
With all the changes going on in the way the different
parts of Great Britain are run, which of the following
do you think would be best for England
... READ OUT ...
56.1 ...for England to be governed as it is now, with laws
      made by the UK parliament,
19.7 for each region of England to have its own assembly
      that runs services like health,
17.0 or, for England as a whole to have its own new
      parliament with law-making powers?
1.7   (None of these)
5.2   (Don't know)
0.3   (Refusal/Not answered)

Q447 [HearRAss]
In recent years, the government has set up chambers or
assemblies in each of the regions of England. How much
have you heard about the work of the (government
office region chamber or assembly) ...
READ OUT ...
%
1.3   ... a great deal,
5.5   quite a lot,
30.4 not very much,
60.9 or nothing at all?
1.7   (Don't know)
0.3   (Refusal/Not answered)

Q448 [SayInRgE]
From what you have seen or heard so far, do you think
that having (regional chamber or assembly) for
(government office region) will give ordinary people
... READ OUT ...
%
25.4 ... more of a say in how (government office region) is
      governed,
3.3   less say,
59.2 or, will it make no difference?
11.8 (Don't know)
0.3   (Refusal/Not answered)

Q449 [ERegEcon]
And as a result of having (regional chamber or
assembly) for (government office region) will the
region's economy become better, worse or will it make
no difference?
IF BETTER/WORSE: Is that a lot better/worse or a
little better/worse?
%
2.7   A lot better
18.6 A little better
59.8 No difference
2.9   A little worse
1.1   A lot worse
14.6 (Don't know)
0.3   (Refusal/Not answered)

Education

ASK ALL

Q454   [EdSpend1]   N=3435
       CARD D1
       Now some questions about education.
       Which of the groups on this card, if any, would be
       your highest priority for **extra** government spending on
       education?

       IF ANSWER GIVEN AT [EdSpend1]

Q455   [EdSpend2]
       CARD D1 AGAIN
       And which is your next highest priority?

	[EdSpend1] %	[EdSpend2] %
Nursery or pre-school children	10.4	11.6
Primary school children	18.2	23.0
Secondary school children	28.5	22.9
Less able children with special needs	26.9	23.6
Students at colleges or universities	14.1	16.5
(None of these)	0.6	0.2
(Don't know)	1.2	0.2
(Refusal/Not answered)	0.1	0.0

ASK ALL

Q456   [PrimImpl]
       CARD D2
       Here are a number of things that some people think
       would improve education in our schools.
       Which do you think would be the **most** useful one for
       improving the education of children in **primary** schools
       - aged (5-11/5-12) years? Please look at the whole
       list before deciding.

Q450   [DoesInfE]
       CARD (E15/E5)
       Taking your answers from this card, which of the
       following do you think currently **has** most influence
       over the way England is run?

%	
1.8	English regional chambers or assemblies
71.1	The UK government at Westminster
7.1	Local councils in England
14.0	The European Union
5.8	(Don't know)
0.3	(Refusal/Not answered)

Q451   [OughInfE]
       CARD (E16/E6)
       Taking your answers from this card, which do you think
       ought to have most influence over the way England is
       run?

%	
11.0	English regional chambers or assemblies
12.3	A new English parliament
48.6	The UK government at Westminster
20.0	Local councils in England
1.6	The European Union
6.2	(Don't know)
0.3	(Refusal/Not answered)

Q458   **IF ANSWER GIVEN AT [PrimImp2]**
[PrimImp2]
CARD D2 AGAIN
And which do you think would be the **next** most useful one for children in **primary** schools?

	[PrimImp1]	[PrimImp2]
	%	%
More information available about individual schools	0.8	1.5
More links between parents and schools	8.1	11.6
More resources for buildings, books and equipment	14.1	21.9
Better quality teachers	16.2	14.8
Smaller class sizes	40.5	20.3
More emphasis on exams and tests	0.8	1.6
More emphasis on developing the child's skills and interests	15.2	22.0
Better leadership within individual schools	1.8	3.8
Other (WRITE IN)	1.1	0.9
(Don't know)	1.2	0.5
(Refusal/Not answered)	0.0	-

Q460   **ASK ALL**
[SecImp1]
CARD D3
And which do you think would be the **most** useful thing for improving the education of children in **secondary** schools - aged (11-18/12-18) years?

Q462   **IF ANSWER GIVEN AT [SecImp1]**
[SecImp2]
CARD D3 AGAIN
And which do you think would be the **next** most useful one for children in **secondary** schools?

	[SecImp1]	[SecImp2]
	%	%
More information available about individual schools	1.3	1.0
More links between parents and schools	5.5	6.3
More resources for buildings, books and equipment	13.8	14.6
Better quality teachers	18.1	13.9
Smaller class sizes	26.7	15.7
More emphasis on exams and tests	4.1	5.4
More emphasis on developing the child's skills and interests	12.7	17.5
More training and preparation for jobs	12.1	19.2
Better leadership within individual schools	2.8	3.5
Other (WRITE IN)	1.3	0.9
(Don't know)	1.5	0.4
(Refusal/Not answered)	0.0	1.5

Q464   **ASK ALL**
[SchSelec]
CARD D4
Which of the following statements comes closest to your views about what kind of **secondary** school children should go to?

%
48.9   Children should go to a different kind of secondary school, according to how well they do at primary school
48.5   All children should go to the same kind of secondary school, ro matter how well or badly they do at primary school
2.5   (Don't know)
0.1   (Refusal/Not answered)

Q465

[PrimBet]
From what you know or have heard, do you think that **primary schools** in the area where you live are
... READ OUT ...

%
30.5 ... getting better,
11.0 getting worse
37.8 or, staying much the same?
20.6 (Don't know)
0.1 (Refusal/Not answered)

Q466

[SecBet]
And from what you know or have heard, do you think that **secondary schools** in the area where you live are
... READ OUT ...

%
25.5 ... getting better,
20.9 getting worse
34.2 or, staying much the same?
19.3 (Don't know)
0.1 (Refusal/Not answered)

Q467

[PrimTest]
Thinking now of **tests and exams** in schools, from what you know or have heard, do you think that **primary school pupils** have to take
... READ OUT ...

%
39.9 ... too many,
7.3 too few,
38.5 or, about the right number of tests and exams?
14.3 (Don't know)
0.0 (Refusal/Not answered)

Q468

[SecTest]
And, from what you know or have heard, do you think that **secondary school pupils** have to take
... READ OUT ...

%
25.9 ... too many,
9.5 too few,
52.9 or, about the right number of tests and exams?
11.7 (Don't know)
0.0 (Refusal/Not answered)

Q469

[Advise16]
Suppose you were advising a 16 year old about their future.
Would you say they should ... READ OUT ...

%
50.5 ... stay on in full-time education to get their (A levels (or A2 levels) / Highers (or Higher Stills)),
10.8 or, study full-time to get vocational, rather than academic, qualifications,
9.7 or, leave school and get training through a job?
28.5 (Varies/depends on the person)
0.4 (Don't know)
0.0 (Refusal/Not answered)

Q470

[VocVAcad]
In the long-run, which do you think gives people more opportunities and choice in life ... READ OUT ...

%
37.9 ... having good practical skills and training,
31.5 or, having good academic results?
30.2 (Mixture/depends)
0.4 (Don't know)
0.0 (Refusal/Not answered)

Q471

ASK RESPONDENTS WHO HAVE OWN CHILD AGED 5-18 IN HOUSEHOLD   N=818
[ChimpCom]
CARD D5
How important is the use of computers in helping your child(ren) to do well in their school work?

%
57.2 Very important
33.3 Fairly important
7.5 Not very important
1.5 Not at all important
0.3 (No child(ren) at school)
0.1 (Don't know)
- (Refusal/Not answered)

ASK ALL

Q472 [WWWLearn]
CARD D5 (AGAIN)   N=3435
How important do you think the internet is for
learning new knowledge or skills?

%
33.1   Very important
42.0   Fairly important
14.3   Not very important
2.7   Not at all important
7.9   (Don't know)
0.0   (Refusal/Not answered)

Q473 [HEdOpp]
Do you feel that opportunities for young people in
Britain to go on to **higher education** - to a university
or college - should be increased or reduced, or are
they at about the right level now?
IF INCREASED OR REDUCED: a lot or a little?

%
24.3   Increased a lot
21.9   Increased a little
45.3   About right
4.1   Reduced a little
1.2   Reduced a lot
3.1   (Don't know)
0.1   (Refusal/Not answered)

**ASK RESPONDENTS WHO HAVE OWN CHILD AGED 5-18 IN
HOUSEHOLD**   N=818

Q474 [ChLikUni]
CARD D6
Taking your answers from this card, how likely do you
think it is that any of your children who are still at
school will go to university?

%
37.7   Very likely
36.6   Fairly likely
16.3   Not very likely
4.3   Not at all likely
3.0   (No child(ren) at school)
2.1   (Don't know)
-   (Refusal/Not answered)

Classification

Housing and local area

ASK ALL   N=3435

Q476 [Tenure1]
Does your household own or rent this accommodation?
PROBE IF NECESSARY
IF OWNS: Outright or on a mortgage?
IF RENTS: From whom?

%
27.3   Owns outright
46.4   Buying on mortgage
11.4   Rents: local authority
0.1   Rents: New Town Development Corporation
4.3   Rents: Housing Association
1.4   Rents: property company
0.3   Rents: employer
0.9   Rents: other organisation
0.6   Rents: relative
5.8   Rents: other individual
0.1   Rents: Housing Trust
0.3   Rent free, squatting
0.7   Other (WRITE IN)
0.3   (Don't know)
0.3   (Refusal/Not answered)

VERSION C: ASK ALL   N=1150

Q479 [ResPres]
Can I just check, would you describe the place where
you live as
... READ OUT ...

%
8.3   ... a big city,
26.9   the suburbs or outskirts of a big city,
44.2   a small city or town,
17.5   a **country village**,
2.5   or, a farm or home in the country?
0.6   (Other answer (WRITE IN))
0.0   (Don't know)
-   (Refusal/Not answered)

Religion, national identity and race

Q485		Q488	
ASK ALL		**IF NOT REFUSED AT [Religion]**	
[Religion]	N=3435	[FamRelig]	
Do you regard yourself as belonging to any particular religion?		In what religion, if any, were you brought up?	
IF YES: Which?		PROBE IF NECESSARY: What was your family's religion?	
CODE ONE ONLY - DO NOT PROMPT		CODE ONE ONLY - DO NOT PROMPT	
%		%	
41.1	No religion	12.2	No religion
5.9	Christian - no denomination	6.4	Christian - no denomination
9.1	Roman Catholic	13.7	Roman Catholic
30.7	Church of England/Anglican	48.1	Church of England/Anglican
1.1	Baptist	1.6	Baptist
2.2	Methodist	4.5	Methodist
3.0	Presbyterian/Church of Scotland	5.6	Presbyterian/Church of Scotland
0.2	Other Christian	0.3	Other Christian
0.8	Hindu	0.9	Hindu
0.6	Jewish	0.7	Jewish
2.2	Islam/Muslim	2.2	Islam/Muslim
0.2	Sikh	0.2	Sikh
0.1	Buddhist	0.1	Buddhist
0.3	Other non-Christian	0.2	Other non-Christian
0.1	Free Presbyterian	0.1	Free Presbyterian
0.0	Brethren	0.2	Brethren
0.3	United Reform Church (URC)/Congregational	0.8	United Reform Church (URC)/Congregational
1.3	Other Protestant	1.4	Other Protestant
0.3	Refused	0.0	Refused
0.2	(Don't know)	0.4	(Don't know)
0.2	(Not answered)	0.2	(Not answered)

Q493 [ChAttend]
IF RELIGION GIVEN AT [Religion] OR AT [FamRelig]
Apart from such special occasions as weddings, funerals and baptisms, how often nowadays do you attend services or meetings connected with your religion?
PROBE AS NECESSARY.

%
10.6 Once a week or more
2.4 Less often but at least once in two weeks
5.5 Less often but at least once a month
9.2 Less often but at least twice a year
5.2 Less often but at least once a year
4.4 Less often than once a year
49.5 Never or practically never
1.0 Varies too much to say
0.0 (Don't know)
0.5 (Refusal/Not answered)

ASK ALL
Q494-Q501
CARD F1
Please say which, if any, of the words on this card describes the way **you** think of **yourself**. Please choose as many or as few as apply.
PROBE: Any other?
Multicoded (Maximum of 8 codes)

%
71.1 British   [NatBrit]
49.8 English   [NatEng]
12.0 European   [NatEuro]
2.4 Irish   [NatIrish]
0.6 Northern Irish   [NatNI]
10.0 Scottish   [NatScot]
0.1 Ulster   [NatUlst]
5.3 Welsh   [NatWelsh]
2.5 Other answer (WRITE IN)   [NatOth]
1.1 (None of these)   [NatNone]
1.2 **EDIT ONLY:** OTHER - ASIAN MENTIONED   [NatAsia]
0.0 **EDIT ONLY:** OTHER - AFRICAN /CARIBBEAN MENTIONED   [NatAfric]
0.3 (Don't know)
0.2 (Refusal/Not answered)

Q515 [NationU]
IF MORE THAN ONE ANSWER GIVEN AT [NationJ]
[BNationJ]
CARD F1 AGAIN
And if you had to choose, which one **best** describes the way you think of yourself?

ASK ALL
Q518 [RaceOri2]
CARD F2
To which of these groups do you consider you belong?

%
1.1 BLACK: of African origin
1.5 BLACK: of Caribbean origin
0.2 BLACK: of other origin (WRITE IN)
1.3 ASIAN: of Indian origin
1.3 ASIAN: of Pakistani origin
0.3 ASIAN: of Bangladeshi origin
0.2 ASIAN: of Chinese origin
0.7 ASIAN: of other origin (WRITE IN)
90.9 WHITE: of any European origin
0.9 WHITE: of other origin (WRITE IN)
0.7 MIXED ORIGIN (WRITE IN)
0.4 OTHER (WRITE IN)
0.3 (Don't know)
0.3 (Refusal/Not answered)

Education

Q524　[RPrivEd]
Have you ever attended a fee-paying, **private** primary or secondary school in the United Kingdom?
'PRIVATE' PRIMARY OR SECONDARY SCHOOLS INCLUDE:
* INDEPENDENT SCHOOLS
* SCHOLARSHIPS AND ASSISTED PLACES AT FEE-PAYING SCHOOLS
THEY EXCLUDE:
* DIRECT GRANT SCHOOLS (UNLESS FEE-PAYING)
* VOLUNTARY-AIDED SCHOOLS
* GRANT-MAINTAINED ('OPTED OUT') SCHOOLS
* NURSERY SCHOOLS

%
11.1　Yes
88.4　No
0.2　(Don't know)
0.2　(Refusal/Not answered)

IF NO CHILDREN IN HOUSEHOLD (AS GIVEN IN HOUSEHOLD GRID)
Q526　[OthChld3]
Have you ever been responsible for bringing up any children of school age, including stepchildren?

%
31.4　Yes
34.9　No
0.1　(Don't know)
0.4　(Refusal/Not answered)

IF CHILDREN IN HOUSEHOLD (AS GIVEN AT HOUSEHOLD GRID) OR 'yes' AT [OthChld3]
Q525　[ChPrivEd]
And (have any of your children/has your child) ever attended a fee-paying, **private** primary or secondary school in the United Kingdom?
'PRIVATE' PRIMARY OR SECONDARY SCHOOLS INCLUDE:
* INDEPENDENT SCHOOLS
* SCHOLARSHIPS AND ASSISTED PLACES AT FEE-PAYING SCHOOLS
THEY EXCLUDE:
* DIRECT GRANT SCHOOLS (UNLESS FEE-PAYING)
* VOLUNTARY-AIDED SCHOOLS
* GRANT-MAINTAINED ('OPTED OUT') SCHOOLS
* NURSERY SCHOOLS

%
9.0　Yes
55.6　No
0.1　(Don't know)
0.4　(Refusal/Not answered)

ASK ALL
Q528　[Tea]
How old were you when you completed your continuous full-time education?
PROBE IF NECESSARY
'STILL AT SCHOOL' - CODE 95
'STILL AT COLLEGE OR UNIVERSITY' - CODE 96
'OTHER ANSWER' - CODE 97 AND WRITE IN

%
30.7　15 or under
27.6　16
9.2　17
9.3　18
19.5　19 or over
0.3　Still at school
2.6　Still at college or university
0.4　Other answer (WRITE IN)
0.2　(Don't know)
0.3　(Refusal/Not answered)

Q531 [SchQual]
CARD F3
Have you passed any of the examinations on this card?

%
64.9 Yes
34.6 No
0.4   (Don't know)
0.2   (Refusal/Not answered)

Q532-
Q535

IF 'yes' AT [SchQual]
CARD F3 AGAIN Please tell me which sections of the card they are in?
PROBE: Any other sections?
CODE ALL THAT APPLY
Multicoded (Maximum of 4 codes)

%
30.3 Section 1:   [EdQual1]
      GCSE Grades D-G/Short course GCSE
      CSE Grades 2-5
      GCE O level Grades D-E or 7-9
      Scottish (SCE) Ordinary Bands D-E
      Scottish Standard Grades 4-7
      School leaving certificate (no grade)

46.7 Section 2:   [EdQual2]
      GCSE Grades A-C
      CSE Grade 1
      GCE O-level Grades A-C or 1-6
      School Certificate or Matriculation
      Scottish SCE Ordinary Bands A-C or pass
      Scottish Standard Grades 1-3 or Pass
      Scottish School Leaving Certificate Lower Grade
      SUPE Ordinary
      Northern Ireland Junior Certificate

22.6 Section 3:   [EdQual3]
      GCE A level, S level, A2 level, AS level
      Scottish Higher Grades
      Scottish Higher-Still
      Scottish SCE/SLC/SUPE at Higher Grade
      Scottish Higher School Certificate
      Certificate of Sixth Year Studies
      Northern Ireland Senior Certificate

2.8   Section 4:   [EdQual4]
      Overseas school leaving exam or certificate
-     (Don't know)
0.6   (Refusal/Not answered)

Q536 ASK ALL
[PSchQual]
CARD F4
And have you passed any of the exams or got any of the qualifications on this card?

60.3 Yes
39.2 No
0.3   (Don't know)
0.2   (Refusal/Not answered)

Q537-
Q559

IF 'yes' AT [PSchQual]
[PSchQFW]
CARD F4 AGAIN Which ones? PROBE: Which others?
PROBE FOR CORRECT LEVEL

%
2.5 **Modern** apprenticeship **completed**   [EdQual126]
5.3 Other recognised trade apprenticeship **completed**   [EdQual127]
7.0 RSA/OCR - Certificate   [EdQual128]
2.7 RSA/OCR - (First) Diploma   [EdQual129]
1.5 RSA/OCR - Advanced Diploma   [EdQual130]
0.7 RSA/OCR - Higher Diploma   [EdQual131]
1.1 Other clerical, commercial qualification   [EdQual132]
6.3 City&Guilds Certif - Part I   [EdQual122]
6.6 City&Guilds Certif - Craft/Intermediate/   [EdQual122]
     Ordinary/Part II
3.8 City&Guilds Certif - Advanced/Final/   [EdQual123]
     Part III
1.7 City&Guilds Certif - Full Technological/   [EdQual124]
     Part IV
4.9 BTEC/EdExcel/BEC/TEC General/Ordinary   [EdQual125]
     National Certif (ONC) or Diploma (OND)
5.4 BTEC/EdExcel/BEC/TEC Higher/Higher National   [EdQual10]
     Certif (HNC) or Diploma (HND)
3.6 NVQ/SVQ Lev 1/GNVQ/GSVQ Foundation lev   [EdQual11]
5.9 NVQ/SVQ Lev 2/GNVQ/GSVQ Intermediate lev   [EdQual17]
4.1 NVQ/SVQ Lev 3/GNVQ/GSVQ Advanced lev   [EdQual18]
                                                                  [EdQual19]

0.4	NVQ/SVQ Lev 4	[EdQual20]
0.4	NVQ/SVQ Lev 5	[EdQual21]
5.1	Teacher training qualification	[EdQual22]
3.3	Nursing qualification	[EdQual13]
5.6	Other technical or business qualification/ certificate	[EdQual14]
15.7	Univ/CNAA degree/diploma	[EdQual15]
8.6	Other recognised academic or vocational qual (WRITE IN)	[EdQual16]

VERSION B AND C: ASK ALL MARRIED OR LIVING AS MARRIED
N=1468

Q589 [STea]
How old was your (husband/wife/partner) when (he/she) completed (his/her) continuous full-time education?
PROBE IF NECESSARY
'STILL AT SCHOOL' - CODE 95
'STILL AT COLLEGE OR UNIVERSITY' - CODE 96
'OTHER ANSWER' - CODE 97 AND WRITE IN

%
29.4 15 or under
31.7 16
5.8   17
10.0 18
19.5 19 or over
-     Still at school
0.1   Still at college or university
0.1   Other answer (WRITE IN)
2.9   (Don't know)
0.3   (Refusal/Not answered)

Q592 [SSchQual]
CARD F5
Has your (husband/wife/partner) passed any of the examinations on this card?

%
59.3 Yes
35.6 No
4.7   (Don't know)
0.3   (Refusal/Not answered)

IF 'yes' AT [SSchQual]
[SSchQFW]
Q593- CARD F5 AGAIN Please tell me which sections of the card
Q596 they are in?
PROBE: Any other sections?
CODE ALL THAT APPLY
Multicoded (Maximum of 4 codes)

%
23.6 **Section 1:** [SEdQul1]
GCSE Grades D-G/Short course GCSE
CSE Grades 2-5
GCE O level Grades D-E or 7-9
Scottish (SCE) Ordinary Bands D-E
Scottish Standard Grades 4-7
School leaving certificate (no grade)
43.6 **Section 2:** [SEdQul2]
GCSE Grades A-C
CSE Grade 1
GCE O level Grades A-C or 1-6
School Certificate or Matriculation
Scottish SCE Ordinary Bands A-C or pass
Scottish Standard Grades 1-3 or Pass
Scottish School Leaving Certificate Lower Grade
SUPE Ordinary
Northern Ireland Junior Certificate
21.9 **Section 3:** [SEdQul3]
GCE A level, S level, A2 level, AS level
Scottish Higher Grades
Scottish Higher-Still
Scottish SCE/SLC/SUPE at Higher Grade
Scottish Higher School Certificate
Certificate of Sixth Year Studies
Northern Ireland Senior Certificate
2.6   **Section 4:** [SEdQul4]
Overseas school leaving exam or certificate
0.8   (Don't know)
5.0   (Refused/Not answered)

Q597 [SPSchQul]

VERSION B AND C: ASK ALL MARRIED OR LIVING AS MARRIED

CARD F6

And has your (husband/wife/partner) passed any of the exams or got any of the qualifications on **this** card?

56.2	Yes
39.6	No
3.8	(Don't know)
0.3	(Refusal/Not answered)

Q598- [SPSchQFW]
Q620

IF 'yes' AT [SPSchQul]

CARD F6 AGAIN Which ones? PROBE: Which others?

PROBE FOR CORRECT LEVEL

Multicoded (Maximum of 23 codes)

%

2.6	**Modern Apprenticeship completed**	[SEdQul26]
4.8	Other recognised trade apprenticeship completed	[SEdQul27]
3.6	RSA/OCR - Certificate	[SEdQul28]
2.0	RSA/OCR - (First) Diploma	[SEdQul29]
1.3	RSA/OCR - Advanced Diploma	[SEdQul30]
0.4	RSA/OCR - Higher Diploma	[SEdQul31]
1.9	Other clerical, commercial qualification	[SEdQul32]
5.5	City&Guilds Certif - Part I	[SEdQul22]
5.4	City&Guilds Certif - Craft/Intermediate/ Ordinary/Part II	[SEdQul23]
3.1	City&Guilds Certif - Advanced/Final/ Part III	[SEdQul24]
2.0	City&Guilds Certif - Full Technological/Part IV	[SEdQul25]
3.2	BTEC/EdExcel/BEC/TEC General/Ordinary National Certif (ONC)or Diploma (OND)	[SEdQul10]
4.5	BTEC/EdExcel/BEC/TEC Higher/Higher National Certif (HNC)or Diploma (HND)	[SEdQul11]
2.1	NVQ/SVQ Lev 1/GNVQ/GSVQ Foundation lev	[SEdQul17]
2.8	NVQ/SVQ Lev 2/GNVQ/GSVQ Intermediate lev	[SEdQul18]
1.3	NVQ/SVQ Lev 3/GNVQ/GSVQ Advanced lev	[SEdQul19]
0.6	NVQ/SVQ Lev 4	[SEdQul20]
0.4	NVQ/SVQ Lev 5	[SEdQul21]
4.1	Teacher training qualification	[SEdQul12]
3.8	Nursing qualification	[SEdQul13]
6.2	Other technical or business qualification/certificate	[SEdQul14]
15.2	Univ/CNAA degree/diploma	[SEdQul15]
7.2	Other recognised academic or vocational qual (WRITE IN)	[SEdQul16]
0.2	(Don't know)	
4.1	(Refusal/Not answered)	

Internet use

ASK ALL

Q650 [Internet]

Does anyone have access to the Internet or World Wide Web from this address?

N=3435

%

51.9	Yes
47.7	No
0.2	(Don't know)
0.2	(Refusal/Not answered)

Q651 [WWWUse]

Do you yourself ever use the Internet or World Wide Web for any reason (other than your work)?

%

49.9	Yes
49.7	No
0.2	(Don't know)
0.2	(Refusal/Not answered)

Q652 [WWWHrsWk]

IF 'yes' AT [WWWUse]

How many hours a week on average do you spend using the Internet or World Wide Web (other than for your work)?

INTERVIEWER: ROUND UP TO NEAREST HOUR

Median: 2 hours

%

-	(Don't know)
0.9	(Refusal/Not answered)

Partner's job details

Q675

ASK ALL MARRIED OR LIVING AS MARRIED   N=2184
[SeconAct]
CARD F8
Which of these descriptions applied to what your
(husband/wife/partner) was doing last week, that is the
seven days ending last Sunday?
PROBE: Which others? CODE ALL THAT APPLY
Multicoded (Maximum of 11 codes)

%
0.3	In full-time education (not paid for by employer, including on vacation)
-	On government training/employment programme
65.3	In paid work (or away temporarily) for at least 10 hours in week
0.3	Waiting to take up paid work already accepted
1.0	Unemployed and registered at a benefit office
0.6	Unemployed, **not** registered, but actively looking for a job (of at least 10 hrs a week)
0.4	Unemployed, wanting a job (of at least 10 hrs a week) but **not** actively looking for a job
4.1	Permanently sick or disabled
16.6	Wholly retired from work
10.1	Looking after the home
0.7	(Doing something else) (WRITE IN)
-	(Don't know)
0.6	(Refusal/Not answered)

Q676

**ASK ALL MARRIED OR LIVING AS MARRIED AND PARTNER NOT
IN PAID WORK OR WAITING TO TAKE UP WORK**   N=752
[SLastJob]
How long ago did (he/she) last have a paid job of at
least 10 hours a week?
GVT. PROGRAMS/SCHEMES DO NOT COUNT AS `PAID JOBS'.

%
11.5	Within past 12 months
23.5	Over 1, up to 5 years ago
21.9	Over 5, up to 10 years ago
22.6	Over 10, up to 20 years ago
14.2	Over 20 years ago
3.9	Never had a paid job of 10+ hours a week
0.7	(Don't know)
1.7	(Refusal/Not answered)

Q653-
Q661   [WWWWhat]
CARD F7
For which of the following do you personally use the
internet or World Wide Web (other than for your work)?
Multicoded (Maximum of 9 codes)

%
20.5	Shopping	[WWWShop]
2.9	Chat rooms	[WWWChat]
37.0	E-mail	[WWWEmail]
13.4	News and current affairs	[WWWNews]
14.3	Training, education and learning	[WWWEduc]
20.9	Travel and weather information	[WWWTrav]
6.7	Keeping in touch with groups I belong to	[WWWGroup]
32.5	General information	[WWWInfo]
1.8	Other (PLEASE SPECIFY)	[WWWOther]
0.3	(None of these)	[WWWNone]
0.8	**EDIT ONLY:** Banking and bill-paying	[WWWBank]
0.5	**EDIT ONLY:** Downloading music	[WWWMusic]
0.5	**EDIT ONLY:** Sports information	[WWWSport]
0.3	**EDIT ONLY:** Games	[WWWGames]
0.5	**EDIT ONLY:** Job search	[WWWJobS]
-	(Don't know)	
0.4	(Refusal/Not answered)	

ASK ALL WHERE PARTNER'S JOB DETAILS ARE BEING COLLECTED
Partner's job details are collected if respondent is not working or waiting to take up work, but partner is working or waiting to take up work.   N=278

Q677   [Title] **(NOT ON DATAFILE)**
Now I want to ask you about your (husband's/wife's/partner's) (present/future) job. What (is his/her job? / Will that job be?) PROBE IF NECESSARY: What (is/was) the name or title of the job?

Q678   [Typewk] **(NOT ON DATAFILE)**
What kind of work (do/will) (he/she) do most of the time?
IF RELEVANT: What materials/machinery (do/will) (he/she) use?

Q679   [Train] **(NOT ON DATAFILE)**
What training or qualifications are needed for that job?

Q680   [PEmploy]
In your (husband's/wife's/partner's) (main) job (is/will) (he/she) (be) ... READ OUT ...
%
80.7   ... an employee,
17.1   or self-employed?
-      (Don't know)
2.2   (Refusal/Not answered)

Q682   [Psuperv]
In your job, (does/will) (he/she) have any formal responsibility for supervising the work of other (employees/people)?
DO NOT INCLUDE PEOPLE WHO ONLY SUPERVISE:
- CHILDREN, E.G. TEACHERS, NANNIES, CHILDMINDERS
- ANIMALS
- SECURITY OR BUILDINGS, E.G. CARETAKERS, SECURITY GUARDS
%
38.2   Yes
59.2   No
0.4   (Don't know)
2.2   (Refusal/Not answered)

IF 'yes' AT [Psuperv]
Q683   [PMany]
How many?
Median: 7 (of those supervising any)
3.9   (Don't know)
2.6   (Refusal/Not answered)

ASK ALL WHERE PARTNER'S JOB DETAILS ARE BEING COLLECTED AND PARTNER IS EMPLOYEE
Q685   [Psupman2]
N=230
Can I just check, (is/will) (he/she) (be) ... READ OUT ...
%
26.9   ... a manager,
10.7   ... a foreman or supervisor,
59.8   or, not?
-      (Don't know)
2.6   (Refusal/Not answered)

Q686 [PocSect2]
CARD F9
Which of the types of organisation on this card
(does he/she / will he/she be working) for?

%
72.3 PRIVATE SECTOR FIRM OR COMPANY Including, for example, limited companies and PLCs
2.9 NATIONALISED INDUSTRY OR PUBLIC CORPORATION Including, for example, the Post Office and the BBC
20.5 OTHER PUBLIC SECTOR EMPLOYER
Incl. e.g.: - Central govt/Civil Service/Govt Agency
- Local authority/Local Educ Auth (incl. 'opted out' schools)
- Universities
- Health Authority/NHS hospitals/NHS Trusts/GP surgeries
- Police/Armed forces
1.2 CHARITY/ VOLUNTARY SECTOR Including, for example, charitable companies, churches, trade unions
0.5 Other answer (WRITE IN)
- (Don't know)
2.6 (Refusal/Not answered)

Q688 ASK ALL WHERE PARTNER'S JOB DETAILS ARE BEING COLLECTED
[EmpMake] (NOT ON DATAFILE) N=278
IF EMPLOYEE: What does (his/her) employer make or do at the place where (he/she) (usually works/will usually work) (from)?
IF SELF-EMPLOYED: What (does/will) (he/she) make or do at the place where (he/she) (usually works/will usually work) (from)?

[PempWork] N=278
IF EMPLOYEE: Including (himself/herself), how many people are employed at the place where (he/she) usually (works/will work) (from)?
IF YES: PROBE FOR CORRECT PRECODE.
(DO NOT USE IF EMPLOYEE/ No employees)
Q692
%
15.6 Under 10
11.0 10-24
18.5 25-99
18.3 100-499
17.0 500 or more
7.3 (Don't know)
2.2 (Refusal/Not answered)

VERSIONS B AND C: ASK ALL WHO ARE MARRIED OR LIVING AS MARRIED AND WHOSE SPOUSE/PARTNER IS IN PAID WORK
[SWkJbrHrI] N=952
How many hours does (he/she) normally work a week in (his/her) main job - including any paid or unpaid overtime?
ROUND TO NEAREST HOUR.
IF RESPONDENT CANNOT ANSWER, ASK ABOUT LAST WEEK.
IF RESPONDENT DOES NOT KNOW EXACTLY, ACCEPT AN ESTIMATE.
Q697
FOR 95+ HOURS, CODE 95.
Median: 40 hours
%
1.3 (Varies too much to say)
1.9 (Don't know)
1.1 (Refusal/Not answered)

Q698   [SWkJbHrX]
What are your (husband's/wife's/partner's) **basic or contractual hours** each week in (his/her) main job – **excluding** any paid and unpaid overtime?
ROUND TO NEAREST HOUR.
IF RESPONDENT CANNOT ANSWER, ASK ABOUT LAST WEEK.
IF RESPONDENT DOES NOT KNOW EXACTLY, ACCEPT AN ESTIMATE.
FOR 95+ HOURS, CODE 95.
FOR 'VARIES TOO MUCH TO SAY' OR DOES NOT APPLY (E.G. SELF-EMPLOYED), CODE 96.
Median: 37 hours

%
7.4   (Varies too much to say)
6.2   (Don't know)
0.2   (Refusal/Not answered)

Income

ASK ALL
Q730   [AnyBN3]
CARD F10   N=3435
Do you (or your husband/wife/partner) receive any of the **state** benefits or tax credits on this card at present?

%
57.8   Yes
41.6   No
0.3   (Don't know)
0.3   (Refusal/Not answered)

Q748   **IF 'yes' AT [AnyBN3]**
CARD F10 AGAIN
Which ones?
PROBE: Which others?

%		
20.3	State retirement pension (National Insurance)	[BenefOAP]
0.6	War Pension (War Disablement Pension or War Widows Pension)	[BenefWar]
1.1	Bereavement Allowance/ Widow's Pension/ Widowed Parent's Allowance	[BenefWid]
2.7	Jobseeker's Allowance/Unemployment Benefit/ Income Support for the Unemployed	[BenefUB]
5.8	Income Support (other than for unemployment)/ Minimum Income Guarantee for pensioners	[BenefIS]
27.0	Child Benefit (formerly Family Allowance)	[BenefCB]
4.4	Child Tax Credit	[BenefCTC]
4.8	Working Families Tax Credit/ Childcare Tax Credit	[BenefFC]
6.9	Housing Benefit (Rent Rebate/Rent Allowance)	[BenefHB]
8.2	Council Tax Benefit (or Rebate)	[BenefCT]
5.0	Incapacity Benefit/Sickness Benefit/ Invalidity Benefit	[BenefInc]
0.1	Disabled Person's Tax Credit	[BenefDWA]
4.6	Disability Living Allowance (for people under 65)	[BenefDLA]
2.0	Attendance Allowance (for people aged 65+)	[BenefAtA]
0.7	Severe Disablement Allowance	[BenefSev]
1.6	Invalid Care Allowance	[BenefICA]
0.5	Industrial Injuries Disablement Benefit	[BenefInd]
0.5	Other state benefit (WRITE IN)	[BenefOth]
0.0	(Don't know)	
0.7	(Refusal/Not answered)	

Q769   ASK ALL
[MainInc]
CARD F11
Which of these is the **main** source of income for you
(and your husband/wife/partner) at present?

%
64.0 Earnings from employment (own or spouse/partner's)
8.9 Occupational pension(s) - from previous employer(s)
11.9 State retirement or widow's pension(s)
1.9 Jobseeker's Allowance/Unemployment benefit
3.9 Income Support/Minimum Income Guarantee for pensioners
3.1 Invalidity, sickness or disabled pension or benefit(s)
0.6 Other state benefit or tax credit (WRITE IN)
1.0 Interest from savings or investments
1.4 Student grant, bursary or loans
1.6 Dependent on parents/other relatives
0.8 Other main source (WRITE IN)
0.4 (Don't know)
0.6 (Refusal/Not answered)

ASK ALL WHO ARE NOT WHOLLY RETIRED AND MALE AGED 65 OR
UNDER WOMAN AGED 60 OR UNDER
Q772   [PenXpct1]
N=2613
CARD F12
When you have retired and have stopped doing paid
work, where do you think **most** of your income will come
from?
INTERVIEWER: IF RESPONDENT SAYS 'SPOUSE/PARTNER'S
COMPANY/OCCUPATIONAL PENSION', CODE AS 'A
COMPANY/OCCUPATIONAL PENSION'.
SIMILARLY FOR STATE AND PERSONAL/STAKEHOLDER PENSIONS.

%
23.4 State retirement pension
42.5 A company or occupational pension
17.6 A personal or stakeholder pension
12.4 Other savings or investments
1.0 From somewhere else (WRITE IN)
EDIT ONLY: Earnings from job/still working
0.3
2.7 (Don't know)
0.2 (Refusal/Not answered)

IF 'company or occupational pension' OR 'personal or
stakeholder pension' AT [PenXpct1] AND RESPONDENT IS
MARRIED, LIVING AS MARRIED, SEPARATED, WIDOWED OR
DIVORCED
Q774   [PenOwn1]
And would that be your own pension or your (husband's/
wife's/partner's/ex-husband's/ex-wife's/late
husband's/late wife's) pension?
%
23.2 Own pension
9.6 Spouse/partner's pension
12.9 (Both)
0.1 (Don't know)
3.0 (Refusal/Not answered)

ASK ALL WHO ARE NOT WHOLLY RETIRED AND MALE AGED 65 OR
UNDER WOMAN AGED 60 OR UNDER
Q775   [PenXpct2]
CARD F12 AGAIN
And which do you think will be your **second most**
important source of income?
INTERVIEWER: IF RESPONDENT SAYS 'SPOUSE/PARTNER'S
COMPANY/OCCUPATIONAL PENSION', CODE AS 'A
COMPANY/OCCUPATIONAL PENSION'.
SIMILARLY FOR STATE AND PERSONAL/STAKEHOLDER PENSIONS.
%
27.7 State retirement pension
16.0 A company or occupational pension
11.1 A personal or stakeholder pension
29.6 Other savings or investments
1.7 From somewhere else (WRITE IN)
9.3 (None)
0.8 **EDIT ONLY:** Earnings from job/still working
3.6 (Don't know)
0.1 (Refusal/Not answered)

ASK ALL IN PAID WORK   N=2011

Q779 [REarn]
CARD F13 AGAIN
Which of the letters on this card represents your own gross or total **earnings**, before deduction of income tax and national insurance?

%
4.6 Less than £3,999
4.6 £4,000-£5,999
5.2 £6,000-£7,999
5.7 £8,000-£9,999
7.6 £10,000-£11,999
11.3 £12,000-£14,999
8.8 £15,000-£17,999
4.9 £18,000-£19,999
7.2 £20,000-£22,999
7.1 £23,000-£25,999
5.9 £26,000-£28,999
5.2 £29,000-£31,999
4.5 £32,000-£37,999
2.5 £38,000-£43,999
1.9 £44,000-£49,999
1.0 £50,000-£55,999
5.5 £56,000 or more
4.9 (Refused information)
1.5 (Don't know)
-    (Not answered)

IF 'company or occupational pension' OR 'personal or stakeholder pension' AT [PenXpct2] AND RESPONDENT IS MARRIED, LIVING AS MARRIED, SEPARATED, WIDOWED OR DIVORCED

Q777 [PenOwn2]
And would that be your own pension or your (husband's/wife's/partner's/ex-husband's/ex-wife's/late husband's/ late wife's) pension?

%
11.0 Own pension
5.7   Spouse/partner's pension
4.1   (Both)
0.1   (Don't know)
11.1 (Refusal/Not answered)

ASK ALL   N=3435

Q778 [HHincome]
CARD F13
Which of the letters on this card represents the total income of your household from **all** sources **before tax**? Please just tell me the letter.
NOTE: INCLUDES INCOME FROM BENEFITS, SAVINGS, ETC.

%
1.7 Less than £3,999
5.9 £4,000-£5,999
5.6 £6,000-£7,999
5.0 £8,000-£9,999
4.6 £10,000-£11,999
5.7 £12,000-£14,999
5.4 £15,000-£17,999
4.1 £18,000-£19,999
4.1 £20,000-£22,999
5.2 £23,000-£25,999
4.8 £26,000-£28,999
4.2 £29,000-£31,999
6.7 £32,000-£37,999
5.9 £38,000-£43,999
4.5 £44,000-£49,999
3.2 £50,000-£55,999
10.4 £56,000 or more
6.4 (Refusal/Not answered)
6.6 (Don't know)
-    (Not answered)

Administration

ASK ALL

Q781   [PhoneX]

Is there a telephone in (your part of) this   *N=3435*
accommodation?

%
95.6   Yes
3.9   No
0.2   (Don't know)
0.2   (Refusal/Not answered)

IF 'yes' AT [PhoneX]

Q782   [PhoneBck]

A few interviews on any survey are checked by a
supervisor to make sure that people are satisfied with
the way the interview was carried out. In case my
supervisor needs to contact you, it would be helpful
if we could have your telephone number.
ADD IF NECESSARY: Your 'phone number will **not** be
passed to anyone outside the National Centre.
IF NUMBER GIVEN, WRITE ON THE ARF
NOTE: YOU WILL BE ASKED TO KEY IN THE NUMBER IN THE
ADMIN BLOCK

%
90.4   Number given
5.2   Number refused
0.0   (Don't know)
0.4   (Refusal/Not answered)

ASK ALL

Q783   [ComeBac2]

Sometime in the next year, we may be doing a follow-up
survey and may wish to contact you again. Could you
give us the address or phone number of someone who
knows you well, just in case we have difficulty in
getting in touch with you.
IF NECESSARY, PROMPT: Perhaps a relative or friend who
is unlikely to move?
WRITE IN DETAILS ON ARF

%
40.7   Information given
54.8   Information not given (other than code 3)
0.3   DO NOT PROMPT: Outright refusal ever to take part again
0.1   (Don't know)
    (Refusal/Not answered)

Versions B and C

Employment and caring

VERSIONS B AND C: ASK ALL CURRENT EMPLOYEES

Q353　[TimeOff]
CARD C9　　　　　　　　　　　　　　　　*N=1184*

And now some more questions about your job.
I'd like you to think about the person at work you go
to if you have to take time off - this may be your
supervisor, your line manager or someone else. How
understanding would this person be if you had to take
time off for family or personal reasons?

%
61.6　Very understanding
27.9　Fairly understanding
4.7　Not very understanding
2.3　Not at all understanding
1.1　Varies too much to say
1.8　(Doesn't have to ask anyone if takes time off)
-　(Don't know)
0.2　(Refusal/Not answered)

IF NOT 'doesn't have to ask anyone' AT [TimeOff]
Q354　[ManWoman]
Is this person a man or a woman?

%
59.8　Man
37.5　Woman
0.3　(Don't know)
0.6　(Refusal/Not answered)

VERSIONS B AND C: ASK ALL CURRENT EMPLOYEES

Q355-　[LostTime]
Q358　CARD C10
Say you had to take a day off work, with little notice,
for family or personal reasons. In general, which of
the things on this card would you do to cover the lost
time?
Which others?
INTERVIEWER: CODE ALL THAT APPLY

%
44.3　Multicoded (Maximum of 4 codes)
12.7　Use holiday or flexi hours *[LTHoli]*
Put in extra effort within normal working
34.1　hours *[LT3ffort]*
23.4　Work extra hours afterwards *[LTExtrHr]*
16.5　Take unpaid leave *[LTUnpaid]*
0.1　None of these *[LTNone]*
0.6　(Don't know)
(Refusal/Not answered)

Q359　[LoseMony]
And if you took time off work for family or personal
reasons would you ...
READ OUT ...

%
18.6　... usually lose money as a result,
12.2　sometimes lose money,
65.6　or, not usually lose money as a result?
2.0　(Varies too much to say)
0.9　(Don't know)
0.6　(Refusal/Not answered)

Q360   [UpLadder]
CARD C11
I'd like you to think about how people in your kind of job move up the ladder at your workplace - for example, by getting themselves promoted. Do you agree or disagree that people who want to do this usually have to put in long hours?

%
16.7   Agree strongly
31.1   Agree
10.8   Neither agree nor disagree
31.7   Disagree
3.5   Disagree strongly
4.4   (No-one moves up ladder/gets promoted)
0.8   (It depends)
0.4   (Don't know)
0.6   (Refusal/Not answered)

Q361   [MovLaddr]
CARD C12
And do you agree or disagree that people in your kind of job who want to move up the ladder at your workplace have to be prepared to move from one part of the country to another?

%
9.1   Agree strongly
23.0   Agree
10.4   Neither agree nor disagree
36.0   Disagree
9.9   Disagree strongly
5.6   No other workplace to move to
3.8   (No-one moves up ladder/gets promoted)
1.2   (It depends)
0.3   (Don't know)
0.1   (Refusal/Not answered)

Q362   [ImpLaddr]
CARD C13
Speaking for yourself, how important is it that you move up the career ladder at work?

%
14.7   Very important
27.7   Fairly important
36.5   Not very important
20.1   Not important at all
0.4   (Don't know)
0.6   (Refusal/Not answered)

Q363   [TOSNProb]
CARD C14
How much do you agree or disagree that if you take time off work at short notice it makes things difficult for the people you work with?

Q364   [LongHrs]
CARD C14 AGAIN
How much do you agree or disagree that people in your kind of job are expected to work longer hours these days than they used to?

	[TOSNProb]	[LongHrs]
	%	%
Agree strongly	24.6	22.7
Agree	44.6	33.1
Neither agree nor disagree	12.0	16.3
Disagree	15.1	23.8
Disagree strongly	3.0	2.5
(Don't know)	0.1	1.1
(Refusal/Not answered)	0.6	0.6

Version C

Transport

Q225 **VERSION C: ASK ALL**   N=1150
[TransCar]
(May I just check ...) ... do you, or does anyone in your household, own or have the regular use of a car or a van?
IF 'YES' PROBE FOR WHETHER RESPONDENT, OR OTHER PERSON(S) ONLY, OR BOTH
%
28.7 Yes, respondent only
15.9 Yes, other(s) only
38.3 Yes, both
17.1 No
-     (Don't know)
-     (Refusal/Not answered)

IF 'yes' AT [TransCar]
Q226 [NumbCars]
How many vehicles in all?
%
44.7 One
29.6 Two
6.4   Three
1.7   Four
0.6   Five or more
-     (Don't know)
-     (Refusal/Not answered)

VERSION C: ASK ALL
Q227 [TrfPb6U]
CARD B1
Now thinking about traffic and transport problems, how serious a problem **for you** is congestion on motorways?

Q228 [TrfPb9U]
CARD B1 AGAIN
(And how serious a problem **for you** is ...) traffic congestion in towns and cities?

Q229 [TrfPb10U]
CARD B1 AGAIN
(And how serious a problem **for you** are ...) exhaust fumes from traffic in towns and cities?

Q230 [TrfPb11U]
CARD B1 AGAIN
(And how serious a problem **for you** is ...) noise from traffic in towns and cities?

	[TrfPb6U]	[TrfPb9U]	[TrfPb10U]	[TrfPb11U]
	%	%	%	%
A very serious problem	12.7	23.5	24.1	12.5
A serious problem	18.5	33.7	35.4	25.3
Not a very serious problem	32.7	27.5	25.8	38.2
Not a problem at all	35.1	15.2	14.3	23.7
(Don't know)	0.9	0.1	0.3	0.3
(Refusal/Not answered)	-	-	-	-

IF 'yes, respondent', 'yes, both', DON'T KNOW OR REFUSAL AT [TransCar]
Q231 [GETABB1]
CARD B2
I am going to read out some of the things that might get people to **cut down** on the number of car journeys they take. For each one, please tell me what effect, if any, this might have on how much **you yourself** use the car to get about.
... gradually doubling the cost of petrol over the next ten years.

Q232 [GETABB2]
CARD B2 AGAIN
(What effect, if any, might this have on how much **you yourself** use the car?)
... greatly improving **long distance** rail and coach services?

Q233 [GETABB3]
CARD B2 AGAIN
(What effect, if any, might this have on how much **you yourself** use the car)
... greatly improving the reliability of **local** public transport?

Q234 [GETABB4]
CARD B2 AGAIN
(What effect, if any, might this have on how much **you yourself** use the car)
... charging all motorists around £2 each time they enter or drive through a city or town centre at peak times?

Q235 [GETABB6]
CARD B2 AGAIN
(What effect, if any, might this have on how much **you yourself** use the car)
... making parking penalties and restrictions much more severe?

Q236 [GETABB7]
CARD B2 AGAIN
(What effect, if any, might this have on how much **you yourself** use the car)
... special cycle lanes on roads around here?

	[GETABB1]	[GETABB2]	[GETABB3]
	%	%	%
Might use car even more	0.2	0.5	0.1
Might use car a little less	21.5	19.0	18.9
Might use car quite a bit less	13.5	15.4	19.5
Might give up using car	5.2	3.0	4.8
It would make no difference	26.4	28.8	23.5
(Don't know)	0.0	0.2	0.1
(Refusal/Not answered)	0.1	-	-

	[GETABB4]	[GETABB6]	[GETABB7]
	%	%	%
Might use car even more	0.1	0.2	0.1
Might use car a little less	16.2	14.1	8.5
Might use car quite a bit less	11.3	9.2	4.8
Might give up using car	5.2	4.1	1.2
It would make no difference	33.8	39.2	52.2
(Don't know)	0.2	-	0.1
(Refusal/Not answered)	0.1	0.1	-

Q237 [Drive]
May I just check, do you yourself drive a car at all these days?
%
Yes 70.0
No   30.0
(Don't know) -
(Refusal/Not answered) -

IF 'yes' AT [Drive]
Q238 [TRAVEL1]
CARD B3
How often nowadays do you **usually** travel
... by car as a driver?

Q239 [TRAVEL2]
CARD B3 AGAIN
(How often nowadays do you **usually**)
... travel by car as a passenger?

Q240 [TRAVEL3] *
CARD B3 AGAIN
(How often nowadays do you **usually**)
... travel by local bus?

Q241 [TRAVEL4]
CARD B3 AGAIN
(How often nowadays do you **usually**)
... travel by train?

Q242 [Travel6]
CARD B3 AGAIN
(How often nowadays do you **usually**)
... travel by bicycle?

Q243 [Travel9]
CARD B3 AGAIN
(How often nowadays do you **usually**)
... go somewhere on foot at least 15 minutes' walk away?

	[TRAVEL1]	[TRAVEL2]	[TRAVEL3]
	%	%	%
Every day or nearly every day	47.8	11.2	7.3
2-5 days a week	16.4	23.4	12.3
Once a week	3.4	25.1	8.8
Less often but at least once a month	1.4	12.8	10.3
Less often than that	0.5	12.1	13.1
Never nowadays	0.5	15.4	48.3
(Don't know)	-	-	-
(Refusal/Not answered)	-	-	-

	[TRAVEL4]	[TRAVEL6]	[TRAVEL9]
	%	%	%
Every day or nearly every day	3.2	2.7	32.7
2-5 days a week	2.9	4.1	24.0
Once a week	3.9	3.2	15.2
Less often but at least once a month	12.9	5.4	6.7
Less often than that	31.5	6.3	4.3
Never nowadays	45.7	78.3	17.1
(Don't know)	-	-	-
(Refusal/Not answered)	-	-	-

Q244 [TrnNear]
CARD B4
About how far do you live from your **nearest** railway station?

	%
Less than ½ mile (15 mins walk)	21.4
½ up to 1 mile (15-30 mins walk)	18.2
Over 1 mile, up to 3 miles	27.1
Over 3 miles, up to 10 miles	22.9
Over 10 miles	10.0
(Don't know)	0.4
(Refusal/Not answered)	-

BRITISH SOCIAL ATTITUDES 2002 SELF-COMPLETION QUESTIONNAIRE VERSION A

N=2929

[MONEYGO]
1. Which one of these two statements comes closest to your own view?

PLEASE TICK **ONE BOX ONLY**

	%
If the money is there, I find it just goes	25.3
OR I always try to keep some money in hand for emergencies	69.2
Can't choose	4.9
(Not answered)	0.6

[NEVBORRO]
2. And which of these two statements comes closest to your own view?

PLEASE TICK **ONE BOX ONLY**

	%
People should never borrow money	11.1
OR There is nothing wrong with borrowing money as long as you can manage the repayments	85.9
Can't choose	2.5
(Not answered)	0.5

[MONEYRET]
3. And which of these two statements comes closest to your own view?

PLEASE TICK **ONE BOX ONLY**

	%
Young people should spend their money while they are young and worry about saving for retirement when they are older	20.8
OR Young people should start saving for their retirement as soon as they can even if they have to cut back on other things	63.2
Can't choose	15.4
(Not answered)	0.7

4. Please tick one box for each statement to show how much you agree or disagree with it.

PLEASE TICK **ONE BOX** ON EACH LINE

		Agree strongly	Agree	Neither agree nor disagree	Disagree	Disagree strongly	Can't choose	(Not answered)
[CREDPLAN] a.	Credit makes it easier for people to plan their finances	2.4	32.4	22.6	30.3	7.1	2.3	2.9
[BOROHARD] b.	It should be made much harder to borrow money even if this means that more people can't get credit	9.0	41.2	20.1	22.3	2.4	2.5	2.5
[CREDSPND] c.	Credit encourages people to spend far more money than they can really afford to	31.5	52.4	8.6	4.3	0.4	1.0	1.7

[SINGMUM1]
5. Thinking about a single mother with a child **under school age**. Which one of these statements comes closest to your view?

*PLEASE TICK **ONE** BOX ONLY*

	%
She has a special duty to go out to work to support her child	14.3
She has a special duty to stay at home to look after her child	23.1
She should do as she chooses, like everyone else	51.7
Can't choose	10.1
(Not answered)	0.8

[SINGMMC2]
6. Suppose this single mother did go out to work. How much do you agree or disagree that the government should provide money to help with child care?

*PLEASE TICK **ONE** BOX ONLY*

	%
Agree strongly	26.2
Agree	47.0
Neither agree nor disagree	11.4
Disagree	8.7
Disagree strongly	2.1
Can't choose	4.0
(Not answered)	0.7

[SMUMSCH1]
7. And what about when the child reaches school age? Which one of these statements comes closest to your view about what the single mother should do?

*PLEASE TICK **ONE** BOX ONLY*

	%
She has a special duty to go out to work to support her child	45.3
She has a special duty to stay at home to look after her child	4.0
She should do as she chooses, like everyone else	43.7
Can't choose	6.4
(Not answered)	0.6

[SMUMSCH2]
8. Suppose this single mother did go out to work. How much do you agree or disagree that the government should provide money to help with child care outside school?

*PLEASE TICK **ONE** BOX ONLY*

	%
Agree strongly	16.7
Agree	44.0
Neither agree nor disagree	17.1
Disagree	13.7
Disagree strongly	2.5
Can't choose	5.4
(Not answered)	0.6

[COUPMUM1]
9. And finally thinking about a **married** mother with a child **under school age.** Which one of these statements comes closest to your own view?

*PLEASE TICK **ONE** BOX ONLY*

	%
She has a special duty to go out to work to support her child	6.4
She has a special duty to stay at home to look after her child	30.6
She should do as she chooses, like everyone else	56.0
Can't choose	6.4
(Not answered)	0.7

[COUPMUM2]
10. Suppose this married mother did go out to work. How much do you agree or disagree that the government should provide money to help with child care?

*PLEASE TICK **ONE** BOX ONLY*

	%
Agree strongly	12.2
Agree	37.6
Neither agree nor disagree	18.9
Disagree	21.5
Disagree strongly	3.4
Can't choose	5.7
(Not answered)	0.8

[BEN500]
11a. Consider this situation:
An unemployed person on benefit takes a casual job and is paid in cash. He does not report it to the benefit office and is £500 in pocket. Do you feel this is wrong or not wrong?

*PLEASE TICK **ONE** BOX ONLY*

	%
Not wrong	1.7
A bit wrong	9.9
Wrong	40.4
Seriously wrong	44.5
Can't choose	2.8
(Not answered)	0.6

[BEN500DO]
b. And how likely do you think it is that you would do this, if you found yourself in this situation?

*PLEASE TICK **ONE** BOX ONLY*

	%
Very likely	6.4
Fairly likely	12.1
Not very likely	29.1
Not at all likely	46.1
Can't choose	5.5
(Not answered)	0.8

[PAY500]

12a. Now consider this situation:

A person in paid work takes on an extra weekend job and is paid in cash. He does not declare it for tax and so is £500 in pocket. Do you feel this is wrong or not wrong?

*PLEASE TICK **ONE** BOX ONLY*

	%
Not wrong	11.6
A bit wrong	25.8
Wrong	40.8
Seriously wrong	15.9
Can't choose	5.2
(Not answered)	0.6

[PAY500DO]

b. And how likely do you think it is that you would do this, if you found yourself in this situation?

*PLEASE TICK **ONE** BOX ONLY*

	%
Very likely	10.2
Fairly likely	18.5
Not very likely	30.1
Not at all likely	33.9
Can't choose	5.9
(Not answered)	1.3

[COHAB500]

13. And now consider this situation:

A person on benefit moved in with his girlfriend and her young daughter a year ago. He does not report this to the benefit office and so the couple are £500 in pocket. Do you feel this is wrong or not wrong?

*PLEASE TICK **ONE** BOX ONLY*

	%
Not wrong	1.9
A bit wrong	11.8
Wrong	51.4
Seriously wrong	30.4
Can't choose	3.7
(Not answered)	0.8

[GOVBEN]

14. Which is it more important for the government to do?

*PLEASE TICK **ONE** BOX ONLY*

	%
To get people to claim benefits to which they are entitled	27.9
OR	
To stop people claiming benefits to which they are not entitled	61.1
Can't choose	10.2
(Not answered)	0.7

[INFORMBN]

15. How much do you agree or disagree with this statement?

"People who know someone is cheating the benefit system should always report this."

*PLEASE TICK **ONE** BOX ONLY*

	%
Strongly agree	17.4
Agree	37.2
Neither agree nor disagree	26.0
Disagree	7.5
Strongly disagree	1.8
Can't choose	9.3
(Not answered)	0.8

N=1928

16. From what you know or have heard, please tick a box for each of the items below to show whether you think the National Health Service in your area is, on the whole, satisfactory or in need of improvement.

*PLEASE TICK **ONE** BOX ON EACH LINE*

		In need of a lot of improvement	In need of some improvement	Satis-factory	Very good	Can't choose	(Not answered)
[HSAREA1] a. GPs' appointment systems	%	17.3	34.5	36.4	10.2	0.1	1.5
[HSAREA2] b. Amount of time GP gives to each patient	%	10.5	26.0	50.7	10.9	0.1	1.8
[HSAREA5] c. Hospital waiting lists for non-emergency operations	%	40.9	41.4	14.1	0.7	0.2	2.6
[HSAREA6] d. Waiting time before getting appointments with hospital consultants	%	49.1	36.1	11.2	0.8	0.2	2.6
[HSAREA7] e. General condition of hospital building	%	18.2	35.7	35.9	7.4	0.1	2.7
[HSAREA13] f. Waiting areas in accident and emergency departments in hospitals	%	21.4	37.1	34.6	3.4	0.3	3.3
[HSAREA14] g. Waiting areas for out-patients in hospitals	%	12.1	37.1	44.0	3.7	0.2	2.9
[HSAREA15] h. Waiting areas at GPs' surgeries	%	4.2	15.6	63.9	13.6	0.1	2.6
[HSAREA16] i. Time spent waiting in out-patient departments	%	25.3	48.1	22.6	1.1	0.2	2.7
[HSAREA17] j. Time spent waiting in accident and emergency departments before being seen by a doctor	%	45.7	35.8	14.0	1.5	0.4	2.6
[HSAREA18] k. Time spent waiting for an ambulance after a 999 call	%	9.3	29.0	46.4	9.6	1.3	4.5

17. In the last twelve months, have you or a close family member …

PLEASE TICK ONE BOX ON EACH LINE

		Yes, just me	Yes, not me but close family member	Yes, both	No, neither	(Not answered)
[GPUSESC] a.	… visited an NHS GP?	% 22.8	13.4	56.3	5.8	1.7
[OUTPUSSC] b.	… been an out-patient in an NHS hospital?	% 22.0	25.2	14.0	35.0	3.8
[INPUSSC] c.	… been an in-patient in an NHS hospital?	% 11.3	18.9	4.2	60.0	5.6
[VISTUSSC] d.	… visited a patient in an NHS hospital?	% 16.1	13.7	24.9	41.5	3.8
[PRIVUSSC] e.	… had any medical treatment as a private patient?	% 6.9	7.4	2.4	80.0	3.3

N=2929

18. From what you know or have heard, please tick one box on each line to show how well you think **state secondary schools** nowadays …

PLEASE TICK ONE BOX ON EACH LINE

		Very well	Quite well	Not very well	Not at all well	Can't choose	(Not answered)
[STATSEC1] a.	… prepare young people for work?	% 4.1	43.7	42.6	6.4	0.4	2.8
[STATSEC2] b.	… teach young people basic skills such as reading, writing and maths?	% 15.3	56.1	21.5	4.1	0.4	2.7
[STATSEC3] c.	… bring out young people's natural abilities?	% 6.2	41.4	40.5	8.4	0.4	3.0

19. Please tick one box on each line to show how much you agree or disagree with each of these statements about secondary schooling

PLEASE TICK ONE BOX ON EACH LINE

		Agree strongly	Agree	Neither agree nor disagree	Disagree	Disagree strongly	(Not answered)
[SECSCHL1] a.	Formal exams are the best way of judging the ability of pupils	% 4.6	42.5	20.3	27.3	3.2	2.0
[SECSCHL2] b.	On the whole pupils are too young when they have to decide which subjects to specialise in	% 9.6	53.3	20.2	13.9	0.8	2.2
[SECSCHL3] c.	The present law allows pupils to leave school when they are too young	% 3.6	24.6	30.1	36.9	2.6	2.1
[SECSCHL4] d.	So much attention is given to exam results that a pupil's everyday classroom work counts for too little	% 12.8	51.0	19.7	13.1	1.1	2.2

20. Please tick one box on each line to show how important you think each of these are:

PLEASE TICK ONE BOX ON EACH LINE

		Very important	Fairly important	Not very important	Not at all important	Can't choose	(Not answered)
[UNISPEC] a.	… that parents encourage children to go to university	% 28.8	46.8	15.3	2.3	5.2	1.6
[UNISTEC] b.	… that teachers encourage more children to go to university	% 28.4	46.8	15.7	2.0	5.2	2.0
[UNISWEC] c.	… that more people from working class backgrounds go to university	% 34.9	40.4	14.5	2.4	5.9	1.9

[UNIBCKGR]
21. Suppose two young people with the same A/A2 level (or Scottish Higher) grades apply to go to university. One is from a well-off background and the other is from a less well-off background. Which one do you think would be more likely to be offered a place …

PLEASE TICK ONE BOX ONLY

	%
… the young person from the well-off background,	42.7
the young person from less well-off background,	2.9
or would they both be equally likely to be offered a place?	44.4
Can't choose	8.8
(Not answered)	1.3

22. Please tick one box on each line to show how much you agree or disagree with each of these statements.

PLEASE TICK ONE BOX ON EACH LINE

		Agree strongly	Agree	Neither agree nor disagree	Disagree	Disagree strongly	Can't choose	(Not answered)
[UNIKNOW] a.	I feel I know quite a lot about what sort of work is done in universities	% 9.2	23.4	20.7	28.5	5.5	10.7	2.0
[UNILINKS] b.	My local university has good links with the community	% 2.5	20.8	34.0	13.3	2.2	25.0	2.3
[UNIWNTC] c.	Universities do enough to encourage working class young people to study there	% 2.4	25.0	28.9	20.2	3.5	17.9	2.0
[UNITENC] d.	Teachers give children enough encouragement to go to university	% 2.8	29.0	30.7	16.5	2.6	16.5	1.9

N=1928

[BRPRIOR1]

23a. Looking at the list below, please tick the box next to the one thing you think should be Britain's highest priority, the most important thing it should do.

*PLEASE TICK **ONE** BOX ONLY*

Britain should ...

	%
Maintain order in the nation	38.7
Give people more say in government decisions	30.3
Fight rising prices	9.5
Protect freedom of speech	9.3
Can't choose	10.8
(Not answered)	1.5

[BRPRIOR2]

b. And which one do you think should be Britain's next highest priority, the second most important thing it should do?

*PLEASE TICK **ONE** BOX ONLY*

Britain should ...

	%
Maintain order in the nation	23.0
Give people more say in government decisions	26.5
Fight rising prices	18.5
Protect freedom of speech	16.3
Can't choose	13.9
(Not answered)	1.7

N=2929

24. Please tick one box to show how much you agree or disagree with each of these statements.

*PLEASE TICK **ONE** BOX ON EACH LINE*

	Agree strongly	Agree	Neither agree nor disagree	Disagree	Disagree strongly	Can't choose	(Not answered)
[MPSPROM] a. Whatever their party, most politicians try to keep their promises.	% 1.6	16.6	22.0	41.9	12.5	3.5	1.7
[ENGRGDEV] b. Now that Scotland has its own parliament, and Wales its own Assembly, every English region should have its own elected assembly too.	% 5.2	21.3	22.7	28.7	8.7	11.6	1.8

N=1928

25. On the whole, do you think it should be or should not be the government's responsibility to ...

*PLEASE TICK **ONE** BOX ON EACH LINE*

	Definitely should be	Probably should be	Probably should not be	Definitely should not be	Can't choose	(Not answered)
[GOVRESP1] a. ... provide a job for everyone who wants one	% 33.1	39.4	13.7	6.5	5.2	2.2
[GOVRESP2] b. ... keep prices under control	% 52.8	38.2	3.4	0.6	2.0	3.0
[GOVRESP3] c. ... provide health care for the sick	% 84.0	11.6	0.6	0.2	1.4	2.1
[GOVRESP4] d. ... provide a decent standard of living for the elderly	% 78.7	16.7	1.2	0.2	1.2	2.0

26. Regardless of whether you think it should be the government's responsibility, how successful do you think governments have been in recent years at ensuring ...

*PLEASE TICK **ONE** BOX ONLY*

	Very successful	Fairly successful	Neither successful nor unsuccessful	Fairly unsuccessful	Very unsuccessful	Can't choose	(Not answered)
[GOVSFUL1] a. ... that everyone who wants a job has one	% 2.2	34.1	28.6	22.6	7.3	2.8	2.4
[GOVSFUL2] b. ... that prices are kept under control	% 4.2	31.3	22.6	26.4	10.4	2.6	2.6
[GOVSFUL3] c. ... that everyone has good access to adequate health care	% 2.3	32.3	20.1	26.8	14.4	1.9	2.3
[GOVSFUL4] d. ... that all elderly people have a decent standard of living	% 1.7	18.3	21.2	32.3	22.5	2.2	1.9

[LABFAVOR]

27. How often would you say Labour does favours for people or companies who give the party large sums of money?

*PLEASE TICK **ONE** BOX ONLY*

	%
Very often	23.7
Fairly often	33.8
Not very often	16.2
Never	2.9
Can't choose	22.2
(Not answered)	1.3

[CONFAVOR]
28. How often would you say the Conservatives do favours for people or companies who give the party large sums of money?

PLEASE TICK ONE BOX ONLY

	%
Very often	25.8
Fairly often	33.6
Not very often	13.9
Never	2.7
Can't choose	23.0
(Not answered)	1.2

29. Please tick one box for each statement to show how much you agree or disagree with it.

N=2929

PLEASE TICK ONE BOX ON EACH LINE

	Agree strongly	Agree	Neither agree nor disagree	Disagree	Disagree strongly	Can't choose	(Not answered)
	%						
[WELFHELP] a. The welfare state encourages people to stop helping each other	4.2	25.9	36.8	27.8	2.7	0.0	2.6
[MOREWELF] b. The government should spend more money on welfare benefits for the poor, even if it leads to higher taxes	6.7	37.2	27.2	23.3	3.2	0.0	2.5
[UNEMPJOB] c. Around here, most unemployed people could find a job if they really wanted one	15.4	49.3	18.0	13.6	1.6	0.1	2.0
[SOCHELP] d. Many people who get social security don't really deserve any help	7.5	28.3	30.8	27.8	3.3	0.1	2.2
[DOLEFIDL] e. Most people on the dole are fiddling in one way or another	8.6	29.4	31.3	25.3	3.1	0.1	2.2
[WELFFEET] f. If welfare benefits weren't so generous, people would learn to stand on their own two feet	9.9	33.9	23.9	25.3	4.6	0.1	2.3
[DAMLIVES] g. Cutting welfare benefits would damage too many people's lives	9.2	44.1	26.5	15.9	2.2	0.0	2.1
[PROUDWLF] h. The creation of the welfare state is one of Britain's proudest achievements	16.0	36.6	31.4	11.1	2.7	0.0	2.1

30. Please tick one box for each statement below to show how much you agree or disagree with it.

PLEASE TICK ONE BOX ON EACH LINE

	Agree strongly	Agree	Neither agree nor disagree	Disagree	Disagree strongly	Can't choose	(Not answered)
	%						
[REDISTRB] a. Government should redistribute income from the better-off to those who are less well off	10.9	27.6	25.2	26.6	7.1	0.1	2.5
[BIGBUSNN] b. Big business benefits owners at the expense of workers	13.7	43.2	24.6	13.2	2.1	0.1	3.1
[WEALTH] c. Ordinary working people do not get their fair share of the nation's wealth	12.7	50.0	22.5	10.9	1.3	0.1	2.6
[RICHLAW] d. There is one law for the rich and one for the poor	18.3	43.0	18.7	15.3	2.6	0.1	2.1
[INDUST4] e. Management will always try to get the better of employees if it gets the chance	16.7	43.7	21.2	14.0	1.7	0.1	2.5

31. Please tick one box for each statement below to show how much you agree or disagree with it.

PLEASE TICK ONE BOX ON EACH LINE

	Agree strongly	Agree	Neither agree nor disagree	Disagree	Disagree strongly	Can't choose	(Not answered)
	%						
[TRADVALS] a. Young people today don't have enough respect for traditional British values	20.1	47.8	19.7	9.6	0.7	0.0	2.1
[STIFSENT] b. People who break the law should be given stiffer sentences	31.7	45.7	15.1	5.3	0.2	0.0	1.8
[DEATHAPP] c. For some crimes, the death penalty is the most appropriate sentence	29.1	26.3	14.8	16.1	11.9	0.1	1.8
[OBEY] d. Schools should teach children to obey authority	30.4	51.5	10.7	4.4	0.8	0.0	2.2
[WRONGLAW] e. The law should always be obeyed, even if a particular law is wrong	8.1	31.1	30.5	24.5	3.6	0.0	2.2
[CENSOR] f. Censorship of films and magazines is necessary to uphold moral standards	18.5	44.1	18.1	12.9	4.3	0.1	2.0

BRITISH SOCIAL ATTITUDES 2002 SELF-COMPLETION QUESTIONNAIRE VERSION B

N=1984

1. To begin, we have some questions about women. Do you agree or disagree?

PLEASE TICK **ONE** BOX ON EACH LINE

	Strongly agree	Agree	Neither agree nor disagree	Disagree	Strongly disagree	Can't choose	(Not answered)
[WWRELCHD] a. A working mother can establish just as warm and secure a relationship with her children as a mother who does not work	% 20.7	43.7	10.3	17.9	4.6	1.7	1.1
[WWCHDSUF] b. A pre-school child is likely to suffer if his or her mother works	% 5.7	30.3	18.2	34.6	8.2	1.6	1.3
[WWFAMSUF] c. All in all, family life suffers when the woman has a full-time job	% 7.1	27.5	19.2	33.5	9.8	1.6	1.3
[WANTHOME] d. A job is all right, but what most women really want is a home and children	% 3.4	20.1	24.8	33.3	13.7	2.9	1.8
[HWIFEFFL] e. Being a housewife is just as fulfilling as working for pay	% 8.3	35.7	22.2	23.7	5.8	2.6	1.6
[FEMJOB] f. Having a job is the best way for a woman to be an independent person	% 10.1	42.6	21.3	20.2	2.5	1.9	1.5

2. And do you agree or disagree … ?

PLEASE TICK **ONE** BOX ON EACH LINE

	Strongly agree	Agree	Neither agree nor disagree	Disagree	Strongly disagree	Can't choose	(Not answered)
[BOTHEARN] a. Both the man and the woman should contribute to the household income	% 18.9	39.8	24.4	12.7	1.2	1.7	1.1
[SEXROLE] b. A man's job is to earn money; a woman's job is to look after the home and family	% 3.9	13.5	17.5	43.6	19.6	0.8	1.2
[MENMORE1] c. Men ought to do a larger share of household work than they do now	% 10.5	49.2	26.7	9.3	1.0	1.8	1.5
[MENMORE2] d. Men ought to do a larger share of childcare than they do now	% 8.9	52.2	26.8	7.9	0.8	2.1	1.4

3. Do you think women should work outside the home full-time, part-time or not at all under these circumstances?

PLEASE TICK ONE BOX ON EACH LINE

		Work full-time	Work part-time	Stay at home	Can't choose	(Not answered)
[WWCHLD1] a.	After marrying and before there are children	% 78.2	7.7	1.3	10.6	2.1
[WWCHLD2] b.	When there is a child under school age	% 3.4	34.1	48.1	11.7	2.7
[WWCHLD3] c.	After the youngest child starts school	% 15.2	65.6	5.4	11.7	2.1
[WWCHLD4] d.	After the children leave home	% 62.0	19.2	1.3	15.1	2.4

4. Do you agree or disagree ...?

PLEASE TICK ONE BOX ON EACH LINE

		Strongly agree	Agree	Neither agree nor disagree	Disagree	Strongly disagree	Can't choose	(Not answered)
[MARVIEW1] a.	Married people are generally happier than unmarried people	% 6.1	17.1	40.0	23.8	7.1	4.6	1.2
[MARVIEW5] b.	It is better to have a bad marriage than no marriage at all	% 0.4	1.8	5.0	43.1	46.6	1.7	1.4
[MARVIEW6] c.	People who want children ought to get married	% 14.0	37.1	16.6	21.8	7.9	1.3	1.3
[MARVIE10] d.	One parent can bring up a child as well as two parents together	% 6.9	32.3	17.7	32.8	7.7	1.2	1.4
[MARVIE11] e.	It is all right for a couple to live together without intending to get married	% 17.9	50.6	14.5	10.8	3.5	1.2	1.4
[MARVIE12] f.	It is a good idea for a couple who intend to get married to live together first	% 14.8	46.2	22.4	10.5	2.5	2.2	1.4
[MARVIE13] g.	Divorce is usually the best solution when a couple can't seem to work out their marriage problems	% 10.9	47.7	20.2	14.0	3.2	2.7	1.3

5. Do you agree or disagree ...?

PLEASE TICK ONE BOX ON EACH LINE

		Strongly agree	Agree	Neither agree nor disagree	Disagree	Strongly disagree	Can't choose	(Not answered)
[CHDVIEW2] a.	Watching children grow up is life's greatest joy	% 35.1	42.6	15.1	2.9	0.8	2.6	0.8
[CHDVIEW6] b.	People who have never had children lead empty lives	% 3.8	9.8	24.1	43.2	15.7	1.9	1.5

6. Do you agree or disagree ...?

PLEASE TICK ONE BOX ON EACH LINE

		Strongly agree	Agree	Neither agree nor disagree	Disagree	Strongly disagree	Can't choose	(Not answered)
[MATLEAVE] a.	Working women should receive paid maternity leave when they have a baby	% 41.0	47.8	4.8	4.2	0.6	0.7	0.9
[CHLDCRBN] b.	Families should receive financial benefits for child-care when both parents work	% 20.6	33.3	17.3	21.2	4.4	1.9	1.4

[MARDNOW2]
7. Are you ...

PLEASE TICK ONE BOX ONLY

	%	
... married or living as married	67.5	ANSWER Q.8
or not?	31.8	GO TO Q.16
(Not answered)	0.7	

N=1339

PLEASE ANSWER Q.8 TO Q.15 IF YOU ARE MARRIED OR LIVING AS MARRIED.

[CPLINCOM]
8. How do you and your spouse/partner organise the income that one or both of you receive? Please choose the option that comes closest.

PLEASE TICK ONE BOX ONLY

	%
I manage all the money and give my spouse/partner his or her share	8.4
My spouse/partner manages all the money and gives me my share	8.6
We pool all the money and each take out what we need	53.9
We pool some of the money and keep the rest separate	16.6
We each keep our own money separate	10.2
(Not answered)	2.3

9. In your household who does the following things …?

PLEASE TICK ONE BOX ON EACH LINE

		Always me	Usually me	About equal or both together	Usually my spouse/ partner	Always my spouse/ partner	Is done by a third person	Can't choose	(Not answered)
[HHJOB21] a.	Does the laundry	% 29.3	17.9	14.7	18.0	17.9	1.5	0.3	0.4
[HHJOB22] b.	Makes small repairs around the house	% 17.9	23.6	16.8	26.1	10.6	3.6	0.3	1.1
[HHJOB23] c.	Looks after sick family members	% 14.8	17.3	35.6	12.9	6.3	1.4	8.7	3.0
[HHJOB24] d.	Shops for groceries	% 13.1	17.1	45.1	15.2	7.4	0.9	0.1	1.1
[HHJOB25] e.	Does the household cleaning	% 17.6	20.2	29.5	18.9	8.1	4.5	0.3	1.0
[HHJOB26] f.	Prepares the meals	% 16.8	22.5	29.1	20.7	9.1	0.9	–	1.0

[RHOMEWRK]
10a. On average, how many hours a week do you personally spend on household work, not including childcare and leisure time activities?

Hours (median) 9

[SHOMEWORK]
b. And what about your spouse/partner? On average, how many hours a week does he/she spend on household work, not including childcare and leisure time activities?

Hours (median) 6

N=1339

[CHORESHR]
11. Which of the following best applies to the sharing of household work between you and your spouse/partner?

PLEASE TICK ONE BOX ONLY

	%
I do much more than my fair share of the household work	21.4
I do a bit more than my fair share of the household work	17.3
I do roughly my fair share of the household work	37.3
I do a bit less than my fair share of the household work	14.4
I do much less than my fair share of the household work	8.2
(Not answered)	1.5

[CHOREARG]
12. How often do you and your spouse/partner disagree about the sharing of household work?

PLEASE TICK ONE BOX ONLY

	%
Several times a week	3.9
Several times a month	8.6
Several times a year	11.1
Less often/rarely	34.3
Never	37.6
Can't choose	3.4
(Not answered)	1.1

[DECDKIDS]
13. Who usually makes/made the decisions about how to bring up your children?

PLEASE TICK ONE BOX ONLY

	%
Mostly me	10.3
Mostly my spouse/partner	5.9
Sometimes me/sometimes my spouse/partner	8.0
We decide/decided together	49.1
Someone else	0.5
Does not apply	24.3
Can't choose	0.5
(Not answered)	1.4

14. When you and your spouse/partner make decisions about the following, who has the final say?

PLEASE TICK ONE BOX ON EACH LINE

		Mostly me	Mostly my spouse partner	Sometimes me/ sometimes my spouse/partner	We decide together	Someone else	(Not answered)
[WHOSAY1] a.	Choosing shared weekend activities	% 8.5	6.8	22.4	60.7	0.2	1.4
[WHOSAY2] b.	Buying major things for the home	% 10.4	9.5	14.4	63.6	0.1	2.0

[INCHIGH]
15. Considering all sources of income, between you and your spouse/partner, who has the higher income?

PLEASE TICK ONE BOX ONLY

	%
My spouse/partner has no income	6.3
I have a much higher income	17.5
I have a higher income	17.9
We have about the same income	12.2
My spouse/partner has a higher income	25.5
My spouse/partner has a much higher income	13.4
I have no income	4.2
Don't know	1.3
(Not answered)	1.7

16. *EVERYONE PLEASE ANSWER*
Do you agree or disagree?

N=1984

PLEASE TICK ONE BOX ON EACH LINE

		Strongly agree	Agree	Neither agree nor disagree	Disagree	Doesn't apply	Strongly disagree	Can't choose	(Not answered)
[TIMEGON1] a.	There are so many things to do at home, I often run out of time before I get them all done	% 15.9	40.1	13.3	19.0	2.3	5.4	1.4	2.6
[NOSTRES1] b.	My life at home is rarely stressful	% 6.3	37.4	18.4	26.6	5.6	2.2	0.7	2.8
[TIMEGON2] c.	There are so many things to do at work, I often run out of time before I get them all done	% 10.6	26.9	13.4	15.8	1.9	25.5	1.1	5.0
[NOSTRES2] d.	My job is rarely stressful	% 1.9	16.2	9.9	27.4	12.6	25.3	1.4	5.3

17. How often has each of the following happened to you during the past three months?

PLEASE TICK ONE BOX ON EACH LINE

		Several times a week	Several times a month	Once or twice	Never	Doesn't apply/ no job	Can't choose	(Not answered)
[HOMETRD] a.	I have come home from work too tired to do the chores which need to be done	% 15.4	18.9	23.3	7.0	31.4	0.2	3.7
[HOMEHARD] b.	It has been difficult for me to fulfil my family responsibilities because of the amount of time I spend on my job	% 4.8	10.8	20.0	24.0	35.3	0.2	4.9
[WORKTRD] c.	I have arrived at work too tired to function well because of the household work I had done	% 1.0	2.2	14.7	44.7	32.4	0.2	4.7
[WORKDIFF] d.	I have found it difficult to concentrate at work because of my family responsibilities	% 1.4	3.1	24.0	32.6	33.9	0.2	4.8

[RUHAPPY2]
18. If you were to consider your life in general, how happy or unhappy would you say you are, on the whole?

PLEASE TICK ONE BOX ONLY

	%
Completely happy	13.5
Very happy	35.3
Fairly happy	37.7
Neither happy nor unhappy	8.2
Fairly unhappy	2.4
Very unhappy	0.8
Completely unhappy	0.3
Can't choose	0.8
(Not answered)	1.1

[JOBSAT]
19. All things considered, how satisfied are you with your (main) job?

PLEASE TICK ONE BOX ONLY

	%
Completely satisfied	7.2
Very satisfied	15.7
Fairly satisfied	28.4
Neither satisfied nor dissatisfied	7.0
Fairly dissatisfied	4.5
Very dissatisfied	2.2
Completely dissatisfied	1.2
Can't choose	31.0
Doesn't apply/no job	0.4
(Not answered)	2.5

[FAMSAT]
20. All things considered, how satisfied are you with your family life?
PLEASE TICK ONE BOX ONLY

	%
Completely satisfied	21.1
Very satisfied	37.8
Fairly satisfied	28.2
Neither satisfied nor dissatisfied	5.5
Fairly dissatisfied	2.8
Very dissatisfied	0.6
Completely dissatisfied	0.2
Can't choose	2.2
(Not answered)	1.7

[MTHRWRKD]
21. Did your mother ever work for pay for as long as one year, after you were born and before you were 14?
PLEASE TICK ONE BOX ONLY

	%
Yes, she worked for pay	53.7
No	36.0
Don't know	9.1
(Not answered)	1.2

[CHLDEVER]
22. Have you ever had children?
PLEASE TICK ONE BOX ONLY

	%	
Yes	68.3	ANSWER Q.23
No	31.2	GO TO Q.25
(Not answered)	0.5	

PLEASE ANSWER Q.23 AND Q.24 IF YOU HAVE EVER HAD CHILDREN.

23. Did you work outside the home full-time, part-time, or not at all …
PLEASE TICK ONE BOX ON EACH LINE

N=1354

		Worked full-time	Worked part-time	Stayed at home	Does not apply	(Not answered)
[RMARWRK1] a.	After marrying and **before** you had children? %	81.2	5.3	3.7	7.3	2.5
[RMARWRK2] b.	And what about when a child was **under school age**? %	42.5	20.5	29.1	3.5	4.4
[RMARWRK3] c.	After the **youngest** child started school? %	42.3	27.2	12.1	13.5	4.9
[RMARWRK4] d.	And how about **after** the children left home? %	36.6	11.7	4.6	41.2	6.0

24. What about your spouse/partner at that time – did he/she work outside the home **full-time, part-time**, or **not at all**?
PLEASE TICK ONE BOX ON EACH LINE

N=1984

		Worked full-time	Worked part-time	Stayed at home	Does not apply	(Not answered)
[SMARWRK1] a.	After marrying and **before** you had children? %	80.1	4.7	3.8	8.4	3.0
[SMARWRK2] b.	And what about when a child was **under school age**? %	55.6	11.9	21.6	5.8	5.0
[SMARWRK3] c.	After the **youngest** child started school? %	50.2	18.4	10.2	15.6	5.7
[SMARWRK4] d.	And how about **after** the children left home? %	36.9	9.0	4.6	43.5	6.0

EVERYONE PLEASE ANSWER
[WOMWORK]
25. Do you think that women should work outside the home full-time, part-time or not at all, when a couple has not yet had a child?
PLEASE TICK ONE BOX ONLY

	%
Work full-time	72.1
Work part-time	8.4
Stay at home	1.4
Can't choose	17.0
(Not answered)	1.1

[PAIDWRK]
26. Have you ever had a paid job?
PLEASE TICK ONE BOX ONLY

	%	
Yes	97.8	ANSWER Q.27
No	1.7	GO TO Q.29
(Not answered)	0.5	

PLEASE ONLY ANSWER Q.27 AND Q.28 IF YOU HAVE EVER HAD A PAID JOB.

[IMPEMP1]
27a. Have you ever changed your hours or working arrangements to look after any of the following people?
PLEASE TICK ONE BOX ONLY

N=1939

	%
No	59.8
Yes, for: Children (own/step)/foster	25.6
Husband/wife/partner	3.6
Father, mother, grandparent	4.5
Father-in-law/mother-in-law/grandparent-in-law	0.2
Grandson/granddaughter	0.6
Other relative	0.7
Other non-relative	0.5
(Not answered)	4.4

[IMPEMP2]

27b. Have you ever given up work to look after any of the following people? Please do not include any time spent on maternity leave.

PLEASE TICK ONE BOX ONLY

	%
No	76.0
Yes, for: Children (own/step/foster	15.3
Husband/wife/partner	2.1
Father, mother, grandparent	2.9
Father-in-law/mother-in-law/grandparent-in-law	0.2
Grandson/granddaughter	0.3
Other relative	0.7
Other non-relative	0.1
(Not answered)	2.3

[FAMWORK]

28. How much, if at all, do you think your family responsibilities have got in the way of your progress at work or your job prospects?

PLEASE TICK ONE BOX ONLY

	%
A great deal	5.0
Quite a lot	7.0
A bit	11.2
Not very much	15.5
Not at all	52.7
Can't say	7.5
(Not answered)	1.2

EVERYONE PLEASE ANSWER

N=1984

29. How much do you agree or disagree with the following statements?

PLEASE TICK ONE BOX ON EACH LINE		Strongly agree	Agree	Neither agree nor disagree	Disagree	Strongly disagree	(Not answered)
[LADDERWF] a	It is important to move up the ladder at work, even if this gets in the way of family life	% 1.4	9.3	20.0	52.2	14.7	2.4
[HOUSEHUS] b	It is not good if the man stays at home and cares for the children and the woman goes out to work	% 3.1	11.9	28.1	41.5	13.3	2.1
[COPEWORK] c	If a person cannot manage their family responsibilities they should stop trying to hold down a paid job	% 4.0	28.7	31.9	29.3	3.6	2.5

NOTE:

Questions B30-60 are the same as questions 1-31 on version A of the self-completion.

BRITISH SOCIAL ATTITUDES 2002 SELF-COMPLETION QUESTIONNAIRE VERSION C

N=1001

NOTE:
Questions C1-29 are the same as questions 1-29 on version B of the questionnaire.
Questions C30-44 are the same as questions 1-15 on version A of the questionnaire.

45. Now some questions about Britain's railways. By railways we mean **train** services, and not metro or underground services. If you don't use trains regularly please answer according to what you know or have heard from other people.

Please tick one box on each line to show how much you agree or disagree with the following statements.

*PLEASE TICK **ONE** BOX ON EACH LINE*

		Agree strongly	Agree	Neither agree nor disagree	Disagree	Disagree strongly	Can't choose	(Not answered)
[TRAINS1] a.	It is easy to find out what time trains run	%	7.0	51.8	12.9	18.0	2.6	6.5	1.2
[TRAINS2] b.	Trains generally run often enough	%	1.9	37.9	15.3	30.1	5.1	7.8	1.9
[TRAINS3] c.	Trains generally run on time	%	0.4	19.2	15.6	44.7	12.4	6.2	1.5
[TRAINS4] d.	Train fares are fairly reasonable	%	0.9	15.2	11.0	42.1	22.9	6.5	1.4
[TRAINS5] e.	Trains are a fast way to travel	%	5.6	53.8	15.2	15.1	3.2	5.3	1.8
[TRAINS6] f.	It is difficult to find out the cheapest train fares	%	10.9	43.8	16.4	15.8	3.0	8.0	2.1
[TRAINS7] g.	Trains have a good safety record	%	2.3	29.1	23.1	28.6	9.4	5.4	2.0

[TOWNTRAN]
46a. Now some questions on roads and public transport.
Thinking first about **towns and cities**. If the government **had** to choose . . .

*PLEASE TICK **ONE** BOX ONLY*

	%
. . . it should improve roads	36.6
OR	
. . . it should improve public transport	62.0
Don't know	0.1
(Not answered)	1.4

[CTRYTRAN]
46b. And in **country areas**, if the government **had** to choose ...

PLEASE TICK **ONE** BOX ONLY

	%
... it should improve roads	31.1
OR	
... it should improve public transport	67.1
Don't know	0.1
(Not answered)	1.6

47. Please tick **one** box to show how much you agree or disagree with each of these statements.

PLEASE TICK **ONE** BOX ON EACH LINE

	Agree strongly	Agree	Neither agree nor disagree	Disagree	Disagree strongly	I never travel by car	Can't choose	(Not answered)
[CARWALK] a. Many of the short journeys I now make by car I could just as easily walk	% 5.1	31.4	10.2	32.3	9.5	7.1	3.5	1.0
[CARBUS] b. Many of the short journeys I now make by car I could just as easily go by bus	% 2.8	24.6	7.6	40.0	15.0	5.6	2.9	1.4
[CARBIKE] c. Many of the short journeys I now make by car I could just as easily cycle, if I had a bike	% 4.2	32.4	9.1	28.8	13.9	5.6	4.2	1.8

48. Please tick one box for each statement to show how much you agree or disagree.

PLEASE TICK **ONE** BOX ON EACH LINE

	Agree strongly	Agree	Neither agree nor disagree	Disagree	Disagree strongly	Can't choose	(Not answered)
[BUSNOOTH] a. I would **only** travel somewhere by bus if I had no other way of getting there	% 10.1	52.7	5.4	24.1	5.0	1.5	1.2
[BUS4POOR] b. Travelling by bus is mainly for people who can't afford anything better	% 2.1	12.5	12.9	54.7	15.5	0.9	1.4
[CARTAXHI] c. For the sake of the environment, car users should pay higher taxes	% 3.7	10.8	11.5	48.2	22.1	2.0	1.6
[CARCONV] d. Driving one's own car is too convenient to give up for the sake of the environment	% 4.9	32.8	22.1	27.1	5.5	5.5	2.1
[CARALLOW] e. People should be allowed to use their cars as much as they like, even if it causes damage to the environment	% 3.3	16.7	25.3	38.2	9.8	5.3	1.4

[CUTCARS]
49a. How important do you think it is to **cut down the number of cars** on Britain's roads?

PLEASE TICK **ONE** BOX ONLY

	%
Very important	26.9
Fairly important	47.6
Not very important	13.4
Not at all important	4.3
Can't choose	6.7
(Not answered)	1.0

[PTIMPRIM]
b. And how important is it **to improve public transport** in Britain?

PLEASE TICK **ONE** BOX ONLY

	%
Very important	71.5
Fairly important	23.3
Not very important	2.0
Not at all important	0.7
Can't choose	1.6
(Not answered)	0.8

50. Many people feel that public transport **should** be improved. Here are some ways of finding the money to do it. How much would you support or oppose each one, as a way of raising money to improve public transport?

PLEASE TICK **ONE** BOX ON EACH LINE

	Strongly support	Support	Neither support nor oppose	Oppose	Strongly oppose	Can't choose	(Not answered)
[PTIMPR1] a. Gradually doubling the cost of petrol over the next ten years	% 2.5	9.3	11.6	37.8	32.5	4.4	1.9
[PTIMPR2] b. Charging all motorists around £2 each time they enter or drive through a city or town centre at peak times	% 7.9	30.0	12.5	23.7	19.8	4.2	1.8
[PTIMPR3] c. Cutting in half spending on new roads	% 3.9	16.5	15.9	34.3	20.9	5.7	2.8
[PTIMPR4] d. Cutting in half spending on maintenance of the roads we already have	% 1.4	6.1	11.1	45.6	28.0	5.5	2.4

51.   Please tick **one** box for **each** of these statements below to show how much you agree or disagree with it.

PLEASE TICK **ONE** BOX ON EACH LINE		Agree strongly	Agree	Neither agree nor disagree	Disagree	Disagree strongly	Can't choose	(Not answered)
[BUSPRIOR]								
a.	Buses should be given more priority in towns and cities, even if this makes things more difficult for car drivers	%	14.6	47.7	15.5	16.2	2.6	2.3	1.1
[CYCPEDPR]								
b.	Cyclists and pedestrians should be given more priority in towns and cities even if this makes things more difficult for other road users	%	16.7	43.5	17.4	14.6	3.4	2.9	1.4

NOTE:

Questions C52-56 are the same as questions 18-22 on version A of the questionnaire.
Question C57 is the same as question 24b on version A of the questionnaire.
Questions C58-60 are the same as questions 29-31 on version A of the questionnaire.

Subject index

measurement of 134-137
see 131-159 *passim*
Road congestion *see* Car use

S

Sample design 261-262
Sample size 262
Sampling
  errors 270-273
  frames 261, 275-276
  points 262
Scales: *see* Attitude scales
Schools: *see* Primary schools; Secondary
  schools; Teaching profession
Scottish Social Attitudes survey xxii
Secondary schools
  assessments of their performance 124-
  125
  measures to improve 117-118, 123, 129
  reducing class sizes in 118, 128-129
  satisfaction with 4, 12, 24, 124-5, 129
  selective/specialist 109, 123
  see also: Education
Self-completion questionnaire 338
September 11th 2001 192, 199
Social class
  and differences in attitudes 256
  and impact on life chances 255
  changing composition of 147-148
  definition of 265-266
Socio-Economic classification, *see*
  National Statistics Socio-Economic
  Classification (NS-SEC)
Socio-Economic Group 267
Social security
  dependency on 1-2
  means-testing 2
  support for 255
  reform of 1
  see also: Benefits
Standard Industrial Classification (SIC)
  267
Standard Occupational Classification
  (SOC) 265
Stratification 261-262
**Stuck in our cars? Mapping transport
  preferences 45-70**
Student loans *see* Higher education
Student maintenance grants *see* Higher
  education

T

Tabulations, Notes on the 279

Tax credits 75
Taxation xxi, 1, 3, 24, 75, 90, 234, 243-
  245, 255
  see also: Public spending
Tax system 75, 89
Teaching profession
  perceptions of 110, 126-127
  recruitment and retention in 110, 125
Technical details of the survey 261-277
Technological change xx-xxi
'Thatcher's children' 11, 75
'Thatcherism' 73-75, 77, 91, 235
Trade unions, membership of xix
  and education level 97
Tradition, decline of 255
Transport *see* Public transport
Trends in racial prejudice 189-214
Trust in government 83, 226, 229
Tuition fees *see* Higher education

U

Unemployment
  and responsibility for supporting
  unemployed people 23
  benefits for 13-15, 234-236, 242-245,
  256
  level of xix, 14

V

Values: *see* 131-159 *passim*
Voting: *see* Election turnout
Voting behaviour: *see* Election turnout

W

Walking 50
Weighting 263-264
Welfare state
  consensus about 2
  pride in 10
  privatisation / role of private sector in 2,
  19, 24
  reform of 2
  support for 10, 24, 256-259
Welfarism scale 269
**What we want from the welfare state 1-
  28**
Will we ever vote for the Euro? 215-232
**A woman's place... Employment and
  family life for men and women 161-
  187**
Women
  and discrimination 162
  and educational attainment 161